RETHINKING AMERICAN ART

ALSO BY THEODORE E. STEBBINS JR.

(Many with distinguished co-authors)

American Master Drawings & Watercolors: A History of Works on Paper from Colonial Times to the Present

American Paintings at Harvard, Volume One: Paintings, Watercolors, and Pastels by Artists Born Before 1826

American Paintings at Harvard, Volume Two: Paintings, Watercolors, Pastels, and Stained Glass by Artists Born 1826–1856

A Book by Anselm Kiefer

Boston Collects: Contemporary Painting and Sculpture

Close Observation: Selected Oil Sketches by Frederic E. Church

Edward Weston: Photography and Modernism

John James Audubon

The Lane Collection

The Last Ruskinians: Charles Eliot Norton, Charles Herbert Moore, and Their Circle

The Life and Work of Martin Johnson Heade: A Critical Analysis and Catalogue Raisonné

Life As Art: Paintings By Gregory Gillespie and Frances Cohen Gillespie

Lure of Italy: American Artists and the Italian Experience, 1760–1914

Martin Johnson Heade

A New World: Masterpieces of American Painting, 1760–1910

The Photography of Charles Sheeler: American Modernist

Sheeler: The Photographs

Ray Spillenger: Rediscovery of a Black Mountain Painter

Weston's Westons: California and the West

Weston's Westons: Portraits and Nudes

RETHINKING AMERICAN ART

COLLECTORS, CRITICS, AND THE CHANGING CANON

Theodore E. Stebbins Jr.

WITH THE RESEARCH ASSISTANCE OF

SUSAN R. STEBBINS

GODINE / BOSTON

Published in 2025 by
GODINE
Boston, Massachusetts
www.godine.com

LIBRARY OF CONGRESS CATALOGING-IN-PUBLICATION DATA
Names: Stebbins, Theodore E. author | Stebbins, Susan Ricci researcher
Title: Rethinking American art : collectors, critics, and the changing canon / Theodore E. Stebbins Jr. ; with the research assistance of Susan R. Stebbins.
Identifiers: LCCN 2025009916 (print) | LCCN 2025009917 (ebook) | ISBN 9781567928341 hardcover | ISBN 9781567928358 epub
Subjects: LCSH: Art and society—United States—History | Aesthetics, American—History
Classification: LCC N72.S6 S675 2025 (print) | LCC N72.S6 (ebook) | DDC 701/.030973—dc23/eng/20250518
LC record available at https://lccn.loc.gov/2025009916
LC ebook record available at https://lccn.loc.gov/2025009917

FIRST PRINTING, 2025
Printed in Canada

CONTENTS

De gustibus non est disputandum
(In matters of taste, there can be no disputes)

—LATIN DICTUM

Acknowledgments

I owe heartfelt gratitude to Susan Ricci Stebbins for her skillful editing of the text, for her research, her ideas, her assistance in countless ways, and for her constant support; she has made this book possible. I am deeply grateful to Bruce Robertson, Kathleen A. Foster, Carol Troyen, and Virginia Anderson for undertaking careful readings of parts of my text and for making invaluable suggestions, in addition to answering my frequent inquiries along the way. I offer special thanks to Marc Simpson and Rob Leith for their helpful reading of early drafts. Emily Sweet has been my right arm throughout this project, and has skillfully managed the footnotes, our book-borrowing, and all of the necessary permissions and images for the illustrations. One of the great pleasures of preparing this book has been the opportunity to be in touch with many old and new friends and former students and colleagues, some in mid-career, others nearing retirement. I feel moved and humbled by all the extraordinary aid I have received. I am especially thankful to Erica Hirshler, Horace Ballard, and Elizabeth Prelinger for their helpful responses to my many inquiries. I am grateful to my college classmates, Daniel Horowitz and Monroe Price, and to Aimée Brown Price and Joseph Helman, for our long talks about art collecting and the meaning of life. Alice Walton has been wonderfully responsive to my questions about Crystal Bridges and Art Bridges. Warren Adelson has generously told me the story of Ray and Margaret Horowitz and their collection and foundation; James Maroney has shared his trove of memories about landmark sales and other key events, and Michael Altman has been enormously helpful over many years. Bryan Lincoln has been my special agent in the field. I benefitted from my conversations with Alan Wallach, as I have from his writings. I owe special thanks to Matt Becker of the University of Massachusetts Press for his early encouragement of this project.

I offer profound thanks to Clark Abt, Alexander Acevedo, Derek Alderman, Barbara and Ted Alfond, Michael Altman, Thomas and Catherine Codman Ball, Linda Bantel, Paul Barolsky, Ross Barrett, Christopher Benfey, Graham Boettcher, Peter R. Brown, Kayla Carlsen, Sara Cavanagh, Carol Clark, Thomas Colville, Nancy and Laurence Coolidge, Margi Conrads, Judith and Ronald Davenport, Eleanor (Bobo) Devens and Robert Devens, Brett Donham, Robert W. Doran, Charles Eldredge, Stuart P. Feld, Jerald D. Fessenden, Ilene Fort, Michael Fried, Abigail Gerdts, Warren and Charlynn Goins, Howard Godel, Charles Giuliano, Karen Haas, Bruce Haverberg, Ena Heller, Cate Hitchings, Margi Hofer, Harry Hollins, Jane Kamensky, Irene Katz, Franklin Kelly, Jodi Knox, Arie L. Kopelman, William Kopelman, Betty Krulik, Sarah Lewis, Bryan Lincoln, Margaretta Lovell, Peter Lunder, Peter Lynch, Peter Lyons, Gigi de Manio, Richard Manoogian, Leo Mazow, Liz McGranaghan, Jill Medvedow, Honorable William A. Middendorf, Dara Mitchell, Fern Nesson, Kimberly Orcutt, Susan W. Paine, Regina Palm, Kimberly Probolus, Tom Ragle, Alfred Rankin Jr., Peter Rathbone, Melissa Renn, Atea Ring, Bruce Robinson, Mitchel Rose, MacKenzie Moon Ryan, Lou Salerno, Andrew Schoelkopf, Sanford Schwartz, George Shackelford, Brenda Shapiro, Lewis Sharp, Gwendolyn DuBois Shaw, Susan Standen, Morgan Stebbins, Isabel Taube, Joan and W. Nicholas Thorndike, William H. Truettner, John Walsh, Nicholas Fox Weber, Catherine Whalen, and my late friends William H. Gerdts, Peter Tillou, John Wilmerding, and Joy Wolf.

I am also deeply indebted to the late Alan Shestack, Matthew Teitelbaum, Ethan Lasser, Laura C. Luckey, Jonathan L. Fairbanks, Gerald Ward, Clifford Ackley, Ben Weiss, Frederick Ilchman, Maureen

Melton, Robert Mowry, Hee Jung Lee, Elliot Bostwick Davis, Pat Loiko, Michael Bramwell, Nonie Gadsden, Marina Tyquiengco, and especially Erica Hirshler, Layla Bermeo, and Julia McCarthy, all formerly or presently at the Museum of Fine Arts, Boston, my home base for many years. At the Yale University Art Gallery, Stephanie Wiles, Keely Orgeman, Patricia Kane, L. Lynne Addison, John Stuart Gordon, Laurence Kanter, and especially Jules D. Prown, who gave me my first job, have been very helpful. I offer special thanks to Martha Tedeschi, Francine Flynn, Megan Schwenke, Miriam Stewart, and Horace Ballard at the Harvard Art Museums. Max Hollein, Vanessa Erbe, Kate Lester Thompson, Denise Murrell, Stephanie Herdrich, the late Barbara Weinberg, and especially Sylvia Yount and Elizabeth Mankin Kornhauser (now at Olana) at the Metropolitan Museum of Art, have been very generous colleagues, as have Stephan Wolohojian and Asher Miller in European Paintings. The excellent staff at Crystal Bridges, including Austen Barron Bailly, Mindy Besaw, Diane Carroll, Juli Goss, and especially Paul Provost, have been very cooperative. And I am deeply grateful to Eric Widing (Christie's), Timothy A. Burgard (Fine Arts Museums of San Francisco), Stephanie Mayer Heydt and Katherine Jentleson (High Museum), Erin Corrales-Diaz (Toledo Museum), Margi Hofer and Linda Ferber (The New York Historical), John Klein (Washington University), Patricia Hickson (Wadsworth Atheneum), Dominic Molon (RISD), Katie Wood Kirchhoff (Shelburne Museum), Karen Quinn (The New York State Museum, Albany), Peter B. Rathbone and Dara Mitchell (Sotheby's), Kenneth Myers (Detroit Institute of Art), the late John Driscoll (Babcock Gallery); Brenda Shapiro, James Rondeau, and Bart Ryckbosch (Art Institute of Chicago); Kaylin Weber and Alison de Lima Greene (Museum of Fine Arts, Houston); Aimee Ng (The Frick Collection), Karen Pfefferle (Wellington Management Foundation), Pilar Tompkins Rivas (Lucas Museum of Narrative Art), Amy Zinck (Terra Foundation), Gordon Wilkins (Addison Gallery, Andover, Massachusetts), Stephanie Sparling Williams (Brooklyn Museum), Bea Garvan (Philadelphia Museum), and Eleanor Jones Harvey (Smithsonian American Art Museum).

This book could not have been written during the COVID years and after without the Boston Athenaeum and the wonderful staff in its Library and Special Collections, especially Arnold Serapilio. Also important for my work were the Isabella Stewart Gardner Museum Archives; Fine Arts Library, Harvard University; Schlesinger Library, Harvard University; Megan Schwenke and Michelle Interrante, Archives, Harvard Art Museums; Barbara S. Meloni and Edward Copenhagen, Harvard University Archives; Massachusetts Historical Society; Elise Kenney, Yale University Art Gallery Archives; Beinecke Library, Yale University; and Timothy J. DeWerff, Century Association.

Finally, I am forever indebted to David Allender of the house of Godine, who made a bold, and I hope wise, decision to take me and this project on. David led me to Mike Levine, the most gifted and kindest of editors, who has helped me smooth out several chapters, especially the introduction and the postscript, and to Daniel Tortora, a tireless enemy of inconsistencies and misspellings and an extraordinary copyeditor.

I close with an apology for all the errors of fact and interpretation that inevitably remain in the following pages, for having omitted the stories of the many museums that I have been unable to visit, and all the outstanding scholars, curators, dealers, and collectors who go unmentioned here for reasons of time and space.

For My Teachers

Ben Long
Henry W. Bragdon
Jakob Rosenberg
John Coolidge

With everlasting gratitude

Introduction

This world is change; this life, opinion.

—MARCUS AURELIUS, *Meditations* (ca. 175–180)

THE ROOTS of this book go back to the fall of 1968 when I was taking up my new curatorial position at Yale. I began by reading through the files of my predecessors, the distinguished scholars John Hill Morgan and Theodore Sizer, and I found that their every letter dealt with the portraits and history paintings of Gilbert Stuart, John Trumbull, and a few of their contemporaries. I wondered, hadn't they ever heard of the Hudson River School, or the nineteenth-century genre and still life painters? Their taste seemed woefully outdated, and I excitedly began to try to fill the gaps in the collection with the artists that we younger scholars were just discovering. Frederic Edwin Church, Martin Johnson Heade, and Fitz Henry Lane seemed giants to us; how could they have overlooked their work?

Only later did I realize that the change from my predecessors' veneration of early portraits to my interest in landscape, genre, and still life paintings evidenced a regular, generational shift in taste. Their favorites, or their canon, focused on the leading colonial and federal painters. Those were the artists that excited them; they were the ones they studied, collected, and wrote about. In the 1960s, when my cohort of young scholars entered the field, we knew the paintings of Copley and Stuart; they were hanging in every museum. We admired them, but we didn't find them exciting. Research on their work had been going on since the Hudson–Fulton Celebration at the Metropolitan Museum of Art in 1909, volumes had been written, and we believed those painters had had their day. In Church, Heade, and Lane we found unexplored territory, talented painters whose pictures were little known and whose importance was unrecognized. David C. Huntington led the way with his work on Church, while Barbara Novak took on Asher B. Durand, John Wilmerding, Lane, and I started researching Heade while other scholars took up Albert Bierstadt, Sanford Gifford, and their peers. We read the little that had been written about our subjects, searched for their paintings and their descendants, wrote dissertations, and organized pioneering exhibitions. The dealers joined the hunt, pleased to have fresh material for a growing group of collectors. It wasn't until years later that I realized my friends and I had helped develop a new canon, and it took even longer for me to understand that this kind of development happens regularly and inevitably, as each succeeding generation sees the world differently and rethinks many of the views of its predecessors. I use the term "rethinking" in my title to indicate these generational shifts, and also to reflect my own development: This book is far different from one I might have written a quarter century ago. The world has changed, and I have changed with it, moving from the narrowness and prejudice I grew up with to an embrace of far healthier modern values.

This book describes these cyclical changes, from the early nineteenth century to the present, and the people who created the evolving standards of taste or were deeply affected by them: the art historians and critics, and the artists and collectors. In studying the early canon, I rely on William Dunlap, the author of the first history of American art in 1834, and on his successors who recorded each succeeding era.[1] For events of the last sixty years, a period when I was an active museum curator, I add my own experiences, observations, and memories. I feel lucky to have played a role in the rediscovery of American art in the

1960s and in the blossoming of interest over succeeding decades, and to have known many of the players. Regarding the last quarter century, a time that saw the emergence of new aesthetic standards based on race, justice, and an embrace of diversity, I no longer write as an insider, but rather as a keenly interested observer.

I prepared for my career at Harvard's graduate school at what was known for years as "the Fogg," the name of Harvard's art museum. There were no courses on American art being offered in my two years of residence, so I studied American art on my own, by reading and by looking, mainly at the Museum of Fine Arts, the Vose Galleries, and other dealers. At Harvard the emphasis was on connoisseurship, the close looking at works of art. I learned from Sydney Freedberg, a specialist in the Italian Renaissance, Max Loehr, who taught early Chinese paintings, and especially from Jakob Rosenberg, an authority on Rembrandt and on master drawings. In the latter's seminar, we examined pairs of similar-looking drawings, always comparing originals from the Fogg's rich collection: We were asked, in which is the line more fluent, more effective, more confident, or more descriptive? Professor Rosenberg's book *On Quality in Art* of 1967 helped establish my lifetime of concern with the question of quality and with the varying methods that have been employed to discern it over many years.[2] In it, Rosenberg examined a number of experts and their ranking of painters, starting with Giorgio Vasari, the Florentine whose book *Lives of the Most Eminent Painters, Sculptors, and Architects* of 1550 established a model for the future. Sadly, Rosenberg fell into the same trap that had bedeviled earlier writers, as he tried to understand why each critic had made the mistakes he had. He asked why had Roger de Piles in the seventeenth century, for example, rated Raphael so much higher than Michelangelo, how could he have judged Rubens to be far superior to Rembrandt, and why weren't Durer and Caravaggio recognized more fully?

Both art experts and the public make the same error today. People are inclined to view past changes in taste as unique misjudgments that will not happen again; they are incredulous that Botticelli was forgotten and Vermeer overlooked until the late nineteenth century. They cannot imagine how foolish people were to reject the paintings of Van

Gogh or of Picasso and the Cubists, or how angry the Armory Show made many art lovers. How unthinking, how stupid, they think, not realizing that the pattern has been repeated again and again in the past, and will be in the future. We now recognize that the process is a continual one. Each past canon was established for good reason; there are no mistakes, there is only history. Many of the favored artists of any period, including our own, will drop from favor, something that art dealers never tell their clients, or museum curators their boards.

My first attempt to affect the American art canon (though I wouldn't have put it that way at the time) came during my internship at the National Gallery of Art. During my Harvard studies, I had been introduced to the art market and the museum world in John Coolidge's Museum Course, a class that changed my life.[3] After my course work, Professors Coolidge and Rosenberg recommended me for a Chester Dale Fellowship at the National Gallery of Art in Washington, where I served as a low-ranking intern in 1967–68. The National Gallery had spent two decades focused on Dunlap's canon, and had acquired important works by Copley, Stuart, and West, but had not yet embraced the nineteenth century. One day in New York, while exploring the dealers, I saw a wonderful Thomas Cole landscape, *Notch of the White Mountains* (fig. 1), at a New York gallery. I knew that the National Gallery lacked even a single example by Cole, founder of the Hudson River School, and so I boldly made an appointment with the eminent director John Walker, showed him a transparency of the painting, and suggested he buy it.[4] Amazingly, Mr. Walker agreed. I still feel a special thrill when I see the Cole hanging there, or whenever I see one of "my" paintings on view at a museum I have served. Bringing great works to public view is deeply gratifying, just as it is teaching students and friends about the breathtaking insights and pleasure to be found in art.

The ups and downs of the reputation of Thomas Cole's student and successor Frederic Edwin Church provide a perfect example of the changing canon. Church was the most lauded and highest priced American landscape painter during from the 1850s to the late seventies, with his *Niagara* selling for a then-magnificent price of $12,500 to William Corcoran in 1876. Then, by 1900, Church's stock had dropped precipitously; his work remained out of fashion until the 1950s and '60s

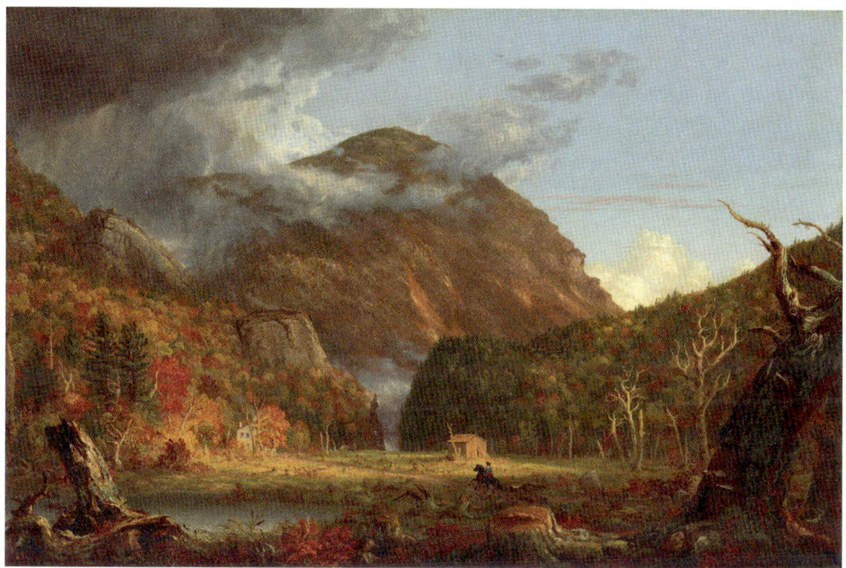

Fig. 1. THOMAS COLE,
A View of the Mountain Pass Called the Notch of the White Mountains (Crawford Notch), oil on canvas, 1839. National Gallery of Art.

when he was rediscovered by the scholar David C. Huntington and the dealer Robert Weimann. Every museum and collector suddenly had to have one. One of my greatest acquisitions was buying his *Mt. Ktaadn* for Yale for $75,000 in 1969; within a few years, its value was in the millions. In recent years, interest in the painter has lagged as the Hudson River School sank, but now the Olana Partnership, the owner of Church's great house on the Hudson and its collection, have set about restoring the artist's renown. "Frederic Church 200," led by the eminent scholar Elizabeth Mankin Kornhauser, has been established, and nearly every museum that owns a Church—thirty-eight of them as I write—has been enlisted in the celebration of the painter's birth in 1826. Several of them, including the National Gallery and the Wadsworth Atheneum, are planning their own exhibitions, and Kornhauser and two colleagues are organizing a major show focused on Church as a "Global Artist."[5] This project is unique in its scope, and one waits with anticipation to see whether it will prove a success.

We are more accustomed to hearing about the canon in literature than in art, especially in university settings where core courses and Great Books courses are still taught. Professor Allan Bloom in *The Closing of the American Mind* (1987) and other books argued for a fixed truth and an unchanging list of classic texts. Increasing arguments in favor of including talented Black and women writers led to heated rebuttals by Bloom and others as they asked, "Do you want us to leave out Milton or Dante?" This argument parallels the current one in the art world, for Bloom argued that books are not to be read for their social, political, or historical content, but rather, strictly for the "aesthetic pleasure" they bring.[6] It was implicit that any major writer must be a white male; one sees this when the scholar F. O. Matthiessen struggled with Emily Dickinson, whose poetry he admired. In the end, he found that she cannot be great, as he found her work to be only "personal and lyric," rather than having the necessary masculine qualities he found in Melville, "the vigorous thrust of his mind and the strengths of his passion."[7] Questioning the canon established by Matthiessen and Bloom were scholars like Jane Tompkins who in her book *Sensational Designs: The Cultural Work of American Fiction, 1790–1860*, argued against the "intrinsic merit" of the classics in favor of opening the list to once-popular, sentimental works by Susan Warner and other women.[8] Tompkins's reasoning, shocking at the time, prefigures today's debates about artistic quality. In her concluding chapter (entitled "But Is It Any Good?") she writes, "Great literature does not exert its force over and against time, but changes with the changing currents of social and political life."[9]

Early in my career I watched as Abstract Expressionism, which for many during the fifties appeared to represent the triumph of American modernism, was suddenly challenged by Pop Art. De Kooning, Rothko, and their colleagues were left behind as the sixties unfolded, and their backers were outraged. The leading American critic, Clement Greenberg, who had discovered Jackson Pollock in the forties, overnight found himself on the outside swimming against a new tide that he didn't understand. One finds such changes happening throughout our history. In the early nineteenth century, William Dunlap understandably felt proud that the US had produced artists like Benjamin West and Washington Allston who gained prominence in the English art world, but today few share his admiration for those painters. The Western landscapes of Albert Bierstadt, lauded for a century, are now faulted as celebrations of Manifest Destiny and the destruction of Indigenous tribes. After the Civil War, taste turned dramatically to France and the enthusiastic patronage of such now-forgotten American academic painters in Paris as Frederic A. Bridgman, William Dannat, and Daniel Ridgway Knight. Then, for years, it was said that American landscape painting had reached its peak with the work of Homer D. Martin, Alexander Wyant, and George Inness; of the three, only Inness is remembered today. And whatever happened to George Fuller and the Tonalists, or the vaunted American muralists of the early twentieth century? Every canon stems from the politics, economics, and culture of its period, and our ways of seeing are constantly being revised as the nation itself changes.

The changes in aesthetic standards that occurred in the twenty-first century, and that have accelerated since the death of George Floyd, seem more dramatic than any of those in the past as they involve a sea change in our culture. Even the most radical past developments, including the coming of Cubism and abstraction, occurred within the boundaries of the Anglo/European tradition, while now we view art globally. Today, American art means the work of both men and women in the entire Western Hemisphere, including the productions of the Spanish viceregal states and those of the Indigenous peoples of the Southwest and Northwest US. Moreover, the old hierarchies of race and gender, and of locale, medium, and style have been largely rejected: Quilts by the Black women at Gee's Bend, pots and blankets of the Navajo, and carvings made from tree roots by Bessie Harvey, are recognized today as equally worthy of consideration as the paintings of John Singleton Copley and Jackson Pollock.

I employ the word "canon," as it is still in widespread use, though I am aware that both traditional art history and the very notion of canons are under attack. For me, the canon refers both to the short list of artists most valued by any generation and to the aesthetic standards of each period. Art history, with its grand narrative describing "the evolution of movements, schools, styles, periods, and eras" and its concomitant definition of a number of painters and sculptors as representing "the highest achievements of European and later Euro-American material cultures"—the old canon, in other words—have been derided by highly articulate, widely respected scholars. Adriano Pedrosa, director of the São Paolo Museum of Art and organizer of the important recent exhibition "Afro-Atlantic Histories," argues powerfully that "art-historical colonization and imperialism" imposes "hierarchies of race, gender, and class" that downgrade the work of non-white peoples and those who do not work in the Anglo-European tradition.[10] I hope I have avoided the perils of such a narrow definition of the canon by using the term nonjudgmentally to refer to the most highly respected art and methodology of each period.

Art museums, libraries, and symphony halls often have the names of canonical figures inscribed on their walls. In Washington, DC, for example, one sees carved into the frieze of the former Corcoran Gallery (built in 1897) the names of eleven artists then thought to be all-time immortals: Phidias, the ancient Greek sculptor, followed by seven important European painters ranging from Giotto to Rubens, all of whose work is still widely respected. But the list concludes with three artists once greatly admired but known only to specialists today: Reynolds, Ingres, and Allston. Sir Joshua Reynolds, first president of the Royal Academy and author of the famous *Seven Discourses*, has lost his position of eminence. The classical master Jean-Auguste-Dominique Ingres still ranks high, but would no longer be chosen by many as the premier representative of France's incredibly productive nineteenth century. And Washington Allston, the only American on the list, though once highly regarded, is now unfamiliar to most. No Asian, Hispanic, or Indigenous name, no African American, no woman.[11] Looking back through history, we learn that canons are often thought to be permanent enough to carve in stone, but they are actually far from it. They should be written in sand. And we remember that the Corcoran itself is now gone.

---

[1] William Dunlap, *History of the Rise and Progress of the Arts of Design in the United States*, 3 vols. (Benjamin Blom, 1834).

[2] Jakob Rosenberg, *On Quality in Art: Criteria of Excellence, Past and Present* (Princeton University Press, 1967).

[3] Professor John Coolidge, director of Harvard's Fogg Museum (now part of the Harvard Art Museums), taught the "Museum Course" from 1950 to 1972. This was modeled on the course that Paul J. Sachs had famously led from 1922 to 1948. See Sally Anne Duncan and Andrew McClellan, *The Art of Curating: Paul J. Sachs and the Museum Course at Harvard* (Getty Research Institute, 2018), and Sybil Kantor, ch. 2, "The Fogg Method and Paul J. Sachs," in *Alfred H. Barr Jr. and the Intellectual Origins of the Museum of Modern Art* (MIT Press, 2002).

[4] At the time, I didn't quite understand the layers of authority I had bypassed with my actions, including the assistant to the director, the curator, the deputy director, and various others, none of whom greeted the acquisition or me warmly after that. I was thrilled to see the Cole illustrated in an article by Milton Esterow on February 28, 1968, entitled "Prices Soar for 19th-Century American Art," *New York Times*, February 28, 1968.

[5] Information courtesy of Elizabeth Mankin Kornhauser, November 13, 2024. For a wide-ranging effort to resurrect a large group of forgotten artists, see Charles C. Eldredge, ed., *The Unforgettables* (University of California Press., 2022).

[6] Dinitia Smith, "Harold Bloom, Critic Who Championed Western Canon, Dies at 89," *New York Times*, October 15, 2019.

[7] F. O. Matthiessen, *American Renaissance: Art and Expression in the Age of Emerson and Whitman* (Oxford University Press, 1941), 431.

[8] Jane Tompkins, *Sensational Designs: The Cultural Work of American Fiction, 1790–1860* (Oxford University Press, 1985).

[9] Tompkins, 192.

[10] Adriano Pedrosa, "History, Histórias," in *Afro-Atlantic Histories* (DelMonico Books, 2022), 22–23.

[11] See Jane Kamensky, "Two Cheers for the Nation: An American Revolution for the Revolting United States," *Reviews in American History* 47, no. 3 (2019): 308–18.

PART ONE

CRITICS AND CANONS

1

Changing Canons in the Nineteenth Century

One of the most central, dramatic, even alarming issues raised by any consideration of the vagaries of artistic taste: the manner in which such changes, while appearing to be the outcome of a most intimate and personal choice, may in fact be predetermined by external circumstances against our very wills.

—FRANCIS HASKELL, *Rediscoveries in Art,* 1976

THE NINETEENTH century saw each generation defining its own aesthetic standards as the nation itself searched for its identity and its guiding myths. The first important art historian in the US was William Dunlap, a playwright, theater manager, historian, and painter; his groundbreaking survey of 1834, *History of the Rise and Progress of the Arts of Design in the United States,* records the taste of his time.[1] Dunlap prepared biographies for 270 painters, sculptors, architects, and engravers, many of their names unfamiliar to us now. He devoted dozens of pages to each of the painters he considered outstanding starting with Benjamin West, Washington Allston, John Singleton Copley, and Gilbert Stuart, while single phrases sufficed for those he could learn little about, as when he simply recorded that "in the year

1760. . . . Cain. Exercised his profession in Maryland."[2] Dunlap's writing, like John Ruskin's a half century later, is worth reading for its elegant phrasing and its wit, and his biographies remain useful, providing details of the artists' lives entertainingly interspersed with rumors, tall tales, critical comments, and frequent grudge-settling asides.

Dunlap's heroes were Benjamin West, who had taught Dunlap in London, and Washington Allston (fig. 2), whom he saw as the greatest living painter. He viewed West as "the most distinguished painter of the age in which he lived."[3] Dunlap acknowledged West's flaws—"the hardness of his outline, the dryness of his manner"—but he found the nobility of his subject matter and his own sterling character to out-

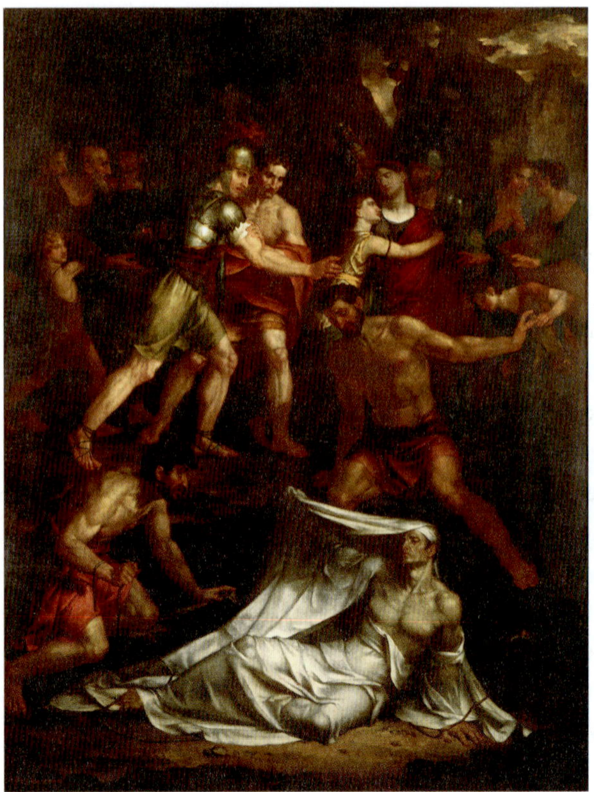

Fig. 2. **WASHINGTON ALLSTON,**
The Dead Man Restored to Life by Touching the Bones of the Prophet Elisha,
oil on canvas, 1811–1813. Pennsylvania Academy of the Fine Arts.

weigh everything else. He found Allston even more impressive, as the possessor of "the highest mental powers united to the keenest physical perception of the good and the beautiful."[4] Central to Dunlap's outlook was his view of history painting as the noblest artistic enterprise, and his emphasis on the character of the artist.[5] These criteria foreshadow the way in which contemporary critics stress the biography and socially relevant subjects of the painters they most admire.

Dunlap's successor was the talented essayist, poet, and Italophile Henry T. Tuckerman, who surveyed the state of American art in his *Book of the Artists* of 1867.[6] Relying on Dunlap's work for the early artists, Tuckerman goes on to discuss the living painters and sculptors of New York, Boston, and, to a lesser extent, Philadelphia. Like Dunlap, he was part of the scene, and he knew it well. He was the first to pay special attention to the important group of collectors that developed in New York and other Eastern cities just as Thomas Cole and Asher B. Durand were coming to artistic maturity: Few collectors have ever had their choices of contemporary painters confirmed by posterity in the way that Luman Reed, Robert L. Stuart, and Robert Gilmor have.[7]

Not being a painter himself, Tuckerman had fewer of the personal conflicts and jealousies that Dunlap evidences, and he was less inclined to throw doubt on the integrity and character of the artists. Tuckerman knew many of them. His method is largely biographical following the example of Dunlap (and Vasari before him); though many more artists were at work in his time, he cast a smaller net than the earlier author as he devotes chapters to just 24 painters and 3 sculptors whose work he deemed most significant, along with an additional 150 practitioners he thought worthy of briefer mention. While Dunlap had ranked history painting and portraiture most highly, Tuckerman favored landscape and genre. He especially admired the painters of what would later be called the "Hudson River School" including John F. Kensett, Sanford Gifford, Worthington Whittredge, and their colleagues, but singled out for extended comment only the two archrivals, Frederic Edwin Church and Albert Bierstadt.[8] He saw Church as a flawless painter, and while he praised Bierstadt's *Rocky Mountains* ("no more genuine and grand American work has been produced . . ."), he also noted that he was "a true representative of the Dusseldorf school" with its "hard and dry" color, where skill often "prevailed over imagination."[9]

Tuckerman was less dogmatic and more open-minded than many historians before and after his time. He wrote, for example, "We are told that painters like Church are scientific and painters like Inness soulful, but their diversity is greatly exaggerated."[10] This was surely a jibe at the collector and writer James Jackson Jarves, whose own book, *The Art-Idea,* had recently appeared.[11] Jarves was a pioneering voice who advocated the new French style of Jean-François Millet and the Barbizon School and especially the work of William Morris Hunt and John La Farge, and thus disagreed with nearly every one of Tuckerman's evaluations.[12] The future of American painting, Jarves believed, lay not in the "cleverness" of the realists but rather in the moodiness of the "idealists" whom he considered "our most profound artists."[13] He rejected Frederic Edwin Church with his "laborious" work, while praising the young painters who had taken up the Barbizon manner for their "warmth, delicacy of execution, and refinement."[14] It would be more than a decade before Jarves's views were widely accepted, but one sees here hints of the next reversal of taste.

In 1864, the same year that Jarves's book was published, the Baltimore entrepreneur and art collector William T. Walters (1820–1894) abruptly decided to sell his fine small collection of Hudson River School paintings. His paintings included Frederic Edwin Church's *Twilight in the Wilderness* of 1860 (Cleveland Museum), which came to be regarded a century later as one of the masterpieces of the genre, and Sanford Gifford's *Castle of Chillon* of 1859 (Morse Museum of American Art); each boasted the special clarity of detail and light that marks the landscape school at its height. Walters replaced them with evocative academic pictures by Jean-Léon Gérôme and Lawrence Alma-Tadema, by the Barbizon masters Jean-François Millet and Theodore Rousseau, and by a few Americans like Julius Stewart. This put Walters at the forefront of the new taste, one that held sway through the rest of the century.

The developments that Jarves prophesied came to pass in the 1870s as the embrace of French art grew stronger. The Hudson River School style—after a relatively short heyday of some twenty years—began to appear literal and old-fashioned. Its canvases, large and small, had celebrated the "empty" American wilderness, the glory of Manifest Destiny, and the myth of carefree rural life. The end of the Civil War and a new ease of travel led more and more artists and wealthy collectors to venture abroad. French influence and the coming of a new landscape style were described by Samuel G. W. Benjamin in his book of 1880, *Art in America,* which outlined the transition from the realistic manner of the Hudson River School to a new one that featured the "subtle effects" of Alexander Wyant and "the vague suggestions, the symbolism and sympathy with the soul" of Jervis McEntee.[15] Benjamin lauded the forward-looking roles of La Farge and William Morris Hunt, viewing the latter as "a key promoter of the new art."[16] He was also ahead of his time in admiring Winslow Homer's "masterly watercolor sketches."[17] In Philadelphia he discovered some of the "new movement's powerful allies," singling out Thomas Eakins (while criticizing the "bloody thigh and crimson finger" in the *Gross Clinic*) and he was almost alone in admiring Mary Cassatt, whom he praised for the "superb treatment and composition of some of her works."[18] Benjamin also commented on what he called "the intellectual pendulum," shrewdly noting "that the time will come when they [the French-influenced paintings] in turn will be either sneered at or forgotten."[19] Benjamin was the most far-sighted observer of his era, and he was among the first American critics to understand that taste is constantly changing.

In the later seventies, American collectors became enamored of figurative paintings by the leading French academic masters. Prime evidence of this turnabout is found in Edward Strahan's massive three-volume tome of 1879, *The Art Treasures of America,* a compendium of the holdings of the leading collectors from across the nation.[20] The book had a thousand paying subscribers, and included chapters on thirty-four collectors, including William A. Corcoran, Mrs. A. T. Stewart, Robert L. Stuart, Collis P. Huntington, William T. Walters, and John Jacob Astor. The author covered the east coast thoroughly and included sections on the art lovers of Cincinnati, St. Louis, and San Francisco as well. It is surprising how all the leading collections looked alike, as they do in every era: Nearly all the collectors were buying Romantic period pieces and Orientalist scenes by the most respected Paris artists, including Jean-Léon Gérôme, Édouard Detaille, Paul Delaroche, William-Adolphe Bouguereau, and Alexandre Cabanel, along with a smattering of works by such Americans as Frederic A. Bridgman, Albert Bierstadt, Frederic Edwin Church, and Sanford Gifford.

Why the turn to Europe and especially France? The Union had won the war, commerce and industry were booming in the North, railroads united East and West in 1869, and suddenly the steamship made Europe far more accessible. France had been supportive of the Union cause, while England, with its reliance on Southern cotton, had hedged its bets. The scholar Barbara Weinberg saw the turn to France as evidence of a new American confidence, and she points to the rejection by an American jury of Bierstadt's *Last of the Buffalo* from the 1889 Paris Exposition as being the final nail in the coffin of the Hudson River School.[21] As in every era, there was an old guard lamenting change: As late as 1898, one finds Frederic Edwin Church plaintively writing his friend Martin Johnson Heade, "I hope French influence will die out."[22] He would have been pleased that his hope would shortly come true.

Most important for the American painters and collectors, Paris had become the center of the art world by the seventies. The competitive annual Salon, opening in May, was the major event of the season, and was open to foreign artists. As Lois Fink points out in her invaluable study, a thousand American artists exhibited at Salons between 1872 and 1899. In 1886, for example, the huge show of over five thousand works included 115 American painters and sculptors, followed by the Belgians, Swiss, English, and Italians.[23] The hope of the American painters in Paris was to have their work accepted at the Salon, both for the honor of it and to boost their chances of sales either in France or the US. They studied with the most successful French painters and naturally emulated their subjects and their styles, ones based on mastery of composition and the human figure, though the Americans eschewed the idealized nude subjects of the Europeans.[24] John Singer Sargent was just one of the many Americans who exhibited regularly at the Salon, where he experienced both success and failure. In 1882, he showed *El*

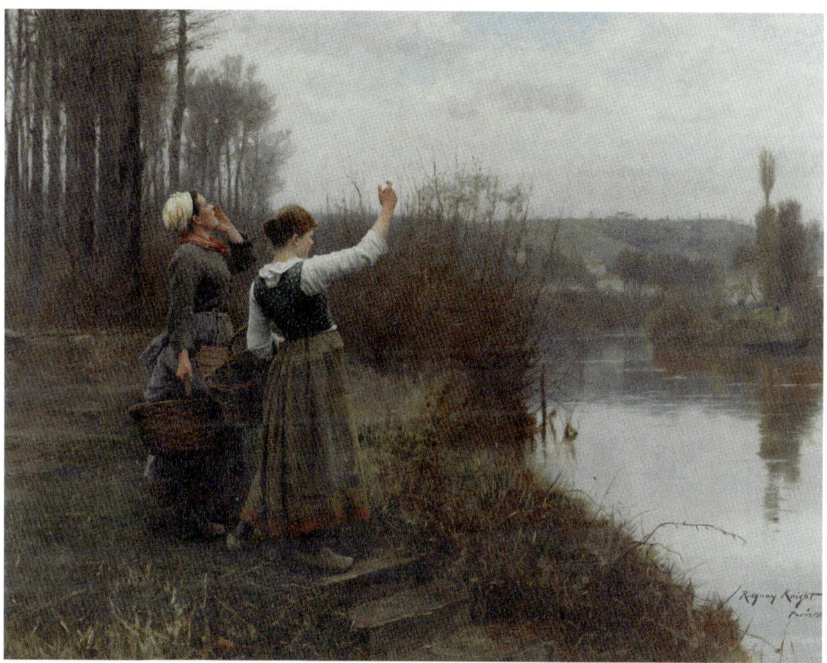

Fig. 3. DANIEL RIDGWAY KNIGHT,
Hailing the Ferry, oil on canvas, 1888. Pennsylvania Academy of the Fine Arts.

Jaleo there, and had the good fortune of having it quickly purchased by a traveling Bostonian, as I describe in the next chapter. But in 1884, he exhibited *Madame X* at the Salon, where it was harshly criticized, an experience that in part caused his move to London.

The prolific New York critic George W. Sheldon had begun as a champion of the old school: His *American Painters* of 1879 described the work of fifty painters, mostly landscapists, starting with Asher B. Durand. But within a few years, he totally reversed course. In his *Recent Ideals of American Art* of 1888, responding to the private collections being built in New York, he rejected the paintings he had once admired, criticizing the Hudson River School for its "blazing sunsets" and its "rush to the grandiose,"[25] while focusing instead on a group of younger American painters in Paris. Sheldon's favorites were Daniel Ridgway Knight (fig. 3) and Charles Sprague Pearce, both of whom painted rural workers and society women, followed by Francis D. Millet, a realist figurative specialist,

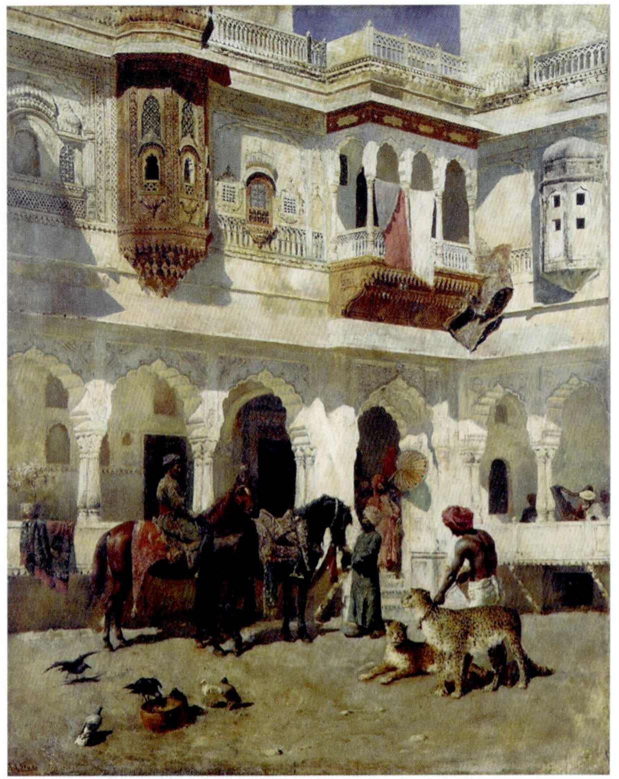

Fig. 4. EDWIN LORD WEEKS,
The Rajah Starting on a Hunt, oil on canvas, ca. 1885.
Metropolitan Museum of Art.

and Pinckney Marcius-Simons, who made colorful Symbolist paintings, along with Frederic A. Bridgman and Edwin Lord Weeks (fig. 4), Orientalists who painted scenes of India and the Near East.

What made the American artists American for Sheldon was strictly their place of birth; he found their residence abroad to be no handicap, and he preferred French subjects, saying "The American spirit, wherever its activities are displayed, is still American."[26] He opined that Julius Stewart's "'Portrait of Mme. La Comtesse de G—' . . . will retain its interest as long as it and our civilization last."[27] Sheldon made no mention of Frederic Edwin Church, and in his stead one finds him proclaiming that Frederick Stuart Church (fig. 5)—a New Yorker who had not trained in France—"has done more than any other American toward the establishment of a truly national school of American art."[28] This Church (no relation to Frederic Edwin) was an illustrator whose *Aesop's Fables* was much admired; his paintings feature dreamy, angelic young women often seen in the company of gentle lions and tigers. In *Recent Ideals*, Sheldon illustrated the work of 111 painters of the 1880s, but amazingly, to our eyes, he could not find a place for Eakins, Sargent, Whistler, or La Farge. The paintings he admired were skillfully painted;

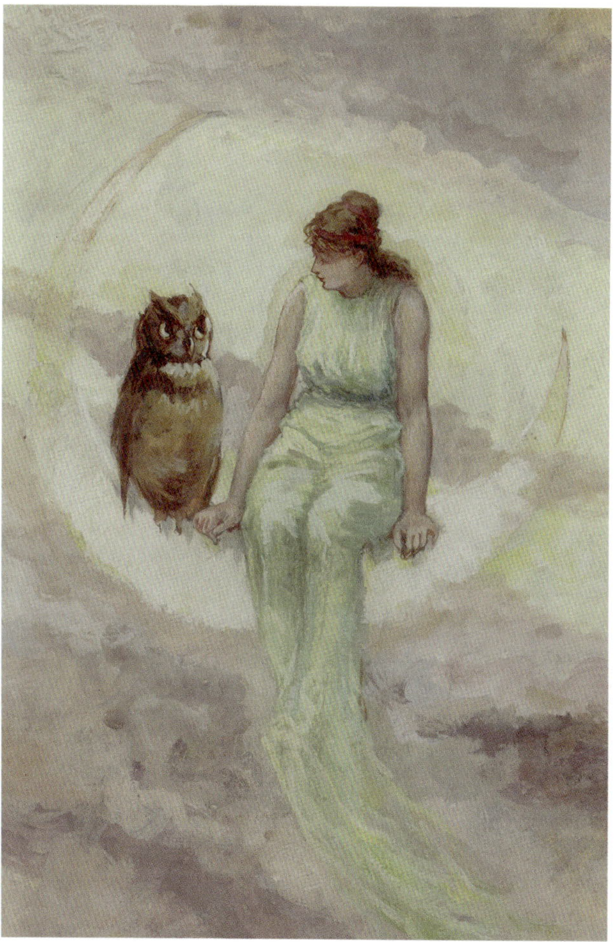

Fig. 5. **FREDERICK STUART CHURCH,**
The Witch's Daughter, detail, watercolor, 1881. Smithsonian American Art Museum.

they had all the quality one could want except for the one that the collectors began demanding around 1900, and that was Americanness.

Sheldon's book was illustrated exclusively with works owned by prominent private collectors, including William T. Evans, Thomas B. Clarke, Benjamin Altman, and other wealthy New Yorkers, and it seems likely that the collectors funded the lavish book. Sheldon viewed high prices as indicators of quality, as many are wont to do today. He reported enthusiastically on the extravagant amounts being paid for the most admired French painters as a way of justifying the collectors' enthusiasm for their lesser-priced American followers. Sheldon cited the record auction price of $45,500 paid for Jules Breton's *Communicants* in 1886, then the new record of $66,000 brought by Ernest Meissonier's *Battle of Friedland, 1807*, a very large, highly detailed depiction of Napoleon saluting his victorious troops, at the 1887 sale of Mrs. A. T. Stewart's collection, while noting that the buyer had quickly presented the work to the Metropolitan Museum. At the same sale, Cornelius Vanderbilt paid $53,000 for Rosa Bonheur's *Horse Fair* (fig. 6), for years the most popular painting in the world, one also given to the Met. Taste has turned dramatically against these paintings, though the *Horse Fair* still hangs at the Met, while the Meissonier does not. Finally, Sheldon records the bidding war in 1889 that resulted in France not allowing the

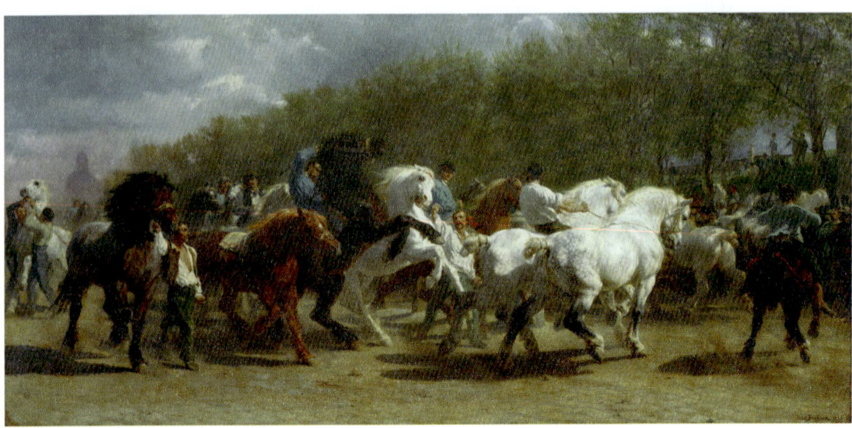

Fig. 6. ROSA BONHEUR,
The Horse Fair, oil on canvas, 1852–1855. Metropolitan Museum of Art.

hugely admired *Angelus* by Jean-François Millet to fall into American hands, at a cost of some $110,000 (nearly $3.5 million today).[29] Art lovers think of this period as the age of Impressionism, but in actuality Cézanne, Monet, and their peers were still largely unknown and wouldn't become widely admired until the twentieth century, while the American Impressionists were still unnoticed.

One wonders where all of the hundreds of once-admired Salon paintings have gone, as today there are almost none of them in American museums either on view or in storage. It would seem that most of the European works found their way back to the European market, while the ones by the Americans appear simply to have vanished. Rarely has a new art been embraced so passionately, then rejected so completely. However, Sheldon spoke for his generation, and many of his contemporaries agreed with his views. The important critic Clarence Cook, best known as an early friend of the American Pre-Raphaelites, published his own ambitious six-volume survey in 1888, *Art and Artists of Our Time*, that covered the painters of Europe and the US, with emphasis on the French, German, and British schools from Fragonard and Feuerbach to Rossetti and the Pre-Raphaelites. Cook had a jaundiced view of the Americans, taking up American art only in his sixth and final book where he wrote that "The history of art in America, from the earliest time to the present, is little more than a reflection of the art of different countries of Europe."[30] He reserved his highest encomiums for Sheldon's artists, including Charles Sprague Pearce, Daniel Ridgway Knight, Frederic A. Bridgman, and Julius Stewart, but also found space to admire the work of both Sargent and Whistler.

In 1889 the Boston writer Walter Montgomery edited and produced an equally ambitious though more insular two-volume work entitled *American Art and American Art Collections* that included essays on some sixty-eight artists and a variety of other topics by leading critics, including Samuel Benjamin and Mariana Griswold Van Rensselaer. Montgomery's authors agreed with the new taste for figurative paintings and illustrations but did so through a broad group of artists living in the United States, including Frederick Stuart Church, J. Francis Murphy, and Seymour Guy. Sheldon, Cook, and Montgomery all agreed that being an American painter meant being as sophisticated, as well trained, and as European-looking as possible.[31]

The Paris Exposition of 1889, both in its selection of 336 American works, and its awarding of honors and prizes to many Americans, closely echoed the views of Sheldon and Cook.[32] Chair of the Paris Committee was the much-admired Frederic A. Bridgman, who had been made a chevalier (or knight, the highest honor) a decade earlier at the 1878 Exposition. A majority of the American works were genre scenes by Paris-trained artists, paintings of rural or society figures or of exotic "characters," or ones set in the Near East or India; there were many landscapes as well, along with some portraits and religious scenes. Three of Sheldon's most admired artists received gold medals: William T. Dannat, Alexander Harrison, and Daniel Ridgway Knight, all Paris residents.[33] Today's critics consider their work "academic kitsch," and they are rarely collected or exhibited.[34] Yet there were also some surprises in the 1889 show. John Singer Sargent and James McNeill Whistler, painters then at the height of their careers, whose work earlier had gone unnoticed by Sheldon and the other American critics, both won high honors in Paris, Sargent as a chevalier, Whistler (exhibiting in the British section) with a gold medal. One wonders how Sheldon could have missed them; the answer I believe is that their work looked so different from the mainstream style, and was found to be of dubious merit precisely because of its originality.

The New York dry goods merchant William T. Evans (1843–1918) became interested in art when his wife gave him George Sheldon's book, *American Painters* of 1879. He became the biggest buyer of the day and eventually owned over eight hundred American pictures, all listed in William Truettner's exemplary article on the collector.[35] He was both a seller (with auctions in 1900 and 1913) and a generous donor to what is now the Smithsonian Museum of American Art and to the Montclair Art Museum. Sadly, he lacked an adventurous eye, and as time went on and the reputations of Homer and others rose, Evans kept on buying a canon already going out of fashion, including forty-one paintings and watercolors by Sheldon's favorite, Frederick Stuart Church. He also owned Alexander Wyant, Will H. Low, Otto W. Beck, and Henry Ward

Ranger in depth.[36] However, he did have eleven pictures by Homer, including *A Visit from an Old Mistress* of 1876. By today's standards or even those of his era, it was a mediocre collection, and Evans was also flawed himself, as someone who used company money to fund his art buying to the tune of some $700,000 (about $22 million today). Truettner describes how he was forced to sell both art and real estate to repay the firm.[37] He was far from the last collector to get into this kind of trouble.

The outstanding collector-dealer of the late nineteenth century was Thomas B. Clarke of New York, a manufacturer of collars and cuffs. Barbara Weinberg's excellent article about him includes a list of the entire collection, accompanied by the dates each work was bought or sold.[38] Clarke began in the early seventies by buying genre and still life paintings by Eastman Johnson and William Harnett along with such members of the Hudson River School as Thomas Cole, Albert Bierstadt, and Homer D. Martin, before moving in the early eighties to Sheldon's favorite figurative, Paris-trained artists, including Frederic A. Bridgman, and Robert Wylie along with some Barbizon-influenced landscapists. In the nineties he fell in love with the work of George Inness—he would own sixty-four examples—and Winslow Homer, buying thirty-eight of his paintings and watercolors. His Homers included *Two Guides* (Clark Art Institute); *Dressing for the Carnival* and *Maine Coast* (Metropolitan Museum of Art); *Eight Bells* (Addison Gallery, Andover); and *The Lookout—"All's Well"* (MFA, Boston).[39] He also purchased Blakelock and Wyant in depth. He owned just one Eakins, a genre picture, and nothing at all by Sargent, Whistler, or Cassatt; their work was just being discovered by American collectors.[40] Still, Clarke's range of interests and his discernment were extraordinary.

Clarke sold 372 works at auction in 1899 in the most important auction of American art of those years; it signaled the start of a new era marked by the rise of Winslow Homer and George Inness. The latter's works led the way with a top price of $10,000, followed by two now-forgotten figures, Homer D. Martin and George Fuller; the surprise came with four Winslow Homer oils that realized handsome prices from $2,585 to $4,500. Appreciation of the Tonalists was on the rise, with landscapes by

Murphy, Wyant, Ryder, and Tryon all bringing amounts in the $2,000 range, while prices for Sheldon's favorite Paris-trained painters were already sinking. By this time, the Hudson River School had lost almost all of its value: Many pictures barely reached $100. The sale also saw *The Ironworkers' Noontime* by Thomas Anshutz, now one of the treasures of the Rockefeller Collection in San Francisco, mustering a bid of just $150. Yet even the top prices for the American works failed to approach the price levels that French pictures were bringing at other sales. French works were still far more sought-after by wealthy Americans than the art of their own country; at the Schaus Sale in 1896, for example, a Theodore Rousseau brought $25,000 and a Constant Troyon $24,500.[41] However, that taste would shortly fade away.

The selection of American paintings at the Paris Exposition of 1900 confirmed the trends established by the Clarke Sale and established a radically new aesthetic. Just as the Paris exhibition of 1889 was a celebration of French influence on American art, the 1900 exposition celebrated Americanness. Critic after critic did an about-face, now praising homespun qualities, with one writing that the Americans who employed French style and subjects "have exchanged their birthright for a mess of pottage."[42] Another writer opined in 1900, "There is a sanity, a virility, a wholesome element in much of the home art that is lacking in that done in the Old World."[43] Yet despite this development, Sargent and Whistler were again recognized as the preeminent Americans. The critics acknowledged that their paintings were "not on the surface American," but rationalized that they were American enough by virtue of their American roots and the fact that their work did not resemble the French or any other school.[44] However, six others, including Winslow Homer, also won gold medals, and it was Homer whose work was most often singled out by the critics. He was well represented at the Paris Exposition and was doubly honored when *A Summer Night* was purchased by the French government for the Musée du Luxembourg.[45] A *New York Times* editorial proclaimed, "The veteran Winslow Homer is the most American of all."[46] The American commissioner general of the fair distinguished Homer as "one of our strongest and most distinctively national American painters."[47] The quality of his work had been briefly acknowledged by both Sheldon and Benjamin, but a consensus would have placed him no higher than the top two or three dozen American painters; suddenly, he was one of the stars of the Clarke sale and the Paris Exposition, and his reputation would continue to rise.

By 1900, mainstream taste had seen three major changes: First was the rise of Cole and Church at mid-century and the rejection of Dunlap's roster; then by 1875, came the replacement of those painters with a dramatically different taste, one that valorized French-influenced landscape and figurative art executed by Americans. Finally, around 1900, there developed a new preference for native artists exemplified by the rugged outdoor scenes of Winslow Homer. This dramatic reversal was marked by a new emphasis on Americanness and its corollaries, the search for manliness and originality, standards that would impact criticism during much of the following century.

---

[1] William Dunlap, *History of the Rise and Progress of the Arts of Design in the United States*, 3 vols. (Benjamin Blom, 1834).

[2] Dunlap, 1:149.

[3] Dunlap, 1:107, 109.

[4] Dunlap, 2:163.

[5] Dunlap, 3:150, 159. Dunlap was also generous to several promising younger artists, including John James Audubon (whom he disliked personally while still praising his work), William Sidney Mount, and Thomas Cole, among others. He famously records the occasion on which he, Trumbull, and Asher B. Durand discovered three of Cole's landscapes in a shop window in New York; he quickly published this account and credits himself with Cole's ensuing patronage.

[6] Henry T. Tuckerman, *Book of the Artists: American Artist Life, Comprising Biographical and Critical Sketches of American Artists: Preceded by a Historical Account of the Rise & Progress of Art in America* (G. P. Putnam & Sons, 1867).

[7] On the early collectors, see Linda S. Ferber and Margaret R. Laster, eds., *Tastemakers, Collectors, and Patrons: Collecting American Art in the Long Nineteenth Century* (Pennsylvania State University Press, 2024).

[8] Tuckerman, *Book of the Artists*, 371.

[9] Tuckerman, 392, 395.

[10] Tuckerman, 530.

[11] James Jackson Jarves, *The Art-Idea* (Harvard University Press, 1864).

[12] Jarves.

[13] Jarves, 233, 251, 249.

[14] Jarves, 232, 233, 222.

[15] S. G. W. Benjamin, *Art in America: A Critical and Historical Sketch* (Harper & Brothers, 1880), 82, 98, 75, 105, 103.

[16] Benjamin, 194.

[17] Benjamin, 117.

[18] Benjamin, 208, 209, 210.

[19] S. G. W. Benjamin, *The Life and Adventures of a Free Lance* (Free Press, 1914), 323.

[20] Edward Strahan, *The Art Treasures of America* (George Barrie, 1879). Strahan was a pseudonym for the Philadelphia art critic Earl Shinn, himself a painter and a friend of Thomas Eakins.

[21] H. Barbara Weinberg, "The Lure of Paris: Late-Nineteenth-Century American Painters and Their French Training," in *A New World: Masterpieces of American Painting, 1760–1910,* ed. Theodore E. Stebbins Jr. et al. (Museum of Fine Arts, 1983), 16–31.

[22] Theodore E. Stebbins Jr., *The Life and Work of Martin Johnson Heade: A Critical Analysis and Catalogue Raisonné* (Yale University Press, 2000), 116.

[23] Lois Marie Fink, *American Art in the Nineteenth-Century Paris Salons* (Cambridge University Press, 1990), 113, 132.

[24] As Fink also points out, the major teaching studio, the École des Beaux-Arts, was closed to women, who were treated unfairly in other ways as well. Fink, 135–37.

[25] George William Sheldon, *Recent Ideals of American Art* (D. Appleton, 1888), 43.

[26] Sheldon, 145.

[27] Sheldon, 114. For a contrary interpretation of this period, see Randall C. Griffin, *Homer, Eakins, and Anshutz: Search for Identity in the Gilded Age* (Pennsylvania State University Press, 2004). Griffin notes "the flood of European art into the United States" and the declining market for the Hudson River School and stresses "the outpouring of anti-European criticism," 12.

[28] Sheldon, 71.

[29] Sheldon, 122, 124. See also George W. Sheldon, *Ideals of Life in France, or, How the Great Painters Portray Women in French Art* (D. Appleton, 1890). This is another lavish book devoted to the salon painters.

[30] Clarence Cook, *Art and Artists of Our Time,* vol. 6 (Selmar Hess, 1888), 12.

[31] Montgomery included a number of illustrators, many of whom specialized in images of sweet, charming children at play. Like Sheldon, Montgomery admired the "large and free" style of Winslow Homer, and Benjamin in his essay that concludes the book opines that Homer's watercolors were now leading the field.

[32] For a good summary of the American painters at the fairs in London and Paris from 1851 to 1900, see Daniel Horowitz, "American Art at International Fairs in Europe, 1851–1900" (Honors thesis, Yale University, 1960).

[33] See the excellent catalogue by Annette Blaugrund and others, *Paris 1889: American Artists at the Universal Exposition* (Harry N. Abrams, 1989).

[34] See Lois M. Fink, "American Art at the 1889 Paris Exposition: The Paintings They Love to Hate," *American Art Journal* 5, no. 4 (1991): 34ff.

[35] William H. Truettner, "William T. Evans, Collector of American Paintings" *American Art Journal* 3, no. 2 (1971): 50ff.
[36] Theodore E. Stebbins Jr. et al., *A New World: Masterpieces of American Painting, 1760–1910* (Museum of Fine Arts, 1983), 16.
[37] Truettner, "William T. Evans," 62.
[38] H. Barbara Weinberg, "Thomas B. Clarke: Foremost Patron of American Art from 1872 to 1899," *American Art Journal* 8, no. 1 (1976): 52ff.
[39] Clarke later became involved in the production and sale of British portraits doctored to look American, as Richard Saunders describes in his essay, "Caveat Emptor: The Trade in American Historical Portraits in the Early Twentieth Century," in *Tastemakers, Collectors, and Patrons: Collecting American Art in the Long Nineteenth Century,* ed. Linda S. Ferber and Margaret R. Laster (Pennsylvania State University Press, 2024).
[40] See Stebbins, *A New World.*
[41] *Collector,* March 1, 1896, 136.
[42] K. C., "American Art in Paris: Its Standing in the City and the Exposition," *New-York Tribune,* July 7, 1900.
[43] C. F. Browne, "The Editor," *Brush and Pencil* 5, no. 3 (1899): 199–200, as quoted in Rodolphe Rapetti, "Assimilation and Resistance" in *Americans in Paris, 1860–1900,* ed. Kathleen Adler et al. (National Gallery, 2006), 181.
[44] K. C., "American Art in Paris."
[45] Nicolai Cikovsky Jr. and Franklin Kelly, *Winslow Homer* (Yale University Press, 1995), 402. See also David Park Curry, "American Art, American Power at the Paris Expositions Universelles," in Adler et al., *Americans in Paris.*
[46] "Paris Edition, *New York Times*: Nationality in Art," *New York Times,* July 17, 1900.
[47] John B. Cauldwell, "Report of the Department of Fine Arts," in *The Commissioner-General for the United States to the International Universal Exposition, Paris, 1900,* vol. 2 (Government Printing Office, 1901), 553.

2

The Rise of Museums and Professional Critics

Let us not, in the pride of our superior knowledge, turn with contempt from the follies of our predecessors. The study of the errors into which great minds have fallen in the pursuit of truth can never be uninstructive. As the man looks back to the days of his childhood and his youth, and recalls to his mind the strange notions and false opinions that swayed his actions at the time, that he may wonder at them; so should society, for its edification, look back to the opinions which governed ages that fled.

—CHARLES MACKAY, *Memoirs of Extraordinary Popular Delusions and the Madness of Crowds,* 1841

I suppose the picture-habit which I seem to have is as bad as the morphine or whiskey one . . .

—ISABELLA STEWART GARDNER, 1896

MUSEUMS BEGAN to collect nineteenth-century American paintings seriously in the first decade of the twentieth century, while increasingly able writers started devoting themselves to the field. It was taken for granted that the artists were white males based in New York or other urban centers. The audience grew, though for years to come it would consist largely of the educated elite of the northeast. Small-circulation journals beginning with *The Crayon* in 1855, the *Cosmopolitan Art Journal,* and *The Aldine* began to popularize art with a broader public, but only in the later years of the nineteenth century were art reviews appearing regularly in the newspapers and periodicals.[1] Books aimed at the growing audience began to be published. In 1900 came *Twelve Great Artists* by the Boston critic William Howe Downes, one of the first considerations of American artists as peers of the great European masters.[2] After describing the work of Rembrandt, Rubens, and others, the author examined the four best American painters in his judgment, Homer, Inness, La Farge, and Sargent. He praised Homer above all others for depicting "with nobility and simplicity, the continental American type of manliness." A few years later, he would write a handsome monograph on the painter.[3] Downes admired Homer for what he saw as the lack of outside influence on his work, his isolated lifestyle, and the vitality of his brushwork. The good critics are always nimble, and this writer used quite different terms to describe the greatness of Inness: Rather than manliness or Americanness, he found the key to Inness in his "master passion of love, the power of exaltation, the susceptibility to a great and uplifting emotion, a divine flight of the soul."[4] Downes viewed La Farge with equal enthusiasm; he fairly swooned over his South Seas watercolors and the stained-glass windows in Boston and Cambridge, works that would have been far less accessible to out-of-town writers.[5] Finally, he added a fourth painter to the canon, one whose paintings he had only recently come to know: This was John Singer Sargent. He based his new "aesthetic intoxication" on the exhibition of Sargent's portraits held in Boston in 1899.[6] He quickly recognized him as "the most spirited, dashing and brilliant of portrait painters," finding portraits like *Mrs. Carl Meyer and Her Children* of 1896 (Tate Britain) to be "unsurpassingly great" while criticizing the "harshness" of some of his male portraits.[7]

The four-man canon proposed by Downes is still recognizable today. Homer and Sargent remain among the most admired American painters, and while Inness and La Farge retain some of their former reputations, they gradually lost stature as Eakins and Whistler came to replace them in the top rank. Downes's small book was quickly followed by several ambitious surveys of the whole field: In quick order came Sadakichi Hartmann's *History of American Art* (1901),[8] two books by Charles H. Caffin (1902 and 1907),[9] and Samuel Isham's *American Painting* (1905).[10] Their publication tells us that American art was finding a wider audience. The writers all began by rejecting the older canons as defined by Dunlap and Tuckerman. Hartmann reported that West's history paintings "have become absolutely unpalatable to our modern generation," while Caffin described them as "pompous and pretentious."[11] All three found Washington Allston insignificant, Hartmann calling him "a sublime botcher and an imitator all his life," while Isham concluded that "it is as unlikely in Allston's case as that of West that posterity will ever renew its interest in his works."[12]

Hartmann, who wrote criticism for the *New York Evening Post* and for Alfred Stieglitz's *Camera Work*, set the stage for the work of Lloyd Goodrich and numerous later historians when he wrote that "the beginning of a native art" is found in the work of Winslow Homer and Thomas Eakins—"native" for him meaning white men born in the US. He found Homer's art to be "crude and angular, but classic in its dignity and strength"; when he came upon *The Gulf Stream* at the Knoedler Gallery several years before its purchase by the Met, he proclaimed it "one of the greatest pictures ever painted in America."[13] Similarly, he found in Eakins's pictures an "unbridled masculine power." He observed brutality in *The Gross Clinic*, but—perhaps taking a jab at Boston's favorite painters, Tarbell, Benson, and Paxton—he suggested that "our American art is so effeminate at present that it would do no harm to have it inoculated with some of that brutality."[14] Yet Hartmann surprisingly viewed Homer and Eakins as representing the past: While noting that both men were still active and that their work had "increased in interest," he believed nonetheless that their approach "has been superseded by other aims and ideals of art."[15] By this he meant the now-forgotten George Fuller, whose "idealized visions of shadowy outlines and soft rich color, rising from vague backgrounds" made him "the greatest genius which the art of our country has produced."[16] Though older than Homer or Eakins, Fuller was seen as representing the future. Fuller was the Ozymandias of his day; once so greatly admired, his work has virtually disappeared from museum walls.[17] Following Jarves and Benjamin, Hartmann valued suggestiveness in art. He rejected the Hudson River School as having "dealt wholly with externals," and embraced the Barbizon-influenced landscape painters, including George Inness ("our greatest landscape painter"), Alexander Wyant, Homer D. Martin, and Dwight Tryon, with their emphasis "on nature itself, the poetry and mystery of its simpler moods."[18] Hartmann was a photography critic, and this was an era when Pictorial photography, with its blurred images and its symbolic, emotional qualities, represented the height of modern art, like the landscape paintings he admired.

Two books by the Oxford graduate and art critic Charles H. Caffin, *American Masters of Painting* (1902), with its chapters on thirteen contemporary figures, and *The Story of American Painting* (1907), a survey from John Smibert to George Luks, share many views with Downes and Hartmann.[19] Caffin saw the landscape school much as Hartmann had, favoring George Fuller while ignoring Cassatt. In both books he wrote fulsomely about Whistler's work, and admired the work of Hassam and Twachtman ("the most modern note in painting"),[20] and he followed Downes in his admiration of Eakins, Homer, and Sargent, finding in the latter's portraits "the thrill of life," despite discerning in some "an elegant shallowness," thus foreshadowing some later critics.[21]

The third major writer of this decade, Samuel Isham, was cut from a different cloth, as a member of a wealthy New York family and an accomplished painter who had studied and exhibited in Paris after giving up a career in the law. His well-written *History of American Painting* of 1905 served as a standard text for decades. Like Hartmann and Caffin, he admired Homer's work unreservedly, but barely mentioned Eakins, finding his paint-handling "inelegant." However, because of his own experience abroad, he was the first to take heed of all three artists later grouped together as the "American expatriates." Isham singled out Sargent's "direct, fluent painting," and his "purity and brilliancy of color."[22] He concluded that he was the best portraitist since Reynolds and Gainsborough, and observed that "no one has read everyday character as minutely and completely as Sargent."[23] He made equally positive observations on the work of Whistler, who had died two years before, summing up his work as expressing "a sentiment of beauty most delicate, subtle, rare, almost impalpable and like that of no other man."[24] And unlike the other critics, he praised Cassatt, calling her the only American follower of Manet, and was puzzled about her lack of renown: "her painting is painters' painting, and makes its strongest appeal to members of her own craft," but, he went on, "the great public stands aloof, indifferent or hostile."[25] Isham found her mothers and children far more subtly executed than the popular ones of her French contemporary William-Adolphe Bouguereau. Thus, he implicitly replaced Eakins with Cassatt in the canon, the only important writer of this period to do so; this was understandable given the high value he placed on elegant brushwork and subtle coloration. Like Hartmann, Isham also held the Paris-trained Americans in high regard: Frederic A. Bridgman, Edwin Lord Weeks, and Daniel Ridgway Knight all are mentioned for the beauty and integrity of their work. Isham was also the only one of these writers to mention Henry Ossawa Tanner, whose work he would have known in Paris and whose paintings are so much admired today; he briefly described Tanner's scriptural subjects as being "painted with all the Oriental surroundings, but with strong, religious feeling."[26] Tanner was better recognized abroad than in the US, as evidenced by his *Resurrection of Lazarus* being purchased by the French government after winning a silver medal at the Paris Exposition of 1900; it is now at the Musée d'Orsay in Paris.

The first decade of the twentieth century saw the US coming of age as a world power, winning the Spanish–American War and expanding its empire to include the Philippines, Hawaii, and Puerto Rico. Martial values were increasingly celebrated and men's sports, along with hunting and fishing, became ways of building and reasserting one's masculinity as the nation turned from agriculture to become an urban society; outdoor games, hikes, and fitness programs helped men ward off the fear of "feminization." Men of this era became more and more afraid of effeminacy and homosexuality as France became associated with the effeminate.[27] These views are reflected in the contemporary fiction of Bret Harte and Jack London; they also paralleled the health and vitality movement of those years exemplified in the popular mind by the exploits of Theodore Roosevelt and his Rough Riders at San Juan Hill in 1898. As Sarah Burns recounts in her excellent study of the period, Roosevelt was considered a sissy when he was first elected to the New York Assembly in 1882, but he carefully honed a new image of himself as a cowboy/soldier/big game hunter, and he became a spokesperson for the strenuous outdoor life.[28] Roosevelt criticized President McKinley as having "no more backbone than a chocolate éclair."[29] As Burns tells us, fear of the unmanly and the degenerate was symbolized in the growing American distaste for the gay Irish poet Oscar Wilde during the nineties, an aversion that climaxed with Wilde's trial and conviction for "gross indecency" and his imprisonment in 1895. As a *Washington Post* editorial proclaimed on the eve of the Spanish–American war, "A new consciousness seems to have come upon us—the consciousness of strength. . . . The taste of Empire is in the mouth of the people."[30]

Winslow Homer's robust paintings of the Adirondacks and Maine, and Eakins's severe, unflattering portraits, along with his rowers, hunters, and boxers, not to mention Dr. Gross's bloody hand, make it easy to consider their art as being masculine. Homer perfectly reflected the new taste when he said, "I wouldn't go across the street to see a Bouguereau."[31] Whistler and Sargent, on the other hand, proved more difficult to rationalize, given their years abroad and the paucity of American outdoor subjects in their work. But Isham explained that "Whistler's Americanism is based partly on his temperament," while Caffin stressed that in Whistler's work "despite the mystery and spirituality," there is "no lack of virility."[32] Whistler was known as a womanizer, and this surely helped with identifying him as manly, according to the standards of that era. The critics struggled more with Sargent, whom Caffin makes the point of introducing as "an American of New England stock."[33] He praised his portraits for their very lack of "psychological analysis" or "sympathy with the subject," (apparently he saw these as inappropriate, unmanly qualities for an artist) and wrote instead of how "dispassionate" and "relentless" he was.[34] The writers all emphasize how Sargent worked long and hard in the best American tradition, Caffin describing his "exacting self-criticism and indomitable perseverance" while Isham reported on his "desperate hard work and struggles," and his "heads painted and scraped out thirty and forty times."[35] From this we see how the critical rationale for admiring the work of both Homer and Sargent has changed dramatically over the years.

Just as a new canon was being established after the turn of the century, the major American art museums began to build their collections of American paintings. They all acted in unison, following the same playbook: The artists on their minds were primarily Homer, Sargent, and Whistler, with Cassatt, Ryder, and Inness playing lesser roles, and Eakins following slightly later (just as nearly every museum today feels it must own work by Henry Ossawa Tanner, Kehinde Wiley, and David Drake). It is extraordinary how the art world always functions as a single organism, as it continues to do today. The Philadelphia Art Museum and the Art Institute of Chicago were buying boldly, but arguably the most farsighted institutional collecting in these years was done by the Metropolitan Museum of Art, which heretofore had demonstrated little interest in living American artists despite having had several painters among its founders. However, the donations of the wealthy New York merchant George A. Hearn (1835–1913) between 1906 and 1913 changed everything, for Hearn not only presented the museum with a group of landmark paintings but also provided an endowed purchase fund for works by living American painters that has proven useful ever since. Hearn was typical of his day in collecting both American and European pictures: His European works were of mixed quality, judging by present standards, but he did better with the contemporary Americans.[36] Of his fifty-six American paintings (I include here the works bought with his purchase fund during his lifetime, as he apparently instigated each one), thirteen remain on view at the Met, and only two have been deaccessioned. From today's vantage point, his coup was the group of five late Homer oils that he began to buy in 1901 and then gave to the Met in 1906 and 1911.[37] Along with his two paintings by George Inness, including *Peace and Plenty,* Theodore Robinson's *A Bird's-Eye View,* and a large Edwin A. Abbey that was his last purchase, they hang in the museum today, as does the Cassatt *Mother and Child (Baby Getting Up from His Nap)*

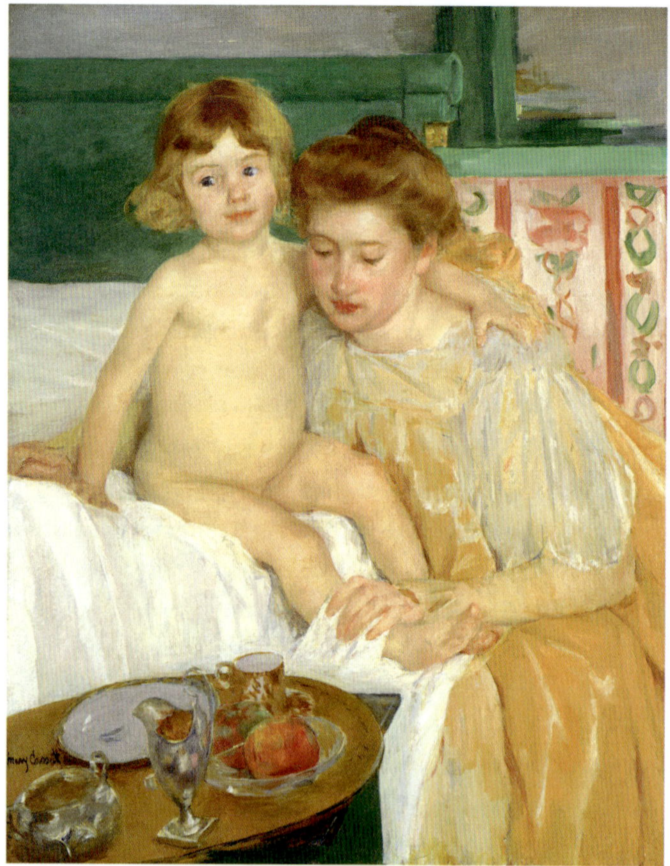

Fig. 7. MARY CASSATT,
Mother and Child (Baby Getting Up from His Nap),
oil on canvas, ca. 1899. Metropolitan Museum of Art.

(fig. 7) that was bought with his fund in 1909.[38] The latter was the museum's first Cassatt; the Met's collection of her work is not as strong as one would expect, for her friend Mrs. Louisine Havemeyer—who left such extraordinary French Impressionist pictures to the museum—never collected Cassatt's work seriously. Three of Hearn's Homers had come from Thomas B. Clarke, including the magnificent *Maine Coast* (fig. 8). Hearn was a rarity, a collector who thought for himself; his Homers were his triumph, and make up for his having only mediocre examples by Sargent and Whistler, and no Eakins at all. Hearn also bought Tonalist land-

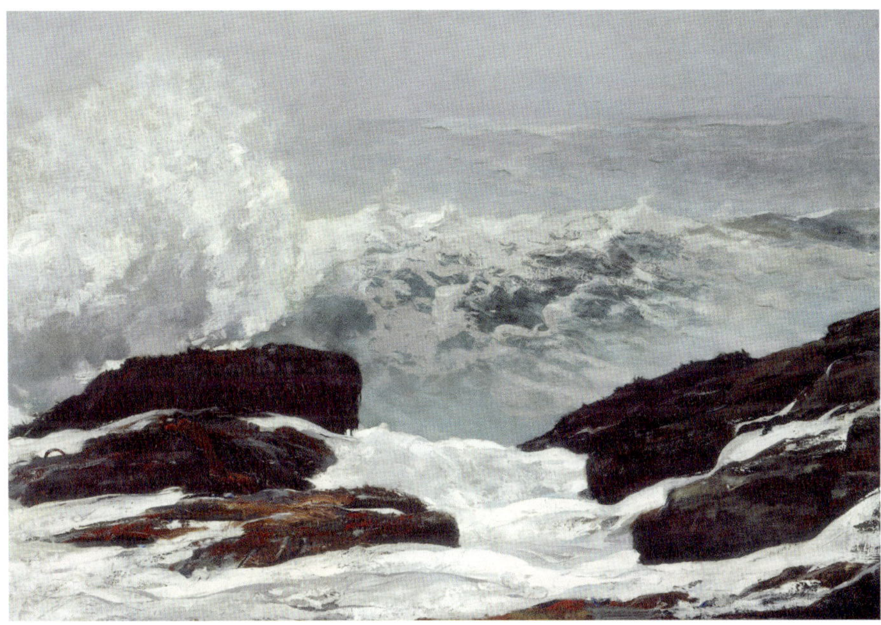

Fig. 8. WINSLOW HOMER,
Maine Coast, oil on canvas, 1896. Metropolitan Museum of Art.

scapes in depth, but his paintings by such once-popular artists as Louis Paul Dessar, Elliott Daingerfield, and Horatio Walker have mostly disappeared from the Met's galleries, not because they are poor examples but rather because taste turned so strongly against that school. At the end of his life, it was said that Hearn's two favorite artists were Winslow Homer and Alexander Wyant (fig. 9); there is no better illustration of how taste changes, for Homer continues to be considered one of the greats, while Wyant's reputation has plummeted.[39] One has trouble imagining how an admirer of Homer's *Maine Coast* could have also bought George Fuller's *The Quadroon* (fig. 10), yet Hearn chose them both.[40] Fuller's work won high praise during his lifetime, with the *Art Amateur* in 1880, for example, finding *The Quadroon* "full of expression, deep feeling, and real sentiment."[41] No painter's reputation has declined more completely.[42]

The Met's outstanding collection didn't happen by accident. Great acquisitions are typically the result of a combination of factors: an energetic curator with a passion for the material, an understanding board,

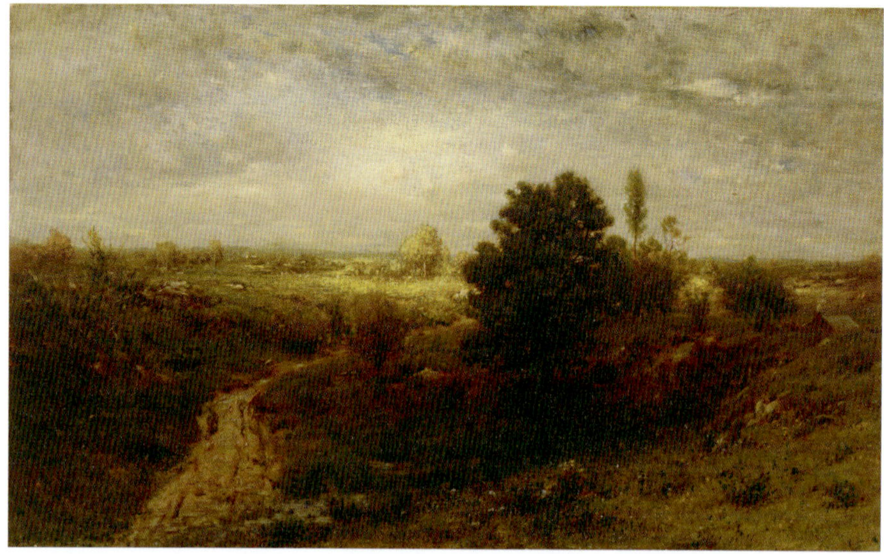

Fig. 9. **ALEXANDER H. WYANT,**
Keene Valley, oil on canvas, ca. 1884–1886. Brooklyn Museum.

a cooperative director, and adequate funding. The Met in 1905 had a new director, Sir Caspar Purdon Clarke, new board leadership under J. P. Morgan, and a new policy favoring the growth of the American collection.[43] At the Met, as at every major museum for years to come, there was a single paintings department, whose curator was typically a Europeanist; thus, the amount of attention accorded to American paintings was always a matter of chance. The curator of paintings from 1906 to 1908 was the gifted British modernist critic Roger Fry, who was just discovering Cézanne and working on his Post-Impressionist exhibition of 1910, but had no interest in American paintings; fortunately for the American collection, he left after a brief stay. Fry's assistant Bryson Burroughs, himself a modestly talented painter and a follower of Pierre Puvis de Chavannes, served as curator of paintings from 1909 to his death in 1934 and was a different story. He was surely one of the great professionals, overseeing as he did the Hearn gifts, encouraging other important donations and bequests, mounting memorial exhibitions of Whistler, Eakins, Homer, Chase, and Ryder, and making a series of extraordinary purchases, besides overseeing the European paintings. I have always thought that the best curators, like Burroughs, should have little plaques in the galleries recognizing their contributions, but alas, they do not.

The Met in 1906 finally purchased Winslow Homer's *Gulf Stream* from Knoedler, after rejecting it earlier, even as Hearn was donating his collection. During the following decade the museum bought Albert Bierstadt's oversized *The Rocky Mountains, Landers Peak,* while bequests brought Frederic Edwin Church's *Heart of the Andes,* and Sanford Gifford's *Kauterskill Clove,* demonstrating the benefits of the museum being in the city where so many major artists had lived and worked.[44] The leading critics of that time considered these painters to

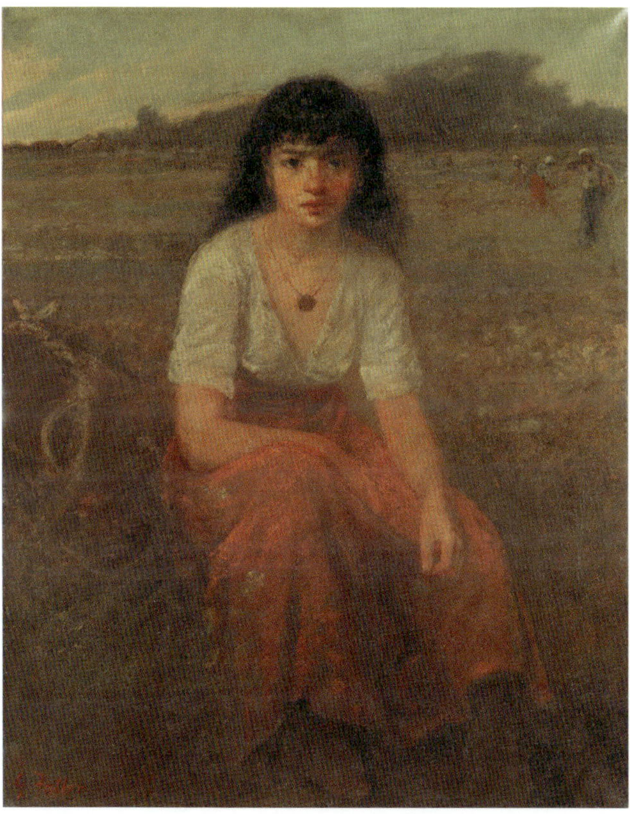

Fig. 10. **GEORGE FULLER,**
The Quadroon, oil on canvas, 1880. Metropolitan Museum of Art.

be totally out of date, but good curators often ignore the critics and listen to what their eyes tell them. Ahead of his time, Burroughs used all three canvases in his 1917 exhibition, "Painters of the Hudson River School."[45] The teens also saw Burroughs purchase three full-length portraits now regarded as landmarks, including John Singer Sargent's *Madame X*, James McNeill Whistler's *Portrait of Theodore Duret*, and Thomas Eakins's *The Thinker*. The Met committed to Eakins before any other museum, even Philadelphia, continuing to buy important paintings by him over the following decades.[46] It had received a Ryder as a gift from George Hearn in 1909, and in the same year bought another, then purchased a third with Hearn's fund in 1915. Ryder was considered a canonical figure through the twentieth century, but, perhaps due to the general rejection of Tonalism, he is no longer. In 1933 came one of the great buys of that or any time when *Fur Traders Descending the Missouri* by George Caleb Bingham was acquired for about $800; this unknown Missouri painter would promptly join the canon. Thus, even before the Met's American Wing was opened in 1924, and long before the museum had a curator of American art, the core of a great collection had been established through a combination of gifts and purchases.

The reputations of the painters judged preeminent by Caffin and Isham held up generally well as the new century went on, with the notable exceptions of George Fuller and John Singer Sargent. Fuller's decline was lasting, while Sargent's was not. Sargent's reputation had risen dramatically in the first decades of the century, due in part to the popularity of his watercolors. In 1909 something of a feeding frenzy began when the Brooklyn Museum bought nearly every work, eighty-three in all, from his first watercolor exhibition in this country, and the Museum of Fine Arts, Boston, and the Worcester Museum followed suit, purchasing large groups of his watercolors respectively in 1912 and 1917. Within a year of Sargent's death in 1925, large-scale memorial exhibitions of his work were mounted in Boston, London, and New York. But then came Roger Fry's scathing review of the London show, where he described Sargent's "uniform superficiality of observation," one "unhampered by aesthetic scruples."[47] Many observers credit that article as sinking the painter's reputation, though the painter's lackluster depictions of the Great War, his turgid murals in Boston and Cambridge, and the growing popular awareness of modernism all surely contributed. Biographies published by Downes in 1926 and by Evan Charteris in 1927 failed to stem the tide, and the painter went quickly from being renowned to being considered a shallow society painter, though a few discerning private collectors like Grenville Winthrop (discussed in chapter 7) continued buying his work. Even forty years later, two leading scholars echoed Fry's judgment. Barbara Novak in her book of 1969, *American Painting of the Nineteenth Century*, devoted just over a page to him, noting how "fashionable success could also divert his natural facility to superficial ends," while John Wilmerding in his survey of a year later wrote of the painter, "At his weakest (for example, in his watercolors), Sargent represented the triumph of superficiality."[48] Thus, within a few years, Sargent went from being one of the most admired of American painters to being thought a lightweight, a charge that lasted until the 1970s when it was roundly rejected by a new generation of critics and collectors.

Boston's Museum of Fine Arts lacked major purchase funds. But unlike New York, Chicago, and Philadelphia, the city already had its colonial and federal pictures and had no need to buy them. In addition, the founders of the museum had proclaimed that it had "a local duty" to collect the works of the leading Boston artists.[49] The museum's first acquisition, in 1870, was the gift of a painting by Washington Allston, while its first purchase of an American work, a few years later, was another picture by Allston; other early donations included important works by Copley, Stuart, and John Trumbull. Over time, the museum has gathered definitive holdings in the work of Copley and Stuart, who today retain their high rank if not their market, and of Allston and Hunt, both of whose work has lost almost all of its onetime luster.

Boston did very well with the "local painters" Homer and Sargent, but was slower to appreciate out-of-town figures such as Whistler and Eakins. Winslow Homer was a native Bostonian, and his work, especially his watercolors, was always popular there. In his case, the Museum of Fine Arts was a decade ahead of the Met, buying *The Fog Warning* in 1894 and *The Lookout—"All's Well"* in 1899, during the painter's lifetime. The MFA in 1899 also became the first museum to buy Homer's watercolors, purchasing *Leaping Trout* at the Thomas B. Clarke Sale in February, then buying three more fishing scenes from his Boston dealer Doll & Richards in May.[50] Important smaller genre paintings were still available a half century later, and were purchased in 1941 and 1953. Then in 1993 I was lucky enough, as curator, to buy Homer's *Driftwood* of 1909 for the museum, his final painting and the last privately owned Prout's Neck oil. I'm still amazed that another museum or one of the aggressive dealers didn't get there before I did.

John Singer Sargent also became a virtual Bostonian, through his successful portrait painting campaigns in the city, the patronage of Mrs. Gardner, and the fact of his being commissioned to paint murals at the Boston Public Library, Harvard, and the MFA itself. In 1905 the museum boldly bought Sargent's remarkable small oil *An Artist in His Studio* that had been executed just the year before, making it the first Sargent to enter the collection. In 1922, the museum purchased two other freshly observed, arguably impressionistic, pictures from opposite ends of the painter's career, *The Pasdeloup Orchestra*, 1876, and *The Master and His Pupils*, 1914. The now-famous family portrait *Daughters of Edward Darley Boit* was donated in 1919, and superb gifts from local families continued to arrive over the years, including a ravishing portrait of Mrs. Charles Inches in 1991. In 1986 the museum at the suggestion of curator Trevor Fairbrother purchased the *Nude Study of Thomas E. McKeller*, a unique portrayal of a Black man and a work whose importance is now widely recognized, and my successors bought *Charles Stewart Carrying the Great Sword of State* of 1904, a grandiose composition that perfectly sums up Sargent's successful career in London. Today the MFA's Sargent collection is rivaled only by the Tate's in London, largely thanks to gifts but also because curators traditionally have liked to build on strength, their aim always being the creation of a definitive holding.

While the Met acquired its fine Mary Cassatts through gifts, including one from the artist herself late in life, the Museum of Fine Arts was largely obliged to purchase her work, something it did effectively starting with *In the Loge* in 1910, a year after the Met had bought its first Cassatt, followed by a pastel in 1932 and then the wonderful oil, *The Cup of Tea,* in 1942. It received the marvelous *Ellen Mary in a White Coat* from a family member in 1982. Several decades after the Met and several other museums had acted, but still in time to procure excellent examples, the MFA began buying important works by major non-Boston artists, including Whistler (1939 and 1942) and Eakins (1935 and 1943), as well as Ryder and Blakelock (1945 and 1946). That these works were available in the forties suggests how slowly interest in American art had grown during the first half of the century. This was an era when important works remained on the market for years, and when there were few collectors, important exhibitions, or scholarly publications in the American field.

In addition, Boston boasted a great collector of its own in the form of Isabella Stewart Gardner, who is known for her old masters but deserves more credit than she has been given as a bold collector of modern art. She was a talented, driven buyer in what had been thought a man's field. She loved art passionately, possessed a keen eye, and didn't mind spending money. "Mrs. Jack," as she was called, fortuitously turned to excellent advisors, including Bernard Berenson, in the years before the mega-rich Frick and Mellon began using him. In 1903 she opened her own museum, just blocks from the Museum of Fine Arts. Henry James introduced Gardner to the young John Singer Sargent in 1886, and she commissioned him to paint her full-length portrait in 1888 when he first visited Boston. Though that work is not one of his most successful, Gardner played an important role in establishing Sargent's reputation in that city, while acquiring another sixty of his works during her lifetime. Gardner in 1886 also bought the first of several paintings by James McNeill Whistler; they became friends and correspondents, and she went on to collect two of his ethereal, nearly abstract oils, along with dozens of his pastels, drawings, and etchings. It is difficult to imagine her ever owning a Homer or an Eakins; her taste was for the genteel, and their art was simply too raw, perhaps too masculine, for her. Mrs. Gardner's taste was consistent; she loved a certain kind of art, and she went after it enthusiastically.

One of Mrs. Gardner's triumphs was her acquisition of Sargent's *El Jaleo* (fig. 11), a work now recognized as one of the greatest American paintings. It was a gift to her from Thomas Jefferson Coolidge II (1831–1920), a major figure in Boston as the operator of textile mills and railroads, ambassador to France, and a relative of hers by marriage. Art was only a minor interest for Coolidge. However, he found himself in Paris in early May 1882 at the end of a long trip to Egypt, and on May 11 he bought *El Jaleo* from the Salon for 10,000 francs. It is a huge picture, eight by eleven feet; its unconventional, sensual subject had few precedents in European painting, and none in American. One guesses that Coolidge took a chance on the young American as he went about filling the large, empty walls in his new house on Beacon Street to go with his pictures by Jean-Léon Gérôme, Adolf Schreyer, and Constant Troyon. Once Mrs. Jack learned of the painting, she persuaded Coolidge to lend it for her new Spanish Cloister then pressed him to make the gift, as he did in 1914.[51]

Just as New York had George Hearn and Boston Isabella Stuart Gardner, so Philadelphia boasted an important collector of European

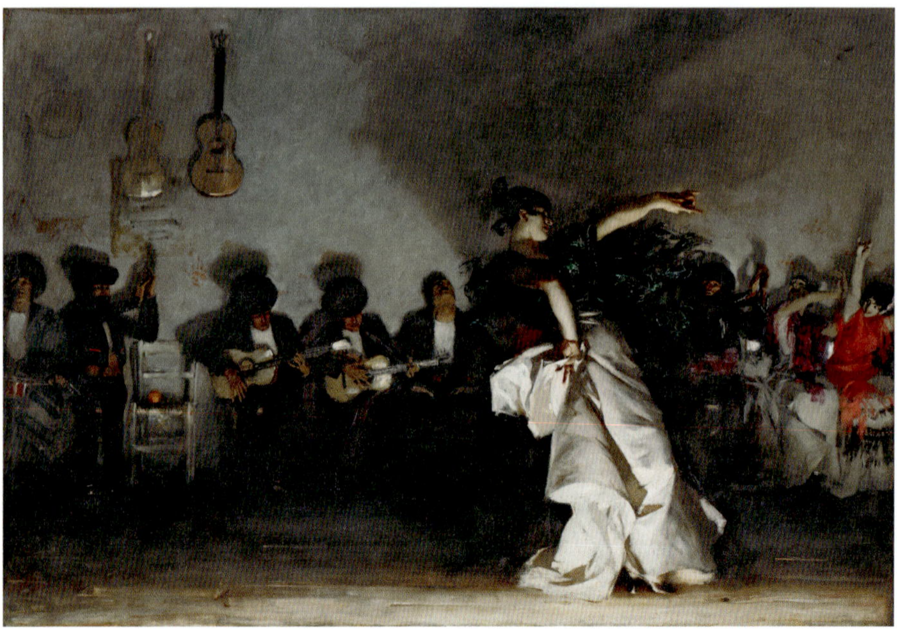

Fig. 11. JOHN SINGER SARGENT, *El Jaleo*, oil on canvas, 1882. Isabella Stewart Gardner Museum.

and American art, John G. Johnson. As early as 1906, Johnson gave the Philadelphia Museum of Art his interesting early oil, *A Balcony in Seville* by Mary Cassatt—making that museum the first to own her work. Then he followed up in 1917 by donating Homer's superb *Winter Coast* and Sargent's *Luxembourg Gardens,* along with two fine Whistler oils. Earlier, in 1895, Philadelphia had purchased Whistler's *Arrangement in Black,* the first painting by the artist to be bought by an American museum; a second pioneering purchase was the acquisition of Henry Ossawa Tanner's *Annunciation* in 1899. The museum then continued to fill out its holdings of all three artists' work, in the twenties buying Cassatt's *Woman and Girl Driving,* two more major Homers—*The Lifeline* and *Huntsmen with Dogs*—and Sargent's superlative *The Rialto,* a highly original view from underneath the legendary Venetian bridge.

The Philadelphia Art Museum, like the Museum of Fine Arts, concentrated for years on building its holdings of local favorites, in its case, the Peale family and Thomas Eakins, just as Boston built its collections of Copley, Sargent, Homer, and the Boston School of Tarbell and Benson. Much of Philadelphia's outstanding Eakins collection came as gifts of 1929 and 1930 from the painter's estate, while paintings by the Peale family arrived regularly as gifts, being supplemented in recent years by donations from the dedicated local collector Robert L. McNeil Jr. In 1945 Philadelphia purchased Charles Willson Peale's trompe l'oeil double portrait, the *Staircase Group,* a landmark picture that anchors its Peale collection. Then in 2006 an even more important purchase took place when the Jefferson Medical School finally—after spurning offers for years—agreed to sell Eakins's *Gross Clinic,* widely regarded as one of the greatest of all American paintings, to Alice Walton's new Crystal Bridges Museum in Arkansas and the National Gallery of Art for $68 million. These partners were brought together by John Wilmerding, Mrs. Walton's advisor and a former curator, donor, and trustee at the National Gallery. The seller agreed to let Philadelphia keep the painting if the funds could quickly be raised, and incredibly, the city succeeded in doing so. A key to this was a temporary alliance of the museum and the Pennsylvania Academy of the Fine Arts, with the institutions embarking on a joint campaign to raise the money, agreeing that the painting would be jointly owned if they succeeded. The Philadelphia Museum's much-loved late director Anne d'Harnoncourt and her board and colleagues led by curator Kathleen Foster persuaded political and civic leaders, wealthy citizens, and some 3,600 donors of the crucial importance of their effort. This is the most impressive example of artistic leadership and civic pride that I know of. The price remains the record for a nineteenth-century American painting, though modern works by Pollock, Warhol, and Lichtenstein have sold for much more, suggesting again how taste has moved to contemporary art.

A visit to Philadelphia's first museum, the Pennsylvania Academy, is necessary if one is to understand the history of American taste, for its collection graphically illustrates Dunlap's old canon. In 1805, the year of its founding, the Academy elected the aged Benjamin West in London, its first honorary member. Three of his most important paintings remain on view at the Academy, including *Death on a Pale Horse* of 1817, a gigantic work of some fifteen by twenty-five feet that the Academy mortgaged itself to purchase in 1836, and one that virtually defines the Romantic style, along with West's equally large classical composition *Christ Rejected,* and his earlier *Penn's Treaty with the Indians* of 1771. Nearby one sees another huge painting that was revered in its day, Washington Allston's *The Dead Man Restored to Life* (fig. 2), an Academy purchase in 1816. Here one also finds a series of other oversized paintings that were long thought to represent the epitome of American art: Charles Willson Peale's iconic *The Artist in His Museum,* Gilbert Stuart's *Lansdowne Portrait,* Thomas Birch's *Perry's Victory on Lake Erie,* Thomas Sully's *George Cooke as Richard III,* John Vanderlyn's *Ariadne Asleep on the Island of Naxos,* C. R. Leslie's *Murder of Rutland,* and John Neagle's *Pat Lyon at the Forge.* Dunlap would be pleased to visit this fine holding of the painters he so much admired, who are little studied by scholars and art lovers today, but not quite as forgotten as Samuel Isham and the others had predicted.

The Pennsylvania Academy completely missed Cole, Church, and the Hudson River School, as those artists hadn't worked in Philadelphia, but its late-nineteenth-century acquisitions illustrate the subsequent canons described by Sheldon and Isham. Purchases from

1881 on include major works by several of the most admired contemporary painters working abroad, including William L. Picknell, Charles Sprague Pearce, George Maynard, and Alexander Harrison. The year 1892 brought to the Academy a talented new director, Harrison Morris, who guided the acquisition of modern works by Frank Duveneck, William Merritt Chase, Thomas Eakins, and Cecilia Beaux. Most remarkable was his snapping up one of the greatest of Winslow Homer's paintings, the *Fox Hunt,* in 1894, the year after it was painted; this was one of the first two institutional purchases of a Homer oil. These works are superbly housed in one of the great American museum buildings, a muscular Victorian monolith designed by Frank Furness, built in 1876 and wonderfully preserved since then. On the negative side, Morris also established a tradition of anti-modernism at the Academy that served it less well over the years.

Chicago, like New York, was more forward-looking than Boston in both its art and architecture. Perhaps because of its early enthusiasm for the French Impressionists, Chicago adopted Whistler's work as representative of modern American art. His paintings and prints were exhibited in the city regularly starting in 1885, and several private collectors began buying his work in the years after the Exposition of 1893.[52] The Art Institute in 1900 purchased its first Whistler oil, *Nocturne: Blue and Gold*; it then went on to build a large collection of the artist's work in all mediums. The city boasted wonderfully adventurous collectors, including the talented, energetic Mrs. Potter Palmer, whose Monets and other French Impressionists, now at the Art Institute, are outstanding; she herself purchased her first Whistler painting, *Gray and Silver,* as early as 1892.[53] In the following year, Chicagoan Arthur J. Eddy commissioned his own full-length portrait from Whistler.[54] The painter early on became well known and widely collected internationally, stemming in part from the purchase of his famous *Mother* by the French government in 1891 after being shown at the Salon a few years earlier: The Whistler boom only increased with the praise showered on his work by the turn-of-the-century writers. Curator/scholar David Park Curry writes that "speculation in Whistler's work was at its height" during the first decade of the twentieth century, a period when the Detroit collector Charles Lang Freer went about creating, with Whistler's assistance, the largest collection in the world of the artist's work in every medium.[55] Thus, in the years before the First World War, Whistler had become the most highly patronized and best known American artist, through the intermingled activities of critics, collectors, and museums, together with those of the self-promoting artist himself.

The Art Institute also embraced the Americans who worked in Impressionist and Impressionist-related styles, acquiring William Merritt Chase's *Alice* by gift in 1893, and in 1910 buying Mary Cassatt's superb *Child's Bath*. 1914 saw the purchase directly from John Singer Sargent of his scintillating painting *The Fountain, Villa Torlonia,* a work at once a portrait of two artist friends, an evocation of Italy, and a demonstration of the painter's pseudo-plein air, Impressionist style. Mrs. Potter's friends, the Ryersons, loved French painting above all, but they also collected an outstanding group of Winslow Homers, all apparently purchased on a single day in early November 1915 from Knoedler. On this amazing outing, the Ryersons bought Homer's impressive oil, the *Herring Net* of 1885, along with about eighteen of that artist's watercolors, including some truly splendid late examples, all later given to the Art Institute. Those were the days.

---

[1] See Anne Farmer Meservey, "The Role of Art in American Life: Critics' Views on Native Art and Literature, 1830–1865," *American Art Journal* 10, no. 1 (1978): 73ff.

[2] William Howe Downes, *Twelve Great Artists* (Little, Brown, 1900).

[3] Downes, 106. See also William Howe Downes, *The Life and Works of Winslow Homer* (Houghton Mifflin, 1911).

[4] Downes, *Twelve Great Artists,* 146.

[5] Downes, 153.

[6] Downes, 165.

[7] Downes, 169–71.

[8] Sadakichi Hartmann, *A History of American Art,* 2 vols. (L. C. Page, 1901).

[9] Charles H. Caffin, *American Masters of Painting* (Doubleday, Page, 1902); Charles H. Caffin, *The Story of American Painting: The Evolution of Painting in America, from Colonial Times to the Present* (Frederick A. Stokes, 1907).

[10] Samuel Isham, *The History of American Painting* (Macmillan, 1905).

[11] Caffin, *Story of American Painting*, 11; Hartman, *History of American Art*, 1:22.
[12] Hartmann, *History of American Art*, 1:38; Isham, *History of American Painting*, 136.
[13] Hartmann, 1:200, 189.
[14] Hartmann, 1:203.
[15] Hartmann, 1:189.
[16] Hartmann, 1:137, 210, 207.
[17] See Percy Bysshe Shelley's sonnet, "Ozymandias" (1818). In the spring of 2024, I found a Fuller hanging at the Addison Gallery of American Art at Andover. It was *Romany Girl*, formerly in the Thomas B. Clarke collection. It had been purchased for the Addison in 1928 when the painter's reputation was still high, for $28,500 (about $500,000 in today's dollars), according to curator Gordon Wilkins.
[18] Hartmann, *History of American Art*, 1:179. For an articulate essay championing these painters, see Frederic Fairchild Sherman, *Landscape and Figure Painters of America* (New York, 1927).
[19] In *American Masters of Painting*, Caffin discusses six painters who still rank high according to current taste (Inness, La Farge, Whistler, Sargent, Homer, and Stuart), along with one who retains a moderate reputation (Brush), and six who are rarely mentioned now (Abbey, Fuller, Martin, Wyant, Tryon, and Walker).
[20] Caffin, *Story of American Painting*, 278.
[21] Caffin, 253.
[22] Isham, *History of American Painting*, 431.
[23] Isham, 434.
[24] Isham, 339.
[25] Isham, 412.
[26] Isham, 417.
[27] See Michael Kimmel, *Manhood in America* (Oxford University Press, 2018), 101ff. See also Monica Rico, *Nature's Noblemen: Transatlantic Masculinities and the Nineteenth-Century American West* (Yale University Press, 2013).
[28] Sarah Burns, *Inventing the Modern Artist* (Yale University Press, 1996), 97.
[29] Kimmel, *Manhood in America*, 95.
[30] As quoted in Howard Zinn, *A People's History of the United States* (HarperCollins, 1999), 299.
[31] Burns, *Inventing the Modern Artist*, 42. The painter who was actually closest to Theodore Roosevelt and the strenuous life was Frederic Remington, who made his first trip west in 1881. He made eighty-three illustrations for Roosevelt's book *Ranch Life and the Hunting Trail* of 1888, and a year later, he won a medal at the Paris Exposition. In 1898 Remington witnessed the Rough Riders' assault on San Juan Hill, and after the war, Roosevelt's soldiers gave him a cast of Remington's *Bronco Buster* as a memento. Yet despite his undoubted credentials as an artist of manly, frontier subjects, Remington failed to win acceptance in the canon until the mid-twentieth century, when wealthy ranchers and oil men like Amon Carter began collecting his work.
[32] Isham, *History of American Painting*, 428; Caffin, *Story of American Painting*, 300.

[33] Caffin, 245.

[34] Caffin, 246.

[35] Caffin, 249; Isham, *History of American Painting,* 431.

[36] They range from a handful of portraits by Raeburn and Beechey, a Richard Wilson Italian view, and an interesting *Angelica and Medoro* by Jacques Blanchard to a variety of undistinguished copies and misattributions, many of which have been sold off by the museum.

[37] Metropolitan Museum of Art accession numbers: *Northeaster* (10.64.5), *Moonlight, Wood Island Light* (11.116.2), *Maine Coast* (11.116.1), *Cannon Rock* (06.1281), and *Searchlight on Harbor Entrance, Santiago de Cuba* (06.1282).

[38] Hearn apparently selected the paintings purchased with his fund. See Amelia Peck and Thayer Tolles, "Creating a National Narrative," in *Making The Met, 1870–2020,* ed. Andre Bayer and Laura D. Corey (Metropolitan Museum of Art, 2020), 114.

[39] See "In Memoriam: George Arnold Hearn, a Trustee of the Metropolitan Museum, 1903–1913," *Metropolitan Museum of Art Bulletin* 9, no. 1 (1914): 2–9. See also *The George A. Hearn Gift to the Metropolitan Museum of Art* (Metropolitan Museum of Art, 1906).

[40] George Fuller's *The Quadroon* makes use of an outdated term meaning a person of mixed race, typically one with one quarter African descent and three quarters European.

[41] *Art Amateur* 3, no. 1 (1880): 2, as quoted in Natalie Spassky, *American Paintings in the Metropolitan Museum of Art,* vol. 2 (Metropolitan Museum of Art, 1985), 152.

[42] Interestingly, curator Sylvia Yount told me that she had hoped to hang it in her reinstalled galleries, but that its compromised condition prevented it. Sylvia Yount, email to the author, July 2, 2024.

[43] Peck and Tolles, "Creating a National Narrative," in Bayer and Corey, *Making The Met,* 47, 110ff.

[44] The year 1907 also saw the purchase of Gilbert Stuart's iconic Gibbs-Channing-Avery likeness of Washington, as well as Stuart's pair of portraits of the extravagantly handsome Matilda and Josef de Jaudenes. These acquisitions marked the start of a continuing campaign to bring the finest of colonial and federal portraiture to the collection.

[45] See Peck and Tolles, "Creating a National Narrative," 263, n. 20.

[46] See Spassky, *American Paintings in the Metropolitan Museum of Art,* 2:584–629.

[47] Roger Fry, "J. S. Sargent at the R. A.," *Nation and Athenaeum,* January 23, 1926, 582–83.

[48] Barbara Novak, *American Painting of the Nineteenth Century: Realism, Idealism, and the American Experience* (Praeger, 1969), 241; John Wilmerding, *American Art* (Penguin Books, 1976), 149.

[49] Theodore E. Stebbins Jr., "A Local Duty: Collecting American Paintings at the Museum of Fine Arts, 1870–1995," in *American Paintings in the Museum of Fine Arts, Boston,* ed. Carol Troyen et al. (Museum of Fine Arts, 1997).

[50] Museum of Fine Arts, Boston, accession numbers 99.24, 99.28, 99.29, and 99.30.

[51] The bill and correspondence with the dealer William Schaus are in the Isabella Stewart Gardner Museum Archives. The entry in Ormond and Kilmurray, no. 772, tells the story of the installation in the Spanish Cloister. Richard Ormond and Elaine Kilmurray, *John Singer Sargent: Figures and Landscapes, 1874–1882* (Paul Mellon Centre for Studies in British Art, 2006), no. 772. See also Morris Carter, *Isabella Stewart Gardner and Fenway Court* (Houghton Mifflin, 1925).

[52] See Sarah K. Oehler, "A Chicago Boy: The Second City Meets James McNeill Whistler," in *Whistler Paintings and Drawings at the Art Institute of Chicago*, ed. Jay A. Clarke and Sarah K. Oehler (Art Institute of Chicago, 2020).

[53] Andrew McLaren Young at al., *The Paintings of James McNeill Whistler* (Yale University Press, 1980), 24.

[54] Arthur Jerome Eddy, *Recollections and Impressions of James A. McNeill Whistler* (Lippincott, 1903). See Vivian Endicott Barnett, *The Chicago Lawyer Arthur Jerome Eddy and His Eclectic Art Collection*, vol. 3, pt. 2 (American Philosophical Society Press, 2022).

[55] David Park Curry, *James McNeill Whistler at the Freer Gallery of Art* (W. W. Norton, 1984), 12–13. Freer bought 130 paintings, 174 pastels, many watercolors and drawings, and nearly 1,000 prints.

3

Important Mid-Century Writers: Goodrich, Sweet, Richardson

Men, it has been well said, think in herds.

—CHARLES MACKAY, *Memoirs of Extraordinary Popular Delusions and the Madness of Crowds*, 1841

AMERICAN ART slowly became a respectable field of study in the mid-twentieth century, as specialist curators and scholars began to take it up. The writings of Frank Jewett Mather Jr., Royal Cortissoz, and Homer Saint-Gaudens were well regarded in their day but go largely unread today, as these writers were simply outshone by a group of younger contemporaries led by Lloyd Goodrich and E. P. Richardson. Yet all five were alike in their nativism, their rejection of Copley and the early painters, their lack of interest in the Hudson River School, their love of mural painting, and their anti-modernism; these were the commonly held views of the day.

Mather was an interesting figure, with his long career as a teacher, museum director, and donor at Princeton between 1912 and 1946. He wrote the text on paintings for the 1927 volume, *The American Spirit in Art*, part of the popular Pageant of America series edited by Yale professor Ralph H. Gabriel, who founded the American Studies department at Yale in 1931. Mather, following Gabriel, saluted American power, prosperity, and patriotism stemming from the First World War victory just as he celebrated Manifest Destiny and the manner in which the Indians "were pushed out of the way as rapidly as possible by the conquering white."[1]

Mather in 1916 and 1931 wrote two other books, both curiously bearing the same title, *Estimates in Art.* The earlier volume includes chapters on nine European painters and just one American, John La Farge, whom he admired as "the most learned" of artists; he celebrated his murals and his stained glass even above his illustrations, his paintings, and his sketches from the South Seas, while puzzling that his greatness was not more widely recognized (fig. 12).[2] Mather's second book with this title was published fifteen years later and includes chapters on the fifteen American painters he deemed most significant; about half his choices are still considered major figures.[3] His favorites were Ryder ("No artist of his time excelled him, and very few of any time"), Homer ("he painted with a force and energy attained by no other artist,") and Eakins.[4] He sensitively described Eakins's tragic sense of character, his rising reputation, his dark manner, and the fact that he painted "thinking and feeling fellow mortals" rather than the magnates or socialites.[5] Mather found *The Gross Clinic* a "very great picture," and he praised the extraordinary composition of *John Biglin in a Single Scull* in the Garvan Collection.[6] Regarding Sargent, he found "a certain emptiness" in the *Boit Children,*[7] while believing his murals at the Boston Public Library to be his greatest achievement. Mather also noted that Sargent's watercolors had earlier been bought "by the scores" by American museums, but he found them "hollow" and "egregiously overrated," a view held by many for years to come.[8]

Mather's fictional short stories and casual essays are more original than his art criticism. They recount the tales of a forger of Corots, a lost Giorgione, a lesser Italian panel that had been "Raphaelized" by a skilled restorer, and an impecunious collector who rashly spent the money he and his bride had been saving for their honeymoon on an ancient silver and enamel cross. Mather was a collector himself, one who haunted the shops and salesrooms, and his essay "On Art

Collecting" of 1912 is a pioneering examination of a field then rarely studied.[9] He abhorred collectors who "give carte blanche to dealers and agents," thereby losing "the real pleasures of the chase" while wasting their funds; for Mather, they were amassers rather than collectors.[10] And he had little patience with collectors who effectively become dealers, describing them as "morally ambidextrous."[11]

Mather's contemporary Royal Cortissoz, the influential art critic for the *New York Herald Tribune,* in 1936 published a new edition of Samuel

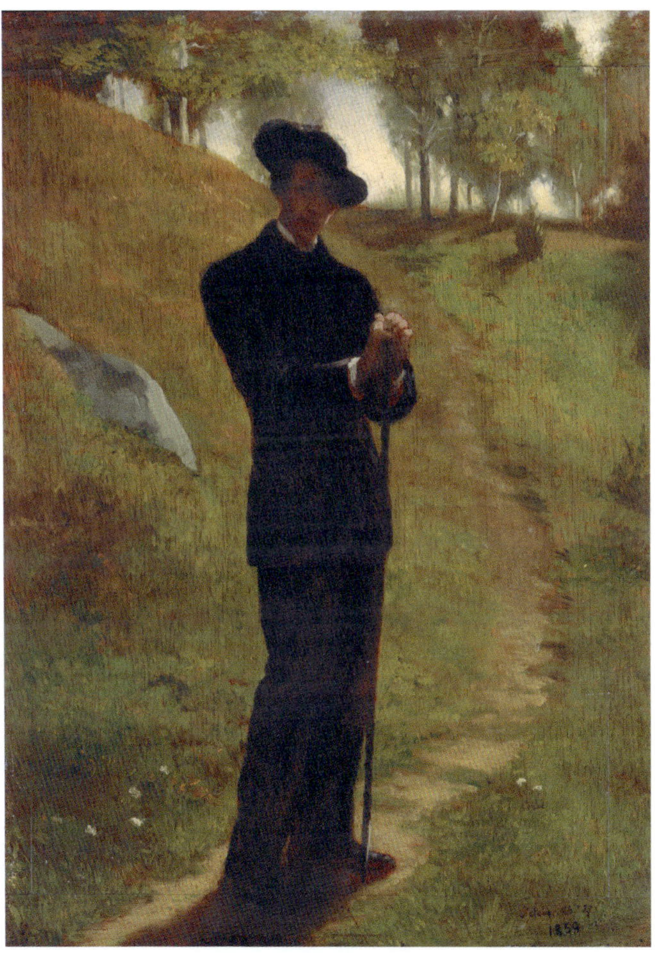

Fig. 12. JOHN LA FARGE,
Portrait of the Painter, oil on wood, 1859. Metropolitan Museum of Art.

Isham's history of 1905. Cortissoz brought Isham "up to date" by adding five supplementary chapters of his own. In them, he endorsed the older writer's canon, praising the work of Homer, Sargent, and Ryder, and finding in Whistler "a vision of beauty such as no man preceding him ever had and no man since has renewed."[12] Cortissoz preferred "the exercise of technical ability touched by delicate feeling," while detesting "the shrill notes of the modernist."[13] He believed that Isham and Mather had been completely correct in finding the work of the mural painters, including Blum, Abbey, and Sargent, the most promising branch of American art, an opinion that would be totally overturned within a few years.

A flamboyant contemporary of these two writers was Homer Saint-Gaudens, longtime director of the Carnegie Institute in Pittsburg and son of the sculptor Augustus Saint-Gaudens. In his book of 1941, *The American Artist and His Times*, he mostly followed the taste of his contemporaries, but unlike Mather and others, he did not relegate Whistler, Sargent, and Cassatt to secondary status but rather called them "our brilliant expatriates." He defended the quality of their work, calling Sargent's portraits "studious and honest," an unusually positive opinion for that time, and one surely influenced by the fact that he and his mother had sat for him.[14] Saint-Gaudens agreed with most of his contemporaries in rejecting the modern as "moronic art bubbles," but wisely concluded that "any prediction in art is blind guesswork and folly at that."[15]

These writers were followed by a younger, abler group of scholars, including Lloyd Goodrich, Edgar Richardson, and Frederick Sweet, all of whom played important roles in raising the standards of the field at mid-century and all of whom I was fortunate to know. Goodrich, the eldest of the trio, had been trained as a painter; he never attended college, but he wrote well and he had keen scholarly instincts. His views were conservative and nativist, not much different in fact than those of Mather and the others, but his undoubted integrity and his hard work enabled him to become the key champion of the American art of his day. Goodrich made the most of his bully pulpit at the Whitney Museum; he spent his career there, starting the year before the museum's founding in 1930 before becoming curator, then associate director, and then director in 1958. He represented the institution well, and he covered the whole field as it was then conceived, with almost no women artists and none of color, with his exhibitions devoted to Homer, Eakins, and Ryder, as well as such contemporaries as his good friend Reginald Marsh and Edward Hopper, the living artist he most admired.[16] One thinks of the Whitney Museum today as dedicated to contemporary art in all its manifestations and as the home of the Whitney Biennial, but it should be remembered that the museum of Goodrich's day had its roots in the Whitney Studio Club (established by Gertrude Vanderbilt Whitney and Julianna Force in 1918) and the figurative tradition. The museum aimed to carry on "a vigorous program of acquisition in the effort to discover fresh talents," like so many institutions that followed, but the collection of realist works that was formed has seemed less and less relevant over the years.[17] Goodrich favored those artists that he saw as truly American, as most independent of foreign influences or training; when he found foreign tendencies in a painter he admired, he found ways to minimize their significance. Yet despite his limitations, Goodrich set an example as one of the preeminent curator/scholar/connoisseurs of his time, and his work on each painter for years remained the starting point for later writers.

At the start of his career, Goodrich began a lifetime of research and writing on Thomas Eakins (fig. 13). That artist's reputation was rising quickly, and such other writers as Henry McBride, Alan Burroughs, and Forbes Watson had already contributed articles on his work. Competition among these critics was keen, but Goodrich got the jump on the others by gaining the trust of Eakins's widow (Susan Hannah Macdowell Eakins) in Philadelphia. He began by publishing an article about Eakins in 1929, then set about preparing a full-scale biography, including a catalogue of all his known paintings, oil sketches, watercolors, and sculpture, 515 works altogether. This well-illustrated, groundbreaking book was published by the Whitney Museum in 1933.[18] Goodrich rationalized his prejudices beautifully: He called Eakins "a pioneer"—a good American word—in going to France to study with Gérôme, then found the latter's work "small, cold, and dry."[19] He

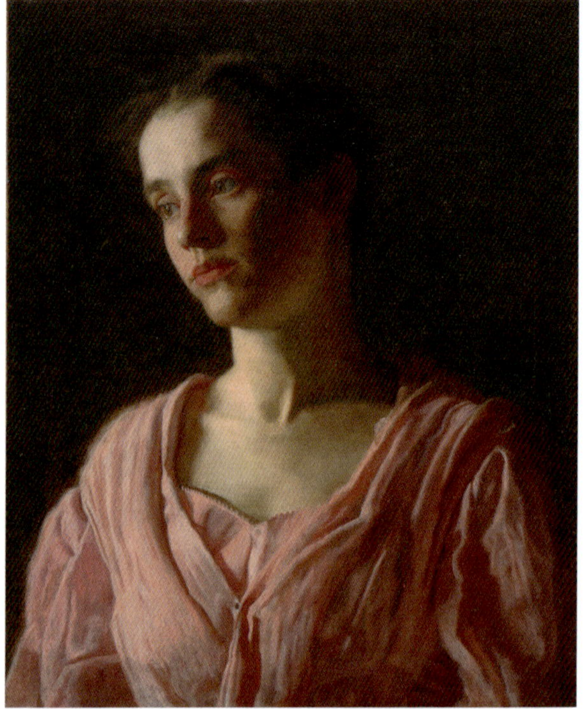

Fig. 13. **THOMAS EAKINS,**
Maud Cook, oil on canvas, 1895. Yale University Art Gallery.

observes that Eakins's early pictures on hunting, sailing, and rowing dealt with "virgin themes," and evidenced "no trace of imitative style."[20] He also celebrated Eakins's "sculptural sense of form" and his deep humanity.[21] Though Goodrich wrote about many painters, Eakins was always his favorite. He ended his career fifty years later with a handsome two-volume study of the artist; it was more nuanced and more detailed than his first book, but his basic view of the painter hadn't changed.[22] Goodrich would be shocked at the way that Homer's work is now more highly regarded than Eakins's, as he would be by the turnabout represented by current scholarship where Eakins is admired for pursuing gender issues.[23]

During the thirties a new canon was gaining rapid acceptance, as evidenced by the Museum of Modern Art's loan exhibition of 1930, "Homer, Ryder, Eakins." Goodrich came to champion this triumvirate.

He had first discussed Homer in a 1924 article, then organized an exhibition of his work for the Whitney in 1936, followed by his biography of 1944. Goodrich, with his typical determination, headed off others who were working on the artist. As before, he made extensive use of letters, dealers' records, museum archives, and contemporary criticism in writing a full-scale biography, and once again his work was published by the Whitney. Goodrich compiled a record of all the painter's works, but in this case, he retained it for future publication.[24] Goodrich wove all his material together to create a heroic portrait of another American individualist, one who painted "certain elemental things" with "extraordinary strength, largeness and truth."[25] He described the continued growth of Homer's art up to the end of the painter's life and accurately connected his growing public recognition with the increasingly high prices his work achieved. Even then, Eakins was always on his mind, as he writes that Homer's figures "did not have the full measure of substance, weight and inner life that Eakins' did."[26] Goodrich especially admired Homer's watercolors, in 1945 organizing an exhibition, "American Watercolor and Winslow Homer," and continued to write about them in numerous later catalogues.[27] He commented that "his oils never caught up with his watercolors in brilliancy, economy of means, or essential artistry," but he upgraded his view of Homer's late paintings in subsequent publications.[28]

Goodrich always venerated the three great "native" painters as he described them, meaning that they were born and bred in the US and were brave and independent, not having succumbed to European training or influence. He had mentioned Ryder in his books on the other artists, and in 1949 wrote an article connecting the three.[29] However, it was only a decade later that he produced a book on Ryder, one in which he found him to be the creator of "the purest poetic imagery in our art of the century" and "the most original plastic artist of his time" (fig. 14).[30] As he had with Eakins and Homer, Goodrich saw Ryder as the product of an old American family. He traced his artistic lineage to "the dark vein of romanticism," to West and Allston and the writings of Poe and Melville. His imagery, Goodrich writes, came from "the unconscious mind," and was thus prophetic of modern art.[31]

A second notable curator-scholar of the same generation was Frederick A. Sweet (1903–1984) who had enjoyed more sophisticated training than Goodrich. He had studied at Harvard with Paul Sachs and Kingsley Porter, had traveled in Europe extensively, and he was conversant with modernism. Sweet spent most of his career as a curator at the Art Institute of Chicago, and perhaps because he was a modest person and wasn't based in New York, he never gained a national reputation. However, he organized two notable pioneering exhibitions for the Art Institute, both of which traveled to New York, one of the Hudson River School in 1945, followed by "Sargent, Whistler, and Mary Cassatt" in 1954.[32] In the former, he celebrated the mid-century landscapists; earlier writers had seen Cole, Church, and the others only as modest predecessors of the giants, Wyant, Inness, and Martin, but Sweet viewed them as central figures. The show was a revelation, including, as it did, thirty works by Thomas Cole, nineteen by Church,

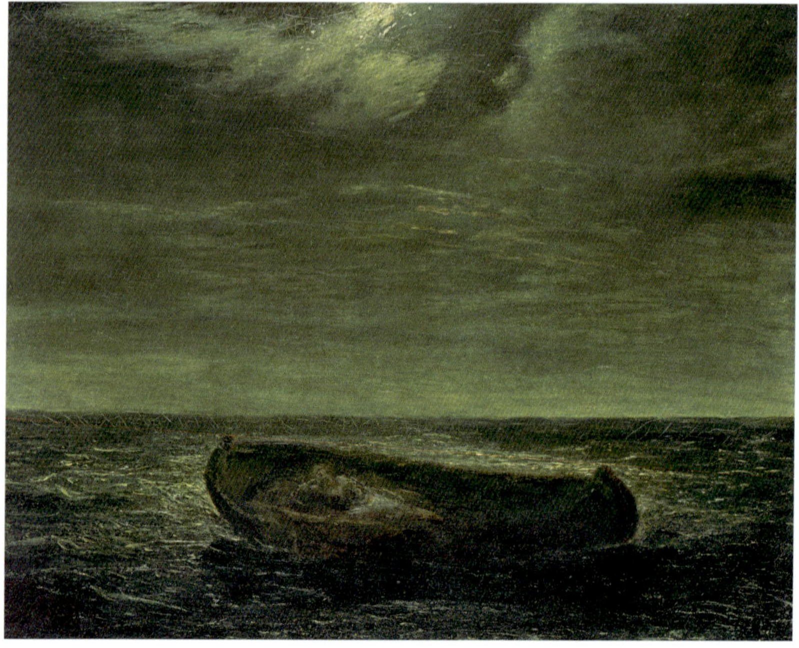

Fig. 14. **ALBERT RYDER,**
Constance, oil on canvas, 1896. Museum of Fine Arts, Boston.

and twelve by Durand, with Kensett, Gifford, and Moran also well represented.[33] The landscapists so highly regarded by earlier writers were mentioned only briefly, while Ryder and La Farge were omitted. This recalibration of the landscape painters represented an important breakthrough, one that helped affirm the new canon that Maxim Karolik was busy collecting at just this time, though there is no evidence that he and Sweet knew one another (see chapter 10).

Sweet's 1954 exhibition devoted to Whistler, Sargent, and Cassatt was even more farsighted. It served as a rebuttal to Goodrich and the "Homer, Eakins, Ryder" troika; Sweet acknowledged that group, but defended his three painters as the best Americans who had worked abroad.[34] Sweet noted that the reputations of Whistler and Cassatt were already rising, then took pains to urge a reconsideration of Sargent as well, urging his readers to consider him as a painter of character rather than simply a facile master of brushwork. There were few exhibitions in those days, and none of today's hectic competition for loans, so Sweet had his choice of paintings; he was able to include *The Boit Children*, *Whistler's Mother*, and the best Cassatts, resulting in an exhibition that has never been equaled. It seems likely that Sweet's exhibition changed some minds among the collectors and his fellow curators and helped lay the groundwork for a gradual reconsideration of all three painters; many today consider them more important than Goodrich's "native" trio.

The third of these major figures was Edgar P. Richardson. Like Lloyd Goodrich, he spent his career working in art museums, mostly at the Detroit Institute, where he served as assistant director and then director between 1933 and 1962. His dour personality, his erudite methodology, and his pretension all made him a less attractive personality than Goodrich, yet I believe he made even more lasting contributions to the field. Perhaps most important was his cofounding of the Archives of American Art in 1954, with the Detroit business executive, collector, and dealer Lawrence A. Fleischman; it became part of the Smithsonian in 1970, and has become the central, indispensable resource for research in the field. Richardson also wrote a good study of Washington Allston in 1944, and he was highly sympathetic to the other early painters touted by Dunlap.[35] In 1956 he published a lengthy survey entitled

Painting in America, a book that served for two decades as the standard textbook in the field.[36] In that volume he listed every possible painter, hundreds of them, describing the major figures at length, the minor ones in a few words. His was a revisionist history, one that made use of Dunlap and other earlier writers while implicitly rejecting Lloyd Goodrich's emphasis on the heroic native American painters; it was the first history since Tuckerman's to mention the landscape and genre artists whose work Francis Garvan, Stephen C. Clark, and Maxim Karolik had begun collecting so actively in the thirties and forties.

Richardson should also be credited as the first generalist to accept modern art. We forget that for many years, modernism appealed only to a small audience, yet Richardson in the mid-fifties wrote sympathetically about Pollock and de Kooning in New York, and David Park and Diebenkorn in the West. His understanding of Cubism and abstraction also led him to accept folk art, or as he called it, "American popular art," and to discuss the work of Edward Hicks, Erastus Salisbury Field, William M. Prior, and several others. He understood that the work of untrained or "naïve" painters could never have been accepted before modernism, with its flat planes, bright colors, and schematic likenesses, had gained a foothold.

---

[1] Frank Jewett Mather Jr., *The American Spirit in Art* (Yale University Press, 1927), 2.

[2] Mather, 245.

[3] The artists are Stuart, Morse, Inness, Vedder, Whistler, Fuller, Martin, Ryder, Homer, Eakins, Sargent, Abbey, Kenyon Cox, Alden Weir, and William Merritt Chase.

[4] Frank Jewett Mather Jr., *Estimates in Art*, series 2 (Books for Libraries Press, 1970), 180.

[5] Mather, 220.

[6] Mather, 217.

[7] Mather, 240.

[8] Mather, 262, 263.

[9] Frank Jewett Mather Jr., "Some Reflections on Art Collecting," in *The Collectors*, ed. Frank Jewett Mather Jr. (Henry Holt, 1912).

[10] Mather, 181.

[11] Mather, 187.

[12] Samuel Isham and Royal Cortissoz, *The History of American Painting: New Edition with Supplemental Chapters by Royal Cortissoz* (Macmillan, 1936), 567.

[13] Isham and Cortissoz, 574, 566.
[14] Homer Saint-Gaudens, *The American Artist and His Times* (Dodd, Mead, 1941), 186, 192. Saint-Gaudens himself had sat for Sargent at the age of ten; dressed in a black suit and wearing pumps, with his mother oddly posed behind him, he looks like the bored brat that he undoubtedly was.
[15] Saint-Gaudens, 220, 317.
[16] He also exhibited and wrote on Yasuo Kuniyoshi, Raphael Soyer, John Sloan, Max Weber, Edward Dickinson, and Georgia O'Keeffe, among others.
[17] See Evelyn C. Hankins, "En/Gendering the Whitney's Collection of American Art," in *Acts of Possession: Collecting in America*, ed. Leah Dilworth (Rutgers University Press, 2003), 163ff.
[18] Lloyd Goodrich, *Thomas Eakins: His Life and Work* (Whitney Museum of Art, 1933). Goodrich gave all his Eakins material to the Philadelphia Museum, where the Department of American Art plans an updated edition.
[19] Goodrich, 15.
[20] Goodrich, 39.
[21] Goodrich, 153.
[22] Lloyd Goodrich, *Thomas Eakins* (National Gallery of Art, 1982).
[23] See Angela L. Miller et al., *American Encounters: Art, History, and Cultural Identity* (Pearson, 2007), 371.
[24] Goodrich gave his records to Abigail Booth Gerdts, who brought them up to date based on her own extensive research and her study of the originals. Her results were published in five volumes as Lloyd Goodrich, *Record of Works by Winslow Homer*, edited and expanded by Abigail Booth Gerdts, 5 vols. (Spanierman Gallery, Goodrich-Homer Art Education Project, 2005–14).
[25] Lloyd Goodrich, *Winslow Homer* (Macmillan, 1944), 204, 113.
[26] Goodrich, 34.
[27] Lloyd Goodrich, *American Watercolor and Winslow Homer* (Walker Art Center, 1945).
[28] Goodrich, *Winslow Homer*, 204.
[29] Lloyd Goodrich, "Realism and Romanticism in Homer, Eakins, and Ryder," *Art Quarterly* 12 (1929): 17–29.
[30] Lloyd Goodrich, *Albert P. Ryder* (George Braziller, 1959), 11.
[31] Goodrich, 1, 11. Lloyd Goodrich became the voice of the Whitney Museum and defined American art for many. His museum's ambition to include all of American art in its exhibitions, publications, and collection, makes it difficult to explain its 1949 decision to sell off all of its pre–1900 holdings. Goodrich reports that the trustees (of which he was one) had decided that it would be impossible to "complete a historical collection equal to those of older institutions," presumably meaning the Met, Boston, Philadelphia, and the like. Then, even more strangely, the Whitney started collecting older material again by the sixties, before remarkably reversing itself for a second time when it sold off that collection at auction in 1987.
[32] Frederick A. Sweet, *The Hudson River School and the Early American Landscape Tradition* (Art Institute of Chicago, 1945). Frederick A. Sweet, *Sargent, Whistler, and*

Mary Cassatt (R. R. Donnelly & Sons, 1954). Sweet also wrote a biography of Cassatt (1966) and organized a full-scale Whistler exhibition (1968).

[33] Sweet, *Hudson River School,* 86, 94.

[34] Sweet, *Sargent, Whistler, and Mary Cassatt,* 8.

[35] Edgar Preston Richardson, *Washington Allston: A Study of Romantic Artist in America* (University of Chicago Press, 1948).

[36] E. P. Richardson, *Painting in America, from 1502 to the Present* (Thomas Y. Crowell, 1956).

4

Americans Discover American Art

The most profound enchantment for the collector is the locking of individual items within a magic circle in which they are fixed as the final thrill, the thrill of acquisition, passes over them.

—WALTER BENJAMIN, *Illuminations*, 1955

THE LAST forty years of the twentieth century witnessed a steady growth of interest in nineteenth- and early-twentieth-century American art as it was then defined. Ambitious exhibitions, handsome scholarly publications, ever-higher auction prices, and a frenzied search for rarities, all played their roles in the years before the epoch came to a climax with the Fraad and Horowitz sales of 2004–5. One looks to the 1960s, when the US audience for art began to expand, for the roots of these developments. In November 1961, art became front-page news for the first time with the New York auction sale of Rembrandt's *Aristotle Contemplating a Bust of Homer* to the Metropolitan Museum for \$2.3 million (about \$23 million in today's dollars), the highest price ever paid for a work of art.[1] By chance, I was there at the invitation of a friend; it was my first adventure in the art world, and it was exciting. Then in January and February 1963, just over a year after the Rembrandt sale, two American museums hosted the first blockbuster exhibition, when the National Gallery and the Met placed Leonardo da Vinci's *Mona Lisa* on view. The painting had been lent by the French government at the request of the First Lady, Jackie Kennedy, who played a key role in bringing cultural awareness to the US. It was shown for three and a half weeks in Washington, then went to the Met for the same length of time, creating a sensation in both cities. Half a million people saw it in Washington, while over a million stood in long lines to savor the experience in New York. People were suddenly hungry for great art, but why? How had the public heard of the *Mona Lisa* or its painter? Art history courses were being taught at many colleges by the fifties and sixties, and a smattering of art books was being published in those years, but these things don't account for the *Mona Lisa*'s amazing appeal. For an explanation we should turn to *Life* magazine, which since its inaugural weekly issue under Henry Luce in 1936 had followed his mandate that every issue feature an art story, because he hoped "to see art become a central part of American culture."[2] *Life*'s photojournalism made the magazine highly popular, with a circulation of over thirteen million copies a week in its heyday. Anticipating the arrival of the *Mona Lisa*, *Life* on January 4, 1963, published a richly illustrated, highly enthusiastic six-page piece about the upcoming loan. The public was suddenly made aware that artistic masterpieces existed, and that ordinary people could view them. Many Americans thus learned about the *Mona Lisa* shortly before it was put on view, and the blockbuster was born.

For the growing audience in the US in the sixties, great art meant Europe, and Europe meant the masters of the Renaissance and of French Impressionism, all of them men. Publication in the mid-sixties of the *Time-Life Library of Art*, with its twenty-eight individual volumes ranging from Giotto and Bernini to Cézanne and Van Gogh, marked a key step for popular education. American art barely figured, with only three of the books devoted to American painters (Copley, Homer, and Whistler), with a final volume titled *American Painting, 1900–1970*, published in 1970 that celebrates the realists (Hopper, Wyeth), the Abstract Expressionists (Pollock, de Kooning, and Kline) and Pop Art. Georgia O'Keeffe was the only woman mentioned, and

Jacob Lawrence the single artist of color. Public interest in American art was limited in those years, and exhibitions and books were few; when the leading scholars published, the subject was likely to be John Singleton Copley, Gilbert Stuart, or John Trumbull, the painters that Dunlap had celebrated years before.

Americans began traveling to Europe and visiting its art museums in greater numbers during the postwar years, one of several reasons that many colleges and universities began teaching art history in the sixties. Numerous courses made use of H. W. Janson's *History of Art*, a survey of world art from prehistoric cave paintings to Jackson Pollock. It was first published in 1962 before being reprinted many times. By the time of the author's death in 1982, it had sold an incredible two million copies, testimony both to the nation's blossoming interest in art and to the prejudices of the era both in its failure to mention a single woman or Black artist and its cursory treatment of American art. Of the book's 848 illustrations, just 10 are devoted to paintings and sculpture made in the US.[3] The omission of women artists began to be corrected only after Janson's death with the third edition, prepared by his son, in 1986.

At the start of the 1960s, American art was still unsung, little studied, and inexpensive, but this changed rapidly over the course of the decade. One of the boldest books of the day was John McCoubrey's short, elegantly written *American Tradition in Painting* of 1963, which described American paintings from colonial times to Abstract Expressionism as having their roots in "the spaciousness and emptiness of the land itself."[4] McCoubrey was a sophisticated nativist and his main point was that American art wasn't European: He effectively compared Franz Kline to Pierre Soulages and Thomas Eakins to Gustave Courbet, always preferring the American. Attitude interested McCoubrey far more than style; in every American artist of every period, he was able to discern a similar fearful reaction to the vastness of the nation. Today his book reads as outdated boosterism, but it usefully appeared just when people were starting to pay serious attention to American art.

A new generation of collectors of American art appeared in the fifties, including Mr. and Mrs. Lawrence Fleischman of Detroit and Mr.

and Mrs. Norman B. Woolworth of New York. Larry Fleischman was a successful business executive who was advised by E. P. Richardson, then director of the Detroit Institute of Arts. The Fleischmans owned a broad historic survey of single examples from Copley, West, and Allston to nearly every member of the Peale family (including the iconic Rembrandt Peale, *Rubens Peale with a Geranium*). They also had a weak group of landscapes and some fine genre paintings, including Thomas Anshutz's *The Ironworkers' Noontime* (fig. 15), along with modest works by Homer and Eakins.[5] Their twentieth-century works were better and included excellent Hoppers and Demuths and the important Charles Sheeler *Classic Landscape*. By contrast, the lesser-known Woolworths (he was an heir to the five and dime fortune) owned a more personal collection, one with outstanding works by major and minor painters, some represented in depth. They had excellent Winslow Homers and were early in buying Childe Hassam, but their special gift lay in buying outstanding works by such lesser figures as E. L. Henry and Levi Wells

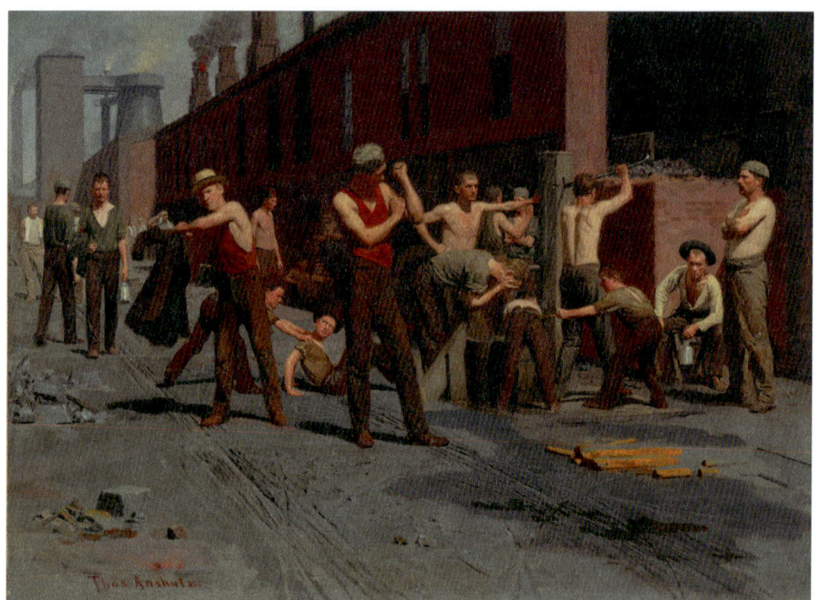

Fig. 15. **THOMAS P. ANSHUTZ,**
The Ironworkers' Noontime, oil on canvas, 1880.
Fine Arts Museums of San Francisco.

Prentice. Mrs. Woolworth also purchased *Rubens Peale with a Geranium* by Rembrandt Peale, now one of the treasures of the National Gallery, when Fleischman sold it in 1966.

New energy came to the American field when Fleischman sold his collection and moved to New York to take over the Kennedy Galleries in 1966 (he then turned personally to collecting Greek and Roman antiquities with controversial results).[6] Larry became a prominent dealer, one who was criticized by some who questioned his ethics but also one with many loyal clients, including the Vatican, Baron Thyssen-Bornemisza, and John D. Rockefeller III.[7] A year later, Stuart P. Feld, also a collector but not yet a well-funded one, left his position as associate curator of American art at the Met to join Kennedy's rival firm, Hirschl & Adler. Feld was an ambitious scholar who did his graduate work at Harvard and who would later amass a splendid personal collection of American drawings, paintings, and decorative arts. In the seventies, Kennedy and Hirschl & Adler ranked as the two leading commercial galleries, with Berry-Hill, Ira Spanierman, James Maroney, Vance Jordan, Richard York, Coe Kerr, and later Thomas Colville, Warren Adelson, and Michael Altman their chief competitors. The two major auction houses were Christie's and Sotheby's, which had taken over Parke-Bernet in 1964, but auctions played a far smaller role in those days. Only a few of these dealers carry on today; the others have gone out of business or have moved to the contemporary field as the supply of good American paintings dried up.

Also active in these years was an interesting group of intimate friends in New York led by Lee Anderson, William H. Gerdts, and James Ricau, who were busy buying more modestly priced paintings, drawings, and watercolors, sculpture, and decorative arts from such dealers as George Guerry and Victor Spark during the fifties on considerably lower budgets. These collectors specialized in order not to compete with one another, Gerdts buying still lifes, Lee Anderson landscapes, and Ricau sculpture; Gerdts bought his first two pictures for $35 apiece in those years, while Anderson was acquiring Thomas Cole's *Falls of Kaaterskill* for $110.[8] These collectors were active in the market for the lower priced, less established American painters that had existed since the twenties and thirties.

Things heated up in the mid-sixties as people with old money, including John D. Rockefeller III, J. William Middendorf, Barbara Babcock Lassiter Millhouse, and John Wilmerding, started buying American paintings. Rockefeller formed a fine collection guided by Larry Fleischman and E. P. Richardson, a survey with good colonial portraits, genre scenes, still lifes, and Hudson River School landscapes. Rockefeller wisely gave the collection to the Fine Arts Museums of San Francisco, rather than seeing it go to the Met, where, he realized, much of it would have been buried in storage. Barbara Millhouse had a superb eye, consulted wisely, and built an outstanding collection of three centuries of American art for Reynolda House in Winston-Salem, North Carolina. Middendorf was, and at one hundred years of age remains, an incredibly avid art collector, but after building a superb group of American paintings, he quickly sold the best ones and moved to Dutch and early Italian paintings. Wilmerding bought excellent works by Lane, Heade, Church, Bierstadt, and Bingham, but then switched course in the seventies, when he let his major Hudson River School pictures go and began acquiring works by Thomas Eakins along with still lifes, watercolors, and drawings. He gave his collection to the National Gallery in 2004.[9] During the late seventies, Baron Hans Heinrich Thyssen-Bornemisza, a Swiss citizen with a Hungarian title, a German fortune, and a Spanish wife (his fifth), and who owned a superb holding of European old masters, dove into the American field. Within a few years, he possessed some three hundred American paintings ranging from Copley to Roy Lichtenstein, with strengths in the Hudson River School and the American moderns, many of them coming from Larry Fleischman. The Thyssen Collection is now housed handsomely in Madrid, and stands as the only European museum with a broad though old-fashioned holding of American art, one that lacks much work by women, Black, Indigenous, or folk artists.

No one at the time had any idea how scarce the great American paintings were. Every collector and every museum were looking for Prout's Neck oils by Winslow Homer, Eakins's rowing scenes, Bingham's rafting pictures, and Mount's genre paintings. When Wilmerding purchased his fine *Boatman* by George Caleb Bingham from Vose for $16,000 in 1965, no one imagined how infrequently such a work would ever come on the market again. When Mrs. Woolworth bought the charming *Rubens Peale with a Geranium* by Rembrandt Peale from Larry Fleischman, no one understood that it was the only remarkable work in the painter's oeuvre. The same was true of Anshutz's *Ironworkers' Noontime*. And though Frederic Edwin Church, Thomas Cole, and many others were prolific, the number of top-notch works by each proved to be small.

The rediscovery of Frederic Edwin Church was led by David C. Huntington, a beloved figure and a helpful colleague to many. David's landmark book of 1966, *The Landscapes of Frederic Edwin Church*, reads like an impassioned sermon, as he speaks of the painter as a prophet for whom nature "was the theater of the world's mystic regeneration."[10] In the same year, David co-curated a brilliant exhibition of Church's work. It included *Twilight in the Wilderness*, a spectacular picture central to Church's oeuvre that Sherman E. Lee, a connoisseur of Asian art and director of the Cleveland Museum, had acquired for his museum the year before for $25,000. The Church exhibition opened at the National Collection of Fine Arts (now the Smithsonian American Art Museum), then traveled to the Albany Institute of History and Art before winding up at Knoedler & Co., the art dealers in New York. That neither the Met nor any other major museum wanted it suggests how narrow the audience for American art was at the time. To cap his early career, Huntington used his passion for the artist to persuade others to join him in saving Olana, Church's magnificent home on the Hudson after it had come close to demolition; the grand Victorian/Moorish building and its collection remain intact, the greatest surviving artist's house in the US.

Other key painters for the younger scholars were Fitz Henry Lane and Martin Johnson Heade, Karolik's discoveries and his favorites. John Wilmerding began working on Lane as a Harvard undergraduate, and he continued as a graduate student. In 1964 the Essex Institute published his short book on the artist that included a checklist of 387 works, including drawings and prints, and in 1966 he organized a Lane exhibition that he rightly subtitled, "The First Major

Exhibition." It was an excellent show that opened at the deCordova Museum in the Boston suburbs, then traveled only to Colby College in Maine, then a minor institution, again suggesting a lack of interest on the part of larger institutions. Things had improved just three years later when I curated the first Heade exhibition. The idea was suggested to me by Bill Gerdts who at the time was director of the gallery at the University of Maryland, which acted as the organizer, but the other two venues he secured were major institutions, the Whitney Museum in New York and the Museum of Fine Arts, Boston.[11] John Canaday's enthusiastic review in *The New York Times* helped bring the painter to widespread attention.[12]

Prices for nineteenth-century paintings rose steadily through the 1960s. Sargent's *Siesta* sold for $24,000 in 1962, while realistic nineteenth-century American paintings were going for twice that. Stuart Feld recalls paying $40,000 for the excellent trompe l'oeil *The Artist's Letter Rack* by Harnett that he bought for the Met from Hirschl & Adler in 1966, and the Met purchased a fine early Twachtman *Arques-la-Bataille* from Spanierman in 1968 for the same amount. The best works of Frederic Edwin Church were attaining even higher levels, with Yale paying $75,000 for Church's *Mt. Ktaadn* in 1969. Around that time Fleischman sold William Sidney Mount's *Cardplayers* to Reynolda House for about $130,000.

The field of nineteenth-century American art had significantly matured by 1970, as evidenced in the scholarship and exhibitions around that time. First came the 1968 publication of Wilmerding's *American Marine Painting*, the first survey of its kind. Barbara Novak's book, *American Painting of the Nineteenth Century: Realism, Idealism, and the American Experience*, followed in 1969. This was a bold attempt to make theoretical sense of the sweep of American art from the portraits of John Singleton Copley to the dark, heavily worked paintings of Albert Pinkham Ryder. Novak defined the core American style as "luminism," with its crisp detail and its evocation of light, a manner she saw as "one of the most truly indigenous styles in the history of American art," as she inventively tried to give new life to the old question, "what is American in American art?" It proved a tough slog for her to make "luminism" fit all the artists.[13] Novak focused on the Karolik painters Fitz Henry Lane and Martin Johnson Heade but neglected Church almost entirely, as she found his paintings "irritating" in their "emotional inflation," recalling for her "the Hollywood spectacular."[14] The well-written book caused a stir, and a good one; in terms of its sophisticated observations on the paintings, it was light years beyond the earlier studies of landscape painting by Wolfgang Born and James T. Flexner. No one was used to discussing the whole of American art in the kind of theoretical terms long employed in the European and modern fields; Novak upped the ante, as it were, though the shelf lives of her theory and her book turned out to be relatively short.

Most significant was the Metropolitan Museum's exhibition of 1970, "19th-Century America: Painting and Sculpture," part of the museum's one-hundredth-anniversary celebration. One forgets how few major exhibitions were presented in those days; they occurred only once every few years, loans were easy to obtain, and people came from around the country to attend the openings. Co-organized by John K. Howat, associate curator in charge of American art at the museum, and John Wilmerding, then a professor at Dartmouth, the sprawling exhibition defined the field as it was then understood. It represented an important transitional moment, one that looked back to the earlier canon of William Dunlap while also celebrating the recent rediscovery of Henry T. Tuckerman's favorite landscape and genre painters. Allston, Vanderlyn, and Morse were still seen as major figures, and the Peale family was well represented. Frederic A. Bridgman, Edwin Lord Weeks, and the other Paris-trained academic painters were omitted, but Emanuel Leutze's gigantic *Washington Crossing the Delaware* had been recalled from the historic site on the Delaware River at Washington Crossing, Pennsylvania, where the Met had lent it for years, and it has been a centerpiece in the American Wing ever since. The best-represented artist was Thomas Cole with seven works; Church, Kensett, Lane, and the other landscapists were seen at their best, and the Hudson River School regained prominence after years of neglect. A number of painters, including Heade, were new to the public; his *Thunderstorm on Narragansett Bay* helped introduce him to a wider audience. These painters, together with the genre specialists William S. Mount and George Caleb Bingham and the masters of still life, Raphaelle Peale and William Harnett, in effect replaced George Fuller, Alexander Wyant, Homer Martin, and the Tonalists in the canon. Not coincidentally, the new artists all worked in crisp, realistic styles, while the previous generation of favorites had painted the subtleties of mystery and mood; taste had turned against blurred imagery and anything that smacked of Symbolism in favor of paintings that hinted at photographic realism. A key factor in the rediscovery of the "new" painters was the growing interest in modern art in those decades: The European Surrealists and Cubists employed relatively bold colors and well-defined outlines, like the nineteenth-century American painters whose work was now finding acceptance. The same circumstances led to an increasing embrace of folk art, and a similar process happened in photography, as the Pictorialists of old were supplanted by Charles Sheeler, Edward Weston, Ansel Adams, and their sharply focused images. Sargent was well represented in the exhibition by four paintings, including *The Boit Daughters* and *Madame X,* but no one yet considered him an Impressionist. However, the show included three outstanding Mary Cassatts—she was the only woman painter represented—as well as two each by William Merritt Chase, Childe Hassam, Theodore Robinson, and J. Alden Weir, evidence of a growing interest in the American version of Impressionism. However, neither Tanner nor any other African American artists were included.

Contemporary American art gained wider public acceptance in the same years, its growing audience paralleling that of the earlier art. The Met's exhibition of 1970, "19th-Century America," summed up the older field, while a Met exhibition of the previous year "New York Painting and Sculpture: 1940–1970" played a similar role for contemporary art.[15] I remember walking through that exhibition in the fall of 1969: The galleries were stunning, and seemed a paean to abstraction with fabulous big paintings by Pollock, Kline, Newman, and the Color Field painters dominating. Of the old Whitney Museum favorites, one found only Edward Hopper and Milton Avery. As in the Met's nineteenth-century show, just one woman made it, in this case the Color Field painter Helen Frankenthaler, and there were no Black artists. The show's gifted young curator Henry Geldzahler was close to Warhol, and he, Johns, Rauschenberg, Lichtenstein, and the other pop artists were well represented while being badly outnumbered; their paintings looked to many like minor offshoots from the main branch of abstraction. Yet within a decade, the Abstract Expressionists and the Pop artists came to dominate the market, the criticism, and the scholarship, as Color Field faded away.

In 1976, John Wilmerding wrote his *American Art,* a survey of the field as he saw it.[16] Making use of long-accepted methodology, with its emphasis on biography, stylistic precedents, and formal analysis, the book effectively summarizes the new nineteenth-century canon, though it weakens when it reaches the art of the twentieth century. Value judgments abound: Church for him represented the "apogee" of landscape, while Eakins was "America's greatest artist."[17] The book is noteworthy in the attention it pays, however briefly, to the art of Indigenous cultures, the art of the Spanish colonies, and to the work of African American painters, including Edward M. Bannister and Henry Ossawa Tanner. Overall, Wilmerding presents a traditional view of American history, describing as he does "the battle for survival and security in the wilderness," the "exuberance and self-confidence" of the Jacksonian era, and "the innocence and single-mindedness of the pre–Civil War decade," all these terms reminding us how much the nation and its historical memory have been transformed in the twenty-first century.

In 1977, the National Gallery appointed Wilmerding as its first curator of American art. The Gallery in prior years had demonstrated only desultory interest in American art after its early acquisitions of portraits and other major works from the old canon like Copley's *Watson and the Shark* and West's *Battle of La Hogue*. This changed dramatically in the era of Wilmerding and his successors, Nicolai Cikovsky Jr. and Franklin Kelly. The most influential museum exhibition following the Met's show of 1970 was Wilmerding's "American Light" at the National Gallery in 1980, an exciting moment that represented the high-water mark for the theory of Luminism as an indigenous, optimistic American landscape style, with Church, Gifford, Heade, and Lane viewed as its major practitioners.[18] Maxim Karolik and John Baur would have been pleased. My revisionist essay in the catalogue argued that Luminism was an international phenomenon rather than an indigenous one, but no one paid much attention to it.[19]

A year after "American Light," Wilmerding organized the Gallery's first exhibition of a private collection of American art, one devoted to the holdings of Jo Ann and Julian Ganz of Los Angeles.[20] The Ganzes began in the sixties; by the time their collection was exhibited at the Santa Barbara Museum in 1973, they owned a decent, generic collection with a little of everything. The next few years saw them weed out many lesser works and focus on tightly painted landscapes, still lifes, and genre paintings, among them superb examples by Raphaelle Peale, Fitz Henry Lane, Seymour Guy, Martin Johnson Heade, and John F. Peto, many of them purchased from Stuart Feld. They also owned a few unimpressive, small-scale figurative works depicting women in classical garb that were mistakenly included in the show of the collection at the National Gallery. The critics unfortunately pounced on the weaker pictures and ignored the many good ones. Hilton Kramer in *The New York Times* wrote a mean, wrongheaded review, calling the collection "stultifying" and lacking "a single major work," while asking, "Has our judgment been corrupted by the will to believe that all American art, whatever its intrinsic quality, has earned a place in our esteem, and thus in our museums?"[21] The Ganzes were stunned, but to their credit, soldiered on and continued to refine their holdings over the next few years. Most important was their decision to go against the rising tide of American Impressionism and sell their sensuous *Sulphur Match* by Sargent to concentrate instead on mid-century realism.[22] The Ganzes used the proceeds to help pay for Harnett's unsurpassed trompe l'oeil, *Mr. Hulings' Rack Picture,* that had been owned by Alice Kaplan (see chapter 13). Through the series of strange events described below, they were also able to acquire the outstanding Frederic Edwin Church *Home by the Lake* at a price far below the "record" auction figure.[23] Together with the Harnett and the sublime examples by Heade, Bierstadt, Lane, and others, with most of the sentimental compositions now gone, their collection became one of the best of its kind. Seeing it in their home in Los Angeles was always an unforgettable experience.

As the National Gallery, the Amon Carter in Texas, the Met, and the MFA, Boston became more active in acquiring and exhibiting nineteenth-century art, one of the traditional leaders of the field, the Whitney Museum in New York, gradually lost interest. However, in 1980, the Whitney presented *American Folk Painters of Three Centuries*, the largest and most scholarly exhibition ever of an area of increasing popularity for collectors. The roots of the American embrace of folk art lie in Alfred Stieglitz's exhibitions of children's art in the teens, the early collecting of Charles Sheeler, the Whitney Studio Club's exhibition "Folk Art" of 1924, and the building of an immense collection in the twenties by modernist sculptor Elie Nadelman.[24] Events of the early thirties brought folk art to a wider audience, with two very different women playing key roles. Abby Aldrich Rockefeller was the wife of one of the world's richest men, John D. Rockefeller Jr., while Edith Gregor Halpert was an Ukrainian Jewish immigrant who became a brilliant, enterprising art dealer as founder of the Downtown Gallery. Mrs. Rockefeller began collecting art in the mid-twenties, and in 1928 created a gallery in her home for her modern works and the folk art together. The following year, she joined two other adventurous women, Lillie Bliss and Mary Quinn Sullivan, in founding the Museum of Modern Art.[25] In 1930, the Newark Museum presented a landmark exhibition of paintings called "American Primitives," organized by Holger Cahill, later director of the Federal Art Project. A year later, Halpert and Cahill established a new business at the Downtown Gallery devoted to folk art, and Mrs. Rockefeller began a buying spree that culminated in a 1932 exhibition of her collection ("American Folk Art") at the Museum of Modern Art, which traveled to six other cities across the country.[26] Her collection eventually became the core holding of the Abby Aldrich Rockefeller Folk Art Museum at Colonial Williamsburg.

The Whitney Museum retained some commitment to earlier American art until 1987, when it sold off the last of its nineteenth-century works. In the seventies, curator Patricia Hills at the Whitney produced a number of influential exhibitions, including one devoted to

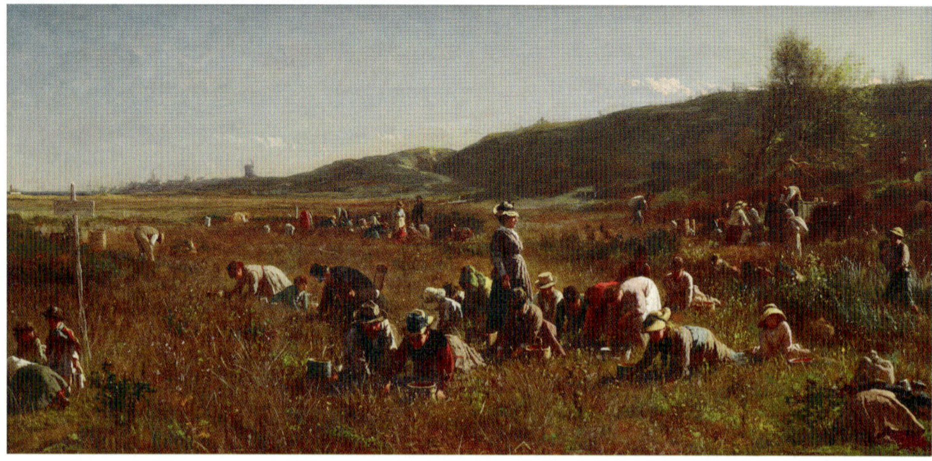

Fig. 16. EASTMAN JOHNSON,
The Cranberry Harvest, Island of Nantucket, oil on canvas, 1880.
Timken Museum of Art.

Eastman Johnson in 1972. His work became a lasting concern for Hills, and her invaluable online catalogue raisonné appeared in 2021. Hills went on to do several other important exhibitions that served to introduce the public to the field, including one of 1974 on genre painting called "The Painters' America: Rural and Urban Life, 1810–1910," and another devoted to "Turn of the Century America" in 1977. She then turned to a wide variety of other subjects, including the work of John Singer Sargent, Alice Neel, and Jacob Lawrence. I should also mention the Brooklyn Museum with its strong curatorial staff and an excellent collection. During this period Brooklyn presented two important exhibitions, both organized by the distinguished architectural historian Richard Guy Wilson: They were "The American Renaissance: 1876–1917," in 1979, and "The Machine Age in America, 1918–1941" in 1986.

The proliferation of books, exhibitions, and collectors led naturally to a rising market for nineteenth-century paintings in the seventies. In 1972, the energetic Connecticut dealer Peter Tillou (also a specialist in folk art, Kentucky rifles, and Dutch seventeenth-century still lifes) found Eastman Johnson's lost masterpiece *The Cranberry Harvest* in England (fig. 16). He got his friend Robert C. Vose, the eminent Boston dealer, to advertise the work. Then Peter offered it for an aggressive $400,000 to the new director at the National Gallery, J. Carter Brown, but Carter had yet to become interested in the American field, and turned it down. He then tried John D. Rockefeller III (Abby's eldest son) who at that time was still committed to the Met, and he obtained a thirty-day option at Tillou's price; the Met's director Tom Hoving loved the picture and hung it in his office, and *The New York Times* printed a piece saying the Met had bought it. But the purchase fell through when Rockefeller's advisor E. P. Richardson attempted to whittle the price down, and the angered Tillou promptly sold the painting instead to the estimable Timken Gallery in San Diego.[27]

These years saw an increasing competition for masterpieces of American art, with each transaction having its own drama and complexities. In 1974, Sotheby's in London purchased a building recently vacated by a shipping company and inside it found a crate containing one of Albert Bierstadt's largest and most dramatic Western scenes, *A Storm in the Rocky Mountains, Mt. Rosalie* of 1866 (fig. 17). In the end,

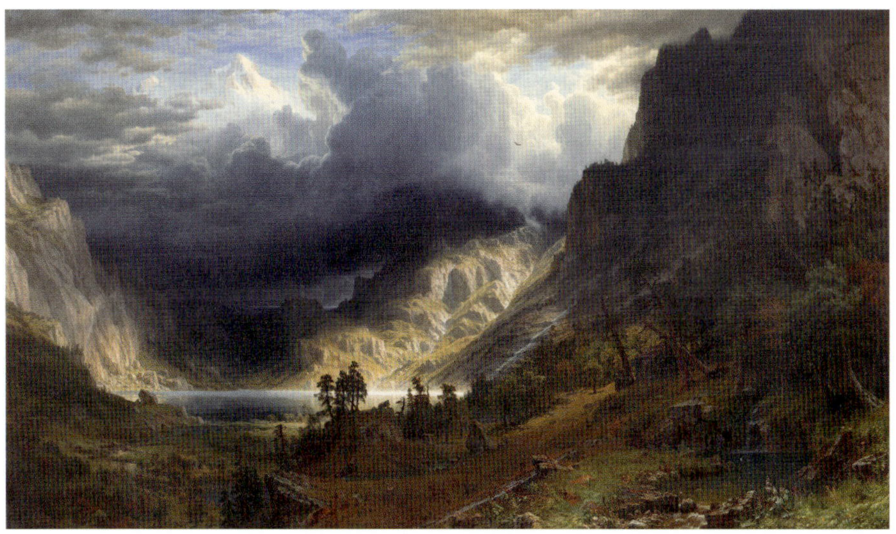

Fig. 17. ALBERT BIERSTADT,
A Storm in the Rocky Mountains, Mt. Rosalie,
oil on canvas, 1866. Brooklyn Museum.

Stuart Feld of Hirschl & Adler sold it to the Brooklyn Museum for $750,000, taking in trade two splendid Winslow Homer watercolors (both fishing scenes, one Canadian and one of Florida), two oils by William Trost Richards, Thomas Eakins's *Oarsmen on the Schuylkill* of about 1873, and $200,000 in cash.[28] Feld and other dealers are simply more practiced and better at these trades than any museum curators; the Eakins alone had a nearly equivalent value to the Bierstadt. The price record set by *Mt. Rosalie* lasted only until 1978, when a late version of George Caleb Bingham's *The Jolly Flatboatmen* brought $980,000 at a Sotheby's auction, with Hirschl & Adler the buyer; they quickly sold it to Daniel Terra, whom I describe in chapter 10. Then, just a year later, another lost painting—something the market loves—was sold at Sotheby's for $2.5 million. This was Frederic Edwin Church's *Icebergs*, a spectacular, large, strange picture that had long been hidden away in a school in rural England. Luckily for the sellers, along came a new collector, Lamar Hunt, who bought it for the Dallas Museum.[29] This run of ever-increasing prices continued in July 1982, when Syracuse University decided to sell Samuel F. B. Morse's large painting *The Gallery of the Louvre* of 1833. Daniel Terra stepped up again, this time paying $3.25 million for an important historic work that had been included in the Met's grand exhibition of 1970. The picture encapsulated Morse's ambition to bring the European old masters to an American audience, a reverse of Terra's own view of himself as carrying the glories of American art to Europe 150 years later.

The market came to a head with Sotheby's auction of May 24, 1989. Coming up for sale was a group of excellent nineteenth-century pictures from the original Thomas B. Walker collection that was being sold by the Walker Art Center in Minneapolis in order to fund modern art purchases, in one of the most misguided museum decisions of that era. The highlight was Frederic Edwin Church's *Home by the Lake* (fig. 18). I had long dreamed of correcting the MFA's lack of an important Church, and we decided to go all out for it; the trustees agreed, and we went to the sale with a nest egg of over $6 million, well over the high estimate. Competition was fierce at the auction, and we were outbid by the dealer Alexander Acevedo, who was bidding for Richard

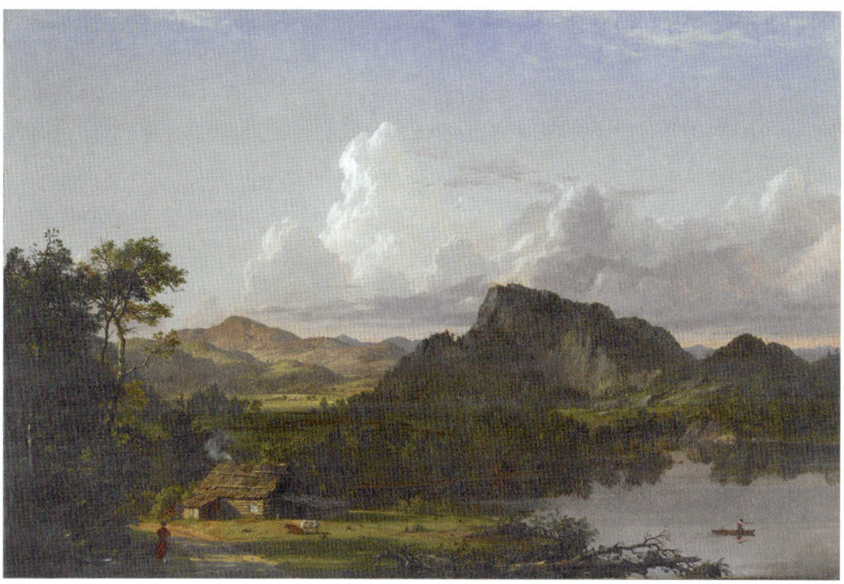

Fig. 18. FREDERIC E. CHURCH,
Home by the Lake, oil on canvas, 1852. Crystal Bridges.

Manoogian, or hoped he was. He won the painting for $8.25 million all in. But Manoogian had only authorized a bid up to five million, and Alex, as he is known, found himself the highly embarrassed owner of a very expensive painting with no way to pay for it. Diana (Dede) Brooks, president of Sotheby's, then sent the work to the MFA, saying we could have it for our top bid. In our galleries, it didn't look as well as I had imagined, and so we turned it down—perhaps a mistake on my part, and in the ensuing confusion Julian and Jo Ann Ganz were able to trade three paintings for it as I describe in chapter 4. The auction price was reported as a new record for an American painting, even though Acevedo never paid for it, and lost several million dollars as a result of having gotten overexcited at the auction.

Numerous major transactions followed. When the Century Association, a private arts-minded club in New York, in 1990 decided to sell *The Power of Music* by William Sidney Mount, it turned first to Jay Cantor, head of American paintings at Christie's, to offer it privately, but the market was down and none of the likely suspects went for it at the $7 million price. These included the Amon Carter, the Met, and the National Gallery, where curators Cikovsky and Kelly were very keen on the painting but director Carter Brown became nervous about buying a painting from a club of which he was a member, and decided against it. Jay Maroney then won control of the work, and offered it to the well-funded Cleveland Museum, where curator Bruce Robertson and director Evan Turner engineered the purchase at $4.5 million. In the same year, for $6 million, Maroney purchased from its longtime owner an even more famous picture, William Harnett's *Old Violin*, long regarded as the artist's masterpiece and one of the classic American paintings. Its sale should have been an easy matter, but the art market had been badly shaken both by an ongoing recession caused by the savings and loan collapse and the Gulf War. Potential buyers became skittish, with the dealer and his partners eventually settling for $4 million from the National Gallery, which thereby acquired another great treasure.

---

[1] Sanka Knox, "Museum Gets Rembrandt for 2.3 Million: Record Price Is Paid by the Metropolitan at Auction Sale," *New York Times*, November 16, 1961.

[2] Melissa Renn, "Life in Color: *Life* Magazine and the Color Reproductions of Works of Art," in *Bright Modernity: Color, Commerce, and Consumer Culture*, ed. Regina Lee Blaszczyk (Palgrave Macmillan, 2017), 181.

[3] Mentioned from the nineteenth century were Bingham, Homer, Eakins, and Whistler; the twentieth-century artists were Joseph Stella, Mark Tobey, Jackson Pollock, and Alexander Calder.

[4] John McCoubrey, *American Tradition in Painting* (George Braziller, 1963), 8.

[5] See *American Painting 1760–1960: A Selection of 125 Paintings from the Collection of Mr. and Mrs. Lawrence A. Fleischman, Detroit* (Milwaukee Art Center, 1960).

[6] Fleischman eventually sold his antiquities to the Getty Museum, many of which had to be returned to the countries of origin because their export was challenged. See D. W. J. Gill and C. Chippindale, "From Malibu to Rome: Further Developments on the Return of Antiquities," *International Journal of Cultural Properties* 14 (2007): 205–40.

[7] When the Rockefeller Collection was exhibited at the Whitney Museum in 1976, a large group of art historians and artists protested its being shown as representative of American art in the bicentennial year. They produced an "anti-catalogue," in which they noted how the catalogue devoted its attention to quality and monetary value while ignoring—for example—the source of John Singleton Copley's sitter William Vassall's wealth (sugar plantations in Jamaica relying on enslaved labor), what was

really happening when Thomas Anshutz painted his *Ironworkers' Noontime* (terrible working conditions leading to the Homestead Strike in 1892), and, regarding George Catlin's paintings of Native Americans, the Rockefeller family's source of wealth in oil taken from Native American lands in Oklahoma and elsewhere.

[8] See William H. Gerdts, "New York Collectors of American Art in the 1950s," in *A Marble Quarry: The James H. Ricau Collection of Sculpture at the Chrysler Museum of Art,* ed. H. Nichols B. Clark (Hudson Hills Press, 1997), 15–26. Henry M. Fuller, a better-funded friend of the group, left his fine small collection years later to the Currier Gallery in Manchester, New Hampshire.

[9] See Franklin Kelly, *American Masters from Bingham to Eakins: The John Wilmerding Collection* (National Gallery of Art, 2004).

[10] David C. Huntington, *The Landscapes of Frederic Edwin Church: Vision of an American Era* (George Braziller, 1966), xi.

[11] Theodore E. Stebbins Jr., *Martin Johnson Heade* (Art Department, University of Maryland, 1969).

[12] John Canaday, "M. J. Heade: American Loner," *New York Times,* November 16, 1969.

[13] Novak, *American Painting of the Nineteenth Century,* 95.

[14] Novak, 94.

[15] Henry Geldzahler, *New York Painting and Sculpture: 1940–1970* (E. P. Dutton, 1969).

[16] John Wilmerding, *American Art* (Penguin Books, 1976).

[17] Wilmerding, 24, 100, 130.

[18] John Wilmerding, ed., *American Light: The Luminist Movement* (National Gallery of Art, 1980).

[19] Theodore E. Stebbins Jr., "Luminism in Context: A New View," in Wilmerding, *American Light.*

[20] John Wilmerding et al., *An American Perspective: Nineteenth-Century Art from the Collection of Jo Ann and Julian Ganz Jr.* (National Gallery of Art, 1981).

[21] Hilton Kramer, "Are the Standards Too Low for American Art?" *New York Times,* November 1, 1981.

[22] The Sargent became one of the best pictures in Hugh and Marie Halff's distinguished collection in San Antonio. See Eleanor Jones Harvey, *An Impressionist Sensibility: The Halff Collection* (Smithsonian American Art Museum, 2006).

[23] The Ganz purchase was made possible when Maroney negotiated a trade between Acevedo, nominal owner of the Church, with the Ganzes giving up good landscapes by Cole, Church, and Bricher in exchange for *Home by the Lake.* I don't know what terms Sotheby's gave Acevedo for paying off the purchase price.

[24] The collection was purchased by the New-York Historical Society (today known as The New York Historical) in 1937.

[25] For a good summary of these events, see Sybil Gordon Kantor, *Alfred H. Barr Jr. and the Intellectual Origins of the Museum of Modern Art* (MIT Press, 2002), 190–95.

[26] In addition, during the forties, Edgar and Bernice Chrysler Garbisch of Maryland were sweeping up some 2,600 folk (or "primitive," or "naïve") paintings and works on paper. This massive collection included such eighteenth-century New England painters as Joseph Badger and Ralph Earl, but was focused unselectively on portraits and

landscapes of the early nineteenth century. Much of it was donated to the National Gallery between 1953 and 1980 after being shown in several exhibitions there, but exactly why the Gallery accepted it remains a mystery.

[27] When Rockefeller's advisor, E. P. Richardson, went to Boston to negotiate the price further, Tillou blew up and took the picture home. Walter Ames, a lawyer who was then director of the new Timken Gallery in San Diego, heard all about this the next day, and phoned to buy the painting sight unseen. Rockefeller called Tillou a day later to say that he'd take it for the full price, and Peter took enormous pleasure in telling him that it had been sold. Peter Tillou, conversation with the author, February 21, 2021.

[28] Lloyd Goodrich, *Record of Works by Winslow Homer*, vol. 5, *1890 through 1910*, edited and expanded by Abigail Booth Gerdts (Goodrich-Homer Art Education Project, 2014), nos. 1727, 1747. A new price level for the best American paintings was established around this time; Maroney sold Church's magnificent *Cotopaxi* to the Detroit Institute for $550,000.

[29] See Eleanor Jones Harvey, *The Voyage of the Icebergs: Frederic E. Church's Arctic Masterpiece* (Dallas Museum of Art, 2002).

5

Celebratory Exhibitions and Publications

The student of visual culture believes that the study of images has been impeded by outmoded tastes for the fine arts, aesthetic experiences, and the recondite art of interpretation.

—CHRISTOPHER S. WOOD, *A History of Art History*, 2019

ONE CAN estimate the importance and popularity of painters in several ways, one being the number of museum exhibitions devoted to their work. The two most venerated nineteenth-century artists during the last quarter of the twentieth century were Winslow Homer and John Singer Sargent. Regarding Homer, one thinks of Helen Cooper's groundbreaking exhibition of his watercolors in 1986,[1] as well as the great survey of 1995 at the National Gallery. Other scholars and institutions, working overtime to cash in on Homer's popularity, turned to ever more specialized sides of his oeuvre: studies of Homer as an angler, a painter of the Civil War, as working in Cullercoats and the Adirondacks, as creator of *The Carnival*, *The Cotton Pickers*, and *The Life Line*, among others; they have all added to our understanding of the artist, alongside weaker explorations of Homer as lover, as photographer, and the like.

Sargent's reputation has had more peaks and valleys than Homer's, but since 1980 he has been the subject of as many books and exhibitions as the painter of Prout's Neck. Richard Ormond, Sargent's great-nephew, made his earliest contribution to the Sargent literature with an exhibition at Birmingham, England, in 1964. Six years later, his first monograph on the painter was published in the US by Harper & Row.[2] This book contained a more sophisticated analysis than the American field was used to. On the whole, relatives should be barred from writing about their artist-ancestors, but Richard was the exception that proved the rule. Since then he and Elaine Kilmurray have gone on to publish a monumental, ten-volume catalogue raisonné starting in 1998, along with numerous other essays on specialized aspects of Sargent's career. I cannot think of another example where a pair of scholars has contributed so much to the understanding of a single painter. Dozens of people have made use of their research, and like Homer, Sargent has been examined from every angle, with the expected mix of results. An outstanding exhibition "John Singer Sargent" was organized by Kilmurray and Ormond for the Tate Gallery in 1998 and traveled to Boston and Washington. The Met, having been left out of the 1998 tour, prevailed upon them to organize "Sargent: Portraits of Artists and Friends" in 2015, another splendid show that featured the painter's more informal works.[3] Most recently, as I discuss in chapter 19, came "Fashioned by Sargent" in Boston in 2023, which included essays by both Kilmurray and Ormond, marking the latter's sixtieth year of distinguished writing about his great uncle.

One of the joys of curatorial work is doing research on a museum's permanent collection. Yet this activity is time-consuming and brings few immediate benefits to the institution, especially nowadays when popular temporary exhibitions are required to bring in the attendance that museums desire. The Met led the way in producing serious, scholarly catalogues of its permanent collection. As early as 1965, Albert T. Gardner and Stuart Feld published the first volume in a planned three-volume series devoted to American paintings. The project was renewed under curator Jock Howat, with superb books appearing in 1980, 1985, and then a new volume by John Caldwell and Oswaldo

Rodriguez Roque replacing the Gardner and Feld volume in 1994.[4] These books set the standard for the field. Similar collection catalogues were produced by the Brooklyn Museum, the Carnegie Museum, the Wadsworth Atheneum, the National Gallery, and the Harvard Art Museums (where I oversaw two catalogues of the collection), among others. Such studies are enormously rewarding for the curators who do them and for interested readers, but high publication costs, the fact that each book is out of date the moment it is printed, the impact of the internet, and the rapidly changing methodology in the field, all suggest that they are likely to be a thing of the past.

American landscape painting was rediscovered in the 1960s, and was celebrated in major exhibitions of the seventies and eighties, before interest in landscape began to decline due to a rising concern with Black and other figurative painters, perhaps together with an increasing awareness of the ongoing destruction of our environment. William H. Gerdts and Linda Ferber authored the first in-depth study of the American Pre-Raphaelites in 1985 for an exhibition at the Brooklyn Museum. The following year saw the exhibition of "American Landscape Before 1830," with a fine catalogue for the Corcoran Gallery by Edward Nygren and Bruce Robertson. In 1987 the Metropolitan Museum presented "American Paradise: The World of the Hudson River School," with a big catalogue including a fine essay by Oswaldo Rodriguez Roque and another by Doreen Bolger Burke and Catherine Voorsanger.[5] "American Paradise" served as a standard reference for years, but is woefully outdated today: The title alone, with its reference to the American wilderness as Eden, disqualifies it for many.[6]

Exhibitions celebrating the work of single landscape painters were a staple of this era. Major exhibitions of the work of John F. Kensett (1985), Fitz Henry Lane (1988), Frederic Edwin Church (1989), Thomas Cole (1994) and the Heade exhibition that my colleagues and I mounted at the MFA in 1999 all testified to the high popular and critical regard for the best of the landscape school. These shows also demonstrated the power of the major Eastern museums, as they were seen only on the Washington to Boston corridor except for Heade, which we shared with the Los Angeles County Museum. The purpose of such exhibitions during their heyday was to celebrate the work of the acknowledged greats, but by the twenty-first century such showings went out of favor as taste changed: Landscape itself fostered less interest than before, as the old canon of artists was downgraded.

Thematic exhibitions also served to expand understanding of the landscape tradition. Several outstanding projects were undertaken by Eleanor Jones Harvey at the Smithsonian Museum of American Art, including *The Painted Sketch* in 1998, her study of the landscape oil sketch; "The Civil War and American Art," an exhibition of 2012; and "Alexander von Humboldt and the U.S." in 2020.[7] All three took on familiar subjects that were already well studied but made use of excellent new research. I hope the same might be said of the exhibition my colleagues and I did in 1992 for Boston, "The Lure of Italy: American Artists and the Italian Experience, 1760–1914."[8] In the process, a good deal of new information was turned up while interesting painters were unearthed from museum cellars, though our work was at variance with the current trend that minimizes the role of Europe in American art. In her years at the Met, curator Barbara Weinberg did a series of exemplary exhibitions of nineteenth- and early-twentieth-century art, including "American Impressionism and Realism," "Americans in Paris," and "American Stories," the last devoted to turn-of-the-century genre painting.[9] She also did a fine show devoted to Childe Hassam in 2004, enlisting twelve other distinguished contributors to the catalogue.[10] The Met has turned to multiple authors more than any other museum: For its fine 1992 exhibition of the work of William Harnett, its four primary authors enlisted eighteen additional writers. Still life painting is far less appreciated than in earlier years, despite excellent exhibitions devoted to John F. Peto and Raphaelle Peale at the National Gallery.[11]

John James Audubon is in a category of his own (fig. 19). He has long been thought one of the greatest of all American artists, and his work has a wide modern audience as seen in the market for the hand-colored period engravings after his work by Robert Havell Jr., by a continuing flow of reproductions in all mediums, and the numerous books about him over the years. However, the scholars, the museums, and the collectors have generally ignored him, largely because his major works are the 435 watercolors for *The Birds of America* that have long been held in a single institution, The New York Historical (formerly known as the New-York Historical Society), where they are minimally exhibited and lent only rarely. The decline of his reputation has been accelerated by the discovery that he owned numerous enslaved people. The National Audubon Society recently described him as "a slaveholder with racist views and treatment of Black and Indigenous people," and considered changing its name before deciding not to, though several local chapters have done so.[12] Yet the works themselves remain as extraordinary as ever.

During the twenty-first century, many of the most ambitious thematic exhibitions dealt with the role of Black artists in various contexts, as I describe in chapters 17 and 19. However, exhibitions of the old canon continue; the Philadelphia Museum of Art is notable for having organized two important shows of traditional nineteenth-century art in recent times. First came Mark Mitchell's ambitious "The Art of American Still Life: Audubon to Warhol" in 2015, followed by Kathleen Foster's extraordinary show "American Watercolor in the Age of Homer and Sargent" in 2017. Foster's massive catalogue, based on her lifetime of research, covered a far broader range of artists, including many more women than I did in my early study of the medium, and achieved the impossible: a scintillating exhibition accompanied by a definitive scholarly text.[13] Neither exhibition traveled; one had to visit Philadelphia to see them. Sadly, fewer and fewer museums now choose to support this kind of exemplary, time-consuming curatorial work and the expensive exhibitions and catalogues that can result.

As twentieth-century art began to displace earlier work in terms of popularity, museums presented an increasing number of impressive exhibitions in the modern field. Noteworthy were Kimberly Orcutt's one-hundredth-anniversary exhibition of New York's Armory Show at the New-York Historical Society in 2013, the Wadsworth Atheneum's impressive Marsden Hartley exhibition, George Bellows at the Los Angeles County Museum of Art (LACMA), Charles

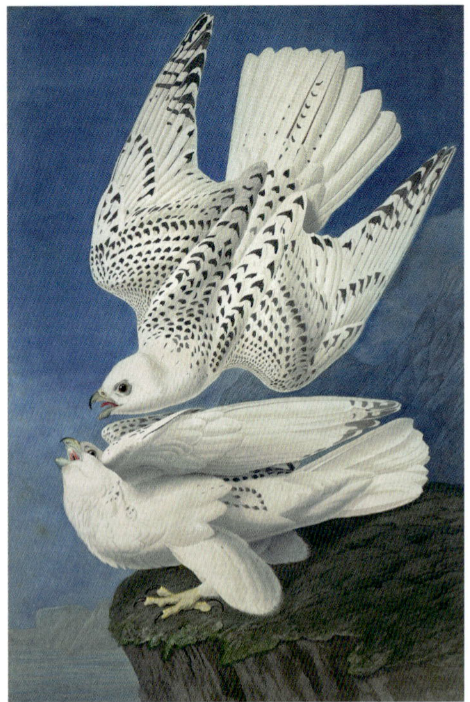

Fig. 19. **JOHN JAMES AUDUBON,**
Gyrfalcon, graphite and gouache on paper, ca. 1835–36.
New York Historical Society.

Sheeler at Boston, Harry Cooper's exhibition devoted to the work of Stuart Davis at the National Gallery, Detroit's exhibition of the Ashcan School in 2007, and the Whitney's show "Edward Hopper's New York" in 2022.[14] Most impressive is the work of curator Barbara Haskell, who has been at the Whitney Museum since 1975. She has survived one director after another, not an easy task for a curator, and in the process has organized nearly two dozen important exhibitions of the American modernists, each with an articulate, well-researched catalogue. Haskell's subjects include Nadelman, Demuth, Dove, Avery, O'Keeffe, Hartley, Joseph Stella, Stuart Davis, and Grant Wood; in addition, she did a comprehensive show of the Mexican muralists ("Vida Americana"), and she summarized the field with her *American Century* in 1997.

I was fortunate to serve from 1977 to 1999 as curator at the MFA, Boston. In the early years, we did two important exhibitions for foreign shores, one for China, the other for Paris. In 1979 the US established diplomatic relations with China, and the State Department was seeking ways to use art as a diplomatic tool. The MFA in 1981 was asked to assemble an exhibition of American art to send to Beijing and Shanghai. I selected fifty-eight paintings from Smibert and Copley to Milton Avery and Edward Hopper, while our curator of modern art, Ken Moffett, added twelve contemporary pictures from Franz Kline to Morris Lewis. An ace intern, Elizabeth Prelinger, wrote many of the entries for the catalogue, published only in Chinese. We sent China some fairly good works along with a handful of treasures, including Winslow Homer's *The Lookout—"All's Well"* and our only Pollock. Carol Troyen reminds me that in Beijing, our paintings were unloaded from their crates at night on a runway lit only by the trucks' headlights. The Shanghai Museum's galleries were threadbare, and I was nervous about the temporary partitions that were installed to hold our heavy framed paintings. But in the end, everything went well, no pictures were damaged, and a great many people, including numerous artists, saw the show in both cities. The biggest thrill for me was wandering around Shanghai and seeing people on the street with our catalogue under their arms. We helped introduce modernism to China; the authorities there were initially reluctant to allow any of our abstract pictures to be shown, but gave in. Now, some forty-five years later, the world has changed dramatically, and China has become the home of many outstanding painters and the world's second largest art market.[15]

The exhibition we organized for Paris in 1983, "A New World: Masterpieces of American Painting, 1760–1910," came about because of my colleague John Walsh's working relationship with Pierre Rosenberg, a distinguished, highly productive scholar of French paintings who was then chief curator at the Louvre, who conceived the idea of an exhibition of the greatest American paintings. My initial idea was to show only the nine or ten best painters in our history, but no matter how I conceived this list, I found that it left out too many great works. In the end, I chose ten artists to be represented by multiple examples (Eakins and Homer leading the way with nine works each, Church with eight), and thirty-nine others with one or two.[16] It was a joy to do; loans were easy to obtain, as Americans were still enthralled with the idea of Paris as the center of the art world if not civilization itself. In addition, the French had no choice but to lend Whistler's famous portrait of his mother; many people came to see that picture specifically, and it made the show into the blockbuster it became in Boston and Washington. This was our attempt to introduce France, and Europe, to the best of American art, but the reaction abroad was only lukewarm.

Moreover, a memorable problem arose when a group of the leading Black artists in Boston protested our failure to include a Black painter in the exhibition. Led by spokesperson Edward Strickland, along with Barry Gaither, Dana Chandler, and John Wilson, they organized a surprise press conference on November 6, 1983, on the steps of the museum to announce their protest, just as the show was ending its run in Boston. Director Jan Fontein then invited the group, about sixteen in number, to meet with us a week later.[17] They were intense, and they were serious. The artists presented their case, and asked that we include a work by Henry Ossawa Tanner at the Paris venue, and reprint the catalogue to include it. Fontein was not his usual decisive self, and turned to me and said, "Well, I think it's up to the curator." I had about fifteen seconds to decide what to do, and fortunately I recognized the rightness of their position and the passion in which they held it. We then asked Bill Cosby for one of his Tanners, *The Thankful Poor* (now in the Art Bridges collection), but he made a point of publicly rejecting our request. Then the Philadelphia Museum quickly agreed to lend us Tanner's *Annunciation*, and the French catalogue included it.[18] I wish I'd chosen a Tanner originally, but I didn't, and in fact no one among our curators or advisors had suggested it. We were simply blind to the racist implications of leaving him out. Tanner seemed to many at that time to be a good painter but not a great one; the revival of his reputation lay just over the horizon. Within a generation, his work became a must for American museums. Our exhibition and the protest it engendered took place on the cusp, just as taste was changing and Americans were becoming aware of our history of racism and the changing standards for judging art.[19]

Other institutions made worthy attempts to export nineteenth-century American paintings abroad, and excellent exhibitions were organized for Paris, London, and Berlin; they served an important purpose in educating scholars and serious art lovers abroad about our art, but none won much in the way of positive criticism or a popular following. Curator Andrew Wilton's "American Sublime" exhibition (Tate Gallery, 2002) and the "Pictures from the New World" exhibition that went to Berlin in 1988, both funded by the Terra Foundation, relied on the "American Light" exhibition in terms of scholarship and inspiration. What people learned, if they hadn't realized it before, is that American art remained provincial up to the late 1940s, and our earlier art on the whole doesn't travel well, in contrast to the European embrace of American modernism beginning with MoMA's traveling exhibitions of the 1950s. The expatriates Whistler and Sargent are exceptions. Sargent's portraits and other works and especially his watercolors can be shown anywhere, as the eminent dealer Warren Adelson found when he sent an outstanding selection to Venice in 2007. The exhibition of around sixty works, all views of Venice, looked very well at the Museo Correr, and proved once again what a sophisticated, truly international artist Sargent was.

Professor Wayne Craven of the University of Delaware in 1994 published the last—and in many ways, the best—textbook of the old era. His well-written, richly illustrated *American Art: History and Culture* covers painting, sculpture, architecture, and photography, with occasional glances at silver and furniture. In it he relies on traditional methodology with its emphasis on biography, artistic movements, and stylistic influences. Craven's book represents an old-fashioned celebration of the old canon and its soon-to-be outdated views: Allston and West were still major figures for him, Manifest Destiny and slavery were mentioned simply as facts, and race goes unmentioned. Craven's methodology can be understood from a single sentence from his book: Regarding Bierstadt's *Rocky Mountains,* he wrote: "This view of exotic aboriginals with all of their colorful costumes and customs seen amid a majestic mountain landscape thrilled Americans with its panoramic vision of a far-distant part of their land."[20] However, he does briefly mention Duncanson, Tanner, Jacob Lawrence, Lois Mailou Jones, and a handful of other artists of color. Craven's volume became outdated almost immediately, as he unknowingly was at work on the cusp of the dramatic changes of the twenty-first century; within a few years, the vastly different textbooks of Frances Pohl and Angela Miller would appear, as discussed in chapter 17.

---

[1] Helen Cooper, *Winslow Homer Watercolors* (Yale University Press, 1986).

[2] Richard Ormond, *John Singer Sargent: Paintings, Drawings, Watercolors* (Harper & Row, 1970).

[3] Richard Ormond and Elaine Kilmurray, *John Singer Sargent: Portraits of Artists and Friends* (Metropolitan Museum of Art, 2015).

[4] Albert Ten Eyck Gardner and Stuart P. Feld, *American Paintings: A Catalogue of the Collection of The Metropolitan Museum of Art* (Metropolitan Museum of Art, 1965); Doreen Bolger Burke, *American Paintings in the Metropolitan Museum of Art*, vol. 3 (Metropolitan Museum of Art, 1980); Natalie Spassky et al., *American Paintings in the Metropolitan Museum of Art*, vol. 2 (Metropolitan Museum of Art, 1985); John Caldwell and Oswaldo Rodriguez Roque, *American Paintings in the Metropolitan Museum of Art*, vol. 1 (Metropolitan Museum of Art, 1994).

[5] Linda S. Ferber and William H. Gerdts, *The New Path: Ruskin and the American Pre-Raphaelites* (Brooklyn Museum, 1985); Edward J. Nygren and Bruce Robertson, *Views and Visions: American Landscape Before 1830* (Corcoran Gallery of Art, 1986); John K. Howat, ed., *American Paradise: The World of the Hudson River School* (Metropolitan Museum of Art, 1987).

[6] Howat, *American Paradise*, 21, 86.

[7] Eleanor Jones Harvey, *The Painted Sketch: American Impressions from Nature, 1830–1880* (Dallas Museum of Art, 1998); *The Civil War and American Art* (Metropolitan Museum of Art, 2012); *Alexander von Humboldt and the United States: Art, Nature, and Culture* (Princeton University Press, 2020).

[8] Theodore E. Stebbins Jr., ed., *The Lure of Italy: American Artists and the Italian Experience, 1760–1914* (Harry N. Abrams, 1992).

[9] H. Barbara Weinberg et al., *American Impressionism and Realism: The Painting of Modern Life, 1885–1915* (Metropolitan Museum of Art, 1994); Kathleen Adler et al., *Americans in Paris, 1860–1900* (National Gallery, 2006); H. Barbara Weinberg and Carrie Rebora Barratt, eds., *American Stories: Paintings of Everyday Life, 1765–1915* (Metropolitan Museum of Art, 2013).

[10] H. Barbara Weinberg, *Childe Hassam: American Impressionist* (Metropolitan Museum of Art, 2004).

[11] John Wilmerding, *Important Information Inside: The Art of John F. Peto and the Idea of Still-Life Painting in the Nineteenth Century* (National Gallery of Art, 1983); Nicolai

Cikovsky Jr., *Raphaelle Peale Still Lifes* (National Gallery of Art, 1988).

[12] Margaret Osborne, "National Audubon Society Votes to Keep the Name of an Enslaver," *Smithsonian Magazine*, March 17, 2023.

[13] Kathleen A. Foster, *American Watercolor in the Age of Homer and Sargent* (Philadelphia Museum of Art, 2017).

[14] Elizabeth Mankin Kornhauser et al., *Marsden Hartley* (Wadsworth Atheneum Museum of Art, 2002); Michael Quick et al., *The Paintings of George Bellows* (Harry N. Abrams, 1992); Carol Troyen et al., *Edward Hopper* (Museum of Fine Arts, 2007); Carol Troyen and Erica Hirshler, *Charles Sheeler: Paintings and Drawings* (Little, Brown, 1987); Harry Cooper et al., *Stuart Davis: In Full Swing* (Prestel Publishing, 2016).

[15] See James P. Sterba, "U.S. Art Exhibition on View in Peking," *New York Times*, September 2, 1981.

[16] Theodore E. Stebbins Jr. et al., *A New World: Masterpieces of American Painting, 1760–1910* (Museum of Fine Arts, 1983).

[17] Jonathan Kaufman, "Protesters at Museum of Fine Arts Score Lack of Black Artists in Show," *Boston Globe*, November 7, 1983.

[18] The French edition of the catalogue employed a different cover design, using Bingham's *Raftsmen on the Missouri*, and included an entry and illustration for the Tanner and four other paintings, all ones shown at the Paris venue only. See *Un nouveau monde: chefs-d'oeuvre de la peinture americaine, 1760–1910* (Editions de la Réunion des musées nationaux, 1984).

[19] Both exhibition projects were funded in part by the Terra Foundation, which has played an important role in spreading the word about pre–World War II art around the world.

[20] Wayne Craven, *American Art: History and Culture* (McGraw-Hill, 1994), 210.

PART TWO

THE COLLECTORS

6

The Wounded Collector: Grenville Winthrop

He had nice tastes certainly, . . . but he seems to me to want digging out and airing. . . . I never was intimate with Grenville—that very word is a contradiction!

—EDITH WHARTON ON GRENVILLE WINTHROP, 1925, as quoted in *Reared in a Greenhouse: The Stories, and Story, of Dorothy Winthrop Bradford*

Nothing appears more improbable or extravagant than the love of curiosities, or that desire of accumulating trifles, which distinguishes many by whom no other distinction could have ever been obtained.

—DR. SAMUEL JOHNSON, *The Idler*, No. 56, 1759

MONEY MAY not bring happiness, but it seems to assuage the misery of many miserable collectors. Obsessive art buying provided a life for Grenville Lindall Winthrop (1864–1943), who without it might not have found one. Winthrop was an extreme case, a wealthy, lonely, reclusive man with virtually no family life, one who cut his descendants out of his will and, on his death in 1943, left his immensely valuable collection to Harvard University. He stands in contrast to Francis P. Garvan, his contemporary and Yale's great collector, in almost every particular except for their shared hunger for art and their reverence for early American history. Winthrop typified his class, as Garvan did his, old money versus new, a passive, highly cultivated, Anglican versus the aggressive, status-hungry Irish Catholic whom I describe in the following chapter.

Winthrop was a ninth-generation descendant of the first John Winthrop, founder and longtime governor of the Massachusetts Bay Colony. He revered his lineage and always kept a copy of the family tree on his desk; he would be shocked to learn that a group of Harvard students in 2023 was demanding the renaming of Harvard's Winthrop House because the original John Winthrop was an enslaver.[1] Grenville's wealth came from his father's success in banking in New York and was due even more to the fortune his wife had inherited from her banker father. Winthrop ranked at the apex of New York society, yet he was a constricted, fearful person, one who exemplified the weakness one can find in families that have boasted great wealth and distinguished ancestors for too many generations. In 1905 he somehow convinced Carrere and Hastings, designers of some of the most sumptuous homes in America, to build him a very plain, large house at Lenox, Massachusetts that he called "Groton Place" after the English birthplace of his ancestors. While taking great care in laying out the grounds and plantings, he ruled out having any flowers at all. His neighbor Edith Wharton insightfully described him in gardening terms, remarking: "He had nice tastes certainly, . . . but he seems to me to want digging out and airing."[2] In a later letter she wrote, "I never was intimate with Grenville—that very word is a contradiction!"[3]

Winthrop's most important college experience and his best grades came in senior year at Harvard when he took two of Charles Eliot Norton's courses in art history, an undertaking that marked his first exposure to art and one that affected the rest of his life. After graduating in 1886, he attended the Harvard Law School then founded a short-lived law firm.[4] In 1892 he married Mary Tallmadge Trevor (1871–1900), a young woman from another wealthy New York family; Mary's family home, "Glenview," in Yonkers, New York, now houses the Hudson River Museum. The marriage itself ended tragically: His twenty-nine-year-old wife abandoned him and their two daughters, seven-year-old Emily and newborn Kate, shortly after the baby's birth, and some months later, she died, a likely suicide.

The unhappy Winthrop became determined to raise his daughters so that they would be spared the dangers of the outside world, an undertaking that predictably failed. Trying to control every aspect of their lives, Winthrop had the girls taught at home by governesses and tutors under his watchful eye. A family member describes the rigidity of Winthrop's household, the formality of strictly vegetarian meals designed to keep the girls from becoming stimulated, and life in the airless home as he attempted to keep his grown daughters uncorrupted from sex even as they grew into adulthood.[5] As a well-meaning but misguided father, Winthrop seems a character out of Balzac or Eugenides, and as in the novels on this theme, the inevitable finally happened. Daughter Emily at thirty-one fell in love with Winthrop's chauffeur, Corey Lucien Miles, while her younger sister Kate, twenty-four, became enamored of the electrician on the property, Darwin S. Morse. Taking advantage of their father's weekend absence in New York in early September 1924, both women eloped with their lovers, each couple driving off in one of Winthrop's fine automobiles. After a carefully planned double wedding performed in Stockbridge by the Reverend John P. Trowbridge at his home, the two couples moved to Santa Barbara, California. Inherited wealth from their maternal grandmother enabled the sisters to fund their new lives.[6]

Kate and Emily thus achieved a perfect rejection of their father, one designed to hurt him in the most painful way possible. The daughters not only eloped but did so with a flourish, making sure that *The New York Times*, the *Chicago Sunday Tribune*, and other major papers carried the story. It became front-page news on September 7, 1924, the day after the event, and the tale was followed in the national press for weeks afterward. In Winthrop's high-WASP social class, where the appearance of having a happy family is paramount, public humiliation of this kind would have been more painful even than the loss of one's fortune. Emily divorced after a few years and became an artist, making modest figurative sculpture and pastels and later designing furniture and jewelry. She remained close to her father and never remarried, while Kate stayed married to Morse and raised two sons; she remained largely estranged from her father, and the boys apparently had but a single meeting with him.[7]

Winthrop had begun collecting art in a desultory way after his marriage, and then became more active after his wife's death in 1900, as he began to purchase early Italian panel paintings of middling quality from his friend Bernard Berenson. He developed an interest in J. M. W. Turner's *Liber Studiorum*, the painter's series of prints in etching and aquatint after his landscape and marine paintings.[8] Then, after suffering the catastrophe of his daughters' joint escape in 1924, Winthrop embarked on a highly obsessive existence in which he paid equal attention to collecting both Western and Eastern Art and to maintaining a busy but rigidly controlled social life. Winthrop's bequest to Harvard in 1943 included over 4,000 objects; his major holdings were in archaic Chinese bronze vessels and Chinese jades, as well as Korean sculpture, European clocks, and Wedgwood ceramics. Of equal interest to him were French and British neoclassic and Romantic paintings and drawings. American art ranked as a tertiary interest at best; nonetheless, his bequest included about 177 works, many of high quality, that form the core of Harvard's American holdings.[9]

Where other collectors turn their passion for objects into a rich social life with dealers, museum curators, and fellow aficionados, Winthrop apparently had no close friends and only one regular human contact except for his servants, and this was his agent Martin Birnbaum, whose photo he always kept on his desk beside the family tree. Birnbaum was born in Hungary, the son of an engraver who moved to New York in 1883. The young Birnbaum attended City College where he met the future muckraker Upton Sinclair, who became a lifelong friend. After law school he discovered the art world, presenting exhibitions of John Sloan, Eugene Higgins, and Albert Sterner, among others, at a German-owned gallery in New York before going to work for a decade for a leading dealer, Scott & Fowles. Birnbaum was a traveler, an adventurer, a sophisticate, and a talented writer as well. He made friends with Gertrude Stein in Paris, with Mrs. Collis P. Huntington in New York, and with the famous, the talented, and the wealthy everywhere.

Birnbaum was close to Charles Ricketts and Charles Shannon, the London designers, and he wrote a sympathetic essay on Oscar Wilde where he found that figure's downfall "shocking and deplorable."[10] He authored excellent catalogues for his exhibitions of Charles Conder, Elie Nadelman, Aubrey Beardsley, Arthur Rackham, and William Blake's watercolors for Dante's *Inferno,* along with a warm memoir of his friendship with John Singer Sargent. He spoke all the necessary languages, and he played the violin brilliantly. Looking back on his life, Birnbaum declared his work with Winthrop "the culmination of my career."[11] All in all, he was one of the most remarkable figures in the art world of that era.

Birnbaum was also a keen student of character. In his memoir, written well after Winthrop's death, Birnbaum describes the collector's weaknesses perceptively, observing that "family and good breeding were perhaps too highly stressed" in Winthrop's makeup, while noting his "ancestor obsession" and his shyness.[12] Birnbaum described Winthrop's evenings alone: "After a lonely dinner, chiefly of fruit and vegetables, he would read some favorite book, or work on a card catalogue of his treasures."[13] Birnbaum found "something poignantly pathetic in the life of one who . . . becomes a solitary lonely figure in spite of great wealth," and thought his character worthy of Proust or Henry James.[14] Winthrop lived not so much through his art as in it. Yet Birnbaum concludes, "under that superficially cold exterior and Puritan poise there was hidden . . . a spiritual hunger for beauty, and a tenderness of spirit."[15] Birnbaum added that when it was discovered that he and Winthrop had purchased a fake or forgery, Winthrop would keep the offending object rather than rushing back to the seller and demanding his money back, as most collectors would have done. A loyal descendant of Puritans, one who always dressed in black, he regarded such events as "costly but useful lessons," according to his agent.[16] Accepting the loss, and retaining such reminders of his own imperfections, was a kind of self-punishment required to keep his deeply conflicted life under control.

Birnbaum chose brilliantly for his wounded client. It is impossible to go through the European paintings and see all of the dreamlike images of suffering, naked men and women in Thomas Couture's *Romans of the Decadence* (fig. 20), Géricault's *Study for the Raft of the Medusa*, Burne-Jones's *Pan and Psyche*, Heim's *Defeat of the Cimbri and the Teutons*, not to mention "the great erotic drawings for Wilde's *Salome*" by Beardsley (as Birnbaum describes them), along with dozens of others by Ingres, Blake, and Moreau, without gaining a sense of Winthrop's inner life, which surely found an outlet in these images.[17] Numerous psychologists have described instances where art collecting functions as a substitute for human sexuality; the deeply hurt and repressed Grenville Winthrop would seem a quintessential example of this.

Winthrop was as obsessive in his social life as in his art collecting. Just as he kept careful duplicate records of each new work of art, so in his guest book he recorded the names of every visitor to his home.[18] Day after day, prominent figures in the international art world and New York society came for lunch or a visit. December 1929 saw the arrival of art historian Philip Hendy from London, the collector Charles Loeser from Florence, and Professor Paul Sachs with thirty-one Harvard students.

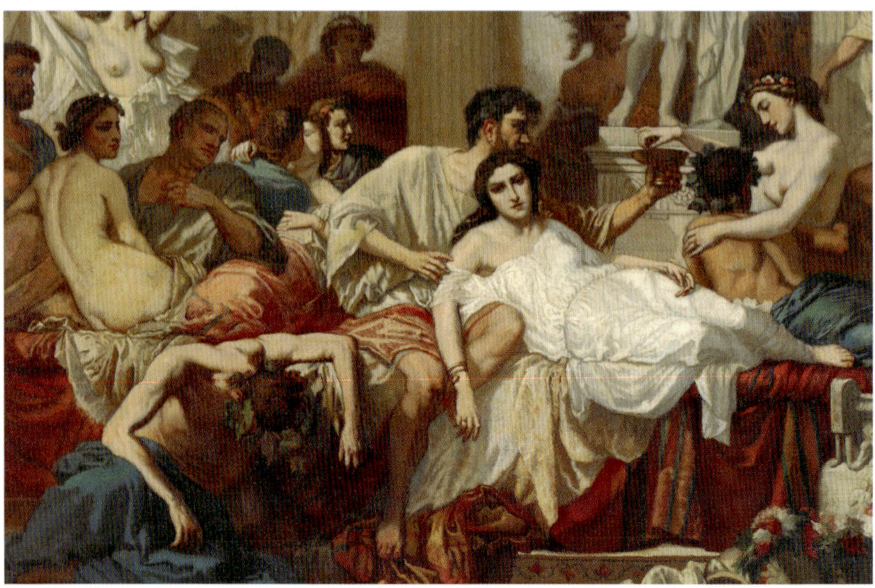

Fig. 20. THOMAS COUTURE,
Romans of the Decadence, detail, oil on canvas, 1847. Harvard Art Museums.

Many of the same people were still visiting in the mid-thirties, but now they included the young Nelson Rockefeller; writer Royal Cortissoz; Kenneth Clark, director of the National Gallery, London; Langdon Warner and Oswald Siren, both scholars of Asian art; and Professor Theodore Sizer from Yale, and his daughter Emily Winthrop Miles, who was always listed as "Miss E. Winthrop." Winthrop not only kept a record of every visitor; astonishingly, he also recorded every lunch or dinner party, whether at his home or at someone else's residence, with a sketch of the dining table showing the placement of each guest.

Many of the visiting museum directors came to plead that their institutions be considered as the eventual recipient of the vast collection.[19] It would have made an important addition to Washington's National Gallery, the Met, or any number of other museums, or it could have become a significant stand-alone institution if left in Winthrop's house a half block from the Met. But the collector had long since decided on his alma mater, Harvard, so all the varied works of art could teach "the younger generation in their impressionable years" about "*Beauty*."[20] Just as Winthrop had tried to control the lives of his daughters, he forbade his works of art from mixing with the outside world when he specified that nothing in his collection could be lent or exhibited outside of Harvard.

In the American field, the works that meant most to Winthrop were very likely the small group of ancestral portraits that he had inherited, and that he, in turn, bequeathed to his nephew Robert C. Winthrop. These included mostly unattributed early portraits of Governor John Winthrop and of his grandson Waitstill Winthrop; their importance for Grenville Winthrop lay in the identities of the family members they portrayed. Robert Winthrop gave them to Harvard in 1964, where they joined the ancestral portraits donated by other members of the family to Harvard's Winthrop House, which became something of a family shrine.[21]

Grenville Winthrop actively sought American paintings and watercolors almost from the beginning of his career as a serious collector. He was never an adventurous buyer, always remaining loyal to the best-known artists, but he nonetheless acquired a number of scintillating works. In 1920 he purchased Charles Willson Peale's compelling portrait of Thomas McKean, a signer of the Declaration of Independence and president of the Continental Congress, as well as an excellent colored drawing by Benjamin West, both through Martin Birnbaum at Scott & Fowles. After this foray, it would be twenty years before Winthrop again took up an interest in early American pictures. Rather, during the twenties, he turned enthusiastically to the work of John Singer Sargent, then to James McNeill Whistler, Winslow Homer, and John La Farge, all established members of the canon whose work had been highly praised by Samuel Isham and Royal Cortissoz. Winthrop frequently entertained Cortissoz, the influential Herald Tribune art critic; the two shared a conservative, anti-modernist outlook and never wavered in their admiration for Sargent, even as his reputation was declining in the late twenties.

Winthrop pursued Sargent's watercolors for some twenty years, work that Birnbaum had described brilliantly in his book on the painter.[22] Fine examples were still available despite all the early museum buying, as Sargent had been immensely prolific with an output of over two thousand watercolors. In 1922 Winthrop bought five views of Venice, Corfu, and the Simplon area, all fresh to the market, at an average cost of $3,000, and four years later he obtained two additional watercolors and his first oil, *The Simplon Valley,* for which he paid $22,000. Eventually Winthrop would buy sixteen Sargents, including two oil studies for *El Jaleo* in 1932 and an evocative, little-known portrait of five-year-old Laura Lister the following year. In 1935, for $5,225, he purchased the exquisite *Breakfast Table* (fig. 21), one of Sargent's small masterpieces and a favorite of the collector, who always hung it in his bedroom. I took pleasure in using it for the cover of the catalogue of the Harvard collection.[23] It is the kind of work—with its fluent brushwork, intimate subject, and reference to Manet—that Margaret Horowitz (whom I discuss in chapter 10) would have described as "a picture to die for." Even in hindsight, it is difficult to imagine a time when it would cost less than a quarter of the price of *The Simplon Valley*; today the ratio would be reversed.

Winthrop's quest for Whistler's work began in 1927 with the purchase of three watercolors and two Venetian pastels, all directed by Birnbaum (who became his agent in 1926), and it concluded in 1941

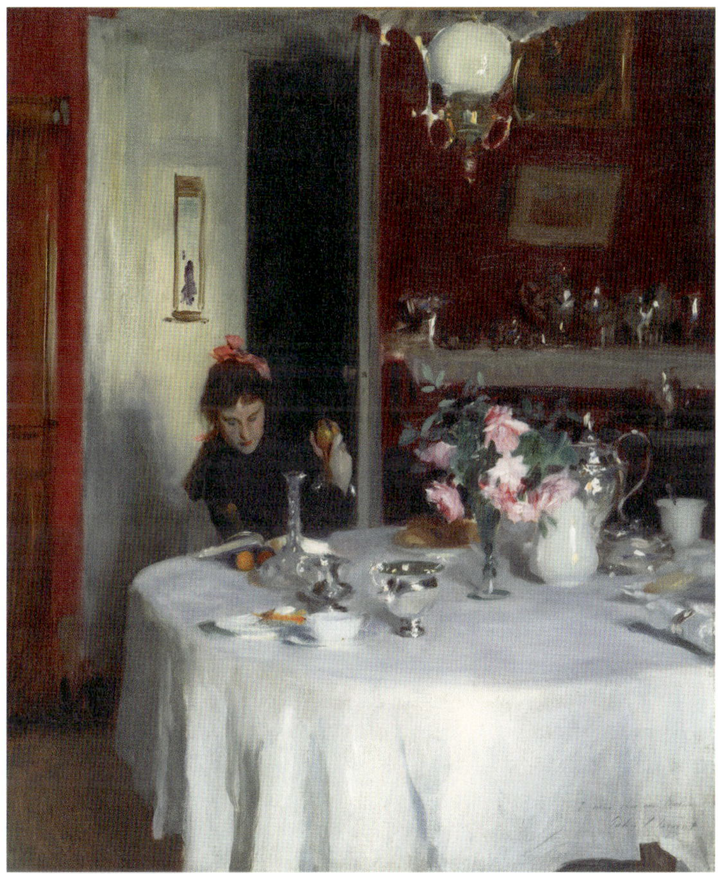

Fig. 21. JOHN SINGER SARGENT,
The Breakfast Table, oil on canvas, 1883–84. Harvard Art Museums.

with the acquisition of sixteen works sold directly to the collector by Tulane University, which had received them in a bequest two years earlier. Winthrop's Whistlers present an anomaly: Most of his twenty-one pastels and watercolors are outstanding, especially the pastels *Sunset, Red and Gold* and *The Storm*, while the sixteen oils as a group are disappointing and rarely on view at Harvard due to their damaged condition. The works on paper typically had had only one owner before Winthrop, and most had apparently never been exhibited, while the oils had been through numerous hands and had had numerous cleanings, each with its own risks to the surfaces. Nonetheless, the oils include the sublime

Nocturne in Blue and Silver, ca. 1871–2, an archetypal work Whistler employed in his lawsuit against the critic John Ruskin in 1877.

Winthrop's Winslow Homer campaign was carried on from 1932 to 1941, with Birnbaum again advising, and with most items coming from Scott & Fowles or Macbeth. The nine watercolors he bought reveal a bewildering range of quality: Some are outstanding by any measure: For the artist at his best, one thinks of the two great Gloucester watercolors from the summer of 1880, as well as the famous *Mink Pond*

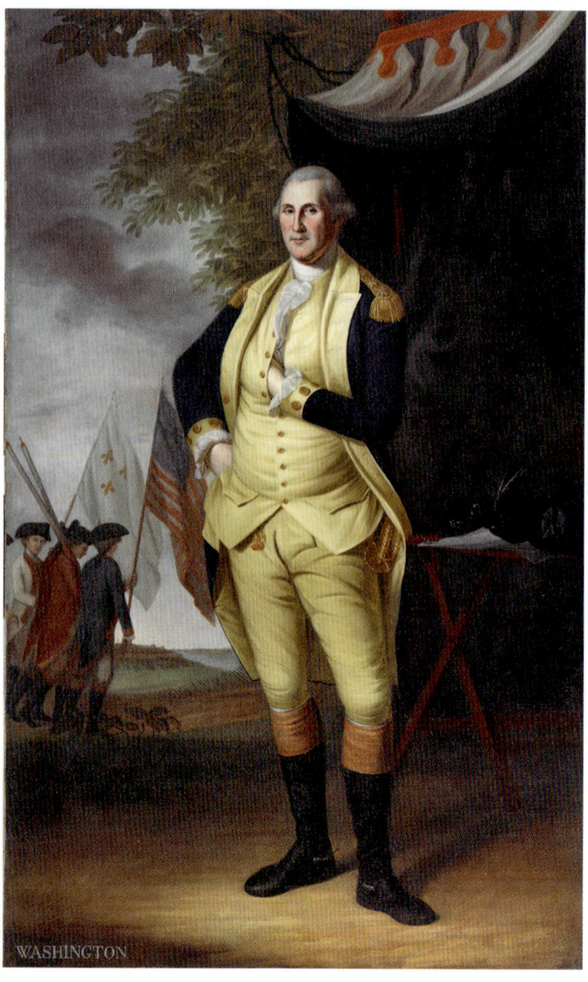

Fig. 22. CHARLES WILLSON PEALE,
George Washington, oil on canvas, 1784. Harvard Art Museums.

and the classic Adirondack fishing scene *Blue Monday*.[24] How could the same sets of eyes have also been attracted by the very faded *Waves*, the mediocre *Palm Trees*, or *The Stag*, a forgery? Looking at Winthrop's Homers and Whistlers, one can only conclude that condition means a great deal more today than it did then. Conservation methods were far cruder at that time, and it had not yet been generally recognized how sunlight can fade the life out of a watercolor.[25] Winthrop rarely bought a European still life; his great Renoir *Spring Bouquet* is an exception. But in American art, he and Birnbaum seem to have sought out floral and other still life subjects, and in doing so, they were ahead of their time. Winthrop's eleven La Farges include the justly renowned *Chinese Pi-Tong*, perhaps the painter's finest floral watercolor. Winthrop also acquired two floral watercolors by J. Alden Weir, as well as the fine early Harnett oil *Still Life with Bric-a-Brac*.

The final months of Winthrop's life saw him making a major effort to shore up Harvard's collection of historic paintings. Even if he had lived, he never would have hung these works at home; they were purchased for their importance in rounding out the Harvard collection. The artists were America's "old masters," as described by William Dunlap a century earlier. In this group are some of the finest works in the collection, including the majestic full-length portrait of Washington on the battlefield at Princeton by Charles Willson Peale (fig. 22); a Benjamin West self-portrait and Copley's superb portrait of West in a red jacket; and Thomas Sully's excellent portraits of Mr. and Mrs. John McAllister Jr. More surprisingly, Winthrop also bought George Inness's *October Noon* of 1891, one of the most successful of that painter's moody late landscapes, and last of all, Charles Bird King's cluttered, remorseful *Vanity of the Artist's Dream*, perhaps the greatest of American *vanitas* pictures and a fitting note on which to end this unusual collector's career.

---

[1] The students also point out that Professor John Winthrop, acting president of Harvard in 1773, owned two enslaved persons. Madeline A. Hung and Joyce E. Kim, "Harvard Students Circulate Petition Calling for Denaming of Winthrop House, Named After Slaveowners," *Harvard Crimson*, February 23, 2023.

[2] Dorothy B. Wexler, *Reared in a Greenhouse: The Stories, and Story, of Dorothy Winthrop Bradford* (Garland, 1998), 222.

[3] Wexler, 222.

[4] Stephan Wolohojian, *A Private Passion: 19th-Century Paintings and Drawings from the Grenville L. Winthrop Collection, Harvard University* (Yale University Press, 2003), 10.

[5] Wexler, *Reared in a Greenhouse,* 228.

[6] Trowbridge told the press that he received the largest fee of his life for his services. The only family members present at the ceremony were the parents of Darwin Morse. "Winthrop Sisters in Dual Elopement; Daughters of Wealthy New York and Lenox Man Wed Chauffeur and Electrician," *New York Times,* September 7, 1924.

[7] Emily Winthrop Miles also became a collector, and in the 1950s she gave her large collection of Wedgwood to the Brooklyn Museum.

[8] Wolohojian, *A Private Passion,* 15. See F. A. W., "The Francis Bullard Memorial," *Bulletin of the Cleveland Museum of Art* 6, no. 3 (1919): 54–56.

[9] Dorothy W. Gillerman et al., *Grenville L. Winthrop: Retrospective for a Collector* (Fogg Museum of Art, 1969).

[10] Martin Birnbaum, *Oscar Wilde: Fragments and Memories* (James F. Drake, 1914), 251.

[11] Martin Birnbaum, *The Last Romantic: The Story of More Than a Half-Century in the World of Art* (Twayne, 1960), 251.

[12] Birnbaum, 180, 182.

[13] Birnbaum, 216.

[14] Birnbaum, 216.

[15] Birnbaum, 183.

[16] Birnbaum, 127.

[17] Birnbaum, 199.

[18] Papers of Grenville L. Winthrop, 1885–2000, Harvard Art Museums Archives, Cambridge, MA.

[19] Wolohojian, *Private Passion,* 45.

[20] Grenville Winthrop to Herbert Friedman, Smithsonian Institution, July 11, 1938, box 98, Paul J. Sachs Papers, Harvard Art Museums Archives.

[21] Theodore E. Stebbins Jr. and Melissa Renn, *American Paintings at Harvard,* vol. 1: *Paintings, Watercolors, and Pastels by Artists Born Before 1826* (Harvard Art Museums, 2014).

[22] Martin Birnbaum, *John Singer Sargent, January 12, 1856: April 15, 1925; A Conversation Piece* (W. E. Rudge's Sons, 1941).

[23] Theodore E. Stebbins Jr., Kimberly Orcutt, and Virginia Anderson, *American Paintings at Harvard,* vol. 2, *Paintings, Watercolors, Pastels, and Stained Glass by Artists Born 1826–1856* (Harvard Art Museums, 2008).

[24] Winthrop in the same years paid $3,600 for *Watching the Tempest,* $3,000 for the light-struck *Waves on a Rocky Coast,* and $4,950 for *Mink Pond,* a work that Birnbaum justifiably touted as one of the artist's greatest.

[25] Stebbins, Orcutt, and Anderson, *American Paintings at Harvard,* 392, 129. Prices, then as now, seem highly irrational. For example, Winthrop in 1940–41 paid $450 for *Sailboat and Fourth of July Fireworks* and three times that for *Schooner at Sunset;* I think of the former as being one of the most perfect watercolors ever, and at least the equal of the sunset view.

7

The Ambitions of Francis P. Garvan

Praise the world to the Angel, not what's unsayable. You can't impress him with lofty emotions; in the cosmos that shapes his feelings, you're a mere novice. Therefore show him some simple object, formed from generation to generation until it's truly our own, dwelling near our hands and in our eyes. Tell him of things.

—RILKE, *Duino Elegies: The Ninth Elegy*, 1912

What we bought was not for ourselves alone, but for the whole country.

—FRANCIS P. GARVAN

FRANCIS PATRICK Garvan (1875–1937) was Yale's greatest collector of American art, as Winthrop was Harvard's, but for Garvan, American art was a single, overriding passion. He collected on a grand scale from the teens to the early thirties, years when Winthrop was also active, eventually presenting Yale with over ten thousand objects, including silver, furniture, paintings, prints, glass, textiles, and ceramics. His background, practice, ambitions, and his temperament could hardly have been more different from Winthrop's; where the conservative, repressed Winthrop viewed the canon as defined by Isham and others as definitive, the flamboyant Garvan set out to collect on his own terms and to redefine the role of the ambitious collector. A Yale publication of 1980 examined Garvan's motivations and practices in each field and recorded the many scholarly publications of the collections, while honoring him and his wife Mabel Brady Garvan, for whom the collection was named, in the time-honored fashion of grateful museums.[1] Garvan's famous collections of decorative arts are well known, but his keen interest in paintings has received little attention, something I would like to help correct.[2]

Garvan's background stands in contrast to Winthrop's, for Garvan was an Irish Catholic whose father Patrick Garvan (1836–1912) had emigrated in 1851 as a boy, one of the thousands fleeing the potato famine. Irish immigrants of that era faced immense barriers of prejudice and discrimination that lasted until the election of John F. Kennedy more than a century later. The Irish were feared for their "alien customs, terrible diseases and despised religion"; these nativist prejudices came to a climax in 1917, when Congress passed a literacy bill barring immigrants who couldn't read.[3] Despite all the obstacles, Garvan Senior lived the American dream, first as a carpenter's apprentice, then becoming a successful contractor and builder in Hartford, Connecticut, before going into the paper business. He married the Irish-born Mary Carroll, and they had ten children. Pat, as he was known, was smart and well-liked; he headed Hartford's Park Commission, became chair of the local school board (though he had never attended college), and won election as a Republican to Connecticut's House of Representatives and then the State Senate.[4] He made the move from poverty to the middle class gracefully, and was ambitious for his children to do even better, sending his two younger sons to Yale after they graduated from East Hartford High. The elder of the two, Edward Joseph Garvan (1871–1910, Yale '94), was a law school graduate who became clerk of the Hartford city court, then a Police Judge, before going into business with his father, while the younger, Francis P. Garvan, became an art collector and a figure of national renown.

Francis P. Garvan was small and feisty, athletic, energetic, highly competitive, a fast talker with an infectious, high-pitched laugh, and one who was popular with his Yale classmates.[5] He stood just five feet, six inches tall and weighed 119 pounds in college; as a member of the varsity track team during his junior and senior years, he ran the 440, a sprint that demands terrific conditioning. He was Yale's best in that event and twice finished second in the intercollegiate championships. His friends called him Pat or Pete, "Anarchist," or "King of Ireland," and in the yearbook he was described as "the Boy Coxey of Yale," after the radical leader of a protest march by unemployed workers that took place in Washington in 1894.[6] An outstanding debater, he was known as "a silver-tongued orator."[7] Going to Yale in the Class of 1897 was the best thing that could have happened to Garvan, and he quickly became a dedicated Yale man. His college room, recorded in photographs of professional quality that he or his dad must have commissioned, provides a virtual self-portrait of the young man, jammed as it was with trophies won at track meets, a pennant signifying his victory in the Harvard Intercollegiate Relay Race on May 9, 1896, dozens of books, a Christian cross, photos of his teams, an oversized American flag, and biggest of all, a Yale '97 banner. In his room, one feels exuberance and energy, the joy of learning and sport, and, above all, his pride in identifying with Yale: All the qualities that would mark his later life can be found here. I never knew Francis Garvan, who died the year before I was born, but I did have the pleasure of meeting his widow Mabel Brady Garvan on several occasions. I also enjoyed knowing their energetic, talented son, Anthony Nicholas Brady Garvan, a longtime, much-admired professor of American Studies at the University of Pennsylvania; other family members told me that he was much like his father in his appearance, his energy, and his mannerisms.

Perhaps the most important event of Garvan's Yale career came when, as a junior, he roomed with freshman Nicholas Brady, a member of an Irish American family far more prominent than his own. The roommates naturally spent time visiting each other's families, with the result that Brady married Garvan's sister Genevieve in 1906, while Garvan married Brady's sister Mabel four years later; thus, the two families became permanently, though not always happily, linked. Garvan's new connection with the Brady family enabled him to move quickly from the Irish American middle class to the highest realms of wealth and prestige in America. By 1912, two years after they married, Francis and Mabel Brady Garvan joined the Winthrops, Bradys, and other established families in the *New York Social Register*. Throughout his life, Garvan was highly ambitious in terms of his status and social class, ambitious in terms of his reputation, his collection, and his wealth.

A place important for Garvan's rise was the Meeting House, an institution I had never heard of until scholar Catherine Whalen kindly brought it to my attention. It was a men's club that met in a house on Forty-Fifth Street in New York owned by Payne Whitney, and it was apparently founded about 1909 by Payne (Yale '98) and his brother Harry Payne Whitney (Yale '94). Its membership of fifteen, its lack of records, and its completely quiet existence suggests that it was modeled on the Yale senior societies; both Whitneys had been members of Skull and Bones. Both were also athletes, Payne as captain of the Yale crew, Harry Payne as an outstanding polo player. Members of the Meeting House were apparently chosen for their accomplishments in finance, sports, and law, or as writers and wits; one has a sense that a primary aim was to have lively conversations around the dinner table. Several were Yale graduates, but the majority had studied elsewhere. The unofficial emblem of the Meeting House was a canvas that Maxfield Parrish painted for it in 1909 entitled *Quod Erat Demonstrandum*, or *QED*, a favorite expression of lawyers meaning, "thus it is proven," or, "argument over"; this supports the notion of it being a debate and discussion society, a perfect environment for Garvan. Dinner meetings there must have been lively and raucous, and very different from the stately meals that Winthrop was serving his guests. The Whitneys, of Puritan stock themselves, unusually for the period were not prejudiced against the Irish or Roman Catholics, hence the election to the club of Robert J. Collier, editor of *Collier's* magazine, Finley Peter Dunne, the humorist and author of *Mr. Dooley in Peace and War*, and Francis Garvan himself. Garvan became close to both Collier and Dunne, serving as a pallbearer at the former's funeral in 1918 while naming his youngest son Peter Dunne Garvan, and paying for Dunne's funeral at St. Patrick's Cathedral in 1936. The members would have been aware of Garvan's outstanding early career, as well as his impending marriage to Mabel Brady, judging from the handsome silver cup they presented him as a wedding present.[8] Another binding theme of the group was its love of horses and especially polo: Both Whitneys played very well, and the other members included two of the greatest American players, J. M. Waterbury Jr., and his brother Lawrence Waterbury. The clubhouse was filled with racing and hunting prints, polo memorabilia, and numerous silver cups and other trophies. Garvan's acceptance into this bastion of the New York establishment marked a key moment in his rise, and the connections and friendships formed there played major roles throughout his life.

Francis Garvan's father-in-law, Anthony Nicholas Brady, was a transportation magnate, the major shareholder of the American Tobacco Company, and one of the wealthiest Americans; on his death in 1913, he left his children a fortune of about $80 million, about the same as J. P. Morgan's estate in the same year. Estate taxes came to just $3.6 million. His two sons, Nicholas and James Cox Brady, received their one-sixth shares outright, while the women—Mabel, her two sisters, and a niece—got theirs in trusts that were managed by the brothers. Each beneficiary's share netted out to $11.5 million, or about $300 million in today's dollars, making Mabel and Francis a wealthy young couple, indeed. Then in 1918, undoubtedly at Garvan's urging, Mabel and her sister Marcia Brady Tucker sued their brothers, alleging mismanagement of the estate, with Garvan's own firm representing the sisters. Garvan was a bloodhound in such matters: He went over every statement and every accounting with a prosecutor's eye, and the resulting settlement added significantly to his wealth. After this, family dinners must never have been the same, if they occurred at all, as one of Mabel's brothers had testified that their father had structured his estate purposely so that it wouldn't fall into the hands of "such persons as the husbands of these contestants."[9]

Garvan took to money like a fish to water, and during the teens he embarked on a house and art collection building campaign that helped establish his family's rank and importance. First came the remarkable "great camp" in the Adirondacks that he purchased from

Alfred G. Vanderbilt in 1915: This was Kamp Kill Kare, a massive rustic complex of some two dozen buildings that was a paean to wealth and to "leisure" in the wilderness. After a damaging fire, Garvan largely rebuilt it with the assistance of the prominent architect, John Russell Pope. The place featured huge pieces of log furniture; fireplaces constructed with local gray granite boulders; a bed made from a tree with its branches still attached; an "Indian Room"; a room "in the style of the Early American Colonists"; a boathouse; and a guest "Kabin" on an island connected by a seven-hundred-foot bridge. There was also a stone chapel where Mass was celebrated on Sundays, a playhouse with bowling alleys and a squash court, and any number of pelts, antlers, guns, and trophy heads on the walls. During summers the camp was served by a staff of thirty to forty, including chefs and assistants, guides and boatmen, farmers, carpenters, grooms for the horses, a blacksmith, and a butler, as well as four college boys serving as bellboys.[10]

In 1919, just as Garvan was embarking on his busiest years with the Chemical Foundation and other enterprises, described below, and before the Brady lawsuit had been settled, he and Mabel purchased "Roslyn House," a sprawling sixty-room mansion in the half-timber Tudor style in Old Westbury, Long Island, near the even larger castle called "Inisfada" that Genevieve and Nicholas Brady were building nearby. Leaving his identity as a tough Irish prosecutor far behind, he, like the Whitneys and his other North Shore neighbors, including the Phippses, Goulds, Woolworths, and Mackeys, along with horseman Ambrose Clark, brother of the art collecting brothers, took on the role of an English country gentleman, with an English butler at the door and a chauffeur for the Rolls. He was promptly elected to the area's most exclusive clubs, including Piping Rock, the Meadowbrook Hunt, and the National Golf Links on Long Island, and the Links in the city. These clubs were snobbish centers of old money, where distaste for the Irish and the nouveau riche was common. But a great fortune helps overcome those problems, and having the Whitney brothers living nearby and very likely sponsoring his applications would have smoothed his way. To demonstrate his new upper-class stature, Garvan commissioned a painting from the equestrian specialist George Ford Morris, *Mrs. Francis P. Garvan on Her Hunter "Alert"* (location unknown), as well as a large, elegant family portrait of 1921, *Mrs. Francis P. Garvan and Her Four Children* by Philip de László (Philadelphia Museum of Art), who emulated Sargent's bravura style and followed his compositional models as well. De László also painted a handsome bust-length portrait of Garvan looking dashing in a white linen jacket (National Portrait Gallery).

Garvan's campaign to establish his family on the Gold Coast of Long Island at the start of the Roaring Twenties recalls F. Scott Fitzgerald's novel, *The Great Gatsby* of 1925. Fitzgerald lived modestly in Great Neck near the Garvans between 1922 and 1924 when he observed all of the area's social life he needed in order to write the book, and he might have brushed shoulders with them at a neighborhood party. However, Garvan, unlike the fictional Gatsby, wasn't a mysterious figure but a well-known one who was unquestionably brilliant, worked enormously hard, and enjoyed what has been described as "a protean career."[11] After law school, he worked for a New York firm, then made use of his political connections to win appointment as assistant district attorney in Manhattan from 1900 to 1910. In that position he helped prosecute playboy Harry Kendall Thaw during the 1906 "trial of the century" for his cold-blooded murder of the architect Stanford White; Garvan thus became widely known. In 1910, the year of his marriage, he founded his own law firm with his partner, George J. Corbett. Highly opportunistic and keenly political, like his father before him, he joined Tammany Hall, the key Democratic organization in New York that helped many Irish in their rise to power, and was active in the reelection campaign of President Wilson in 1916. Catherine Whalen's research sheds important light on Garvan's amazing career that followed, as he was appointed chief investigator for the Alien Property Custodian, then succeeded his friend A. Mitchell Palmer as Custodian early in 1919 when Palmer became the US attorney general.[12]

Garvan also served as Assistant Attorney General under Palmer and as Dean of the Fordham Law School (1919–1923), and in addition in 1919 became president for life of the Chemical Foundation, the organization he had founded to take over the German patents seized during the war, a seemingly impossible array of duties for one person. This foundation grew out of the activities of the Alien Property Custodian, whose mission was established under the wartime Trading with the Enemy Act in October 1917, as amended in November 1918, to confiscate German assets in the US. Garvan saw a continued German threat after the war; he confiscated vast amounts of both real and intellectual property, speaking often about "the German menace." As he and Palmer wrote at the time, "The German chemical industry, which had so thoroughly penetrated our own, was gigantic, perhaps the strongest and most remunerative of all Teutonic industries. The task of identifying and taking over its property in the United States was thus a direct attack on a most formidable opponent. . . ."[13] Understanding the whole of Garvan's role at the Chemical Foundation seems key to understanding him, but unfortunately the details are highly complex and remain unclear. Garvan came under attack for corruption and profiteering from 1919 on, and the attacks intensified once the Republicans and President Harding had taken office in March 1921.[14] In 1923 Harding's Attorney General sued the Chemical Foundation for exercising monopoly control of the industry, and for selling the patents it had seized to DuPont, Dow Chemical, and others at below-market prices. Garvan was viewed by the American chemical industry as a heroic figure who built it, while his opponents saw him as a corrupt figure with "a bullying and often rude personality."[15] He was outraged by the suit and by related civil litigation, and he defended himself energetically, with the help of some of the nation's leading lawyers, against charges of corruption until the Supreme Court finally ruled completely in his favor in 1926.

When Garvan began buying American silver in 1916, he turned to the leading American silver scholar, Francis Hill Bigelow, as his advisor and agent. But unlike Winthrop, Garvan was his own expert, and he took total charge of every transaction. In 1917, for example, he wrote Bigelow that he would only buy an object "after a personal examination by me."[16] He bought vast numbers of American chests, tables, chairs, clocks, and other kinds of furniture, along with silver, pewter, porcelain, and glass, from good to great quality, which he lent to many historic houses and period rooms throughout the east. Like many collectors, he developed an ever-broader view of his aims, rationalizing how he had the public interest in mind ("what we bought was not for ourselves alone, but for the whole country").[17] These were the years when the American Wing at the Met was opened, Colonial Williamsburg and the Henry Ford Museum established, and when Henry Francis du Pont was furnishing his grand house-museum, Winterthur. American antiques seemed to these wealthy men to exemplify the qualities they saw as key to the American character. Garvan's letter to Yale in 1930 makes clear his interrelated Christian and patriotic motives. He wrote that God's glories must not be hidden under a bushel, and continued, "the same is true of every surviving article of historic interest (that) goes to make up our heritage of patriotism and constitutes our Flag."[18] The nativist rationale motivating Garvan and his contemporary museum-builders has been largely discredited today, just as their collections have faded from the limelight; American Wings at the museums have had to reinvent themselves in hemispheric terms in order to maintain their relevance.

Though Garvan's passion was silver and furniture, he was equally interested in American paintings, portrait miniatures, and prints. Unfortunately, Garvan's paintings collection was broken up in order to pay estate taxes, and only a few works went to Yale; however, it can be reconstructed using his records. Buying in the same years as Winthrop, he generally eschewed the established, expensive painters that Winthrop favored, the members of the canon, and instead pursued far less costly pictures that he believed illustrated American life and American democracy. Garvan loved objects that told stories. Just as in the decorative arts, where he sought historic provenances and period inscriptions, so in his paintings and prints he favored scenes representing historic sites or of what was then believed to be everyday life in antebellum rural America.[19] His taste in many ways foreshadowed that of such collectors as Maxim Karolik and Stephen C. Clark, who became active following Garvan's death.

Garvan owned fifteen paintings by Edward Lamson Henry, a post–Civil War specialist in "historic" scenes whose brightly colored, romanticized compositions found a wide audience during the

Victorian era.[20] He also collected numerous genre scenes by such then–little-known painters as Charles Deas, David Gilmour Blythe, Thomas Waterman Wood, W. A. Walker, and J. G. Brown—all artists that Maxim Karolik would collect in the forties. Garvan was also an early collector of pictures by the Missouri painter George Caleb Bingham. He bought the small *In a Quandary, or Mississippi Raftsmen at Cards* of 1851 (Huntington Library, Art Museum, and Botanical Gardens), for $375, then about 1937 he acquired the great *Shooting for the Beef*, 1850 (Brooklyn Museum) (fig. 23), which had been briefly owned by Stephen C. Clark. He purchased four portraits of Native Americans by Charles Bird King, several Homer oils from the 1870s, two Peaceable Kingdoms by Edward Hicks, the *Scissors Grinder* by Eastman Johnson (Fenimore Museum), and a fine full-length Thomas Eakins portrait of the painter John McClure Hamilton (Wadsworth Atheneum), for which he paid $12,000, his largest outlay for a painting. Garvan also bought a number of paintings of deer hunting and game birds by the Adirondack specialist Arthur F. Tait, over a dozen equine portraits by the specialist Edward Troye, as well as landscapes by Thomas Doughty, DeWitt Clinton Boutelle, and George Durrie. In addition, he had a number of figurative paintings by George de Forest Brush, Abbott H. Thayer, and James McNeill Whistler and by the illustrators N. C. Wyeth and Howard Pyle. Only a handful of these works made it to the Yale collection, but one that did, interestingly, was George Fuller's *Mary Chickering*; thus, we learn that Fuller was still in vogue when Garvan was active. He also owned a number of excellent miniatures by Copley, the Peales, and others, a fine group of objects that came to Yale through the generosity of Mrs. Garvan in 1955. In addition, in sculpture he collected several dozen Rogers Groups, the three-dimensional realistic, sentimental genre scenes featuring two or three figures courting, sewing, farming, and going to war.[21]

Garvan made his own decisions on paintings. In the decorative arts, he went after the same kinds of furniture and silver that Henry Francis du Pont, the Met, and many others were pursuing, but the paintings he chose all reflected his own taste for illustrations of American life. Moreover, unlike many of his fellow antiquarians and the leading critics of the day, Garvan wasn't an anti-modernist who

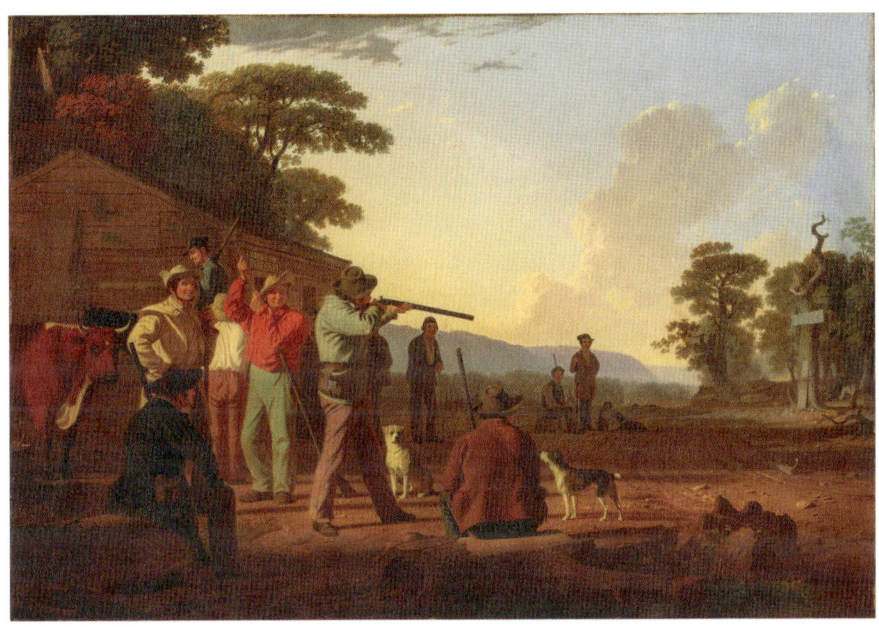

Fig. 23. GEORGE CALEB BINGHAM,
Shooting for the Beef, oil on canvas, 1850. Brooklyn Museum.

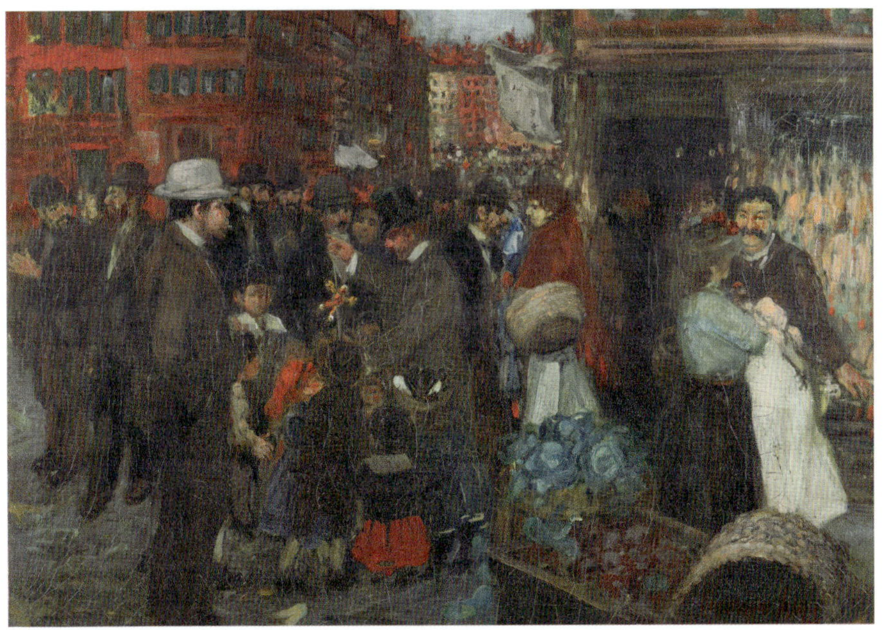

Fig. 24. GEORGE LUKS,
Street Scene (Hester Street), oil on canvas, 1905. Brooklyn Museum.

was afraid of contemporary art. Early on, he was drawn to "Ashcan School" street scenes picturing the urban working classes. He began buying works by John Sloan in the teens, and within a few years acquired a half dozen views of life in the lower East Side by Jerome Myers along with nearly two dozen of his drawings, several fine examples by George Luks, including his outstanding *Hester Street,* now at the Brooklyn Museum (fig. 24), along with excellent examples by Robert Henri. One would love to know exactly why such works appealed to Garvan, whether he saw them simply as illustrating an important part of the American story, or whether he would think, looking at them, how lucky his father and grandfather had been to escape the New York tenements and make it to Hartford.

Garvan cared deeply about the future of his collection. He hoped it wouldn't be "selfishly hoarded in Yale's own halls," which is what actually happened in the end, but rather aimed to have it serve the nation.[22] In his letter to Yale, Garvan described the "Mabel Brady Garvan Institute of American Arts and Crafts" that he planned to establish, an institution that would fund loans to many institutions as well as lectures, travel, publications, and a string of regional centers, an institution much like the ones founded by Alice Walton a half century later. However, Garvan's funds ran low; most of the paintings were sold from his estate after his death in 1937, and his plan to fund the Institute and his other charitable projects, including rebuilding historic Annapolis, didn't come to fruition.[23] How this happened is a mystery. Most wealthy American families suffered only paper losses during the Depression, unlike much of the populace. Garvan and his wife had enormous wealth, and what caused the sales from his estate, whether he had suffered major losses as a result of speculating or buying on margin, or whether his executors erred on the side of caution, is unknown. Whatever the case, his family's lifestyle saw little change; all the vast properties were retained, and the Garvans continued to give lavish balls for their daughters' debuts in 1932 and 1934.[24]

When Garvan decided in 1930 to have his portrait painted, he turned to a prominent New York painter, Augustus V. Tack, who would also be Grenville Winthrop's choice just two years later (fig. 25). Tack

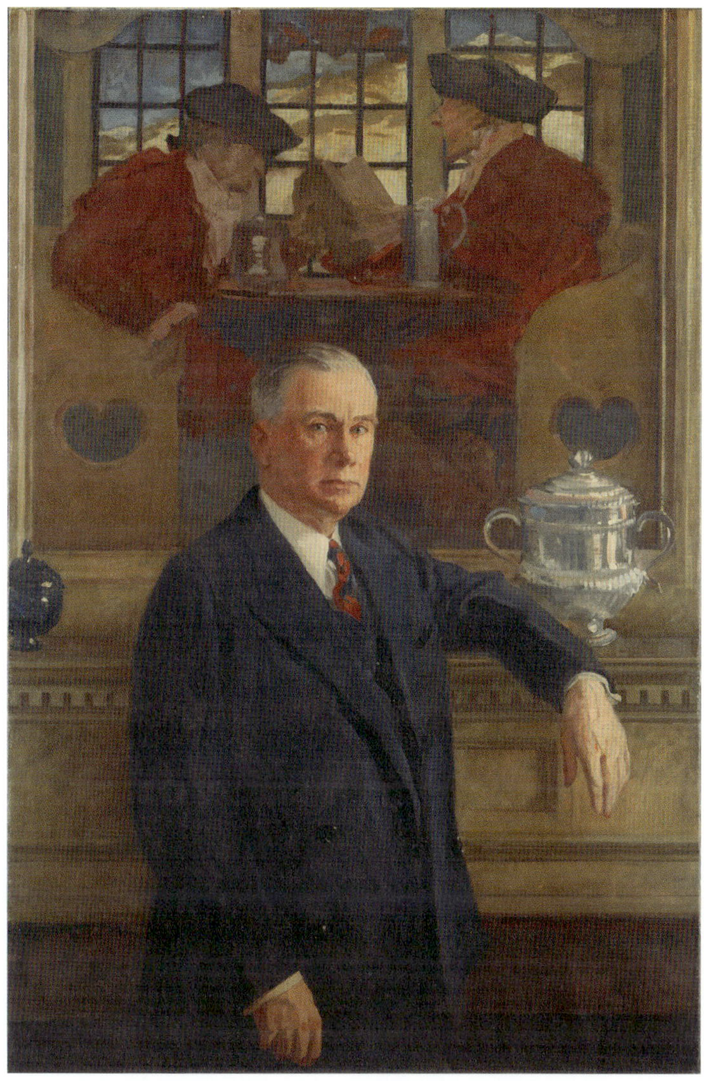

Fig. 25. AUGUSTUS VINCENT TACK,
Portrait of Francis P. Garvan, oil on canvas, ca. 1930. Yale University Art Gallery.

pictures Garvan wearing a double-breasted blue suit whose unbuttoned jacket fails to hide his now considerable weight; the diminutive track star of 1896–97 is long gone, and so, shockingly, is the handsome, confident man of the world painted by Philip de László just a decade earlier. Now, at fifty-five, Garvan seems uncertain, and the artist cannot disguise his pasty complexion or his uncertain gaze; one feels a hint here of his untimely death at sixty-two. This should have been a year of triumph for him, as he had just given Yale some five thousand works of art as "The Mabel Brady Garvan Collection," but one sees here instead a figure with weighty concerns, perhaps related either to his declining health, the strain of litigation, or financial losses. Garvan was portrayed leaning against a mantlepiece, with a lovely covered bowl of cobalt blown glass at left and the superlative *Two-Handled Covered Cup* by silversmith Edward Winslow at the right.[25] Yet the most distinctive element in Tack's portrait is the large painting over the mantle. The work is Maxfield Parrish's *Quod Erat Demonstrandum*, from the Meeting House. When that club disbanded in 1928, Garvan obtained the painting for himself, suggesting how much his membership had meant to him.

It was at the Meeting House dinners and other events that he would have gotten to know Payne Whitney and Harry Payne Whitney. He overlapped with both brothers at Yale, but there is no evidence that they became close friends at college. Harry Payne Whitney (Yale '94) would have been a senior when Garvan entered as a freshman, while Payne (Yale '98) was a year behind him. Nonetheless, in 1932, Garvan presented Yale with The Whitney Collection of Sporting Art, an extraordinary assemblage of about a thousand objects, making the gift in memory of Payne and Harry Payne Whitney. The younger brother, Payne (father of another collector, Ambassador John Hay Whitney, and of Joan Payson, future owner of the New York Mets baseball team) had died suddenly at fifty-one on May 25, 1927, while playing tennis at his Long Island estate, while the older, Harry Payne Whitney, died of pneumonia three years later. Garvan specified the credit line on each object: "Whitney Collections of Sporting Art, given in memory of Harry Payne Whitney, B.A. 1894, and Payne Whitney, B.A. 1898, by Francis P. Garvan, B.A. 1897, M.A. (Hon.) 1922." Garvan timed his gift to coincide with the 1932 opening of Yale's magnificent new Payne Whitney Gymnasium, which Payne had funded, and where much of the collection was initially installed.

The Whitney Collection included 49 paintings, 20 sculptures, and some 885 prints, 486 of them by Currier and Ives, illustrating nearly every sport.[26] In terms of quality, as viewed today, the masterpiece is Thomas Eakins's *John Biglin in a Single Scull* of 1874 (fig. 26), a tightly composed, brilliantly lit portrait of an athlete in action that hung in the rowing area at Yale's gym. Also noteworthy is Eakins's huge boxing picture, *Taking the Count*, another of the three major works that Garvan bought from Eakins's widow in 1928. At the gym as well were

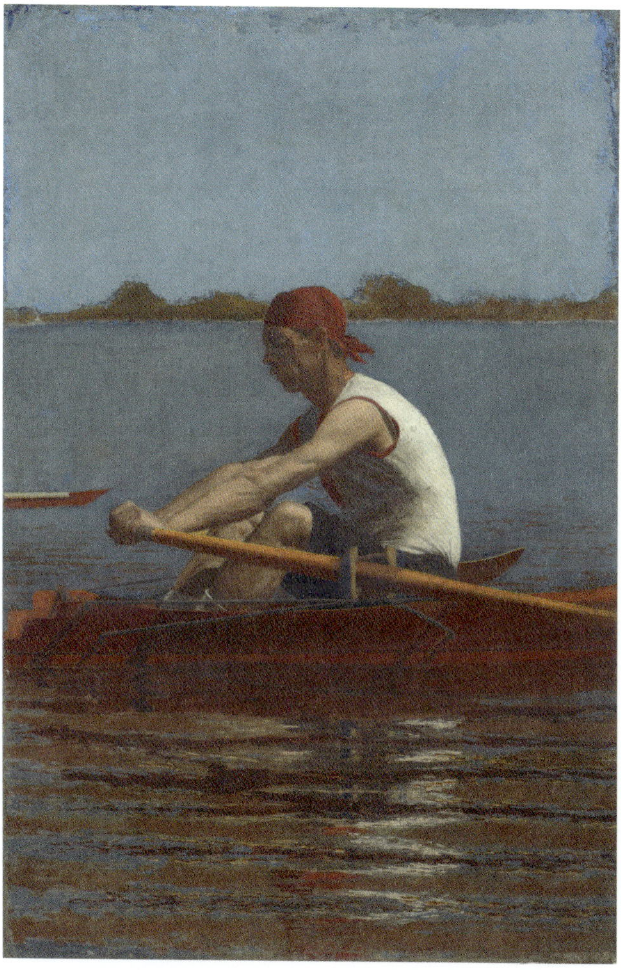

Fig. 26. THOMAS EAKINS,
John Biglin in a Single Scull, oil on canvas, 1874. Yale University Art Gallery.

Frederic Remington's painting *Touchdown, Yale v. Princeton,* and a nearly complete set of George Bellows boxing lithographs.

Garvan's collection of sporting art was dedicated, in his words, to "two of the finest gentlemen and sportsmen" in Yale's history, and it "memorialized a great friendship," his own with the Whitneys.[27] He wrote Yale's President Angell that his two friends believed that "sport is more than play, that it is a proving ground for the development of the laws of right living and fair play," concluding that Yale might "become a great research laboratory . . . for the improvement of the spirit of every boy and girl in this country."[28] This was farsighted, as it would be decades before Yale admitted women as undergraduates. He lauded the Whitneys for their linked success in sport and their integrity in business, thus not so subtly reminding his contemporaries of his own athletic victories at college and by implication his own honorable behavior in his business career. His views echoed those of the Greeks, recalling the ways in which athletic excellence was equated in the *Odyssey* and the *Iliad* with good citizenship and with bravery on the battlefield. Garvan in his youth would surely have been aware of Theodore Roosevelt's reliance on ancient models for his cult of manliness. Roosevelt in 1890 had opined that "Goodness and strength must go hand in hand if the Republic is to be preserved," and he was optimistic about the future: "Already this awakening of interest in manly sports, this proper care of the body, have had a good effect on our young men."[29]

Despite his impressive abilities and his immense accomplishments, Garvan must have always felt like an outsider. He never forgot that he was Irish, and he probably long remembered the slights he had suffered, as when he failed to be elected to the prestigious collecting group, the Walpole Society.[30] He took up much of the Anglophilic lifestyle and longed to be fully accepted by the WASP establishment and yet his son Anthony Garvan years later remembered his father as "deeply anti-British in a colonial Irish sense." In the same year that he gave Yale the Whitney Collections, he also donated to the university his collection of over two thousand books on Ireland in honor of his parents: It included many works on Irish history and especially the Cork area, as well as large numbers of first editions of modern Irish writers, including William Butler

Yeats.[31] Around this time, doubtless at his urging, his wife Mabel Brady Garvan applied for membership in the high-WASP National Society of the Colonial Dames of America, when she submitted extensive material on the Eldred and Carpenter families in Vermont, ancestors of her mother Marcia Myers Brady, through whom she hoped to establish her eligibility. All of the documentation had been gathered by researchers paid by Garvan. In addition, he hoped that his sons would be accepted by the Sons of the Revolution, again through New England antecedents of his wife's mother; he kept the application forms all of his life. These efforts ended in failure. Nonetheless, his magnificent gifts to Yale were part of a bold effort to establish his stature as an American of the highest ethical standards and social standing. In the end, Garvan's ambition to create a collection at Yale of American decorative arts of the highest quality and great breadth was fully realized, even though his paintings had been sold and his dream of having his collections play a national role did not come to fruition.

---

[1] Alan Shestack, ed., *Francis P. Garvan, Collector* (Yale University Art Gallery, 1980).

[2] See Helen A. Cooper, "Francis P. Garvan: Collector of Paintings, Prints & Sculpture," in Shestack, *Francis P. Garvan*.

[3] Ray O'Hanlon, *Unintended Consequences: The Story of Irish Immigration to the U.S. and How America's Door Was Closed to the Irish* (Merrion Press, 2021), 40–43.

[4] John G. Coyle, "Patrick Garvan," *Journal of the American-Irish Historical* Society 12 (1913): 270.

[5] Beatrice Garvan, conversation with the author, June 17, 2017.

[6] Yale University, *Class of 1897 Decennial Record* (Yale University, 1897), box 2, Francis Garvan Papers, Albany Institute of History and Art, Albany, NY. Other Garvan papers are held at the Archives of American Art and at the American Heritage Center, University of Wyoming, Laramie, WY.

[7] Yale University, *Class of 1897*.

[8] Catherine L. Whalen, "The Alchemy of Collecting: Material Narratives of Early America, 1890–1940" (PhD diss., Yale University, 2007), 108; Yale University Art Gallery, accession number 1997.59.1.

[9] Michael Gross, *740 Park: The Story of the World's Richest Apartment Building* (Broadway Books, 2005), 130.

[10] Craig Gilborn, *Adirondack Camps: Homes Away from Home, 1850–1950* (Syracuse University Press, 2000), 273–95.

[11] Whalen, "Alchemy of Collecting," 105.

[12] Whalen, 145.
[13] A. Mitchell Palmer and Francis P. Garvan, *Aims and Purposes of the Chemical Foundation, Incorporated, and the Reasons for Its Organization* (De Vinne Press, 1919), 3.
[14] Gross, *740 Park,* 130.
[15] Kathryn Steen, "Patents, Patriotism, and 'Skilled in Art': USA vs. The Chemical Foundation, Inc., 1923–1926," *Isis* 92, no. 1 (2001): 106.
[16] Francis P. Garvan to Francis H. Bigelow, December 22, 1917, Francis P. Garvan Collection, Yale University Art Gallery Archives.
[17] Susan B. Matheson, *Art for Yale: A History of the Yale University Art Gallery* (Yale University Art Gallery, 2006), 91.
[18] Francis P. Garvan, letter to George P. Day, Yale Treasurer, June 9, 1930, reproduced in Shestack, *Francis P. Garvan,* 67.
[19] See John Stuart Gordon, "For Silver, for Country, and for Yale: Francis P. Garvan and the Politics of Collecting," lecture, Yale University Art Gallery, May 13, 2015.
[20] "(for Mr. G's estate) 1937," *Assets: Paintings Located at Yale University (on Loan),* Francis P. Garvan Collection.
[21] See Helen A. Cooper, "Francis P. Garvan: Collector of Paintings, Prints & Sculpture," in Shestack, *Francis P. Garvan,* 62.
[22] See Gerald W. R. Ward, "A Wide View for American Art: The Goals of Francis P. Garvan, Collector," in Shestack, *Francis P. Garvan.*
[23] Garvan also hoped to restore the Hammond–Harwood House in Annapolis, Maryland, where he made extensive loans of decorative arts, and to undertake an ambitious restoration of "old Annapolis." In the process, he bought many Annapolis properties. He ended the project in 1932. See Charles A. Webb, "Annapolis Colonial Restoration: The Secret Project, 1926–1935," *Maryland Historical Magazine* 115, no. 1–2 (2020): 33–61.
[24] See *New York Daily News,* June 24, 1934, 28.
[25] Yale University Art Gallery, accession numbers 1980.18.1 and 1932.47.
[26] The subjects included hunting for deer and quail, woodcock shooting, trout fishing, football, boxing, wrestling, swimming, polo, horse racing, trotters, skating, rowing, cockfighting, and almost every aspect of track, including the shot put, the javelin, and the sprint.
[27] Cooper, "Francis P. Garvan," 71.
[28] Cooper, 72.
[29] Theodore Roosevelt, "Professionalism in Sports," *North American Review* 151 (1890): 187, 190.
[30] The criteria for membership in this club, founded in 1910 by Henry Francis du Pont and his friends, was "distinction in the collecting of early American objects of the decorative arts and fine arts, or attainment through study or experience in the knowledge of these arts; and the social qualifications essential to the well-being of a group of like-minded persons." It would be fascinating to know on what grounds Garvan was excluded. Full disclosure: I was also blackballed from membership.
[31] See Donald G. Wing, "The Garvan Collection of Books on Ireland," *Yale University Library Gazette* 6, no. 3 (1932): 45–46.

8

The Troubled Clark Brothers

Whenever Willy is unhappy, he goes out and buys something.
—MRS. GEORGE HEARST, on her son William Randolph Hearst

That swine and treacherous sneak.
—ROBERT STERLING CLARK, referring to his brother Stephen C. Clark, 1929

ROBERT STERLING Clark (1877–1956) and Stephen Carlton Clark (1882–1960) were the second and fourth sons of Alfred Corning Clark (1844–1896), the son and heir of Edward Cabot Clark, who amassed one of the great Gilded Age fortunes as the cofounder of the Singer Sewing Machine Company.[1] Robert Sterling Clark's name is renowned for his role as the founder of the Clark Art Institute in Williamstown, Massachusetts, one of the most admired of small American art museums. Stephen Carlton Clark is less well known; though his collection was the equal of his brother's, he split it between several institutions on his death, and his extraordinary paintings quietly became embedded at the Met, Yale, and elsewhere. It was Edward Clark who established the family in Cooperstown, west of Albany in rural New York State. On his death in 1882, he left an estate of some $35 million, the equivalent of $1 billion today. Sterling and Stephen grew up in immense luxury both at the Cooperstown estate and in New York City, where they lived in a mansion on Twenty-Second Street just off Fifth Avenue, and would have also known the nearby flat that was maintained for guests and the sprawling apartment at the Dakota, a massive apartment complex built by their grandfather. The two brothers were always fiercely competitive; their animosity doubtless had its roots in childhood but rose to the surface once they were both collecting.

A key issue in many families, rich and poor alike, is the division of the parents' possessions after their passing, and this became a major bone of contention after their mother's death in 1909, with Sterling feeling he had been shortchanged by Stephen. Objects and possessions have a way of becoming surrogates for deeper emotions. At times the brothers traveled and shopped together in New York and Europe as pals, while on other occasions Sterling was wont to criticize his younger sibling's taste and his lack of guile, as when he told Stephen that an advisor was "sticking it" to him.[2] In his study of the family, Nicholas Weber cites an entry in Sterling's diary where he writes, "This fellow Rehn has bad manners & is an awful bluffer. Just the kind of a man to sell bum pictures to Stephen."[3] Frank Rehn in fact was the dealer for both Hopper and Bellows, and Stephen got some extraordinary pictures from him. Sterling never hesitated to lecture Stephen, as he thought he had an infallible eye, and he quickly came to distrust all other art experts except himself. He particularly disliked the modern artists that Stephen favored, describing his Matisses as "mere daubs of grotesque figures."[4]

Sterling Clark, after army service in China (he won a Silver Star for valor in the Boxer Rebellion in 1900) and the Philippines, settled in Paris in 1910. There he met a French actress, Francine Modzelewska (later changed to Clary), who already had an illegitimate daughter, and she moved into his new house there; only in 1919 did they marry. He had bought old master drawings in Paris, but back in the US in 1912 he began collecting paintings seriously, acquiring fine works by Van Dyck, Holbein, and Jacob van Ruisdael, as well as some superb Renaissance pictures. He paid $100,000 for the sublime *Portrait of a Lady* by Domenico Ghirlandaio that was found for him by his father's sculptor friend George Barnard, and $170,000 for the Piero della Francesca *Virgin and Child Enthroned with Four Angels,* a work that was always his particular pride and joy. The latter is the best of the painter's work in the US, and for years Duveen and others tried to buy it from him. Almost from the start, Sterling conceived of building a museum for his collection, first planning to build it in New York City as a rival to the Frick and then in 1950 changing his mind and settling on Williamstown, Massachusetts, as its location.[5] Once construction had begun there, he poured his energy into planning it. He gave it wonderful works of art including his outstanding old master paintings, sculpture, and drawings, his large holding of French Impressionism, and the great paintings he owned by his favorite Americans, Homer and Sargent.

Sterling began brilliantly with Sargent, buying *A Venetian Interior* in 1913, then over a decade later following it with the closely related *Street in Venice.*[6] Sargent was at his best in these highly original views of 1880–82, where he avoided scenic Venice in favor of depicting the dark interiors and byways and its working class. He also purchased two other paintings dating from Sargent's early years, both from Knoedler, the source of much of his collection, the evocative Orientalist picture, *Fumée d'Ambre Gris* and the equally telling portrait of his teacher, Carolus-Duran. In the mid-twenties, Clark acquired an interesting picture of naked Italian boys on the beach, and the striking small portrait of *Mme. Paul Escudier (Louise Lefevre)* with a large white bow in her hair, but then virtually gave up on the painter. He collected another six oils in the twenties and thirties, but all were minor works. What he had was a group of fine works that show Sargent's early promise, but not his fulfillment. And what seems most difficult to explain, for a collector who loved drawings and watercolors, is that he only owned one weak Sargent watercolor, during a period when Grenville Winthrop and many others were collecting great ones.

Sterling did not make the same mistake when it came to Winslow Homer. Marc Simpson is surely correct in describing his holding as "the finest gathering of Homer's work put together by any one person after the artist's lifetime."[7] He began in 1916 with a superb picture that had belonged to Thomas B. Clarke, *Two Guides,* ca. 1875, a large composition celebrating American wilderness and manhood (fig. 27). The following year, Clark followed with two watercolors in the same vein, including an extraordinary one of men fishing in the violent Saguenay River in Quebec.[8] He took up Homer again with a vengeance in 1923 when he acquired three marine pictures, all from Knoedler; they included *Summer Squall,* which, though relatively small, ranks as one of the artist's most successful renderings of the foaming surf at Prout's Neck. He continued his campaign in 1924 with another first-rate watercolor, *Beach Scene, Cullercoats,* and the unique oil *Undertow,* where two men rescue two women from heavy surf, an important work much discussed in the literature.

Sterling Clark was surely aware that his competition for great Homers was the Metropolitan Museum of Art.[9] There he could see the five powerful marine paintings that George Hearn had given, plus *The Gulf Stream* and a Saguenay River picture that Charles Homer had donated; also in 1922 he would have been aware that the Met had just

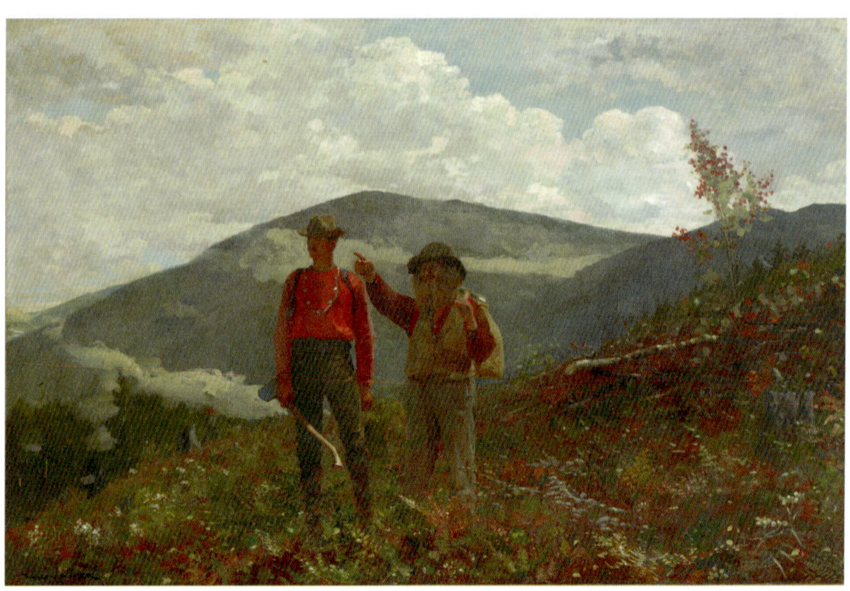

Fig. 27. **WINSLOW HOMER,**
Two Guides, oil on canvas, 1877. Clark Art Institute.

received the gift of *Prisoners from the Front,* and that it had recently purchased *Dressing for the Carnival.* Even at that early date, it must have seemed that the great Homers were disappearing, and that time was of the essence; it thus seems likely that the Met's holdings provided at least partial motivation for his acquisitions of 1923–24. Twenty years later, Homer's *West Point, Prout's Neck,* with its amazing red sky and a single spouting wave, emerged from a private collection onto the market, and when Clark saw it, he wrote in his diary, "Magnificent in the same class as the best in the Metropolitan $37,500."[10] He quickly bought it. Then in 1950 he found the superb early picture *The Bridle Path* on the market after it had been deaccessioned by the Whitney Museum.

In the last decade of his life, Sterling Clark turned to the work of two quite different American painters: Frederic Remington and George Inness. Inness had been part of the canon since 1900, while Remington, the painter of the west, had gained stature more recently when Western collectors embraced his work. Clark's first Remington is a typical action scene, a soldier on horseback leading a group of galloping unmounted horses away from harm in battle. The second, purchased in 1951, is a thoughtful composition depicting a lone, dark-skinned Indian scout on horseback in snow, trying to discern whether some distant figures are friend or foe. It's a simple, beautifully painted work, a study of whites like the Sargent *Fumée d'Ambre Gris* he had bought years before. In this decade, Clark also bought two moving, Tonalist paintings by George Inness, both painted within a few years of the painter's death. *Wood Gatherers: An Autumn Afternoon,* 1891, had earlier belonged to both Thomas B. Clarke and George Hearn, two legendary collectors. A woman and a barely visible child are outdoors, gathering wood; the mood is elegiac, surely winter is coming. The second picture, *Home at Montclair* (fig. 28), is a winter scene of profound emptiness and abstract beauty; no figures are seen, only a few birds hunting for food. It seems no surprise that Clark bought these paintings about loss and death shortly before his own demise.

Turning to Stephen C. Clark: When I first walked through the Yale University Art Gallery in 1968 after going to work there, I kept seeing credit lines on many of the greatest American and European pictures

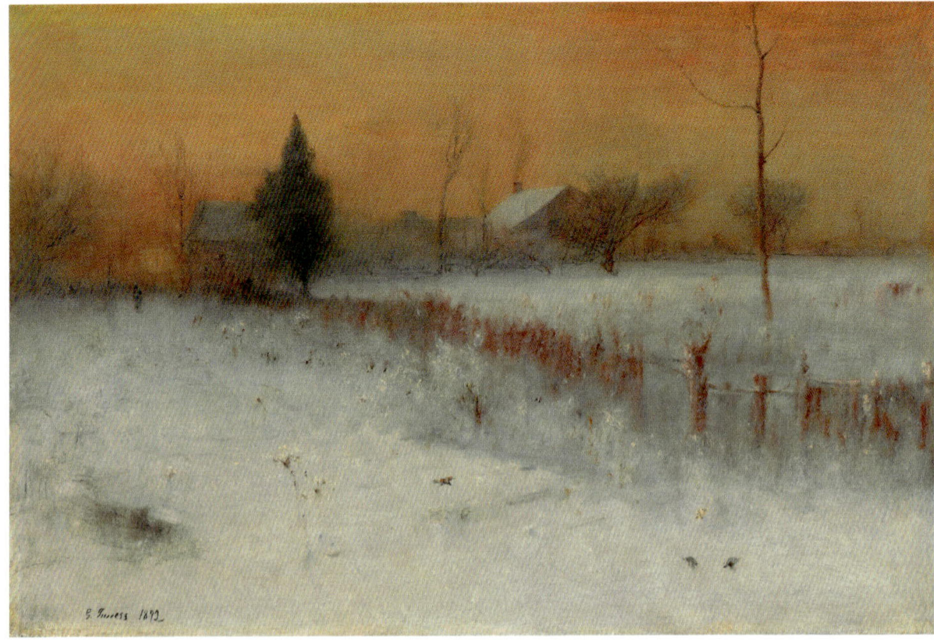

Fig. 28. **GEORGE INNESS,**
Home at Montclair, oil on canvas, 1892. Clark Art Institute.

that read, "Bequest of Stephen Carlton Clark B.A. 1903." The terrific pair of Frans Hals portraits, the world-class masterpiece *Night Café* by Van Gogh, the superb Manet *Young Woman in a Spanish Costume,* the great Corot harbor scene, the two striking Picassos, and then the Americans, with two fine early Winslow Homer oils, a superb group of Thomas Eakins's work from *Rail Shooting* to *Maud Cook,* and finally the best four Hoppers I had ever seen anywhere. How did these paintings that would have been the core collection at any museum in the nation end up at Yale? And who was this collector with seemingly perfect taste, anyway? I had come to Yale to work for the director of the Gallery, Andrew Carnduff Ritchie (1907–1978), a tall, ruddy Scot who was serious about art and had what directors need most: a way with donors. He had headed the department of paintings and sculpture at the Museum of Modern Art from 1949 to 1957, before coming to Yale. He must have known Stephen C. Clark well, for Clark was a powerful trustee at MoMA and the former chairperson of its board. Stephen C. Clark's outstanding collection was made to order for the Museum of Modern Art. In earlier years he had given the museum such key works as Brancusi's iconic *Bird in Space* and Bonnard's *Breakfast Room,* and it had every reason to expect him to continue. Clark was guided by Alfred H. Barr's taste. Barr's inaugural exhibition at the museum in 1929 was "Cézanne, Gauguin, Van Gogh, Seurat," the painters he regarded as the founders of modernism. That exhibition included the superlative Seurat *Circus Sideshow,* a work that Barr badly wanted for the museum. In the end, he couldn't raise the funds, and Clark bought it for himself, and later gave it to the Met.[11] Barr always regarded it as the greatest work in Clark's collection; he ranked Cézanne's *Card Players, Madame Cézanne in the Conservatory,* and the Van Gogh *Night Café,* next. In the end, none of these works, or the Picassos Clark bought later, went to MoMA.[12]

The Yale University Art Gallery began a brilliant collecting campaign in 1956 with an exhibition called "Pictures Collected by Yale Alumni."[13] The lenders comprised a who's who of the American elite, including Robert Lehman, Averell Harriman, John Hay Whitney, J. Watson Webb, and Paul Mellon, with Stephen C. Clark a key organizer. He lent twelve of his best paintings, including the pair of Hals portraits, the Manet, the Eakins *Rail Shooting,* and the Homer *Morning Bell,* all of which he later gave to Yale. In 1958, he gave Yale his two great Picassos, *Dog and Cock* and *First Steps,* the latter a work that Barr had suggested to him, along with two recent paintings by English modernists Stanley Spencer and Francis Bacon. These works would have greatly pleased the Scot Andrew Ritchie, who had trained at the Courtauld in London and who loved modern British art.

Stephen C. Clark pursued American paintings during exactly the same years that he was acquiring world-class modern European works. He was a rarity in being equally interested in the two fields, and he was in the collecting forefront in both areas. In 1930, the Museum of Modern Art confirmed the American canon with its exhibition "Homer, Ryder, Eakins." A few months before the exhibition opened, Clark wrote Eakins's widow (Susan Hannah Macdowell Eakins) introducing himself and asking if he could visit. By February he had purchased four superb pictures from her, including *Rail Shooting* and *Maud Cook* (see fig. 13, page 60); he got there shortly after Francis Garvan bought his pictures.[14] Stephen C. Clark went on to acquire nine more works by Eakins before 1952, all from various New York galleries, thus forming the outstanding private holding of its day.[15] Clark collected Winslow Homer just as avidly, buying twelve oils, a drawing, and a watercolor during the thirties and forties.[16] The greatest of all his Homers was surely *Hound and Hunter* of 1892, where a young guide in a boat holds the antlers of a recently shot deer so the animal won't sink in the lake, while trying to call off an approaching dog. It's a dark picture about violence and death, one that's set on a late Autumn afternoon. I think he responded to Eakins, Hopper, and others for the profundity of their paintings, for the sadness that envelops them. *Hound and Hunter* was not a work that Clark owned for long; he got it from Wildenstein in 1946 and gave it to the National Gallery the following year.[17] The Gallery was just then starting to build up its American holdings, and must have been courting Clark, as he had given it his Eakins of Archbishop Falconio the year before.[18] However, Homer's work in general didn't have the same staying power for Clark as Eakins's did. Most of his other Homers were sentimental paintings from the 1870s, decent pictures but ones he tired of and sold off. Two exceptions were *A Game of Croquet*, 1866, and *The Morning Bell* of 1871, both of which he had purchased in the late thirties. These were carefully executed, almost geometrically composed paintings that generations of Yale students have attempted to interpret.[19]

Stephen C. Clark responded less favorably to the murky visions of the third member of the canonical trio, Albert Ryder, but in the mid-thirties he did buy three of his oils, most notably *The Forest of Arden*, which he bequeathed to the Met. Early in his collecting career, he also tried out the other Americans whose work was being most actively collected during the teens, John Singer Sargent and James McNeill Whistler, but within a few years found that they weren't for him; his consistent taste for profound, crisply painted works stood in contrast to his brother Sterling's preference for loose brushwork. Thus, it was natural for Sterling to collect Homer and Sargent (and of course Renoir) in depth; he also bought works by Inness and Cassatt. Stephen's favorite Americans, on the other hand, were always Eakins and Hopper.

Stephen C. Clark had the methodical mind and dignified demeanor of an old-fashioned estate lawyer; he couldn't abide any kind of sloppiness, and that applied to his paintings. One sees this in his Hoppers particularly. Edward Hopper had been one of his favorites since he began collecting seriously; he bought *House by the Railroad* in 1926, the year after it was painted, then gave it to MoMA in 1930. Next he got *Manhattan Bridge Loop* and a landscape watercolor in 1928, and donated them to Andover and Yale respectively a few years later. He continued to pursue Hopper up to the end of his life, as evidenced by the four outstanding oils he bought between 1945 and 1957, each of them a profound expression of isolation, and each going to Yale in his bequest (fig. 29). Another favorite was George Bellows. He began collecting Bellows's work early on, boldly buying his 1921 portrait of Katherine Rosen the year after it was painted,

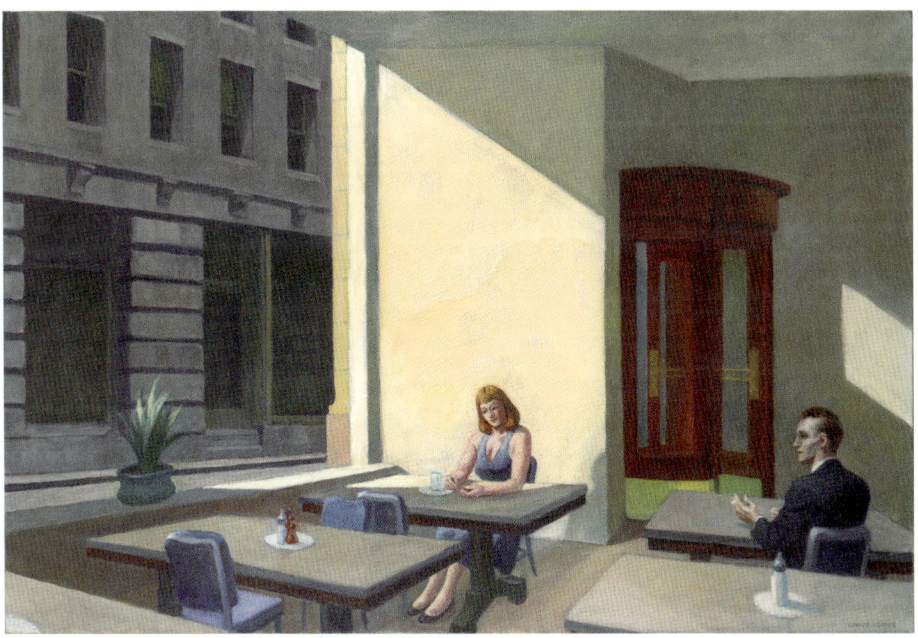

Fig. 29. EDWARD HOPPER,
Sunlight in a Cafeteria, oil on canvas, 1958. Yale University Art Gallery.

and *Lady Jean,* his touching picture of his nine-year-old daughter, a few years later. As with Hopper, these were works that Clark cherished, and he left all his Bellows, three paintings and five drawings, to Yale.[20]

In the late thirties Stephen C. Clark took up another kind of American art, for quite a different purpose. In 1939 he persuaded the New York State Historical Association to move its headquarters to Cooperstown, and in 1944 he gave it "Fenimore House," the handsome stone mansion that had been built by his elder brother Edward Severin Clark (1870–1933). As soon as the move was agreed upon, Clark began searching for mid-nineteenth-century landscapes, genre scenes, and portraits to fill the new museum; he was competing directly with Maxim Karolik, who was buying in the same years from the same dealer, Robert McIntyre at Macbeth Gallery in New York (see chapter 9). These were inexpensive works, ones often costing in the hundreds of dollars rather than the many thousands; he was buying them for illustrative reasons, seeking works that would tell his Cooperstown neighbors something about their rural past and the role of cider makers, scissor grinders, and other forgotten characters and trades. The results were mixed. He obtained a few fine landscapes, including Thomas Cole's *Last of the Mohicans,* which he had to have because it illustrated a scene from the novel by local hero James Fenimore Cooper, but mostly he concentrated on story-telling pictures by James G. Clonney, Eastman Johnson, and others. Just as he was beginning, in 1939, he came across *Eel Spearing at Setauket* by William Sidney Mount at Macbeth (fig. 30). There is no record of whether he realized how extraordinary a work it was, though, given his eye, he might well have. Any museum would have bought it in an instant. The collection he formed for Cooperstown for is a modest one, but *Eel Spearing* is the reason to see it.

Clark also purchased several other outstanding paintings during this campaign, but returned them to the dealer for reasons we can only guess at. All were works that would shortly become part of the canon, but were virtually unknown when he acquired them. In 1939 he purchased *The Ironworkers' Noontime* by Thomas Anshutz, but he tired of it and gave it back to Macbeth five years later. The picture had once belonged to Thomas B. Clarke; it went through numerous hands until

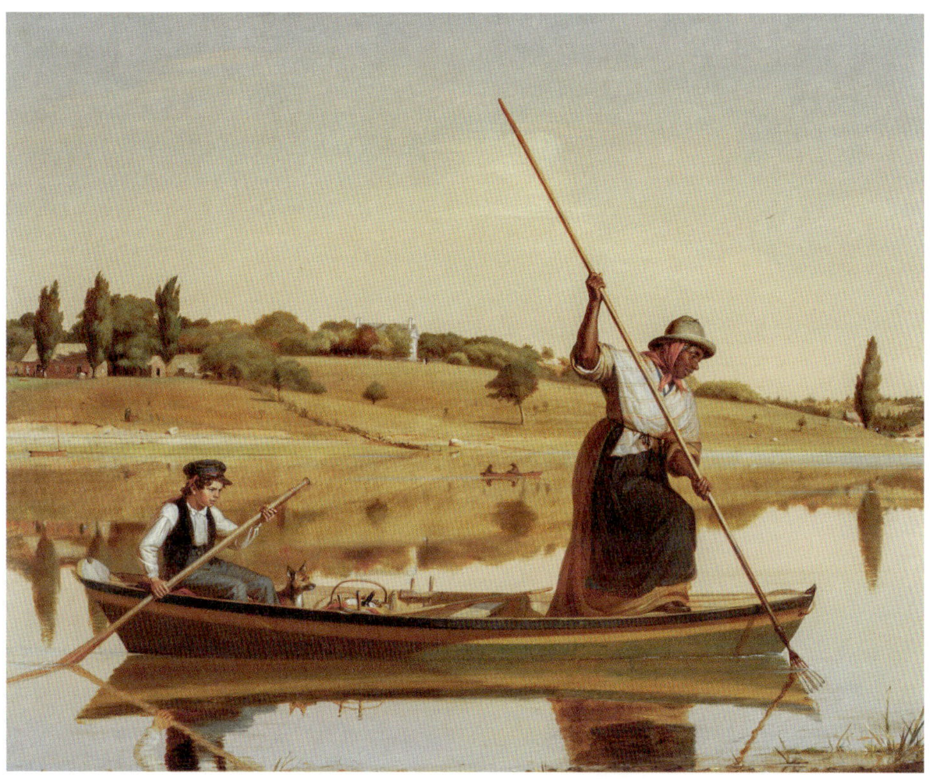

Fig. 30. **WILLIAM SIDNEY MOUNT,**
Eel Spearing at Setauket, oil on canvas, 1845. Fenimore Art Museum.

acquired by Lawrence Fleischman, then by Dr. Irving Burton at whose auction in 1972 it brought $250,000, before going to the Rockefellers the following year. He briefly owned another excellent picture, the Blakelock *Moonlight Sonata* that he obtained from Macbeth in 1942, then returned; the Museum of Fine Arts purchased it in 1945. Several other works that would become celebrated in the future went through Clark's hands in 1944 when he purchased five paintings by Martin Johnson Heade. One surmises that the dealer was favoring Clark over Karolik, giving him first choice of everything due to his immense wealth. Luckily for Karolik, Clark held onto the Heades for only a year before returning them to the gallery. They didn't fit the bill for Clark, who was looking for pictures of homespun American life, but they were exactly what Karolik was seeking: *Approaching Storm: Beach Near Newport,* became the pride of his collection, and he also bought another excellent Clark reject, *Orchids and Hummingbirds.*

Stephen C. Clark's eye led him to purchase these inexpensive paintings, but what led him to sell them? When Clark was buying the Heades, the Mount, the Blakelock, and the Anshutz, no one at the time could have imagined that they would become much admired and highly valuable. Neither collectors nor curators can see into the future, and Stephen C. Clark understandably must have felt that they didn't illustrate the American scene in the way he wanted. Then in 1950, Clark took a final step in building the collection of the Fenimore Museum when he purchased three hundred works of folk art from Howard and Jean Lipman. They were well-known, much-respected collectors in that field, and she was a scholar and the longtime editor of *Art in America.* From the Lipmans, Clark acquired cigar store figures, decoys, weathervanes, whirligigs, Santos figures, tramp art, miniatures, two fine Edward Hicks peaceable kingdoms, and portraits by John Brewster Jr., Ammi Phillips, and a handful of others, as well as some works by twentieth-century outsider artists, including Bill Traylor and Howard Finster. There are a few fine things, but overall the selection looks to me like the lower end of the Lipmans' collection, and one wonders whether Clark even saw the objects before buying them. His rigorous, disciplined eye was nowhere in evidence in this transaction.

Michael Conforti's excellent book of 2006, *The Clark Brothers Collect,* sheds light on the busy collecting lives and philanthropies of both Sterling and Stephen C. Clark. Museum professionals understand that their mission is to portray their founders and benefactors in the best possible light, as Conforti and his colleagues did, while only hinting at the considerable tensions and troubles within the family. But the following year saw the publication of *The Clarks of Cooperstown* by Nicholas Fox Weber, a well-respected author of a dozen books about American artists and patrons.[21] Weber dug deeply, and presented considerable evidence to support his conclusion that Alfred Clark, father of the collectors, led two separate lives, one in Cooperstown and New York as a respected family man and philanthropist, the other a clandestine one, "a passionately homosexual existence" in Europe, where he always spent the four summer months.[22] As a bisexual, Alfred would have been keenly aware of both the social and legal risks of his existence. Any hint of effeminacy would have violated his contemporaries' belief that a father's masculinity and integrity were all-important. New York State didn't repeal the laws that criminalized sodomy until 1965. In Europe, on the other hand, there were neither such laws nor the same risk of disgrace and ostracization. Alfred's first great love was apparently Lorentz Severin Skougaard, a Norwegian tenor, whom he was with for nineteen years starting in 1866, well before his marriage (Alfred named his first son, born in 1870, Edward Severin Clark). He also became very close to the American sculptor George Gray Barnard, whom he commissioned to fashion a marble monument entitled *Brotherly Love,* depicting two naked men, for Skougaard's grave.[23] The ensuing years saw Clark and Barnard traveling through Europe together, with Barnard paying long visits to the Clarks in New York and Cooperstown, where he was welcomed by the entire family, and Clark commissioning more works, and aiding him financially while paying the rent on his Paris studio.

We have no idea what Sterling and Stephen knew or sensed about all this as boys. This was an era when the homosexuality of a prominent married man would have been unthinkable for many, and their lives surely reflected the tensions of growing up in such a bifurcated, secretive atmosphere. Their father was an enormously generous person, an art lover, and a dedicated father, someone described as "sensitive, pensive, and vulnerable," while he also lived with private passions and a hidden double life.[24] In the US he appeared to be a paragon of morality, as when he openly disapproved of "the frivolity, vulgarity—and worse—which today dishonor our stage," while in Europe he enjoyed a far less judgmental culture where he was little known.[25] When he was crossed and he thought principle was involved, he would use all his powers to fight back, something his sons also learned to do. Sterling, the elder, was a prideful adventurer and bon vivant who was loud, entitled, querulous, and hot-tempered. He bought brilliantly early on, but in his later years buying art, silver, books, and other bibelots by the dozen became a way to pass the time rather than a focused enterprise.

Stephen, the youngest son, on the other hand, was a shy, taciturn man, who became both the most respectable citizen and the most adventurous collector of the family. He seems to have been both less damaged and less highly emotional than Sterling. But one senses in the art he loved—in the sad, carefully composed images of Hopper, Eakins, and the others—some of his lifelong effort to keep his own emotions under control. He was also the only one of the four brothers to have children. For both brothers, art had huge importance; it was central for Stephen, while for Sterling it seems to have been almost everything. Seeking the sources of their urge to collect, Weber concludes that "they were intense in their emotional needs, and devoted to artistic objects as the carriers of the creative, the beautiful, and the familial."[26]

In 1927 Sterling broke entirely with his brothers when he sued them, trying to break the terms of a trust so that his wife Francine could inherit family trust funds, and again he lost. A fistfight between Sterling and Stephen marked the end of their relationship. Sterling described his younger brother as "that swine and treacherous sneak," and as Weber writes, "Sterling would sustain his unequivocal rage almost to the end of his life."[27] Weber reports that he became more and more obsessive in his calumnies toward his brothers, his efforts to reduce his income taxes, his buying of vast properties in Kentucky and France, and his declining relations with his wife Francine.[28] Still collecting, he bought more and more mediocrities. His favorite painter was Renoir (he thought him "perhaps the greatest that ever lived") but with few exceptions, he didn't seek out that artist's best works but rather his fleshiest and most titillating ones. He developed a hatred of Franklin D. Roosevelt, and according to Weber, became involved in financing a plot to overthrow him and reinstate the gold standard.[29] That story is long and complicated, but seems credible, given Sterling's strong beliefs and his violent personality. Sterling fits the classic personality profile of the angry collector as a desperately needy, driven figure.

What can we learn from these two troubled art-collecting brothers? It seems that collectors need a certain amount of arrogance if they are to think that they deserve to own the very best; but as numerous observers have suggested, an overweening self-confidence and an inability to listen to others leads to trouble. Sterling Clark bought beautifully early on, and more weakly as his self-regard and his anger grew. His Homers, his early Sargents, and his two Innesses place him among the best collectors of American art of his day, and provide a good reason for visiting his museum. His cache of Homers, together with the Met's, is one of the factors that made Homer's work so difficult to find for later collectors. His brother Sterling (together with the Met and the Philadelphia Museum) did much the same for Eakins. The great examples are simply gone. Neither Sterling nor Stephen collected Sargent in depth. His art remained collectible for years, because he left behind such a large oeuvre, and because his work went out of fashion for nearly half a century. Both Clark brothers concentrated on the canon of their time, buying different aspects of it according to their individual tastes, a canon that remains fairly intact to this day, despite the strenuous efforts of many scholars, collectors, and dealers to dislodge it. Then Sterling, in the early forties, without knowing it, bought and then sold a canon that was on the verge of being established by Maxim Karolik, as we will see in chapter 9.

At the end of the day, the personal foibles of the brothers will be forgotten. Both brothers accomplished greatness through their love of art, Sterling building his wonderful museum at Williamstown, Stephen giving superlative works to his favorite museums, MoMA, the Met, and Yale. Despite their personal troubles, both lived up to their parents' deepest wish that the public benefit from their fortune.[30] But what a shame they didn't reconcile and combine their holdings: Together they could have formed one of the great American museums.

---

[1] On the worldwide importance and vast market for Singer sewing machines, see Jack Buckman, *Unraveling the Threads: The Life, Death, and Resurrection of the Singer Sewing Machine Company, America's First Multi-National Corporation* (Dog Ear Publishing, 2016).

[2] Nicholas Fox Weber, *The Clarks of Cooperstown* (Alfred A. Knopf, 2007), 140.

[3] Weber, 156.

[4] Weber, 183.

[5] Weber, 236ff.

[6] Margaret C. Conrads, *American Painting and Sculpture at the Sterling and Francine Clark Art Institute* (Hudson Hills Press, 1990).

[7] Marc Simpson, "Sterling and Stephen Clark as Collectors of Winslow Homer," in *The Clark Brothers Collect: Impressionist and Early Modern Paintings,* ed. Michael Conforti (Yale University Press, 2006), 242.

[8] Marc Simpson, *Winslow Homer: The Clark Collection* (Yale University Press, 2013), 101.

[9] Simpson, "Sterling and Stephen Clark," 240.

[10] Simpson, 239.

[11] Gilbert T. Vincent and Sarah Lees, "A Life with Art: Stephen Carlton Clark as Collector and Philanthropist," in Conforti, *Clark Brothers Collect,* 150.

[12] Weber, *Clarks of Cooperstown,* 359. Alfred H. Barr was also a huge admirer of Matisse's work; his groundbreaking Matisse exhibition was presented in 1931. Between 1927 and 1934, Stephen C. Clark carried on a Matisse campaign that resulted in his owning fifteen paintings; he gave one to the museum, but sold all the rest in the late forties and early fifties, having fallen out of love with them.

[13] Yale University Art Gallery, *Pictures Collected by Yale Alumni, Exhibition: May Eight to June Eighteen, 1956* (Yale University Art Gallery, 1956).

[14] Conforti, *Clark Brothers Collect,* 140–41.

[15] Stephen C. Clark left Yale eight superb Eakins paintings in his will, while the great portrait of Professor Henry A. Rowland had gone as a gift to Andover, his prep school, in 1931, the year after he bought it from Mrs. Eakins.

[16] Conforti, *Clark Brothers Collect,* 330–31. One of the paintings given to Yale, *Wash Day,* depicting a young Black woman doing wash, is no longer attributed to Homer.

[17] Conforti, 331.

[18] Conforti, 180.

[19] The forties and fifties were virtually the last time when one could buy a great Homer oil, as they had already been pursued by the major museums and a handful of collectors for half a century. The National Gallery was a late entry in the race but was able to purchase two other iconic works during these years: *Breezing Up* in 1943, and *Right and Left* in 1951.

[20] Clark also patronized the work of Eugene Speicher, a portrait, landscape, and still life painter highly regarded in his day but largely forgotten now. Sarah Lees in her indispensable checklist of works collected by Stephen C. Clark lists nineteen works by Speicher, an artist he began buying in the twenties; he gave away these pictures during his life and as bequests to a wide variety of museums. Conforti, *Clark Brothers Collect,* 317.

[21] Weber, *Clarks of Cooperstown.*

[22] Weber, 43.

[23] Weber, 62.

[24] Weber, 127.

[25] Weber, 94.

[26] Weber, 127.

[27] Weber, 173, 238.

[28] Weber, 172ff.

[29] Weber, 185.

[30] Weber, 179.

9

Maxim Karolik, Discovering a New Canon

Tell me whether the painting is good and I will not care who the painter is.

—MAXIM KAROLIK, *M. and M. Karolik Collection*, 1949

This vain, repetitive, consummate megalomaniac.

—PERRY T. RATHBONE, describing Karolik, 1962

MAXIM KAROLIK'S name is known throughout the American art world. It stands for the very best in colonial and federal American furniture and silver as evidenced in the widely admired collection that he and his wife formed in the thirties and it represents the boldest collecting of American paintings and folk art that anyone accomplished at mid-century. No other collector changed the canon in the way Karolik did. Yet it would be impossible to conceive of a more unlikely champion of American art than Maxim Karolik (1893–1963). How did this Orthodox Jew make his way from Akkerman (now Bilhorod-Dnistrovskyi) near the Black Sea to become one of the most insightful of all collectors of American art? What drove a tenor of only moderate abilities to turn a 1927 engagement to perform at the home of the wealthy spinster Martha Amory Codman in Washington, DC, into a marriage with the lady within the year? What accounts for his fluency in English, his eye and his love of art, and his special understanding of meaning and quality in American paintings? And what gave him the courage and the will to continue making extraordinary gifts of art to Boston, where he was never accepted?

Karolik grew up in Akkerman, a prosperous port city of about twenty-eight thousand people on the Dniester Estuary in the southwest corner of Ukraine. Jews made up 20 percent of the population, and the Jewish merchants, grain brokers, and storekeepers and their families were generally accepted, attending the town's two synagogues and many other institutions. Maxim—judging from his earliest letters in Russian and English—was well educated. As a boy he would have gone to one of the Hebrew schools, and then very likely received a college education in the nearby capital city of Odessa. Both Akkerman and Odessa were known for their liberal, westernized cultures; the schools and colleges there were receptive to Jews and offered them a broad education. But if Maxim enjoyed a relatively carefree childhood, it came to a crashing end in October 1905, when, as a boy of twelve, he witnessed a violent pogrom in Akkerman. Trouble had been building since a group of mutineers had seized control of the battleship Potemkin from its officers and anchored the ship at Odessa in June, in open defiance of the Tsarist government.[1] University students and workers organized mass rallies in support of the mutineers and a general strike was called, but then pro-Tsarist mobs on October 19 launched a violent attack on the Jews; uncontrolled by the police, they set fire to 1,600 homes and businesses, raped and pillaged, and massacred at least four hundred people in Odessa. A few days later, local farmers flooded into the markets of Akkerman, and led to extensive looting and burning. However, the Jews in that city had organized a defense force of forty men, and were able to limit deaths to eight. In preparation, the defenders had gathered weaponry, placing two twelve-year-old boys in charge of guarding it; one wonders whether Maxim knew them, or was involved himself.[2] Afterwards, many Jews left the area and scattered widely. Six members of the Karolik family, including Maxim's siblings Abram, nine, and Rosa, five, sailed from Liverpool to New York in 1906, and his sister Frieda, then seventeen, came to the US by a different route in the same year; she soon married the owner of a drugstore and, now Frieda Goulko, came to live a middle-class life in Queens. She and Maxim enjoyed a long, close relationship, and his early letters to her, in Russian, speak of his struggles and provide evidence of her efforts to support his musical career and to help bring him to the US. From them we learn that after the 1917 Revolution Maxim made his way to Italy, and that Frieda financed some singing lessons for him early in 1921 with the well-known baritone Eugenio Giraldoni.[3] By July 27, 1922, Maxim was in London, writing to the famous conductor of the Philadelphia Symphony Orchestra Leopold Stokowski in perfect English, imploring him for an audition. There is no evidence that his request succeeded, but by fall he had made it to New York. In November 1923 he had signed a low-paying contract with the Chicago Opera; he wrote Frieda that he'd suffered "a temporary financial collapse" and implored her to send money so that he could replace his single worn-out suit with a new one. But he was always optimistic; he told her that he knew "my luck will turn," and that he looked forward to "the moment when I'm able to share my wealth with all of my brothers and sisters."[4] Back in New York in 1924–25, Karolik was still struggling financially when he performed with the Popular Civic Opera League for the season.

In early March 1927 Maxim wrote Frieda, "After darkness, light comes," quoting an old Russian proverb.[5] He reported having performed without a fee in January at a large charity concert in Washington, DC, for the Old Russian Red Cross in Bulgaria, and he said, "High society came, and I'm swamped with invitations for private homes."[6] One such invitation came from Martha Amory Codman, an unmarried sixty-eight-year-old, the only child and sole heir of John Amory Codman and Martha Pickman Rogers Codman, who was descended from the merchant Elias Hasket Derby (1739–1799) whom many thought to be the richest man in Boston. Derby had made his fortune from his trade with Russia, the East Indies, and China, and from his numerous privateers.[7] She was thus part of a family well known in Boston for generations of great wealth and high social standing. Martha lived in splendor, residing in winters in an eighteen-thousand-square-foot, four-story brick mansion on Decatur Place in Washington that had been designed and built for her in 1908 by her cousin Ogden Codman Jr., and in summer at the equally grand "Berkeley Villa" in Newport, Rhode Island, in the Colonial Revival style, another Codman design. In 1930 Martha's household staff included nine Irish servants, while a decade later it numbered thirteen.[8] She had begun collecting American art and antiques early on, concentrating on reuniting treasures that had belonged to Elias Hasket Derby while seeking out Amory and Codman family portraits; as early as 1923, she presented the Museum of Fine Arts with two important carved Salem card tables once owned by Derby. She was clearly a bright, strong-minded woman, and one puzzles over her having remained single until her late sixties, but the family records and letters contain no clues about this.[9]

Maxim Karolik was tall, handsome, and thirty-four years of age when he performed at Martha's house on July 21, 1927 (fig. 31). The details of the party where she met Karolik have been lost, but one guesses that it was a musical benefit for one of the many charitable causes she supported. One longs to know what their conversation following Maxim's recital was like. Implausibly, they began a friendship. Perhaps she invited him to return to the house for tea a week or two later. Then who knows what happened? He spent the rest of the summer with her, and Martha in the fall wrote to tell her Aunt Mary (Mrs. Arthur Codman), who lived in Germany, that he was "a gentleman to his fingertips." She told her of their plans to marry, adding, "Of course I know what people will say."[10] The couple was married in France on February 2, 1928; their only wedding gift came from Aunt Mary. Maxim wrote her at her hotel in Zurich on April 26, 1928, thanking her for dinner and signing it "your newly adopted nephew."[11] A week later, Martha also wrote, thanking her aunt for the orchids, telling her that Maxim was pleased she had addressed the flowers to "Mr. and Mrs. Karolik" and reporting that they were going to Paris, then would head home.[12] Maxim wrote her from Paris in mid-May, saying, "I feel that you trust me."[13] On this wedding trip, Martha traveled with seven maids and a nurse; they all sailed from Cherbourg to New York on the SS *Majestic* in late May. In

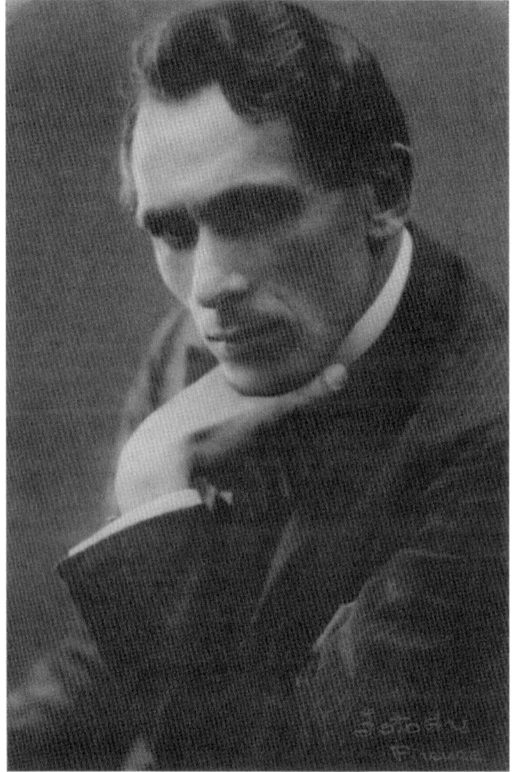

Fig. 31. UNKNOWN PHOTOGRAPHER, *Maxim Karolik*, ca. 1927. Massachusetts Historical Society.

a few months' time, Maxim Karolik had moved from being a penniless immigrant to commanding princely wealth. His voice never gained him great fame or success, but at the concert of his life, it proved good enough to charm Martha Codman. In October he wrote Aunt Mary with the news that he had become an American citizen and told her, "We are happy."[14]

People in Boston were horrified. Karolik would have been described by Boston society as a rogue, an adventurer, a fortune hunter, an outrage, and a Jew. Martha Codman Karolik was immediately dropped from the *Social Register* and from her clubs.[15] Maxim Karolik was never invited to join any of the men's clubs of Boston or Newport, and apparently the couple never received visits or invitations from friends or family. After the gift of the furniture, silver, and other material in 1938, Maxim was appointed to the Decorative Arts Visiting Committee at the MFA, but there would be no offer for him to join the paintings committee even after his extraordinary gifts in the forties or to become an MFA trustee, an honor that would have been taken for granted in normal circumstances. Yet Maxim somehow accepted his status, and forged ahead in good spirits as Martha's partner in art and life, and as someone with a healthy sense of his own self-worth.

At Martha's homes in Newport and Washington, he came face to face with American art for the first time. He would have found them filled with fine eighteenth-century American furniture, silver, paintings, and works in other mediums, some of it inherited from her distinguished ancestors but much purchased from relatives and dealers. She herself was a collector and antiquarian, one who in 1923 had researched and privately published the 1775–77 journal of her ancestor Katherine Greene (Mrs. John) Amory.[16] Martha Codman Karolik quickly came to trust her young husband, even if her family did not. On January 1, 1930, less than two years after marrying, she took a notebook containing an inventory of the paintings she had inherited from her father John Amory Codman, including ancestral portraits by Copley and Stuart along with a group of seventeenth- and eighteenth-century European pictures, and inscribed it in her lovely script as follows: "Everything mentioned in this book I have given to my husband," while signing it "Martha Catharine Karolik."[17] From this time on, their enterprise became a joint one. The Karoliks were highly conscious of the huge disparity in their ages and always took pains to minimize it. Their passports didn't lie, and showed the thirty-four-year difference, but when it came time for the annual census of 1930, Maxim listed his age of thirty-six correctly, while Martha put hers down as fifty-six, subtracting sixteen years, and they did the same in 1940. Also, they seem never to have been photographed together, and there exist no photographs at all of Martha in her later years.

Maxim quickly adopted Martha's interests, and together they began adding to her collection. Their buying was within the established canon, one that looked back to the Hudson–Fulton Celebration of 1909; they had numerous rivals, including Francis Garvan, Henry Francis du Pont, and the Metropolitan Museum of Art. In 1934 or 1935, they decided to expand their collection beyond furniture and silver made in Boston in order to seek objects of the highest quality from New York, Philadelphia, and other major centers, and to do it in collaboration with the Museum of Fine Arts. Despite the Depression, the market had risen a little since Francis Garvan's heyday a decade earlier, and in the mid-thirties, the Karoliks paid $12,000 for a great Philadelphia high chest, the same amount for an excellent bureau dressing table by the Newport cabinetmaker Edmund Townsend, and $17,000 for their most costly object, the famous chest-on-chest (a chest of drawers standing over eight feet high) by Samuel McIntire in Salem that remains one of the museum's treasures today. By 1938, when they offered the gift of the collection to director George Harold Edgell of the MFA, it included 115 pieces of furniture, 40 silver objects, 17 paintings including 8 Copleys, and various prints, drawings, and pastels. The "M. and M. Karolik Collection of 18th Century American Arts" opened to the public in 1941.[18] Maxim had hit on a brilliant alliterative title for the collection, one that gave joint credit to his wife and himself without specifying who came first. Ahead of his time, he insisted that the museum produce a handsome, fully illustrated, scholarly catalogue, and had one prepared by Edwin J. Hipkiss, the MFA's curator of decorative arts, who advised on the later purchases. In his own essay, Karolik demonstrated that he had quickly become an articulate and knowing expert himself, in one instance describing his passion for a favorite Philadelphia tea table while comparing it to lesser examples in the collection, and in another case analyzing Copley's American pictures versus his English ones to the detriment of the latter. Importantly, he explained that the works had been chosen for their artistic quality rather than their historic significance.[19] This was new. Francis Garvan and the early collectors sought works of high quality while also emphasizing provenance, valuing objects that had been owned by signers of the Declaration of Independence or other historic personages, but Karolik instead stressed the aesthetic merit of each work, and thus influenced the field.

Karolik became an American with amazing speed. A few years after the collection went on view at the museum, he expressed his views in an article in the January 1942 *Atlantic* entitled "The American Way."[20] This piece would have given the Boston Brahmins yet another reason to dislike him, as he proclaimed himself a liberal and an internationalist, urging in Rooseveltian terms that the nation aim for a new era of "freedom from want and freedom from fear."[21] He pressed contemporary business leaders to reject money as a value in itself, blamed them for the crash of 1929, and opined that the gaudy "cottages" of Newport, where he lived, "should never have been built."[22] He urged a return to eighteenth-century values, and concluded with the passion of an immigrant that America "is the hope of all liberal, freedom-loving people."[23] Karolik had developed a deep love for the United States and its art; he was articulate and audacious and he wanted to be heard. He believed that the talents and virtues of the Founders were reflected in the arts and crafts of their time, just as he would shortly begin to see nineteenth-century paintings as reflecting the nation's democratic values.

As the first collection neared completion in 1938, Karolik must have wondered where to turn next. Through Martha's love of antiques, he had found a role for himself, and collecting became his life. In fact, he wasn't well qualified for anything else; his voice was never great, and he lacked the temperament and training to succeed in business. As an art collector and museum patron, he became an important personage in the art world. Art dealers become fast friends with anyone with the money and interest, and museum curators—unlike their trustees—cannot afford to be snobs. Maxim was treated with respect everywhere he went, and every letter was addressed to him as "Mr. Karolik." Seeking a new field of interest, he turned first to the paintings of Thomas Birch, the Philadelphia painter of marine views, genre scenes, and history paintings. Birch provided him with a perfect introduction to nineteenth-century American art, as he painted every genre except still life. Moreover, the prices were right, generally in the hundreds of dollars. In 1937 he purchased Birch's *Landing of William Penn* from Charles Childs, who had just opened his gallery in Boston. Other Birches, most of them from Childs, followed shortly, including *Sleigh Ride in the Country*; *Skating*; *New York Harbor*;

and *Seascape*. These works established Karolik's interests, focusing as they did on the countryside and its inhabitants, views of ports and the sea, and bits of local history, all the subjects he would later pursue in depth. Martha Codman Karolik was now over eighty, and while there is every evidence that she believed in the new project, her role was now limited to giving moral and financial support.

Karolik surely saw "Life in America," the important exhibition at the Metropolitan Museum of Art that was on view from April through December 1939, as he lent three paintings to it, Thomas Birch's *New York Harbor*, A. A. Lawrence's *Boat Race*, and James Hope's *Army of the Potomac*. This exhibition coincided with the New York World's Fair, and had a primary aim of informing a wide audience about life in the US. Emphasis was on the bright side, with rural scenes far outnumbering urban ones, and with many more representations of prominent citizens than ones of the working poor and very few likenesses of African Americans. American life was interpreted as pleasurable, bucolic, and white, in *Life* magazine–like terms. Heade and Church were not represented, but Fitz Henry Lane was, and by one of his most beautiful paintings, *Southwest Harbor, Maine*. This would very likely have been Karolik's initial viewing of a large group of American genre pictures, landscapes, and marines, and perhaps his first chance to meet many of the leading collectors and dealers in the field; it also very likely introduced him to many unfamiliar artists. Interestingly, though Francis Garvan himself had died two years earlier, his taste was also much in evidence at the exhibition, as the "Garvan Collection, Yale University" was credited with the loans of the two important Binghams discussed in chapter 7, as well as genre scenes by Eastman Johnson, David G. Blythe, William A. Walker, Worthington Whittredge, and J. G. Brown, all painters that Karolik would start collecting shortly. The "Life in America" exhibition would have been highly gratifying to him and to others who were interested in vernacular art, as most exhibitions of American art in these years were devoted to Homer, Whistler, La Farge, and other members of the canon.

The nineteenth-century landscape and genre paintings had been generally overlooked by the scholars and major museums, where they were typically viewed as second-rate "Americana."[24] Karolik traveled uncharted waters in going after Heade and Lane, but there were at least a dozen dealers who handled the other "lesser" painters, and there were a few institutions and a number of collectors like Garvan and Stephen C. Clark who were pursuing both the folk art and the landscapes and genre pictures. One of Karolik's rivals in the field was Clara Endicott Sears (1863–1960), a Bostonian who opened her Fruitlands Museum in 1914. In the twenties and thirties she collected dozens of modest portraits that she found on her tours of New England; most of them were by painters with a modicum of academic training, while a few were by untrained artists, including Robert Peckham and Winthrop Chandler. Sears purposely avoided what she called "grotesque examples," referring to the striking folk portraits that Abby Aldrich Rockefeller and Edith Halpert were pursuing.[25] In the early forties, the years when Karolik was most active, Sears was also building a collection of landscapes. Her book about her holdings, *Highlights Among the Hudson River Artists* (1947) was more sophisticated than her volume on the "primitives," and suggests her knowledge of the field. It's a weak collection overall, for her eye was not equal to Karolik's, but her Church *Tropical Sunset* and her Robert Weir, *View of the Hudson from West Point,* are better than anything he had by those painters.[26] There were also a handful of museums building collections, most notably perhaps the New Britain Museum of American Art. Its talented director from 1938 to 1964 was Sanford Low, who built a remarkable collection; his standout purchase to my mind was Frederic Edwin Church's *West Rock, New Haven* of 1849, for which Low paid $1,000 in 1950 to Vose Galleries, where he did most of his shopping.

Karolik began his second campaign in earnest in 1943, when he bought two Lanes from Charles Childs: They were *Ships in Ice off Ten Pound Island, Gloucester,* and *Owl's Head, Penobscot Bay, Maine* (fig. 32), and he paid $550 for the pair. Since the 1960s, these have been considered to be two of the painter's masterpieces, each one valued today at well over $1 million. That year he also bought Lane's *Gloucester from Brookbank,* William Sidney Mount's *Bone Player,* Henry Inman's *Dismissal from School* (which he would have seen in the "Life in America" exhibition), and James G. Clonney's *Waking Up,* spreading his business among several dealers. A number of Karolik's paintings depict Black men, but he never owned a work—as far as I can tell—by a Black artist, because the dealers he was frequenting simply were not offering them. At the same time, somewhat surprisingly, he acquired Thomas Cole's biblical scene, *Expulsion from the Garden of Eden,* now a highly regarded work, but one that falls well outside of Karolik's search for homespun, native scenes. He had a special feeling for Cole and also bought several of his Italian scenes.

A second New York exhibition marked another turning point for Karolik: This was "Romantic Painting in America," which opened at the Museum of Modern Art on November 17, 1943. Karolik attended together with the MFA's distinguished curator of paintings, W. G. Constable, onetime Slade Professor at Cambridge and former director of the Courtauld Institute in London, who was best known for his book on Canaletto. This unlikely pair somehow formed an effective partnership in the creation of the new collection. Here they first saw the work of Martin Johnson Heade, whom neither had ever heard of before,

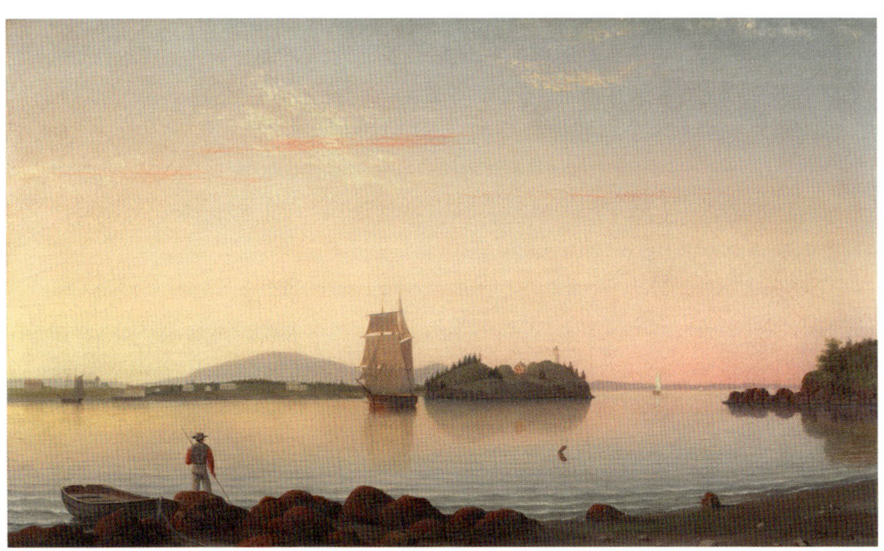

Fig. 32. **FITZ HENRY LANE,**
Owl's Head, Penobscot Bay, Maine,
oil on canvas, 1862. Museum of Fine Arts, Boston.

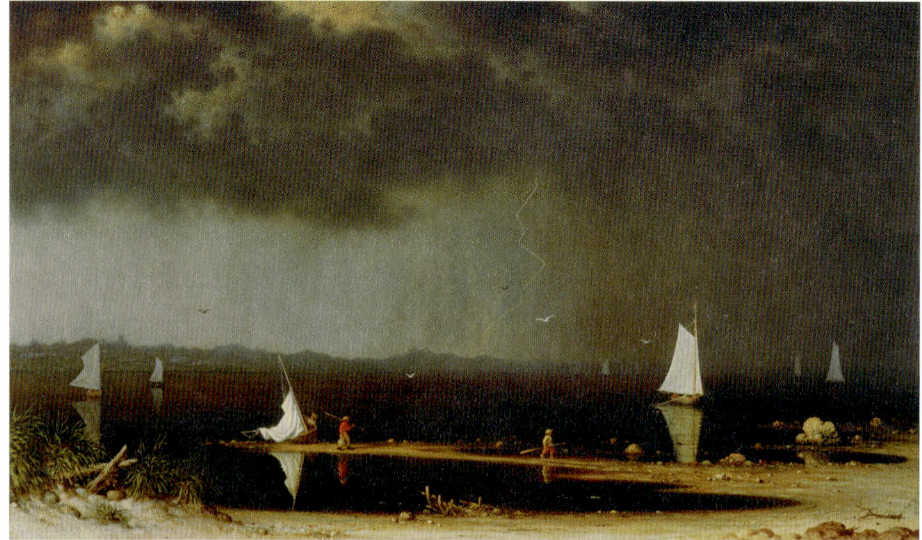

Fig. 33. MARTIN JOHNSON HEADE,
Thunderstorm on Narragansett Bay, oil on canvas, 1868. Amon Carter Museum.

who was represented by his *Thunderstorm on Narragansett Bay* (Amon Carter Museum) (fig. 33). Viewing this painting triggered Karolik's admiration for the artist, and he would spend years pursuing his works, eventually owning over forty of them. Sadly for him, *Thunderstorm* had already been sold by the enterprising New York dealer Victor Spark to a small-time collector named Ernest Rosenfeld for $500.[27] In 1977 dealer Jay Maroney sold it on Rosenfeld's behalf to the Amon Carter Museum for $750,000, a then-record price for any American painting.

None of the New York or Boston dealers had offered Karolik a Heade, because none of them had ever had one. His paintings existed, but they were owned by the painter's relatives or by the descendants of the New England families and Florida tourists that had bought them years before. Now, overnight, because of the appearance of *Thunderstorm over Narragansett Bay*, his work became collectible, and the hunt was on. One of the most enthusiastic seekers was Robert McIntyre of the venerable Macbeth Gallery, as he had been similarly affected by seeing *Thunderstorm*. Karolik purchased nearly a dozen Heades from McIntyre over the next few years, together with a nearly equal number from Victor Spark. By 1948, McIntyre had gathered enough material to write a creditable first biography of the painter, a book financed anonymously by Karolik.[28] In 1944 Karolik bought four of his paintings, then purchased ten more in 1945, including the well-known *Approaching Storm: Beach Near Newport* (once owned by Stephen C. Clark, as described in chapter 9), all at prices of less than $1,000. Victor Spark told him that he was driving up the painter's prices, and as if to prove his point in 1946, he charged him $1,500 for *Orchids and Spray Orchids* and $2,000 for the striking *Magnolia Grandiflora* on red velvet. What seems extraordinary in retrospect is the speed and enthusiasm with which Heade entered the marketplace and the canon.

Though Karolik was working closely with W. G. Constable, it was he who supplied the money and the passion. He had no agents and no scouts except for the dealers, and he was very much on his own. When he first saw Heade's picture at the Museum of Modern Art, he responded immediately even though the painter's name was unfamiliar and he had never seen a painting like it. It was an age of rediscovery and canon change; the nation and the world had been permanently altered by the Depression and the war, and people were ready for new art. In the same months that Heade was being discovered, several people led by the Museum of Modern Art curator James Johnson Sweeney and the collector Peggy Guggenheim had recognized the work of the young Jackson Pollock. Every collector dreams of making such discoveries, but very few have the confidence to take untrodden paths. Nearly all collectors and curators believe they have great "eyes," but most in fact have better ears than eyes, one reason that so many collections in every field contain so many of the same accepted artists. Collectors typically buy by name, wanting their treasures to be recognized by friends and visitors, but Karolik actually followed his own favorite maxim: "Tell me whether the painting is good and I will not care who the painter is."[29]

Karolik, along with the Chicago curator Frederick Sweet (discussed in chapter 3) also played a key role in the early forties in the revival of the Hudson River School, the painters lauded by Tuckerman whose reputations had been in decline since the late 1870s. One of Karolik's favorites was Albert Bierstadt; he gave twenty-two of his paintings to the MFA, including excellent Western pictures and a number of fine oil sketches, a genre he was the first to collect. He also had great depth in Doughty, Cole, Kensett, Whittredge, and Cropsey, with lesser strength in Durand and Church and just one Sanford Gifford. In addition, Karolik is still given little credit for being the adventurous collector of folk art that he was.[30] Karolik expanded the boundaries of the traditional definition of naïve, untrained, or folk art. Besides examples by such accepted folk painters as William M. Prior, John Brewster, and Erastus Salisbury Field, he owned many other works that blur the margins of the old definitions, ones that date to the Civil War years or after, such as the now-famous *Meditation by the Sea*, the evocative urban scene *A Street in Winter*, and the proto-surrealist portrait *Child in Rocking Chair* by E. L. George.

The mystery with Karolik, given his background, is how he came so speedily to become the audacious collector he did. The first collection was Martha's, but the second one was very much his: Here he embarked on a new field, building much of the collection within three years, and almost all of it within five. He called his achievement "The M. and M. Karolik Collection of American Paintings, 1815 to 1865." His aim was "to show the beginning and the growth of American landscape and genre painting."[31] He was adamant about concentrating on "the period between Gilbert Stuart and Winslow Homer," though in fact most of his Heades and quite a few of the other pictures date well after 1865.[32] His taste was for rural art, for the homespun and the local, for the farmers and the workers. He believed, as he said in his *Atlantic* article, that the arts would help produce a "much finer type of citizen" who will build a "Democracy in which worth, not wealth, is the measure."[33] He took another shot at the Brahmins when he wrote in the collection catalogue in his usual colorful style, "You know as I do that the enthusiasm of the average Museum Trustee for the objects with which he is concerned is akin to the enthusiasm of the chief eunuch for the odalisques in his master's harem."[34] This line alone would have guaranteed that he never be elected to Boston's venerable Somerset Club. Karolik rarely expressed his anger, but he had a way with words when he did.

How was Maxim Karolik, a newcomer and an outsider, so quickly able to grasp the quality of paintings that almost no one else was interested in? No well-bred, well-educated New Yorker or Bostonian would have looked twice at these pictures. Karolik possessed the hunger for art that collectors must have, and with his background he surely had a powerful sense of loss and of longing, what is described as "sehnsucht" in German. But where was Karolik's eye formed? Where did his love of art come from? The basic taste of many collectors seems to stem from their teens and early youth, and this was probably true of Karolik as well. He may well have attended the College of Music and the Arts in Odessa, and I believe his taste in art stems from these years. He could hardly have missed the impressive Odessa Art Museum which housed an excellent collection of the so-called Wanderers (or the Peredvizhniki), including a fine group of marine paintings by the preeminent specialist Ivan Aivazovsky, whose works have many affinities with those of both Heade and Lane. Here he would have also found peasant and genre scenes and numerous landscapes by Alexei Savrasov, Ivan Shishkin, Arkhip Kuindzhi, and Vasily Surikov. Russian painters of the last third of the nineteenth century celebrated the land and the people in much the same terms as their American counterparts, and they employed a closely related realist style. The wind-bent trees and stormy skies in the work of F. A. Vasilyev remind one of Inness and Bierstadt; the huge oaks portrayed by Shishkin are very much like Whittredge's; V. V. Pukirev's *Checking the Dowry List* of 1873 (Tretyakov Gallery, Moscow) relates to the many family groups in the Karolik Collection; and Arkhip Kuindzhi's *Lake Ladoga* (State Russian Museum, St. Petersburg), with its menacing, dark clouds, might be mistaken for a painting by Martin Johnson Heade. Karolik could easily have seen these pictures and others like them in the frequent traveling exhibitions organized and circulated by the "Wanderers," a group of realist, anti-academic artists, who circulated their exhibitions regularly, and frequently presented them in Odessa. Thus, when Karolik started looking at mid-nineteenth-century American paintings, they would have seemed familiar to him, as they are so close in style and mood to the Russian pictures he knew. In addition, Karolik would have lived with local Ukrainian folk art since birth, as many houses in Akkerman and its surrounding villages were decorated with the brightly colored floral decorations that were indigenous to the region—hence, I believe, his easy acceptance of American folk painting.[35]

Karolik once again insisted on a handsome scholarly book to accompany the collection. In selecting John I. H. Baur to write the essay, Karolik chose the most capable scholar he could have found. From 1934 to 1952 Baur served as curator at the Brooklyn Museum, where he demonstrated his acumen in a series of scholarly catalogues accompanying exhibitions devoted to American Impressionism, Eastman Johnson, John Quidor, William Sidney Mount, Theodore Robinson, and American marine painting. Baur was one of the leading scholars/curators of the day, but he was never well known; he was shy and lacked the gift for self-promotion that his future boss Lloyd Goodrich enjoyed. Baur recognized the significance of Karolik's great finds—Heade and Lane—and understood that the collection had been formed "with the specific purpose of a re-evaluation" of the canon in mind.[36] The question of changing taste interested him. In the Karolik essay, he asked "Why were Heade and Lane and Blythe and Quidor virtually dropped from the annals of our art, while Church and Cole and Durand and Kensett held their places?"[37] Baur understood how taste changes over time, and he was aware of how his era's appreciation of Surrealism and of modern paintings affected its view of earlier art. Baur commented on how the "pantheistic realism" he observed in Heade and Lane was different enough from the traditional Hudson River School style to account for their neglect.[38] Regarding Lane, he immediately grasped "the almost magic quality which radiates from these serenely polished coastal scenes" and he fully understood Heade's originality and the "sinister" qualities of his marine paintings.[39] Baur then followed up in 1954 with a thoughtful, influential article, "American Luminism," where he examined the works of several mid-century painters before concluding that Heade and Lane were the primary practitioners of the style he had been trying to define.[40] The Karolik catalogue itself was a big, hardbound book, in contrast to the pocket-sized paper catalogues that were the norm in the field. Karolik thus broke new ground with his collection and with its excellent catalogue, and Baur set a new standard with his essay about Karolik's favorite painters.

Karolik constantly weeded and pruned his collection, like many collectors, but of course unlike Grenville Winthrop and Richard Brown Baker. His accounts with the dealers were complicated, as he was buying, trading, and selling at such a rapid rate. In 1948, for example, he sold two paintings by Frederic Edwin Church through one of his favorite dealers, Norman Hirschl at the John Levy Galleries: They were *Tropical Landscape* and *Twilight, 1850*. The first cannot be identified today, but the second is undoubtedly the wonderful *Twilight, "Short Arbiter 'Twixt Day and Night" (Sunset)* that William H. Gerdts remarkably found at the same gallery eight years later when he purchased it for the Newark Museum. One of the Karolik mysteries is why he didn't do better with Church. His fine little view of an Andean peak, *Cayambe*, was bought in 1943 and remains in the collection, while his major example, *The Finding of Moses*, on closer inspection turned out not to be by the artist at all.[41] It would have made a difference to the Boston collection if he had kept *Twilight, "Short Arbiter."* But no collector is perfect, and a full understanding of Church's importance lay nearly twenty years in the future.

Martha Codman Karolik died at ninety in April 1948. Her funeral at Trinity Church was attended by the president, director, and several curators from the Museum of Fine Arts, a number of her old friends, and a half-dozen Codman and Amory cousins, suggesting that some of the family and local gentry were willing at last to show her some respect. A grand catalogue of the new paintings collection was published the following year, and the collection itself opened in refurbished galleries at the MFA on October 2, 1951. It included 233 paintings, with important groups of landscapes by Heade, Lane, Durand, and Cole; excellent genre pictures by James G. Clonney, Eastman Johnson, David Gilmour Blythe, and others; folk paintings by Erastus Salisbury Field and John Brewster, along with many by unknown hands; a good group of academic portraits by Samuel F. B. Morse and Thomas Sully; fine Western scenes by Albert Bierstadt, Alfred Jacob Miller, and Seth Eastman; and a smattering of still lifes by trained and untrained artists. The museum agreed to show them for five years, with no guarantees after that. "Art in America" lavished praise on the collector and the collection in a special issue the next year, and the lofty Preservation Society of Newport, which was dedicated to saving the lavish marble "cottages" Karolik had criticized, gave him one of the ten medals it presented on its tenth anniversary in 1957. In 1958, still dreaming of recognition for his voice, he issued his *Russian Art Songs* through Unicorn Records, but the praise he longed for didn't happen.

The real test of Karolik's character came with Martha's death. Maxim was a handsome, vigorous, and now wealthy fifty-five-year-old. He might well have taken off for the Riviera with a showgirl, as Martha's family doubtless expected, but instead he remained totally loyal to her interests. He proved to be a real collector, one of the best, and he didn't stop. During the fifties, Karolik turned his passion and energy to American drawings in a way no one had before him or has since. Operating quickly once again, he began the third Karolik collection, this one devoted to American drawings and watercolors; he was now working with the MFA's curator of prints and drawings, Henry P. Rossiter. Paul Sachs at Harvard and a few others had occasionally acquired an outstanding American drawing, but Karolik aimed for a definitive collection of the entire field, both the academic and the untrained artists. The dealers got the word and sent him drawings by the dozens. He in turn bought in large batches, 700 going to the museum in 1949, 218 in 1956, and so on. Many he bought in groups (the bill saying only "drawings by William S. Mount" for example), while for some of the best examples he paid prices averaging thirty to fifty dollars. He acquired drawings by the painters in the collection while expanding his range, now including Vanderlyn, Bartlett, and other early masters, and buying watercolors by Inness and Moran from later in the century. He bought about 6,000 drawings, half of them by untrained artists, a far higher percentage than with the paintings; these included Pennsylvania German frakturs, stenciled still life watercolors, topographical drawings, watercolor portraits by self-taught artists, and many works by amateurs. Many of these were very likely the work of women, but it will be impossible to know how many until a great deal more research is done on the unsigned works. There was also a large, impressive group of Civil War drawings by Winslow Homer, Alfred Waud, and many others. The third and last Karolik catalogue was published in two volumes in 1962; it included only about half of the massive holding, hence its title: "Selections from the M. & M. Karolik Collection of American Water Colors & Drawings 1800–1875." It remains the best collection of its kind, though its aim was a broad, democratic survey rather than the acquisition of individual rarities.[42]

Karolik also continued to collect paintings during the 1950s, while he was amassing all the drawings, and some of his greatest acquisitions came in this decade. He began doing more business with the Vose Galleries, which had begun changing its emphasis away from colonial portraits and Barbizon landscapes, and he bought Heade's fine *Lake George* from them. He continued to pursue his favorite artists, adding landscapes by Lane, Thomas Doughty, Alvan Fisher, and others. More importantly, he also acquired two of the greatest of all American folk paintings, *Joseph Moore and His Family*, ca. 1839, by Erastus Salisbury Field (fig. 34) and *The Reverend John Atwood and His Family*, executed six years later by Henry F. Darby. These are a curator's joy, as they are similar in their large size and subject matter and are close in date, and I always hung them on adjoining walls at the museum. They also demonstrate that Karolik in his late sixties had lost none of his willingness to pounce on a great painting when he saw it. The museum accepted his gift of Field's *Moore Family* in January 1958, with director Rathbone not unreasonably calling it "the masterpiece of American primitive portraiture."[43] It was quickly hung, then went to the Brussels World's Fair for the summer.[44] Around the same time, Karolik bought the extraordinary *Pictorial Quilt* made about 1895–98 by an illiterate, once-enslaved woman in Georgia, Harriet Powers. This large, visually captivating piece became one of the first works by a Black American to enter the MFA collection. It is now widely recognized as a masterpiece of American folk art, while providing more evidence of Karolik's amazing acumen.

Karolik also ventured in other new directions in these years, as he came to admire the work of John F. Peto, a late-nineteenth-century

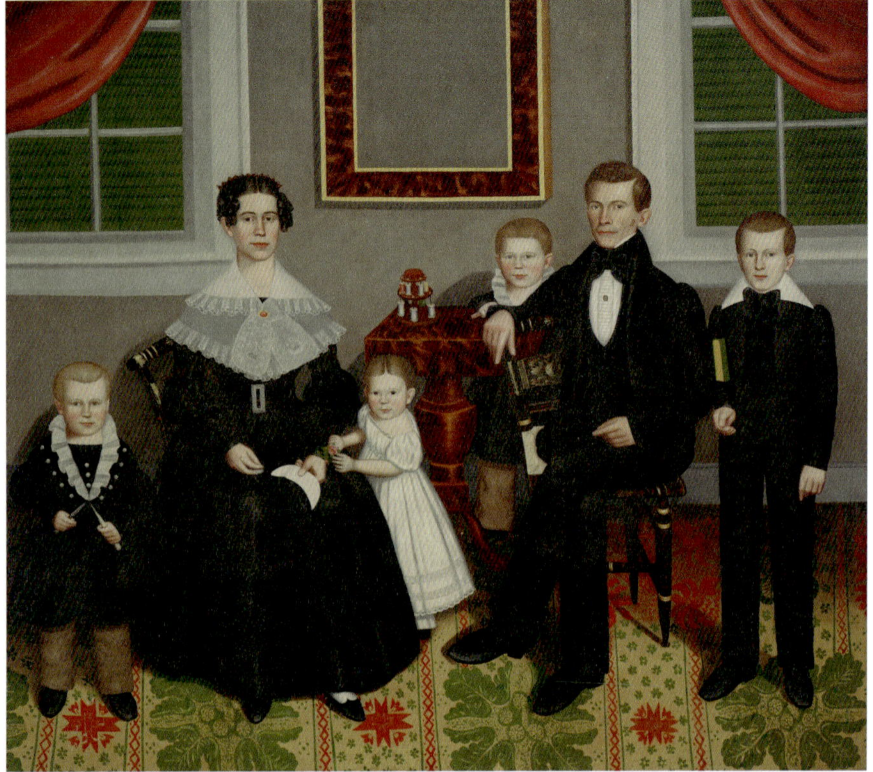

Fig. 34. **ERASTUS SALISBURY FIELD,** *Joseph Moore and His Family,* oil on canvas, ca. 1839. Museum of Fine Arts, Boston.

master of trompe l'oeil and a follower of William Harnett, but one whose more poignant images have their own special qualities. In the few years before his death in 1963, Karolik bought four Petos, including the outstanding *Poor Man's Store* of 1885. Finally, and most surprising of all, he purchased the very large tempera entitled *Soaring* by Andrew Wyeth; this was the only major work he owned by a contemporary painter.

The Karolik Collection of nineteenth-century paintings remained on view at the MFA from 1951 to 1956, then the collection came to national attention when 150 paintings (136 from his gift to the museum and 14 from Karolik's private collection) were sent to twelve museums on a coast-to-coast tour, an unprecedented celebration of a private collector.[45]

The traveling exhibition included almost all of the collector's favorites, including 14 Heades, 7 Lanes, and 10 Bierstadts, though it naturally lacked the Petos and the 2 large family portraits that he was in the process of acquiring. This project must have given him great pleasure, as he accompanied the show everywhere and was feted at every stop. Karolik was a showman at heart. His traveling exhibition introduced the nation to a number of unfamiliar artists just as American art was becoming known. The makeup of the show suggested, as Karolik had insisted all along, that there was little difference between the folk painter and the more trained practitioner. As he had dreamed, the exhibition helped form a new canon, one that included the painters he had discovered, notably Fitz Henry Lane and Martin Johnson Heade.

Another late in life project that surely pleased Karolik was his sale of 117 paintings to Electra Havemeyer Webb for her museum at Shelburne, Vermont; he must have enjoyed taking on the dealer's role for a change. Mrs. Webb apparently visited him at Newport about March 1957, and then the two began a long negotiation, exchanging lists and talking prices. All the pictures she bought were ones that he still had at home; with the exception of the marvelous *Death Struggle* by Charles Deas, and the Wyeth *Soaring*, they were mostly duplicates and lesser works by Heade, Lane, and the others.[46]

Perry T. Rathbone, the new director of the MFA, undoubtedly thinking that Karolik had not been properly honored by the museum, in 1958 appointed him Honorary Curator of American Art. This immediately led to trouble. Karolik interpreted his appointment as making him honorary curator of the three departments responsible for his collections, Paintings, Decorative Arts, and Prints and Drawings, and he frequently made himself welcome at all three. As the discreet, gentlemanly Walter Muir Whitehill wrote in his history of the museum, Maxim "began haranguing various trustees . . . at great length to express views on current museum policies and operations that were often critical of the Director."[47] According to Whitehill, Karolik had not done this before; but with his new appointment, his interference led to "a considerable loss of time and expenditure of patience" on the part of trustees and staff.[48] Those who remember Karolik from his last years recall him as "loud and blustery," as Morton Vose recounted to me some years ago.[49] Carol Troyen tells the story of his refusing to take off his ubiquitous fur coat inside the prestigious Somerset Club.[50] Alice Winchester in a 1957 article on him in *Antiques* wrote that Karolik was "demonstrative in manner and speech," and that he "sometimes gives the impression of playing the buffoon."[51] Director Perry Rathbone, in the privacy of his journal, found him "an insufferable burden . . . [a] vain, repetitive, consummate megalomaniac."[52] But Ralph Lowell, president of the MFA, and a perfect representative of Brahmin Boston, in a letter of 1960 summed up the collector more diplomatically: "Karolik, although rather hard to understand and a good deal of a pest, has been a real friend of the museum."[53]

In December 1960, Karolik hosted a dinner for the MFA trustees and its director at the Club of Odd Volumes on Beacon Hill, its purpose being to celebrate the twenty-fifth anniversary of the start of his and Martha's first collecting project. In normal circumstances, it's a dinner that would appropriately have been given for the collector by the museum. Nearly all of the trustees, including two Gardners, two Coolidges, a Saltonstall, and a Lowell, and one woman, Mrs. Roger H. Hallowell, responded favorably, each one penning a short acceptance note that began, "Dear Mr. Karolik." Apparently, no one was on a first-name basis with him. Among the attendees was Sydney Rabb, son of a grocer, who built the Stop & Shop grocery chain into a great enterprise, and who had broken the ice of the city's anti-Semitism by becoming head of the trustees of the Boston Public Library, and then in 1962 the first elected Jewish trustee of the MFA.[54] Boston remained insular and anti-Semitic far longer than New York or Chicago; even the eminent jurist Louis Brandeis had been earlier rejected by the city's fashionable clubs.[55] Karolik lacked the collegial manner of a Rabb or a Brandeis, and he was considered loud besides, so he would never have been accepted into the Brahmin circles or their clubs; his dinner at the Club of Odd Volumes had to be sponsored by another member.[56] One of the trustees who attended, Samuel Cabot, wrote to Karolik, congratulating him, and closed with a stunningly condescending remark about his collection: "The whole would be considered unique and distinctive for one who comes from the same background as the artists and their work. This is so much more true of one whose background is different."[57] What the foolish Mr. Cabot didn't realize is that only someone with a "different" background could have formed the collection.

Karolik came from a different culture than the Boston Protestants, who were unused to laughter, strongly expressed opinions, or any behavior that drew attention to oneself. The events he had experienced in Akkerman shaped him, and were simply beyond the ken of his wife's family or his new neighbors in Newport or Boston. Martha's family and Boston's elite were shocked by him, by the huge disparity in age with his wife, by his outspokenness, and by his religion. Yet his education and family life must have been the sources of his strength and confidence. What I find most remarkable about Karolik, beside his eye, his passion for art, and his loyalty to Martha, is his courage. He clearly found happiness in his new life, and he was somehow able to ignore being treated rudely by the supposedly well-mannered upper class. His magnificent collections were accepted, but he wasn't. What he had learned early in life about discrimination must have enabled him to view Boston's social rebuffs and its anti-Semitism merely as pathetic annoyances. He had witnessed much worse. From the start he not only adopted American art but American values. He made exemplary use of his new American freedoms to express himself, as he did in his published letters to the MFA directors and his articles. Much as we admire his collections, we should also admire Maxim Karolik for the remarkable human being he was.

---

1 See the film by Sergei Eisenstein, *The Battleship Potemkin* (1925), for a dramatization of these events.

2 Nisan Amitai Stambul, *Akkerman and the Towns of Its District: Memorial Book* (Yizkor Books in Print Project, 1983).

3 Maxim Karolik to Frieda Goulko, May 14, 1921, Maxim Karolik Papers, Smithsonian Archives of American Art, Washington, DC.

4 Maxim Karolik to Frieda Goulko, November 2, 1923, Maxim Karolik Papers.

5 Maxim Karolik to Frieda Goulko, March 1927, Maxim Karolik Papers.

6 Maxim Karolik to Frieda Goulko, March 6, 1927, Maxim Karolik Papers.

7 See Nick DeLuca, "Elias Hasket Derby: The Privateer Who Pioneered the Russian Trade," *Journal of the American Revolution*, February 15, 2018.

[8] US Census Bureau, "Population Schedule," *Sixteenth Census of the United States: 1940*, box 24, Karolik-Codman Family Papers, Massachusetts Historical Society, Boston, MA.

[9] See Catherine and Thomas Ball, *Paradox: Puritans and Epicures in the Codman Family, 1637–1960* (pub. by author, 2020).

[10] Martha Codman to Mary Codman, fall 1927, box 25, Karolik-Codman Family Papers.

[11] Maxim Karolik to Mary Codman, April 26, 1928, box 25, Karolik-Codman Family Papers.

[12] Martha Codman to Mary Codman, May 1, 1928, box 25, Karolik-Codman Family Papers.

[13] Maxim Karolik to Mary Codman, May 17, 1928, box 25, Karolik-Codman Family Papers.

[14] Maxim Karolik to Mary Codman, June 6, 1928, box 25, Karolik-Codman Family Papers.

[15] The *Social Register* began publication in 1886 with a volume devoted to "high society," the wealthy WASP (white Anglo-Saxon Protestant) citizens of New York. It later published annual volumes devoted to the same group in Chicago, San Francisco, and elsewhere.

[16] Katharine Greene Amory, ed., *The Journal of Mrs. John Amory (Katharine Greene) 1775–1777, with Letters from Her Father, Rufus Greene, 1759–1777* (Merrymount Press, 1923).

[17] Martha Catharine Karolik, January 1, 1930, Notebook, box 24, Karolik-Codman Family Papers.

[18] Edwin J. Hipkiss, *Eighteenth-Century American Arts: The M. and M. Karolik Collection* (Harvard University Press, 1941).

[19] Maxim Karolik, "As I Reflect upon the Collection," in *Eighteenth Century American Arts: The M. And M. Karolik Collection*, by Edwin J. Hipkiss (Harvard University Press, 1950).

[20] Maxim Karolik, "The American Way: A Conversation Piece," *Atlantic Monthly*, October 1942, 101–5.

[21] Karolik, 104.

[22] Karolik, 103.

[23] Karolik, 105.

[24] Maxim Karolik, "A Letter to the Director" in *M. and M. Karolik Collection of American Paintings 1815–1865*, ed. Museum of Fine Arts, Boston (Harvard University Press, 1949).

[25] Clara Endicott Sears, *Some American Primitives: A Study of New England Faces and Folk Portraits* (Houghton Mifflin, 1941), v.

[26] Clara Endicott Sears, *Highlights Among the Hudson River Artists* (Houghton Mifflin, 1947).

[27] In a letter to Karolik dated December 31, 1943, Spark said he doubted that Rosenfeld would part with it for $1,200 or $1,500, implying that those amounts represented the highest price he could imagine for Heade's great painting.

[28] Financial Papers, box 27, Karolik-Codman Family Papers.
[29] Karolik, "Letter to the Director," ix.
[30] Gerald W. R. Ward et al., *American Folk* (Museum of Fine Arts, 2001).
[31] Karolik, "Letter to the Director," ix.
[32] Karolik, x.
[33] Karolik, "The American Way," 101–5.
[34] Karolik, "Letter to the Director," xiii.
[35] Elizabeth Prelinger, who has helped me with every aspect of this book, in 1982 as an MFA intern traveled to Russia for me to research these Russian painters; I remain deeply grateful for her help then and now.
[36] John I. H. Baur, "Trends in American Painting, 1815–1865," in Museum of Fine Arts, *M. and M. Karolik Collection*, xv–lix.
[37] Baur, xv.
[38] Baur, xli.
[39] Baur, xliii, xliv.
[40] John I. H. Baur, "American Luminism, a Neglected Aspect of the Realist Movement in Nineteenth-Century American Painting," *Perspectives, USA* 9 (1954): 90–98.
[41] *The Finding of Moses* is included in the Karolik *M. and M. Karolik Collection of American Paintings* catalogue of 1949 (no. 80) as attributed to Church on stylistic grounds, while noting that it had been on the market as "American School." Museum of Fine Arts, Boston, accession number 47.1231. It is a large sunset view with waving palm trees and a group of figures in the foreground, too loosely brushed and lacking the detail to be Church. It is now attributed to the obscure Dutch-Canadian painter Alexander F. Loemans (1818–1894).
[42] Museum of Fine Arts, *Selections from the M. and M. Karolik Collection of American Watercolors and Drawings, 1800–1875* (Museum of Fine Arts, 1962).
[43] Perry T. Rathbone to Maxim Karolik, January 10, 1958, box 26, Karolik-Codman Family Papers.
[44] Two years later, Anne Atwood of New Boston, New Hampshire, wrote Karolik about her family portrait by Darby. He offered her $2,000, and she accepted, trusting the collector to set the value, as she wrote Tom Maytham, longtime assistant in the Department of Paintings. When she began to realize that Karolik had taken advantage of her, she wrote again to complain; Maytham and Karolik went to see her, and somehow persuaded her that the price was reasonable.
[45] The traveling exhibition was accompanied by a modest catalogue entitled *American Paintings 1815–1865*. Twelve museums hosted it for six-week periods, starting with the Whitney Museum in New York (January 9–February 24, 1957), then the Milwaukee Art Institute; the California Palace of the Legion of Honor (San Francisco); LACMA; Seattle; Portland (Oregon); Denver; Munson-Williams-Proctor Arts Institute (Utica, New York); Detroit; Dallas; Art Gallery of Toronto; and Rochester Memorial Art Gallery (New York). The catalogue lists 150 paintings, all from the MFA; however, 14 of these were withdrawn at some point, and Karolik substituted 14 pictures from his private collection, all listed at the end of the catalogue.

[46] Mrs. Webb paid Karolik $83,800 for the group, with the Deas at $15,000 being the highest priced.

[47] Walter Muir Whitehill, *Museum of Fine Arts Boston: A Centennial History* (Harvard University Press, 1970), 730.

[48] Whitehill, 730.

[49] Morton Vose, conversation with the author, October 23, 1979.

[50] Carol Troyen, "The Incomparable Max: Maxim Karolik and the Taste for American Art," *American Art* 7, no. 3 (1993): 65.

[51] Alice Winchester, "Maxim Karolik," *Antiques,* 1957, box 26, Karolik-Codman Family Papers.

[52] As quoted in Perry T. Rathbone, *In the Company of Art: A Museum Director's Private Journals,* ed. Belinda Rathbone (Godine, 2024), 78.

[53] Ralph Lowell to Robert Baldwin, July 7, 1960, Karolik-Codman Family Papers.

[54] Paul Sachs, associate director of Harvard's Fogg Museum, was elected in 1932, but his position at Harvard and his professional standing put him in a different category.

[55] Jonathan D. Sarna, *Jews of Boston* (Yale University Press, 2005).

[56] Lowell to Baldwin, July 7, 1960.

[57] Samuel Cabot to Maxim Karolik, November 2, 1960, box 26, Karolik-Codman Family Papers.

10

Ray & Margaret Horowitz and the Invention of American Impressionism

The best things here are the things your father and I collected, things all that we worked for and waited for and suffered for. Yes, there are things in the house that we almost starved for! They were our religion, they were our life, they were us.

—HENRY JAMES, *The Spoils of Poynton*, 1897

Collecting, looking, reading become an adventure in innovation, in seeing things in new ways, in refashioning and refreshing your ideas about life—and this is what art is all about.

—RAYMOND J. HOROWITZ, "Conversations with Collectors," 1999

AMERICAN IMPRESSIONISM as we know it today is strictly a modern invention. Mary Cassatt is generally considered the first American Impressionist, despite spending most of her life in France. She began as an academic painter, having gone to Paris in 1865 to study with Gérôme before developing her Impressionist style and beginning to exhibit with Degas and the French Impressionists in 1879. John Singer Sargent showed several conventional portraits at the Salon of 1885, then in summer very likely visited Monet in Giverny and painted his loosely brushed, tentatively Impressionist *Claude Monet Painting by the Edge of a Wood*.[1] Theodore Robinson, Willard Metcalf, and numerous others followed in the late eighties and early nineties and under Monet's influence developed their own versions of an Impressionist style twenty years after it had been developed in France. These American Impressionists knew one another, but never formed a group as such, and never exhibited together.

Frank Jewett Mather Jr., Lloyd Goodrich, and the other writers of the twenties and thirties took little heed of the American Impressionists, and it was not until 1937 that the estimable John I. H. Baur, who later wrote the Karolik Collection catalogue, became an early champion of the style with his exhibition "Leaders of American Impressionism: Mary Cassatt, Childe Hassam, John H. Twachtman, and J. Alden Weir."[2] Nine years later, Baur, aiming to correct his omission of Theodore Robinson, organized a show devoted wholly to that painter's work.[3] I have already described Frederick Sweet's 1954 exhibition of Whistler, Sargent, and Cassatt; it must have raised awareness of those painters, yet their work held little interest for the few active buyers of American art before Ray and Margaret Horowitz began collecting.

The Horowitzes were close to Daniel and Rita Fraad, as the men worked closely together on a daily basis: Ray Horowitz was the chief attorney for Dan Fraad's massive enterprise, the Allied Maintenance Corporation (later Ogden Allied) which in 1956 was described as having five thousand employees who cleaned and maintained some fifty-two million feet of building space each day, including Penn Station and the airports, where they also fueled the planes.[4] The Fraads became wealthy from this enterprise, and the Horowitzes did increasingly well thanks to Ray's legal fees. He and Dan Fraad were hardworking, self-made men who stood in contrast to the inheritors of fabulous wealth like Grenville Winthrop and the Clark brothers.

The Fraads started collecting first, as a result of Rita's having taken art classes at Smith College. They made some trial runs with lesser works, then in 1955–57 became serious when they bought paintings by Ryder, Homer, and Eakins, the trio long thought to be the preeminent figures of the nineteenth century, while also acquiring a watercolor by Edward

Hopper. The Fraads then turned to tough, realistic pictures from the early twentieth century, as exemplified by *The Cabby* by George Luks, which they purchased in 1959.[5] The Horowitzes were familiar with the Fraads' growing collection, but they didn't themselves begin until 1961. Early that year the Fraads gave Margaret a gift of $1,000 to buy Ray a present from them for his forty-fifth birthday; after some shopping, she selected a minor Berthe Morisot painting, *Girl Seated, Reading.*[6] This confirms dealer Stuart Feld's theory that "All of these collectors really wanted to be collecting French Impressionism, but they either couldn't afford it, or thought they couldn't."[7] Margaret and Ray began reading voraciously about art. They first bought American drawings, and later in 1961 made their first major purchase, paying Hirschl & Adler $3,000 on time for Robert Henri's *Girl Seated by the Sea,* a bright, cheerful, more or less Impressionist painting. Ray reports that when they saw it, "We were instantly drawn to it," and he went on, "Since then, our taste has remained the same."[8] Very few collectors are fortunate enough to establish their focus early on, and even fewer are disciplined enough to maintain a single direction. In 1961 and 1962 they went on to acquire a self-portrait by Theodore Robinson for $1,900, a watercolor by the same artist for $650, the lovely Robert Vonnoh, *Springtime in France,* for $900, landscape pastels by Robert Henri and Childe Hassam, and Hassam's *Nurses in the Park,* an oil that cost $2,750; these modest prices suggest the state of the market at that time. In the following year, 1963, Margaret and Ray purchased another Henri oil, two Sargent watercolors, and their first work by William Merritt Chase, a watercolor portrait of a young woman dressed in black. Thus, in a very short time, they owned works by their favorite artists; from then on, it was a question of expanding and upgrading.

American Impressionism represented new territory: It was little known, and it was inexpensive. The Fraads, Horowitzes and other beginning collectors in New York would have been aware of the great exhibitions of the French Impressionists and Post-Impressionists being presented at the Museum of Modern Art, including "Seurat" in 1958 and "Monet: Seasons and Moments" in 1960, and they would have known that the lenders to these exhibitions included many of the wealthiest Americans, including Walter Annenberg, Sterling Clark, John Hay Whitney, and Paul Mellon.[9] The Fraads and Horowitzes also could hardly have missed the auction of French art owned by Mr. and Mrs. Norman Woolworth (who also collected American art) at Parke-Bernet in New York in October 1962.[10] Witnessing an uninteresting early Van Gogh and a handsome, small Degas pastel go for $90,000 apiece, with landscapes of moderate quality by Gauguin, Pissarro, and Sisley bringing between $40,000 and $60,000, must have reinforced their opinion that American Impressionist works had comparable quality at a tenth the cost or less. Just as Maxim Karolik two decades earlier had established the market for Heade, Lane, and their cohorts, it was these New York collectors who created the new demand for American Impressionism.

The Fraads, who had introduced their friends to collecting, were influenced by them in turn. After seeing what Margaret and Ray were doing, Rita and Dan started adding Impressionist pictures to their collection, purchasing a colorful Glackens in 1962, five Prendergasts in 1962–3, as well as paintings by Metcalf, Robinson, and Twachtman shortly afterwards. Just as the Horowitzes were acquiring their two Sargent watercolors, the Fraads bought two extraordinary Sargent oils from Hirschl & Adler in 1962 and 1964, first the famous *Siesta* (fig. 35) and then the classic *Venetian Street*, paying $24,000 for the former and $20,000 for the latter.[11] Ray Horowitz had seen *Siesta* first, but said that "we didn't remotely have the money," so he suggested it to the Fraads. He always lamented the loss, commenting that it was "our picture," and going on, "Dan liked the vigorous, forceful kind of painting, and we liked the more lyric."[12] Then, six years later, Ray and Margaret bought an excellent Sargent oil at a more affordable price: *Lady Seated Beside an Alpine Pool* of ca. 1909–11. This was a tougher, darker picture than they were used to, more like something one would find at the Fraads. They hung it in their small library, but they found that it never quite fit in. They let it go at Margaret's urging in 1980, but Ray always regretted the sale. Even for the most thoughtful, serious collectors, the unity of the collection as installed in the home plays a major role, and holding onto one's best pictures turns out to be nearly as much of a challenge as acquiring them.[13]

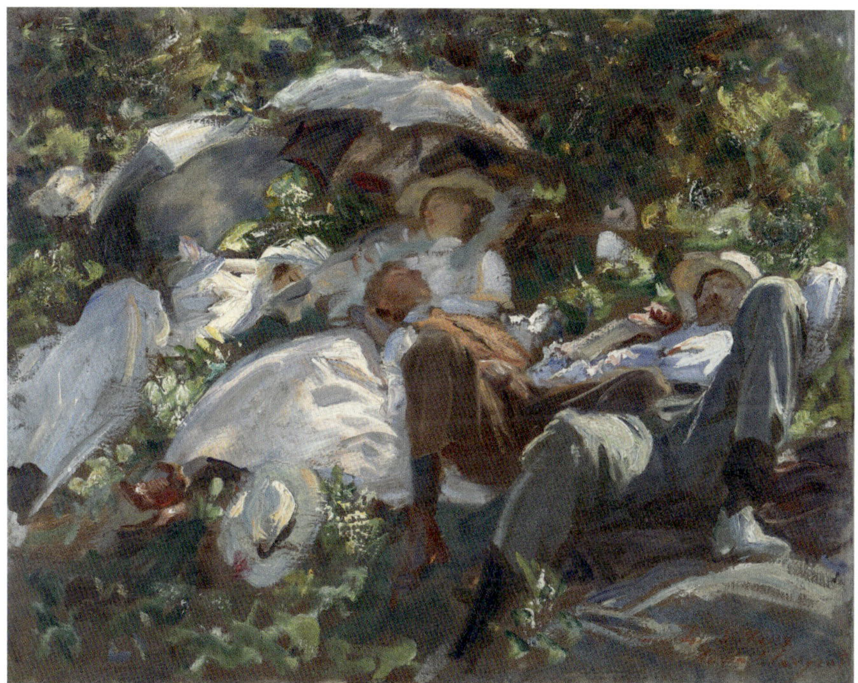

Fig. 35. JOHN SINGER SARGENT,
Group with Parasols (Siesta), oil on canvas, 1904–1905. Private Collection.

Why did the Impressionist pictures appeal to the Fraads and the Horowitzes and such friends as Ralph and Florence Spencer and Vivian and Meyer Potamkin? During these years, the Rockefellers and Middendorfs, along with John Wilmerding and Barbara Lassiter, were all busy collecting mid-nineteenth-century realist and luminist paintings by Bingham, Mount, Lane, and Church. Ray Horowitz and the others were aware of the realist landscapes and genre scenes but weren't drawn to them the way they were with the Impressionists. Why? In college, Ray had already developed his admiration of French Impressionism; now he and Margaret found similar-looking American examples they could afford. The pictures they responded to are bucolic and cheerful; they reflected these families' joy in being Americans, even during the troubled years of the 1960s. The Rockefellers and their peers, on the other hand, were long-established Protestant families that enjoyed summer homes in the Adirondacks, Mt. Desert, and the West; many owned vast tracts of land in Wyoming and Idaho as well. They fished and hunted, sailed and rode their horses during summer vacations; they loved the outdoors and the wilderness and went to great lengths to preserve it, and it's not surprising that they responded to wilderness scenes. The paintings collected by the old families spoke of the conquest of the continent that had been accomplished by their ancestors. The Horowitzes and their friends instead were descended from recent European immigrants; their parents or grandparents had memories of persecution, of pogroms and the ghetto. They were urban people who loved New York and city life.[14] American Impressionist pictures depicted warm, exuberant, colorful, and sometimes sentimental scenes on a domestic scale. Many depicted women and children and the warmth of families. For the Horowitzes and the others, the figures and landscapes of Hassam and Chase exemplified the American dream.

There were no textbooks to guide the new collectors. They could turn only to John I. H. Baur's modest catalogues, to Frederick Sweet's exhibition, and to a scattering of other books and articles. The most recent survey of the field, E. P. Richardson's *Painting in America* of 1956, would have offered little help for he disparaged the Impressionists as "interested in the esthetic rather than the vital."[15] Parenthetically, one finds Richardson still loyal to this prejudice twenty years later, when he was advising the John D. Rockefellers. Their collection, which was given to the Fine Arts Museums of San Francisco in 1979, contains some magnificent mid-century paintings, but no Cassatt, no Whistler, and just two pictures—a Shinnecock Chase and a sunlit scene by Hassam—that could be called "Impressionist." Thus, what the Horowitzes and Fraads did was not to revive past taste so much as to invent a new grouping of painters who quickly became accepted as the "American Impressionists." Much as Thomas B. Clarke, George Hearn, and Maxim Karolik had done decades earlier, the collectors led, and the museums, dealers, and scholars followed.

The young Donelson Hoopes deserves credit as one of the first modern scholars to take this art seriously. In 1964 Hoopes mounted an exhibition at the Corcoran Gallery, where he was serving as curator, called

"The Private World of John Singer Sargent." After its presentation in Washington, DC, this excellent show traveled to the art museums at Cleveland, Worcester, and Utica, all good venues, but none of them in New York or the other major art centers, doubtless because of Sargent's still-lagging reputation. In his foreword to the catalogue, the Corcoran's director Herman Warner Williams observed that he found Sargent's portraits "no longer so convincing," while Hoopes echoed this, saying that the painter had by then fallen "to a position of scorn."[16] By excluding the formal portraits in favor of Sargent's drawings, watercolors, and landscapes, and by stressing his "enormous talent," he aimed to revive his reputation, and I believe this exhibition began the process. Hoopes was the first to mention the painter's "Impressionist interlude."[17] Just as Don's book appeared, the Brooklyn Museum in the summer of 1964 mounted an exhibition of the Fraad Collection, a show that traveled to the Addison Gallery at Phillips Academy, Andover, Massachusetts. Dan and Rita's collection was half formed by then; it already included Sargent's *Siesta* as well as excellent paintings by Sloan, Metcalf, Chase, and Robinson, along with a few less compelling works. However, the poorly installed show had little impact, both because the quality of the paintings and drawings was uneven, and because Brooklyn in those days was not much visited by the leading art lovers, even those who lived across the river in Manhattan.

Hoopes was a good scholar who found an interesting, unstudied area. In 1970 he wrote *Sargent's Watercolors*, which followed his excellent study of the watercolors of Winslow Homer from the previous year. These books drew exclusively from the collections at the Met and the Brooklyn Museum; strangely enough, Don seems to have been unaware of the ambitious private collections then in formation. Then in 1972 Hoopes published *The American Impressionists*, the first book-length examination of this group, preceded only by modest exhibitions at the University of New Mexico in 1965 and at Hirschl & Adler in 1968. He began by describing his terms very broadly—a little too broadly for today's taste: He described Hunt as a forerunner and Inness and Whistler as practitioners of the newly imported style. He found Hassam, Twachtman, Robinson, and J. Alden Weir to be the central figures of the movement, along with Cassatt, while adding Chase and Sargent to the Impressionist canon for the first time. Hoopes describes Sargent's connection with Monet and his work in England in the late eighties, and tells us about the founding of the Society of American Artists in 1877, the important 1886 Durand-Ruel French Impressionist exhibition in New York, and the role of the group of Boston and New York painters called "The Ten" beginning in 1898.[18] Sadly, Don's book was organized haphazardly, with most of the useful comments being found in the entries opposite each illustration, rather than in a single essay. Then in 1974, Richard Boyle, the well-respected director of the Pennsylvania Academy, contributed a survey entitled *American Impressionism*. While this book presented little new information, it was more clearly organized than Hoopes's had been.

If someone had told Ray Horowitz in 1939 as he graduated from the Columbia Law School, that in a little over thirty years he would be one of the most prominent members of the New York art world, he would have laughed with disbelief. He was a progressive, one who subscribed to *The Nation* and *The New Republic*, someone who had suffered the stings of virulent anti-Semitism at school. It was suggested to Ray that he change his name, but he declined. His father Israel S. Horowitz had been born in Russia and had come to the US as a toddler; he became a successful doctor and brought up Ray and his sister in the comfortable middle class. In 1932 Ray entered Columbia College, where he studied political science, but greatly enjoyed what he described as "an exhilarating experience in art and art history" in auditing the lectures of the gifted scholar Meyer Schapiro.[19] Then, after graduation from Columbia Law School, he married Margaret Goldenberg, a bright, feisty person who had earned a master's degree from NYU; her father had begun as an itinerant peddler before becoming wealthy in the woolen business. Ray served as assistant corporate counsel for the City of New York under Mayor La Guardia from 1941 to 1943, then went into private practice advising companies, including Dan Fraad's.

Ray Horowitz was a friendly, quiet man with a warm sense of humor and an engaging manner. He was thoughtful and well-read, a lover of Henry James; he was learned but modest, and everyone liked him at once. Margaret was a different story. She was warm, but exuberant and outspoken. You could hear her shrill voice across a crowded room. At gallery openings, one would hear her calling out, "Ray, don't you think ours is better?" When Ray spoke at a gathering, Margaret would issue corrective comments from the audience. But Margaret's bark was worse than her bite. She was a very kind person with a big heart. She loved the art and the collecting as much as Ray did, or maybe more. Their collecting was a joint enterprise, and they only bought paintings they both agreed on.

Having begun collecting seriously in 1961, Ray and Margaret developed a passion for looking and buying, for getting to know the dealers, the scholars, and their fellow collectors, and they loved the whole process. Rita Fraad and Margaret Horowitz would scout out the galleries during the week, and then on Saturdays they would set out with their husbands and with other collecting couples to show off their finds. None of the collectors in the sixties had any idea that they were making significant investments, and Ray Horowitz said he was pretty sure that he'd never see the money again. Certainly, they couldn't have foreseen the ancillary benefits that owning important collections would bring them. When Margaret Horowitz was smitten by a work, she would pursue it single-mindedly. One day in 1969 she heard from Tony, the friendly jack of all trades and delivery man at the Coe Kerr Gallery, that a fine William Merritt Chase had just come in; she raced over, "almost fainted when she saw it," and then phoned Ray and demanded that he drop everything and come quickly.[20] Ray came, and they bought *The Fairy Tale* (fig. 36) for $30,000 (about $245,000 in today's dollars), paying the asking price as they typically did, while acquiring a perfect Horowitz picture. Chase's warm rendering of a sumptuously dressed mother and child in an idyllic seaside landscape quickly became the centerpiece of their collection. Just seven years earlier, they had been appalled at the price of the Sargent *Siesta,* but now they were willing and able to step up to a new price level. An activity that began as a weekend hobby had become a consuming interest.

During the decade, Margaret and Ray's budget increased along with their ambitions and they began aiming for the best. A month before

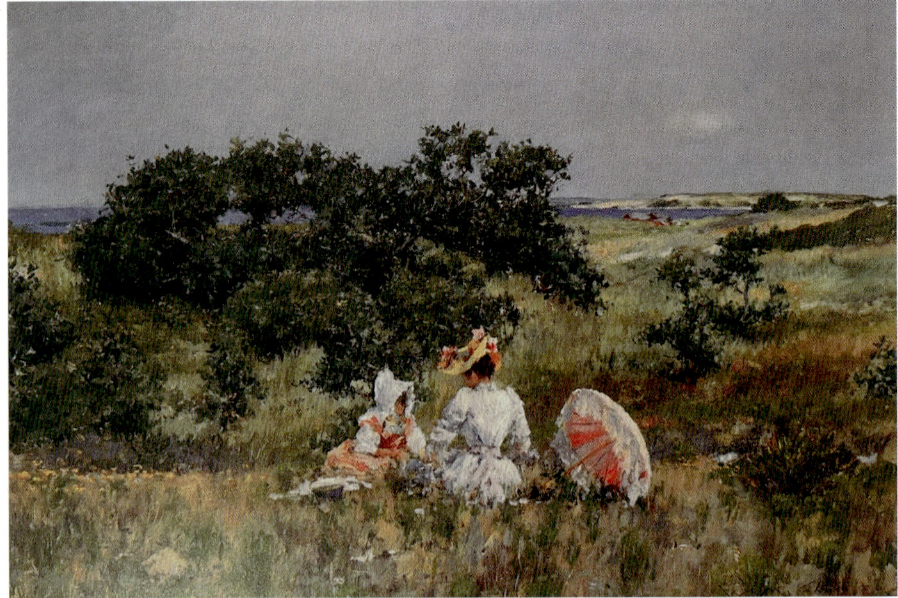

Fig. 36. **WILLIAM MERRITT CHASE,**
The Fairy Tale, oil on canvas, 1892. Private Collection.

they saw *The Fairy Tale,* they found Chase's pastel *Self Portrait,* with its striking yellow background, at a Parke-Bernet auction. They already owned several Chase pastels, but they recognized that this was a masterpiece, and they had to have it. They found themselves bidding against the wealthy Joseph Hirshhorn; with Margaret saying "Bid, bid" to Ray, they kept at it until Hirshhorn finally quit at $16,500, a huge price at the time for a work on paper. Their final acquisitions before the landmark exhibition of their collection at the Met in 1973 included a Bellows portrait, *Emma in a Purple Dress,* that cost another $30,000, a brilliant La Farge watercolor of flowers from Kennedy Galleries, the Maurer *Café Scene* from Babcock, and the Dennis Miller Bunker *Roadside Cottage,* a picture they both loved, that they bought through Perry T. Rathbone in 1972 just after he left the directorship at the MFA, Boston.[21]

The exhibition "American Impressionist and Realist Paintings and Drawings from the Collection of Mr. and Mrs. Raymond J. Horowitz" opened at the Metropolitan Museum of Art in April 1973. American art wasn't then (or ever) a Met priority. The only other American art collection it had exhibited was that of J. William Middendorf II, a prominent Wall Street figure who owned important American historical prints as well as several major landscape paintings by Frederic Edwin Church and some excellent still lifes. The Middendorf show went on view in 1967 at the behest of curator Stuart Feld, just before he left the museum world for the commercial side. By 1973, the American department was headed by John K. (Jock) Howat, a responsible curator but not one who aggressively sought out collectors. However, the Horowitzes had become well known to the Met's American Paintings department in the sixties, having begun making annual gifts of works of art to the museum in 1965. They instinctively knew how the game was played. In 1966 when Ray and Margaret were moving to their new apartment on East Seventy-Fourth Street, Stuart Feld said he'd be glad to store their paintings at the museum in the interim. Fortuitously, a colleague from the European paintings department saw them in storage, and put fifteen Horowitz pictures into the Met's summer loan show along with some privately owned French Impressionists, where they attracted the attention of the dealers and other collectors. Feld had floated the idea of showing their collection, and Jock Howat, who succeeded Feld, proposed an exhibition of their collection. It was the Horowitzes' good luck that the museum was just then preparing for a blockbuster show for 1974, "Impressionism: A Centenary Exhibition," organized in cooperation with the Louvre, and the American show must have been easy for director Tom Hoving to approve as a lead-in to presenting the French paintings. The Horowitz exhibition was installed in the spring of 1973. With its handsome, fully illustrated catalogue written by Dianne Pilgrim (including fifteen of the fifty works in color, an extravagance for the day), it became the talk of Madison Avenue and beyond.[22] It made everyone aware of the American Impressionists, and it helped build knowledge of little-known figures like Twachtman, Robinson, and Bunker. As Ray commented later, "We became unwitting pioneers."[23]

The National Gallery of Art itself presented an excellent exhibition of "American Impressionist Painting" in 1973, drawing on its own collection while borrowing extensively from other museums and a few private collectors, notably Dr. and Mrs. John J. McDonough. After opening in Washington, the show traveled to the Whitney Museum in New York, then to Cincinnati and Raleigh, North Carolina, but it seemed to have very little impact. One wonders whether this was because the New York collectors and dealers were not involved. Dr. McDonough had formed a fine survey collection of American paintings before he sold everything at Sotheby's in March 1978.[24] In many ways, his most interesting work was one he had owned for only a few months, the *Self-Portrait* by William Merritt Chase (fig. 37). When this work first came up at auction, everyone admired it, for it was a ravishing, close-up portrayal of the artist dressed in white, wearing a

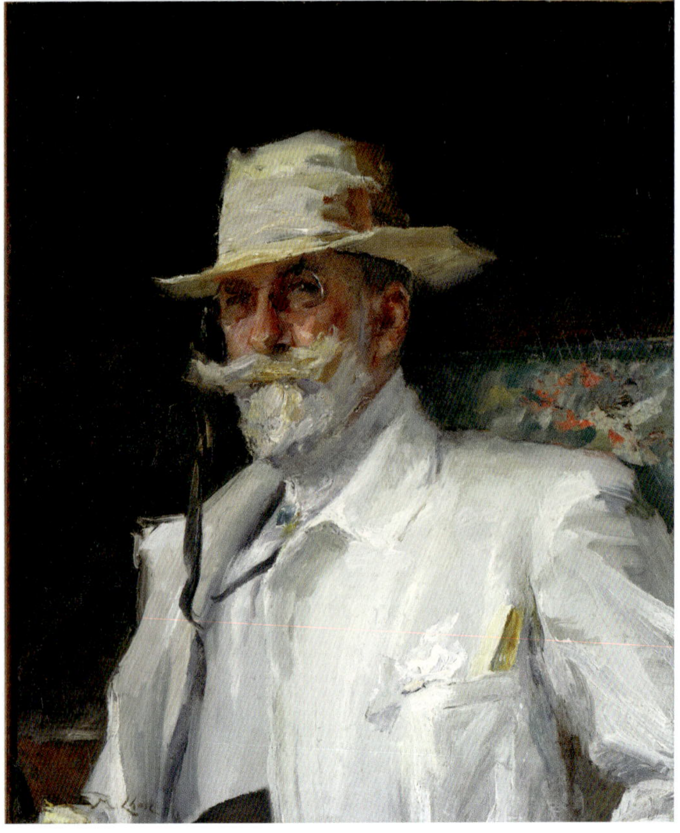

Fig. 37. **ANNIE T. LANG,**
William Merritt Chase, oil on canvas, ca. 1910. Metropolitan Museum of Art.

wide-brimmed hat, directing a piercing gaze at the viewer. Many people, including the Horowitzes, bid on it until it went for $47,500—the record for a Chase—to Dr. McDonough. Then along came Ronald Pisano, who had recently completed his University of Delaware dissertation on the students of William Merritt Chase, and who proved through a published photo that the work had been cut from a larger portrait of Chase by his student and lover Annie Traquair Lang and then inscribed with a Chase signature. Sotheby's quickly refunded the price to McDonough. The painting was then reoffered by Sotheby's as a Lang, and this time was purchased for $3,240 by the Horowitzes, who quickly gave it to the Met. At the time, these events seemed like an embarrassment for the field, and the Met quietly put the picture into storage. But in recent years it has gone on view. It is just as beautiful now as when it was a Chase, and people came to realize that it brought to light a talented, little-known woman painter. All this reflects the field's traditional misogyny and its foolishness, and brings up the question of misattributions and forgeries. The portrait of Chase lost 90 percent of its value when it was reattributed to a supposedly lesser artist: Thus, we conclude that most of the original sales price was for Chase's name, and just 10 percent for the handsome painting itself. We know from this and from numerous other examples that many collectors and dealers don't actually see the work: They are buying the reputation or prestige of a given painter, the signature in other words, while the quality of the painting itself is relatively unimportant.

In 1980 two important players entered the fray, the scholar William H. Gerdts (1929–2020) and the Chicago collector Daniel J. Terra (1911–1996). Both were complicated figures. Gerdts was a brilliant researcher and a prolific writer who worked harder and knew more about American art of the nineteenth century than anyone else in the field. He formed an extraordinarily comprehensive library, one that he put at the disposal of friendly colleagues and former students. I doubt that anyone will ever match his productivity, the depth of his research, or his visual acuity, though he disliked theory and would have hated the current direction of the field. In an early phase of his long career he served brilliantly as curator at the Newark Museum from 1954 to

1966, making a series of farsighted purchases just before prices started to boom. These included the superb *Twilight, "Short Arbiter 'Twixt Day and Night"* by Frederic Edwin Church, a Karolik discard as mentioned above, a fine orchid and hummingbird picture by Heade, excellent landscapes by Cole, Gifford, and Bierstadt, and still lifes by Harnett and the Peales. Bill was also an omnivorous personal collector of American still lifes: He created an encyclopedic holding of mid-century fruit and flower pictures with more regard for broad representation than for quality, though he did have some beautiful examples by George Lambdin, George Henry Hall, and one or two others. One of his most surprising flaws, to my mind, was his conviction that modern art was mostly bogus. His favorite modern painters included such realists as Stephen Scott Young, known for his watercolors of the Bahamas, and Bruce Kurland (1938–2013), a painter of modest still lifes, but the figure he believed to be "the greatest living American painter," as he said in a lecture in 2004, was Charles Alton Pfahl III (1946–2015). Pfahl was a talented realist painter, whose dark, disturbing work features cruelly broken dolls and harshly disfigured women along with skeletons, fish, birds, and self-portraits. My guess is that Bill, an angry, complicated person himself, identified with both his style and his imagery.[25]

American Impressionism was still considered a minor branch of the field in 1980 when Gerdts wrote the catalogue for an ambitious exhibition organized by the Henry Art Gallery at the University of Washington in Seattle. This was also when many people first became aware of Daniel J. Terra, for he had just opened the Terra Museum in Evanston, Illinois, outside of Chicago. On receiving a loan request, Terra offered to pay for all the color plates in the catalogue on the condition that fifteen of his paintings be included in the show. Harvey West, director of the Henry Gallery, quickly agreed; this was justifiable as Terra already owned a number of fine things, including Robinson's *Wedding March* (fig. 38) and Sargent's *Dennis Miller Bunker Painting at Calcot*. I was curator at the MFA Boston at the time, and I agreed to lend six major paintings, including Mary Cassatt's *Cup of Tea*, and Childe Hassam's *Grand Prix Day*, partly because Bill Gerdts took it personally if one failed to lend generously to his exhibitions. The Institute

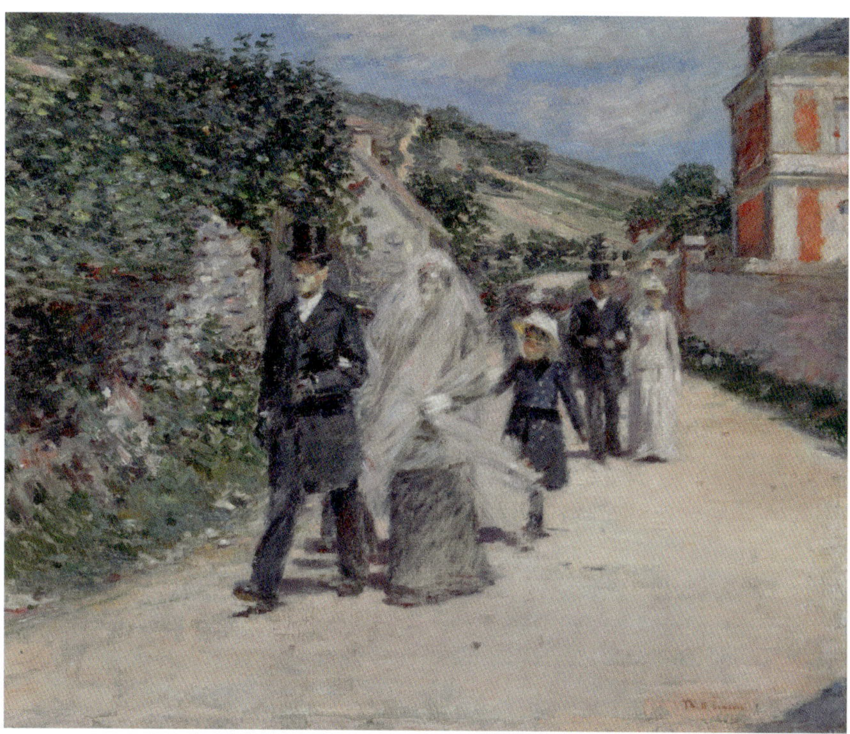

Fig. 38. THEODORE ROBINSON,
The Wedding March, oil on canvas, 1892. Terra Foundation.

of Contemporary Art/Boston (ICA) took the show at my suggestion. One day I received a phone call telling me that the truck bringing all of the paintings from Evanston to Boston had been hijacked and was missing, and this naturally caused considerable alarm among the museum registrars. It turned out that the driver had stopped to get some coffee, leaving his vehicle running; when he came out, the truck was gone. After a few hours of our fearing the worst, imagining a ransom call, or a police chase and the truck overturned and in flames, the vehicle and the paintings were found unharmed, and the collection proceeded to Boston where it boosted the ICA's attendance considerably; people were already drawn to anything Impressionist, even though the painters were not yet well known.

Gerdts barely mentioned Chase in his 1980 essay, but more than made up for that with his next project, his big, handsome book of

1984, *American Impressionism*; it was dedicated to Ray and Margaret Horowitz and featured their Chase *Fairy Tale* on the cover.[26] American Impressionism took off from this point. By then Bill had mastered the field; he knew every public and private collection and illustrated all the best paintings, many in color, and this time he restrained himself concerning the many iterations of the Impressionist style in other nations. All the earlier books and exhibition catalogues on American Impressionism had been modest affairs, but the Gerdts book was designed for the coffee table and not the bookshelf. With its extensive footnotes and bibliography, standard features for Bill's publications, it declared that this was both an art and a scholar to be taken seriously. Over the next decade, more and more galleries, collectors, and scholars turned to American Impressionism and prices rose exponentially. In addition, various dealers and others set themselves up as authors of scholarly catalogues raisonées of even the minor painters, with Gerdts playing a part in several such projects.

Daniel J. Terra, for his part, became an important figure during the 1980s, when he served as President Reagan's ambassador at large for cultural affairs, a reward for his effective fund-raising. Dan became well known as a passionate collector of American Impressionist paintings and as the creator of museums in Chicago and at Giverny, France, where Monet had lived for so long. Terra, the son of Italian immigrants, became a great success story as a chemical engineer who made a fortune as the founder of Lawter Chemicals in Chicago. He and his first wife Adeline Richards Terra (1910–1982) began collecting after they were married in 1937.[27] After thirty years of buying English and French landscapes and minor old masters, in 1971 they bought two oil studies made by Sargent for his *Oyster Gatherers of Cancale,* and from that time on they focused on American art. A 1977 exhibition of the collection at Penn State, Dan's alma mater, suggests that their early taste for Tonalist pictures was by then being supplanted by a growing interest in Impressionist works.[28] In 1978, the Terras founded the Terra Museum of American Art, and shortly thereafter, their sights now raised, they purchased two fine paintings from Hirschl & Adler: the *Wedding March,* 1892, by Theodore Robinson, and *The Jolly Flatboatmen* by

George Caleb Bingham. The two paintings set the tone for the future, with Dan seeking iconic, historic American works like the Bingham on one hand, while becoming increasingly entranced with the American painters who had gone to Giverny to be close to Monet. The Robinson was a perfect Terra painting, picturing as it did a newly married couple, the American painter Theodore Butler and Suzanne Hoschedé, Monet's stepdaughter, walking down a street in Giverny on their wedding day. It was always one of Dan's proudest possessions, and he loved taking visitors to the very place in town that it depicted.

By 1987, Dan had remodeled two adjoining buildings on Michigan Avenue in downtown Chicago and had moved his museum there. For the opening exhibition, someone—perhaps Dan himself—conceived the idea of doing a joint presentation with the venerable Pennsylvania Academy of Fine Arts—an ideal partner, with its important, historic collection and its willingness to send some of its iconic works to the new museum—in exchange for a handsome fee. The idea was to position Dan's new museum as a peer with a much respected though lethargic old one. Dan by then had acquired a second classic painting to go with his Bingham: This was Samuel F. B. Morse's *Gallery of the Louvre*. In the six years since opening at Evanston, Dan had also acquired a handful of excellent landscapes and genre paintings by Lane, Heade, Gifford, Krimmel, and Mount, along with a number of B-level pictures by a wide range of other artists from Copley to Cassatt. For the opening he filled out the collection with numerous Audubon and Cassatt prints, together with twenty-five oils, watercolors, and monotypes of varying interest by Maurice Prendergast. It was an impressive group to have gathered in a short time, though it didn't stand up well to the great loans from Philadelphia, including major works by West, Vanderlyn, and Charles Willson Peale, a group capped by one of the greatest Winslow Homers, the famous *Fox Hunt* of 1893. The exhibition had the intended result and established Dan as a major player in the field.

Dan Terra was a builder and a dreamer who made things happen. He loved the idea of art, the importance of it, and he enjoyed the status and prestige of being a museum founder first in Chicago and then in Giverny, France in 1992. He was highly ambitious for his collection but deeply unrealistic as well. Once, as were walking down the street in Giverny, he said to me, "Well, now I'm number one, don't you think?" I asked what he meant. "Well," he responded, "Number two after the Met, I mean." I mumbled a reply and we moved on.[29] Pride of ownership is a risk for all collectors. Dan thought that a high price guaranteed the quality of a painting, but unfortunately it doesn't. He didn't seek out advice from experts, but mostly relied on a few dealers to steer him, and they frequently took advantage. It became well known in the trade that Dan would pay almost any price for a work connected with France, or especially Giverny, regardless of quality; the idea that some American painters had worked in Monet's town captivated him, and it was the history and the associations rather than the art itself that spoke to him. He acquired some wonderful things, but overall, Terra simply lacked the eye and the judgment of art and people that a great collector needs. My friend and colleague Charles F. Montgomery in 1961 wrote an insightful analysis of the successful collector in which he suggested, "The true connoisseur will cultivate habits of skepticism, humility, and objectivity."[30] Terra was not alone among collectors in totally lacking these qualities. He would be terribly disappointed to find that neither his museum in Chicago nor the one in Giverny survives today.

The twice-yearly auctions at Sotheby's and Christie's were memorable events during the eighties and nineties. Everyone came, the collectors from all over the country, the dealers of course, and even some museum curators like me. A typical sale took place at Sotheby's on May 27, 1993. The experts in charge were the much-respected Peter Rathbone, son of the former MFA director, who headed American Paintings for the auction house from 1972 to 2008—an amazing run—and the flamboyant and canny Dara Mitchell. By this time, the Impressionists had come to dominate the market, and so they came up in the morning sale, while the earlier artists from Gilbert Stuart to Winslow Homer were sold in the afternoon. There was good quality throughout, totally unlike the situation today, some thirty years later. The morning session included numerous works by Hassam, Chase, Prendergast, and Sargent, but everyone quickly focused on two outstanding lots, a large pastel by William Merritt Chase entitled *Peonies* and Childe Hassam's *The Room of Flowers,* a work I regarded as Hassam's best and one I had included in my "New World" exhibition of 1983. Everyone assumed that it would be Terra versus the important Detroit collector Richard Manoogian for these two, and indeed these two battled for both. The Hassam came up first, and was sold to Manoogian for $5,502,500, a record for Hassam or any American Impressionist picture. Next came the Chase *Peonies.* The estimate was $800,000 to $1.2 million, more than had ever been paid for a Chase pastel. Manoogian and Terra went at it again, with Berry-Hill Gallery as usual bidding for Terra. The bidding quickly went above the high estimate and kept going until Dan had paid $3,962,500 for the striking pastel.

Dan and Rita Fraad also amassed an outstanding collection, one in many ways superior to those of Terra or the Horowitzes, and one wonders what the Met was thinking in never offering them an exhibition. Their pictures were shown at the Amon Carter Museum in Fort Worth, Texas, in 1985, and a handsome catalogue was produced, but that was a long way from New York.[31] Like their friends Margaret and Ray, they owned nothing by Cassatt or Whistler; their Eakins was an ungainly oil sketch, and their only Homers minor ones from the 1870s. These painters had been in the canon too long, and their major works were gone. But unlike the Horowitzes, the Fraads had two major Sargent oils as well as several strong paintings by Bellows, together with outstanding ones by George Luks, Everett Shinn, and John Sloan. They preferred tough pictures, rather than the warm ones favored by their good friends. After Rita Fraad's death, the whole collection was sold by Sotheby's. The Bellows *Shore House* and the Sargent *Venetian Street* went first by private treaty at big prices to enormously wealthy collectors, and the other fifty-one works were sold at auction on December 1, 2004. The results were stunning: The sale marked a historic high point in the market, with auction proceeds of $65 million, as against estimates of $31 to $47 million. With the private sales, the value of the collection reached nearly $100 million. The star lot at the sale was the Sargent *Siesta,* the work that Ray Horowitz loved and had suggested to them; it brought an astonishing $23,528,000. The existence of children and grandchildren is typically a determining factor for collectors, and though the Fraads had supported museums in their lifetime, in the end they decided to keep the money in the family.

To conclude the remarkable story of Margaret and Ray Horowitz: Their collection had a second museum showing, this time in 1999 at the National Gallery of Art. Though the Horowitzes were New Yorkers with lifetime ties to the Met, the Gallery mounted a campaign to win their collection, and it nearly succeeded. Ray never became close to the Met's longtime curator Jock Howat or to Philippe de Montebello, the director; rather, he enjoyed curators who got around and knew the market, ones with whom he could argue the merits of this or that painting, dealer, or collector. As Ray explained, "I got attached to the National Gallery because, unlike the Met, it had a human face, and it was a warm place to be at, to go to."[32] He took the director Carter Brown with a grain of salt, describing him later as "transparently insincere but nonetheless engaging."[33] The Horowitz exhibition opened in Washington on a very cold January day in 1999 with the entire American art world in attendance. I saw that some of their weaker pictures had been cut while being replaced by several wonderful acquisitions, including Childe Hassam's view from Celia Thaxter's flower garden on the Isle of Shoals, and William Merritt Chase's *Reflections,* a work that ranks with Chase's best. Unlike *Fairy Tale,* it is an indoor, atypically dark scene with none of the painter's usual pastel tones; rather, the work seems to suggest the interior workings of the mind of his young wife, catching her in mid-thought as she looks up from her newspaper. It made a perfect way for them to cap off their collection as they themselves grew older and contemplated the fate of their beloved paintings.

After the exhibition in Washington, Ray and his advisor and friend Warren Adelson carried on long discussions about the dispersal of the collection, with Ray deciding to distribute it widely rather than favoring either the Met or the National Gallery. By the time of Ray's passing in September 2005, a few months after Margaret's death, their paintings were numerous enough and valuable enough in the booming market to serve multiple purposes. The Met lost the collection but benefitted significantly by receiving the proceeds of the sale of Margaret's favorite painting, the Chase *Fairy Tale,* that went to Bill Gates for over

$10 million, an outcome of their 1969 purchase that earlier would have seemed unimaginable. In return, the Met named two galleries for Margaret and Ray. Next, the estate raised substantial money both for the Mr. and Mrs. Raymond J. Horowitz Foundation for the Arts and for a trust whose income would go to their daughter Judith for her life. Barbara and Ted Alfond bought two superb works by William Merritt Chase, including *Reflections* and the famous pastel *Self-Portrait* on a yellow background, paying handsomely for the pair. Then Alice Walton's Crystal Bridges Museum selected five pictures at high prices, including Frank W. Benson's awkward *Summer Day*, and Twachtman's unresolved *September Sunshine*, along with a superlative La Farge watercolor and a strong oil by Alfred Maurer. Together with the Fraad auction of 2004, these sales marked the height of the boom in American Impressionism; the judgment and good luck of both couples was made manifest.

After the most valuable Horowitz works were sold, many fine ones were left. Following Ray's instructions, their executor Warren Adelson gave them to various museums that Ray and Margaret had admired. During this process, the National Gallery was granted two Horowitz favorites, the Bunker *Roadside Cottage*, and the Chase pastel, *Back of a Nude*, one of the first works one would see on entering their apartment. The Met received several works, good ones, but not quite of the same caliber. Nearly two dozen other museums across the country, from Colby College in Maine and the Norton Gallery in Palm Beach, to the Amon Carter in Texas and the Seattle Museum, to the Santa Barbara Museum and the Huntington Library, all received one or more pictures. Adelson chose them carefully, studying each museum's collection before making his decisions. The MFA received a Horowitz favorite, the Robert Henri *Girl by the Sea*, a type of work it needed, while Harvard, where I was curator at the time, received the lovely Hassam *Nurses in the Park*, which became one of its few American Impressionist paintings. One of the most appropriate gifts, I think, was sending the Prendergast watercolor *Picnicking Children—Central Park* to the Brooklyn Museum, for the Horowitzes had received it as a gift from the Fraads in 1986 after owning it jointly with them since 1962, and Brooklyn was Dan Fraad's favorite museum. Adelson's gifts from the Horowitz collection were impressive in terms of the knowledge and the sensitivity they demonstrated.

Adelson had also begun distributing grants from the Horowitz Foundation about 2009 after it received the proceeds of the sales, then on the death of Judy Horowitz in 2016, the foundation had its funds replenished with the capital from her trust. Altogether, the foundation made 159 grants totaling about $17.5 million, averaging $110,000, before spending down the assets by 2021. The grantees were mostly art museums large and small, from the Met and the National Gallery to such smaller, deserving institutions as the Mattatuck Art Museum and the Black Mountain College Museum.[34] Warren Adelson took no compensation in judiciously spreading the Horowitz funds far and wide in support of American art. Another foundation would have spent enormous amounts of time and money on elaborate grant applications, committee meetings, and staff salaries, but Adelson apparently relied mainly on his own good instincts while acting quickly and effectively.

Only in America. Margaret and Ray, children of immigrants, had come a long way from their beginnings. As novice collectors in 1961, they could never have dreamed that they would be courted by America's two greatest museums, that they would win widespread friends and admirers, and that they would be remembered not only as great collectors but also as major philanthropists and museum benefactors across the country. Their secret was hardly a secret: They loved art, they remained true to their original vision, they were without guile, and they had excellent judgment both in paintings and people. Everything that happened after their deaths reflected their thoughtful, generous spirits.

---

[1] Richard Ormond and Elaine Kilmurray, *John Singer Sargent* (Tate Gallery, 1998), 110, 274.

[2] John I. H. Baur, *Leaders of American Impressionism: Mary Cassatt, Childe Hassam, John H. Twatchman, J. Alden Weir* (Brooklyn Museum, 1937).

[3] John I. H. Baur, *Theodore Robinson, 1852–1896* (Brooklyn Museum, 1946).

[4] Thomas Whiteside, "Holy Smokestacks, What a Mess," *New Yorker,* March 24, 1956.

[5] Much later, Rita Fraad turned to collecting contemporary realist drawings, many of which she gave to Smith College. Rita had a strong aversion to abstract art.

[6] "Conversations with Collectors: Margaret and Raymond Horowitz," interview by Franklin Kelly and Nicolai Cikovsky Jr., National Gallery of Art, January 24, 1999.
[7] Stuart Feld, conversation with the author, February 17, 2021.
[8] "Conversations with Collectors."
[9] Thanks to George Shackleford for telling me about these exhibitions.
[10] Parke-Bernet Galleries, *Impressionism and Other Paintings and Drawings Collected by Mr. & Mrs. Norman B. Woolworth* (Parke-Bernet Galleries, 1964).
[11] Stuart Feld, conversation with the author, February 24, 2017.
[12] "Oral History Interview with Raymond J. Horowitz, 2004 Oct. 20–Nov. 5," interview by Avis Berman, Smithsonian Archives of American Art, November 5, 2004.
[13] I believe that Ray and Margaret didn't realize how good their Sargent was. My guess is that if Richard Ormond and Elaine Kilmurray had published the eighth volume in their catalogue raisonné by this time (*John Singer Sargent, Figures and Landscapes, 1908–1913*), with its wonderful illustrations of the fifty paintings and watercolors of the Simplon Pass that Sargent executed during these summers, they might have decided differently. This overlooked period was one of brilliant creativity for the artist. Seeing them together in Ormond's book makes one realize what a superb painting this is, even though, with the figure of a woman dressed fashionably and incongruously in black, it lacked the warmth of a typical Horowitz picture.
[14] There was one exception: As early as 1951, Dan Fraad purchased a primitive salmon camp on the Gander River in Newfoundland, and he and Rita improved the place and enjoying fishing there with groups of friends every summer. See Linda Ayres, "Remembering Rita Fraad," *American Art* 18, no. 3 (2004): 102.
[15] E. P. Richardson, *Painting in America: The Story of 450 Years* (Thomas Y. Crowell, 1956), 307.
[16] Donelson Hoopes, *The Private World of John Singer Sargent* (Corcoran Gallery of Art, 1964), 2.
[17] Hoopes, 17.
[18] Donelson Hoopes, *American Impressionists* (Watson-Guptill Publications, 1972), 8.
[19] "Conversations with Collectors."
[20] "Conversations with Collectors."
[21] On Perry T. Rathbone, see Belinda Rathbone, *The Boston Raphael: A Mysterious Painting, an Embattled Museum in an Era of Change, and a Daughter's Search for the Truth* (Godine, 2014).
[22] John K. Howat and Dianne H. Pilgrim, *American Impressionist and Realist Paintings and Drawings from the Collection of Mr. and Mrs. Raymond J. Horowitz* (Metropolitan Museum of Art, 1973).
[23] "Conversations with Collectors."
[24] The McDonough sale at Sotheby's took place on March 22, 1978; the collection had been exhibited at the New Orleans Museum of Art in 1975 with a handsome catalogue by John Bullard entitled *A Panorama of American Painting: The John J. McDonough Collection.*

[25] Gerdts's lecture "The Greatest Living American Painter" was presented at a meeting in New York in 2004 organized by Lisa Koenigsberg in her series "Initiatives in Art and Culture."

[26] William H. Gerdts, *American Impressionism* (Artabras, 1984). For the Henry Art Gallery catalogue, see William H. Gerdts, *American Impressionism* (Henry Art Gallery., 1980).

[27] Elizabeth Kennedy, *An American Point of View: The Daniel J. Terra Collection* (Hudson Hills Press, 2002).

[28] John Paul Driscoll, *American Paintings from the Collection of Daniel J. Terra* (Pennsylvania State University, 1977).

[29] Full disclosure: I was a trustee of the Terra Foundation at the time.

[30] Charles F. Montgomery, "Some Remarks on the Practice and Science of Connoisseurship," *Walpole Society Note Book* (1961): 7–20.

[31] Linda Ayres and Jane Myers, *American Paintings, Watercolors, and Drawings from the Collection of Rita and Daniel Fraad* (Amon Carter Museum, 1985).

[32] "Oral History Interview," 2004.

[33] "Oral History Interview," 2004.

[34] Smaller places typically received around $25,000, larger ones $100,000 and more, many of them for specific projects relating to publications on American painters. The largest gift, of $1.5 million, was made to Boston University to fund a professorship in American art, while next were ones of $1 million each to the Bard Graduate Center and to the Yale University Art Gallery. The MFA Boston got $600,000 for various American art projects, Philadelphia $500,000 to help fund the reinstallation of its collection, and so on. The foundation also made grants to worthy art-related organizations such as the Archives of American Art and the International Foundation for Art Research (IFAR), and to Scenic Hudson, which protects the Hudson River environment.

11

Collecting the Canon During the Boom Years

If only I had Mellon's money, I could really collect.

—HENRY J. HEINZ II, chair, H. J. Heinz Co., to the author, 1979

Well! I paid a large sum for that picture and I do not regret it, not a farthing of it. I bought neither beauty nor glamor, no, nor still life, nor a great composition; nothing but art, just pure incandescent art, right out of the crucible; its author heated it over the sacred fire. It seems to me it is not a picture; it is not a portrait, it is an inspiration.

—LOUISINE W. HAVEMEYER, *Sixteen to Sixty: Memoirs of a Collector*, 1961

THE BOOMING market in American art during the eighties and nineties made everyone involved feel smart. During these years, numerous well-funded collectors were competing for a dwindling supply of fine paintings. The best works of Homer, Eakins, Whistler, and Cassatt were long gone, as were those of Church, Bingham, and Mount, but the dealers and their clients were undaunted. Many of the new buyers were attracted to, or were steered to, the American Impressionists and related artists, as the definition of "American Impressionism" expanded to include almost any painter whose brushwork was visible. The galleries needed new material as an ever-richer group of new collectors entered the market, and American Impressionist pictures were plentiful. The dealers should have been saying, "We can offer you second string artists at first string prices," but of course they weren't. Though superb works by Cassatt, Prendergast, Hassam, and Chase do exist, they are nearly all in museums, and only lesser works by them and their contemporaries were generally being offered. The era of American Impressionism came about suddenly and ended nearly as abruptly, as the weakness of many of the painters and the egregiously inflated prices became more and more obvious.

Dan Terra's frequent rival at the auctions in the eighties and early nineties was Richard Manoogian of Detroit, who was, I believe, the ablest buyer of those years; later he became the most skilled seller as well. Unlike Dan, Dick went to all the dealers, he loved art, he was both well-liked and aggressive, and he paid quickly. He bought the best of both minor painters and the major ones, and he never purchased something for the artist's name—a weakness of many collectors. An immensely able business executive who built the Masco Corporation, Manoogian tells me that he started collecting on his own in the sixties and only in the mid-seventies hired the distinguished curator Larry Curry to advise him; as a result, he sold everything and started over.[1] In 1989 his impressive collection was exhibited at the National Gallery, the Met, the Fine Arts Museums of San Francisco, and at the Detroit Institute of Arts; later he lent parts of it to other institutions around the country.[2] Dick collected everything, from still life to landscape, genre, Impressionism, academic, and Western pictures, and he never seems to have owned an uninteresting one; he clearly loves paintings with wall power. He was among the first to buy the expatriates of the 1880s, including Julius Stewart, Francis D. Millet, and Charles Sprague Pearce, the painters whom George Sheldon had rated so highly, but he didn't purchase their typical works but rather their most informal ones. Dick supported the Detroit Institute and other museums, but never made substantial gifts of art, much to the frustration of many curators, and at the height of the market, he began selling the collection, with many outstanding works going to Alice Walton and John S. Middleton.

The best collectors of that era followed the same pattern, seeking high quality and in the process creating their own takes on the canon. Thelma and the late Melvin Lenkin in Washington had bold taste, and they had the funds to compete in the fast-moving market of the eighties. A star of the collection is one of Mary Cassatt's strongest compositions, *Reading "Le Figaro,"* 1878 (fig. 39), an unsentimental portrait of the artist's mother seated in an armchair reading a newspaper. All of the Lenkins'

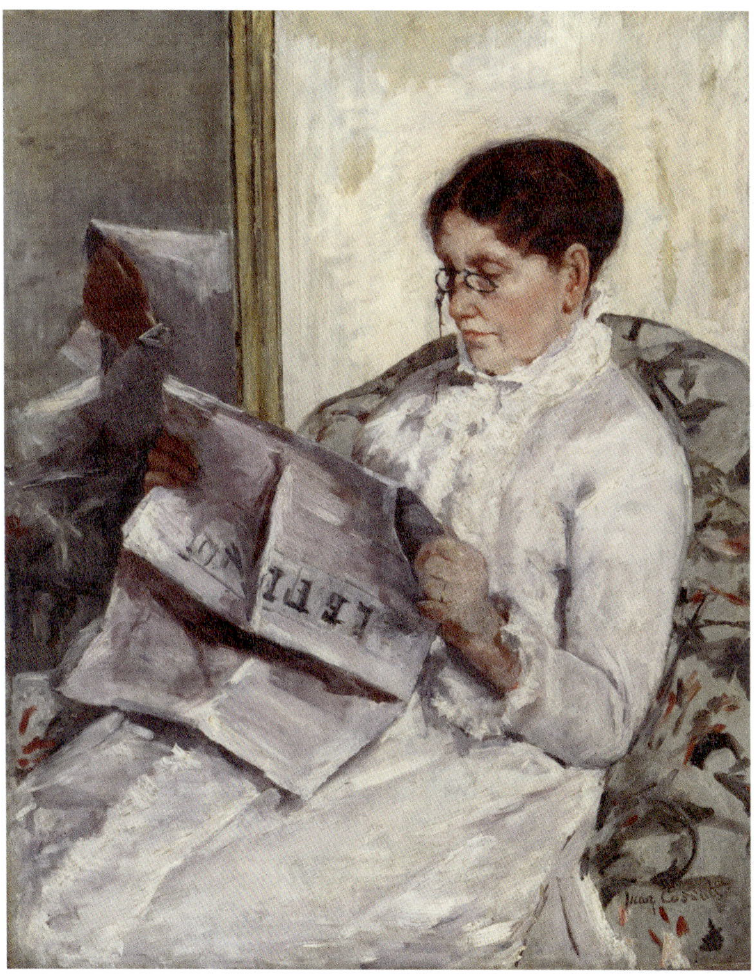

Fig. 39. MARY CASSATT,
Reading "Le Figaro," 1878. Private Collection.

pictures are richly painted; there are no generic ones bought for their signatures. They have a fine Sargent oil sketch of a dancer and one of his garden scenes, and a good Dennis Bunker, but then, like the Fraads and the McGlothlins, they didn't pursue lesser the minor Impressionists but went instead for superb, quickly executed, pictures by Ashcan School painters including Luks, Glackens, Shinn, Sloan, and George Bellows. In their home you also find a magnificent Western watercolor by Thomas Moran, a floral composition by John La Farge, two fine late Homer watercolors, and an amazing group of paintings by Martin Johnson Heade, and a big stained glass three-part screen of hanging autumnal fruits by Louis Comfort Tiffany in the dining room. Terrific paintings were still available in the eighties, for those willing to reach for them.[3]

Several members of a public-spirited Maine family were also collecting on a high level. The Dexter Shoe Company in Dexter, Maine, was founded in 1958 by a brilliant entrepreneur and philanthropist named Harold Alfond. Two of his five heirs were his nephew Peter Lunder and his son Theodore (Ted) Alfond, who with their wives, Paula Lunder and Barbara Alfond, set about acquiring American art in a serious way in the early 1980s.[4] Each of these families built outstanding collections: the Lunders' is familiar because it was given to Colby College in Maine and has been well published, while the Alfonds' holding was broken up and sold. The Lunders decided to build a broad survey for the Colby College Museum of Art, while the Alfonds said from the start that their nineteenth-century works would be dispersed rather than given away.

The Alfonds built a superb holding of mid-century landscapes by Heade, Gifford, Kensett, Church, and Inness before moving into American Impressionism, acquiring terrific watercolors by Maurice Prendergast, several notable Sargents, and two of the great Horowitz Chases as I have described. Having formed an excellent collection, owners can sit back and enjoy the accolades and the visitors, or if they miss the action too much, they can reinvent themselves, sell the art, and plunge into another field. The Alfonds were too energetic to rest, and they loved collecting, so they dispersed the older pictures and turned to contemporary art with a vengeance, this time buying hundreds of paintings and photographs for their alma mater, Rollins College in Winter

Park, Florida. They are drawn to colorful, thoughtful, sometimes witty pictures, often by little-known artists from around the world, many of which have inspiring stories to tell either in the artists' own struggles or in their subject matter. You don't look for tough-minded or difficult works by Anselm Kiefer or Richard Serra here. Once purchased, the paintings and the occasional sculpture immediately become the property of the college, and are used to enhance the public spaces of the Alfond Inn, a lovely hotel the family built near the campus. This is a two-sided philanthropic enterprise: The works of art give Rollins a pleasing, varied collection of recent art for student enjoyment and education, while all the proceeds of the Inn go to funding scholarships at the college.[5] This is an admirable endeavor, but I still feel sorry that their very fine small collection has gone forever; it was one of the best of its kind.

The Lunder Collection is quite different, being purposefully formed as an extensive survey of nineteenth- and early-twentieth-century American art, together with some more recent work.[6] The donors' aim was to help educate the college's students, but as at many academic museums, only a modest amount of teaching from the collection actually occurs. Colby nonetheless has positioned itself as a force in the American field through the activities of the Lunder Institute, an institution within the museum that supports exhibitions, symposia, and other projects with six partner museums, operates an ambitious "Summer Think Tank," and provides fellowships for artists, as well as the Lunder Consortium for Whistler Studies.[7] The Lunder Institute often works with Crystal Bridges and the Terra Foundation as one of a group of institutions with real financial heft that promote diversity, equity, and inclusion in the arts. The Lunders' favorite artist is Whistler. Whistler paintings of high quality have long been a rarity on the market, and the Lunders acquired just one outstanding early oil, *Chelsea in Ice* (fig. 40), together with dozens of fine small oils and pastels, and over two hundred prints, many of them rare impressions. Impressive catalogues of the collection were published in 2013 and 2015, and it has been growing steadily since then. Director Jacqueline Terrassa kindly sent me a list of the 820 acquisitions of 2017–23; one sees the collectors recently turning largely to prints and small studies by canonical painters like Winslow Homer,

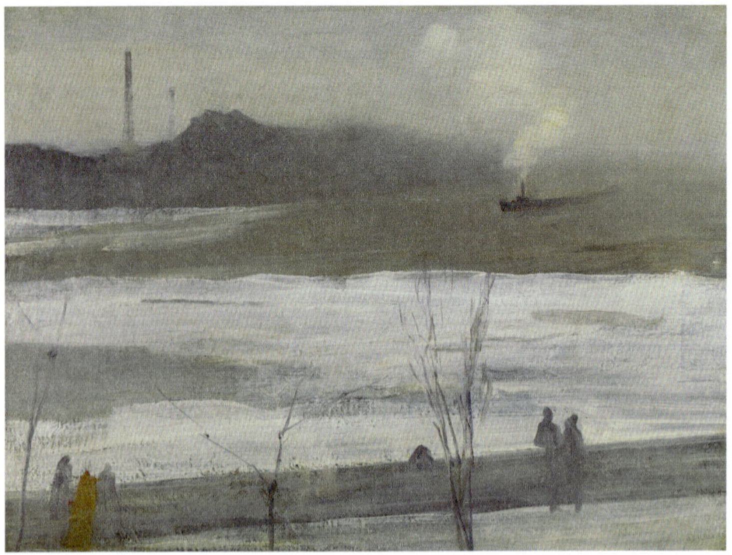

Fig. 40. **JAMES MCNEILL WHISTLER,** *Chelsea in Ice,* oil on canvas, 1864. Colby College Museum of Art.

whose major works can no longer be found. Thus, the list includes some 103 Whistlers, 41 Bellows, and a remarkable 377 works by Arthur Wesley Dow, nearly all of them color woodcuts along with some photographs, as well as large groups of prints by such international figures as Hokusai, Goya, Otto Dix, and Jacques Callot. French influence is often apparent in the Lunders' choices; included in their gift to Colby are paintings by such expatriate Americans as Edwin Lord Weeks and Elizabeth Nourse, as well as works by such French masters as Corot, Daubigny, and Bouguereau. The collection includes rare early Chinese bronzes and pottery. It is also rich in paintings and sculpture of the American West, in American neoclassic marbles and nineteenth-century bronzes, and in twentieth-century art from Georgia O'Keeffe to Jenny Holzer. The collection is a very broad one, with generally good quality overall.

The collectors James W. and Frances Gibson McGlothlin in Virginia are also significant philanthropists. Jim went through Washington and Lee and the W&L law school waiting on tables and then made a fortune in the coal business and other enterprises. By way of full disclosure, I advised them when they were starting out. They started with Hudson River School landscapes, buying two wonderful pictures by Thomas Cole now at Crystal Bridges and others by his contemporaries. Within a few years, after purchasing a difficult, asymmetrical Sargent, *Gathering Blossoms, Valdemosa,* from Vance Jordan, they moved to American Impressionism and the later nineteenth century, just as the Alfonds had. They bought a lovely Cassatt, *Lydia Seated, Crocheting,* that is both a figurative picture and an Impressionist landscape with a wonderful surface on which the artist employed a combination of oil and tempera; it's a painting that Ray and Margaret Horowitz would have loved. Like the Fraads, they were drawn to tough, realist pictures, and they acquired several of the Fraads' strongest Ashcan School pictures, including John Sloan's *Gray Day,* George Luks's *Cabby,* and George Bellows's masterpiece, *Kids* (fig. 41). The McGlothlins also acquired a

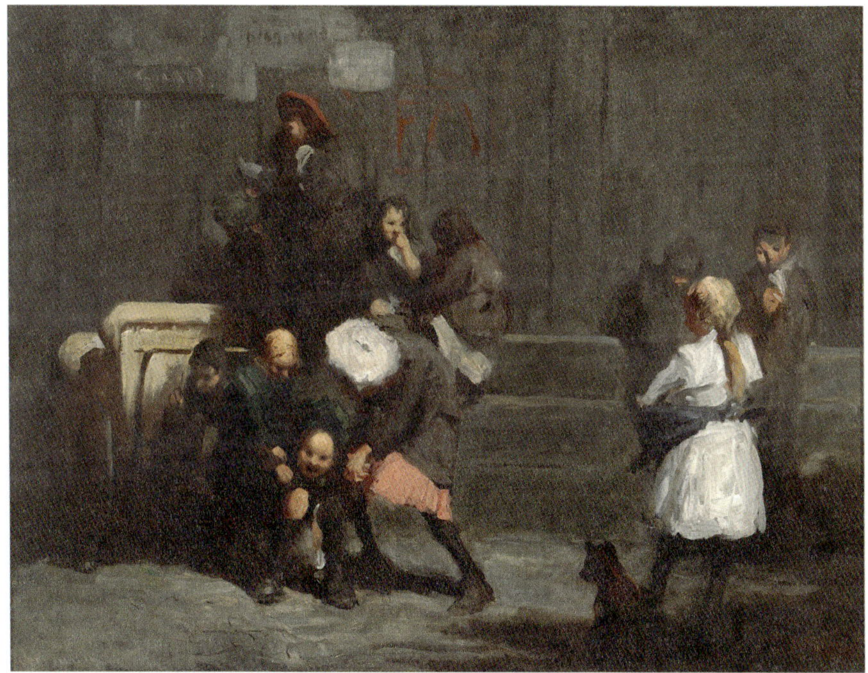

Fig. 41. **GEORGE BELLOWS,**
Kids, oil on canvas, 1906. Virginia Museum of Fine Arts.

group of superb Sargent oils, including *The Venetian Wineshop,* two fine late Homer watercolors, several excellent Childe Hassams, and an outstanding Chase pastel. Like the Alfonds, they often relied on the dealer Michael Altman as they built the collection. Jim and Fran didn't hesitate to pay top prices, but in return, they acquired a superb collection that has significantly enhanced the stature of the Virginia Museum in the American field and is housed in a new wing they built.[8]

Here I should mention two highly important buyers whom I have never met, and whose collection I haven't seen in situ. They are Bill Gates, founder of Microsoft and his now-former wife, Melinda French Gates, two of the wealthiest people in the world. They were advised by Thomas Barwick of Seattle, a much-admired insurance man and a keen collector himself who was close to Bill's dad; his dream was to help form a magnificent collection for the Gates that he hoped would eventually go to the Seattle Art Museum. Barwick enlisted several of the ablest art-finders in the nation, ones who read and researched assiduously, and instructed them to seek only "A" paintings. Between 2000 and 2008, the well-rewarded scouts presented their finds to Barwick, who submitted them to the Gates along with a single paragraph explaining the importance of each. The Gates bought nearly all the recommended pictures, often before actually seeing them, and paid the asking prices, resulting in a collection of some fifty paintings that is better than Alice Walton's, despite the fact that the art was only a minor interest for them. Barwick and his scouts rounded up several of the most celebrated American paintings for the Gates starting with the Homer *Lost on the Grand Banks* and including Chase's *Fairy Tale,* the great *Roomful of Flowers* by Childe Hassam, the Monet-like Sargent *A Morning Walk,* and the Sargent *Venetian Street Scene* from the Fraad Collection. They also unearthed a rarely seen Cassatt, *Mrs. Cassatt Reading to Her Grandchildren,* and an extraordinary little-known Eakins of Professor William A. Forbes sold by the Jefferson Medical School. They somehow bought from David Rockefeller perhaps the greatest of Fitz Henry Lane's works, *Ships and an Approaching Storm Off Owl's Head, Maine,* and they also acquired major landscapes by Sanford Gifford and Thomas Cole. From the early twentieth century, the Gates bought an important picture once in the William H. Lane Collection, Charles Sheeler's *Newhaven*, along with George Bellows's *Polo Group* and his *Shore House* once in the Fraad Collection, and two major paintings by Edward Hopper. All of their fifty paintings are masterpieces, or close to it, judging by the old standards. There are no works by Blacks, and the only women represented are Cassatt and O'Keeffe. Like several other of their very wealthy peers, they also bought several paintings by Andrew Wyeth. Seeking masterpieces on a big budget in just the same years was John S. Middleton, better known as owner of the Philadelphia Phillies. Middleton is a more traditional collector than the Gates, as he is knowledgeable about the art and cares deeply about each work. Just as the Gates relied on Tom Barwick, Middleton has counted on the New York dealer Michael Altman for nearly all of his purchases. His outstanding collection of over 150 works has a broader reach than the one formed by Barwick and the Gates, running as it does from an important Charles Willson Peale of Washington and several superb still lifes including the unequalled Harnett *Mr. Hulings' Rack Picture* to important paintings by de Kooning, Pollock, Johns, and Lichtenstein. He bought the Johns *Flag* at auction in 2010 for $28.6 million, and the Lichtenstein *Sleeping Girl* for nearly $45 million two years later. His earlier pictures include both the Church and the Gifford sold by the National Academy of Design in 2008, the record-setting Sargent *Siesta* that Ray Horowitz had once coveted, and the famous Childe Hassam *Flags, Fifth Avenue*, formerly owned by Brooke Astor.[9] Middleton, the Gates, and Alice Walton and a few others were competing for the same pictures and drove the market to unheard-of heights. The euphoria of those days is now long gone, and the enormous bubble these collectors created has collapsed. The great and even the good paintings are gone. The marketplace and the scholarly world were thus ready for a new canon, one that was not long in coming.

---

[1] Richard Manoogian, conversation with the author, February 23, 2024.

[2] Nicolai Cikovsky Jr., ed., *American Paintings from the Manoogian Collection* (National Gallery of Art, 1989), shown at National Gallery, Fine Arts Museums of San Francisco, Metropolitan Museum of Art, and Detroit Institute of Arts.

[3] The Lenkin collection was never exhibited as a whole, but the Smithsonian American Art Museum, an institution they were long associated with, did exhibit the screen and a few other treasures in 2007, and later showed nineteen outstanding paintings from the collection in 2015.

[4] Full disclosure: I helped advise the Alfonds on mid-century American art, while I know the Lunders only socially.

[5] Three catalogues have been published to date by the Cornell Fine Arts Museum, Rollins College, Winter Park, Florida, each edited by the Alfonds' advisor. Abigail Ross Goodman, *Art For Rollins: The Alfond Collection of Contemporary Art*, 3 vols. (Cornell Fine Arts Museum, 2013–18). Goodman also serves as consulting curator at Rollins.

[6] See Sharon Corwin, ed., *The Lunder Collection: A Gift of Art to Colby College* (Colby College Museum of Art, 2013), and Justin McCann, ed., *Whistler and the World: The Lunder Collection of James McNeill Whistler* (Colby College Museum of Art, 2015).

[7] The Lunder Institute in 2024 funded symposia dealing with the meaning and future of American art at six museums: the de Young Museum, San Francisco; The Broad, Los Angeles; Crystal Bridges, Bentonville; the Addison Gallery, Andover; the Museum of Fine Arts, Boston; and the Whitney Museum, New York.

[8] David Park Curry and Theodore E. Stebbins Jr., *Capturing Beauty: American Impressionist & Realist Paintings from the McGlothlin Collection* (University of Virginia Press, 2005); Sylvia Yount, *Private Passion, Public Promise: The James W. and Frances G. McGlothlin Collection of American Art* (University of Virginia Press, 2010).

[9] Middleton sold 43 paintings, mostly landscapes, at Christie's on January 23, 2025. There were fine examples by Thomas Cole, Raphaelle Peale, and a few others mixed with lesser works. Prices were solid, with only five unsold lots, and were viewed by some as marking a resurgence of the nineteenth-century market.

12

William H. Lane, Champion of Modern American Art

The aesthetic emotion is an emotion about form. In certain people, purely formal relations of certain kinds arouse peculiarly profound emotions.

—ROGER FRY, *Art and Commerce*, 1926

The phenomenon of collecting loses its meaning as it loses its personal owner. Even though public collections may be less objectionable socially and more useful academically than private collections, the objects get their due only in the latter.

—WALTER BENJAMIN, *Illuminations*, 1955

Part One: PAINTINGS

WILLIAM H. Lane (1914–1995) was one of the two donors whose gifts exponentially raised the stature of the Museum of Fine Arts in the field of American art, the other being Maxim Karolik. Lane did his collecting in the early 1950s, just a decade after Karolik, and like Karolik, he was an outsider. Outsiders by necessity form their own approaches to art, not being subject to the constricting rules of upper-class good taste. Bill wasn't born in Bessarabia, but he did come from another place almost as distant from Brahmin Boston: the Irish Catholic middle class of Leominster, Massachusetts. His father William Lane, as a young man, had come to Leominster with his Irish-born parents, and he spent his life there. Mr. Lane senior worked for a comb manufacturer in his youth, just as the industry was moving from the use of bone to the new plastics technology. He founded the Standard Comb Company, which eventually became Standard Pyroxoloid Corporation. Judging from newspaper accounts, Lane Sr. was an able, well-liked person, as president of the Chamber of Commerce, and a member of the Elks, the Knights of Columbus, and the Leominster Sportsmen's Club.

Mr. Lane senior, like Francis Garvan's father, was ambitious for his son, and after his high school graduation, he sent Bill to Tabor Academy for a year to prepare for college. Bill liked Tabor, where he starred as a tackle on the football team. Entering Harvard with the class of 1937, Bill found his courses of little interest; he once told me that he spent most of his time at college reading books of his own choice and attending whatever concerts he could find in the Boston area. His scholastic record was poor: As a freshman, he was placed on probation on November 28, 1933, "for unsatisfactory Nov. record"; he came off probation at the end of June 1934, but after getting all D's and E's in his sophomore year, he was suspended.[1] After a successful summer school term, he was readmitted in the fall, with the requirement that he repeat his sophomore year. Things went almost as badly as before (including a D in Music 4) and he was, in Harvard's terminology, permanently "deprived of privileges" on September 22, 1936.[2] He headed home and went to work for his father. In later years Bill was always ambivalent about Harvard; he took pride in having attended, but felt resentment as well; however, he chose to be listed in the Class of '37 yearbook, as well as in the regular editions of the *Alumni Directory*. Saundra Lane used to tell me that Bill's father had died suddenly, causing him to leave college so that he could run the company, but in fact that wasn't quite the truth. Though Bill's dad had died suddenly of a heart attack, but it was on May 14, 1937, late in what would have been Bill's senior year, and well after he had been dismissed from college. However, Bill did manage the business after his father's death, and ran it well; he never made a great fortune, but put away some substantial funds before closing down the company in 1972.

After I started at the MFA in 1977, I began seeing important pictures at exhibitions that were credited to a lender I didn't know, the Lane Foundation: There were three fine Stuart Davis paintings in a show at the Fogg Museum in 1978, and single, high-quality works at Whitney Museum exhibitions, including "Synchronism" and "Dada," around the same time. I obtained Bill's address and then wrote him, asking if I could visit. A few weeks later, Mr. Lane responded with an invitation to come at twelve noon on December 15, 1980. I drove out with my colleague Carol Troyen, and then at twelve sharp knocked on the door of the yellow farmhouse. It was immediately thrown open, and a big man with a very deep voice glared at us and said, "Where have you been?" I stammered that I thought our date was at twelve, and he said, "No, no. Where has the museum been all this time?" We were on the defensive from the start.

The lovely Saundra Lane appeared, friendly and hospitable as always,

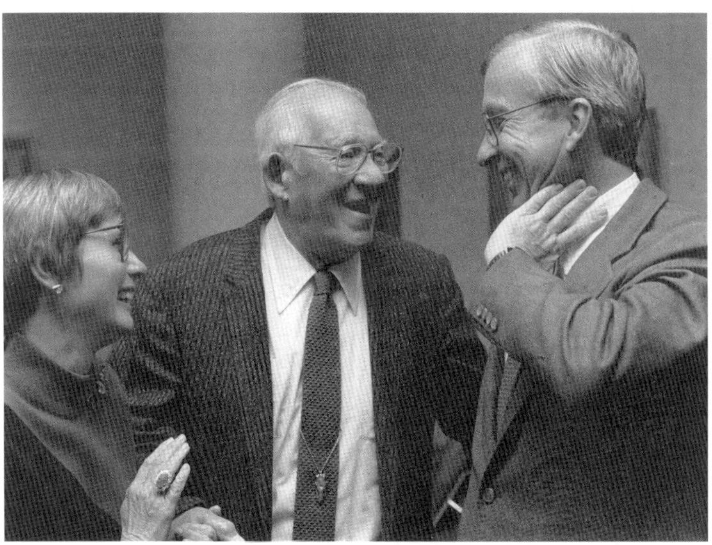

Fig. 42. UNKNOWN PHOTOGRAPHER, *Bill and Saundra Lane with Ted Stebbins*, 1990.

but let him do all the talking (fig. 42). As we went into the living room, I glanced at the piano, as I always do, and was relieved to see it piled high with art books, not photos of brides and young families; if you find the latter, you know there's little chance of getting the collection. In our conversation, we got right to the point, telling the Lanes that we wanted to improve the MFA's holdings in American modernist paintings, and would like their help. Mr. Lane responded angrily, telling us how badly he'd been treated by the museum. He recalled donating a fine Franz Kline in 1974, then having the MFA's curator of contemporary art, Ken Moffett, come for a visit; Moffett apparently looked around, then told Bill that he didn't think he had much that would be of interest to the museum. Years later Bill was still steaming about this, and we spent most of our time telling him that things had changed, and that we were prepared to demonstrate the sincerity of our interest. He didn't soften much during our visit, but he didn't throw us out either, so we left feeling that we had a chance with him.

Lane had told us that a group of his pictures would be on view at the deCordova Museum in March. I went to see the exhibition and found it impressive, with some stunning things, including O'Keeffe's *Deer's Skull with Pedernal* (fig. 43), Sheeler's classic *Newhaven*, and Dove's *That Red One*, all pictures I have loved ever since. Together with the works we had glimpsed in his storeroom at home, it was clear that he had a major collection. I organized a meeting with Jan Fontein, the MFA director, who, from the beginning of my tenure, had trusted my judgment. A Dutch-born scholar of Asian art, Jan was well informed about art from around the world and was gratifyingly open to the unfamiliar. He loved the chase and he quickly understood what the Lane collection could mean to the museum, and so he gave a quick go-ahead to our mounting a major exhibition. On April 8 I wrote Mr. Lane offering to do a show, and then he and I spent nearly a year discussing what to include, with me learning the collection as he pulled more and more things out of his secret storeroom.

Bill had begun collecting in 1952. His first marriage was declining, and he began driving to New York by himself to go to the classical voice concerts and the opera. By accident one day he walked past a group of

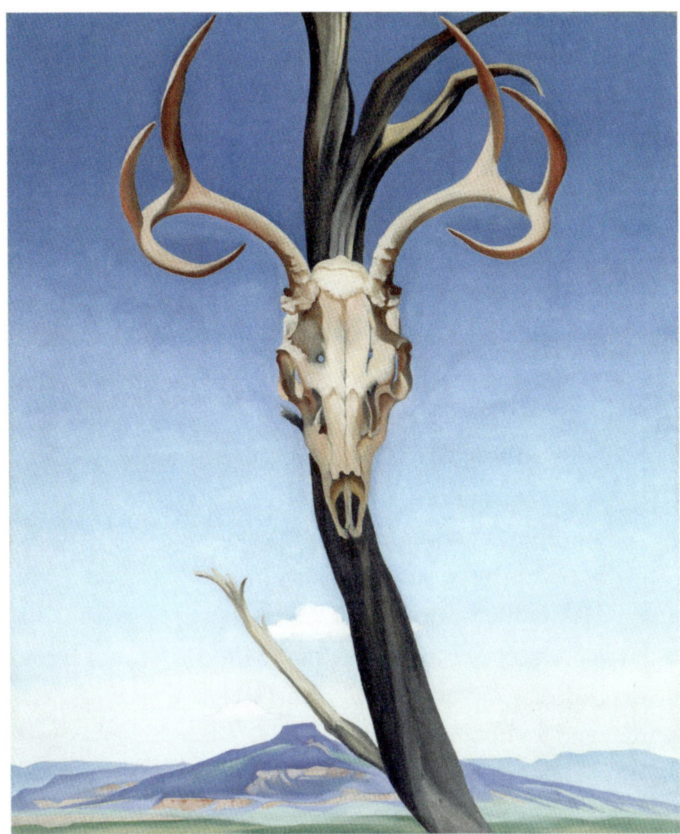

Fig. 43. GEORGIA O'KEEFFE,
Deer's Skull with Pedernal, oil on canvas, 1936. Museum of Fine Arts, Boston.

paintings hanging on a fence in Greenwich Village; he paused to look them over, then bought one. A friend suggested he might do better at the Macbeth Gallery, and there in January 1952 Bill made his first serious purchase, spending $150 on a landscape oil by Jay Connaway, a conventional realist who had worked with William Merritt Chase. In July 1953, at the Shore Galleries in Boston, he found his true direction, and purchased *Integration,* 1944, by Hans Hofmann, a bold, curvilinear abstraction that would be among our selections for the MFA exhibition. Later that month Bill discovered Edith Halpert and her Downtown Gallery; his first acquisition there was the Stuart Davis, *Apples and Jug* of 1923, a terrific small picture that finds the painter at ease with the cubist idiom. The Hofmann cost him $450, the Davis, $600. Those were difficult works, and why Lane responded to them as he did remains a mystery, as it is with every collector.

The Davis and the Hofmann set Lane's direction: He was moved on one hand by the modernists who worked to portray American subjects in styles derived from Cubism, and he was equally drawn to the brushwork and strength of the Abstract Expressionists. He became friendly with Hans Hofmann and purchased several other pictures from him. Bill was always curious about each artist's development, and after acquiring some of his recent pictures, he persuaded Hofmann to sell him his early oil of 1921, *Green Bottle*. In the fall of 1953 he also met Franz Kline and immediately responded to his work. Lane bought seven Klines directly from the artist within a few months; most were colored abstractions from the mid-forties, but he also acquired *Square*, a brilliant black-and-white picture of 1953. He admired some larger Klines, but as he couldn't fit them into his station wagon, he didn't pursue them; the size of the car was always a determining factor for him. He asked Kline what other painters he'd recommend for his collection, and Kline suggested Jackson Pollock and the late Arshile Gorky. A few months later he purchased a fine Gorky oil, *Good Hope Road*, 1945, for $1,500, his biggest outlay yet. He then tried to strike up a relationship with Pollock, going down to the Cedar Street Bar late one afternoon, where Kline had said he would surely find him. But unfortunately, Pollock was already drunk, and he rudely rebuffed Bill's self-introduction. What a shame that he hadn't gone instead to see Sidney Janis, Pollock's dealer, for he lost interest in Pollock after that.

The human connection was important for Lane, and he was always more at ease with talented people than with socially prominent or self-important ones. He met Georgia O'Keeffe by chance in 1948 when he was flying his one-engine plane alone around the west, as he loved to do. He had some engine trouble and put down on a field in New Mexico. Who should drive up in her jeep offering to help but Georgia O'Keeffe? They became fast friends long before he knew her work. A decade later, keenly aware of his growing collection, she gave the Lane Foundation the important painting by Charles Demuth, *Longhi on Broadway*, that we chose as the cover image for our catalogue of the collection. Stuart Davis also knew of Bill, having benefitted from his patronage—by the end of 1957 Bill owned fourteen works ranging in date from 1911 to 1956—and Davis donated *Gloucester Street* to the foundation in 1957. Bill developed an even closer relationship with Charles Sheeler, often visiting back and forth with Sheeler and his wife Musya, with constant conversations about the meaning of art. Bill loved his work, and by 1956 he owned twenty-nine works that Edith Halpert showed that year as "Charles Sheeler Exhibition from the William H. Lane Foundation."

Bill bought steadily from 1953 to 1961, most often going to Edith Halpert's Downtown Gallery but also frequenting the Alan, Willard, and Durlacher Galleries in New York and Boris Mirski in Boston, as he purchased examples by the Mexican painters Orozco and Tamayo, the Boston Expressionists Karl Zerbe and Hyman Bloom, and such important early modernists as Patrick Henry Bruce and Joseph Stella. He became friendly with Halpert, who would regularly come to visit him in Lunenburg, and through her he built up large, definitive holdings of the work of Arthur Dove, Georgia O'Keeffe, Charles Sheeler, Marsden Hartley, and Stuart Davis. Many weekends would see him in New York loading up his big station wagon with paintings. He'd keep some and then bring the rest back in a week or two, so he was constantly looking and looking, refining his eye.

The fact that some of these paintings were still in Halpert's racks in the fifties seems astonishing today, when we are used to things happening overnight. Several of Lane's Doves, including the inventive *Clouds*, had been exhibited by Alfred Stieglitz at his Intimate Gallery in 1927, just after they were painted, but they went unsold; on Stieglitz's death in 1946 they went to Edith Halpert, and they found their first buyer only in 1953 when Lane came along. Duncan Phillips had purchased dozens of Doves in the thirties and early forties, and Ferdinand Howald was buying in the same years, but there were very few other collectors for his work, and thus Lane in the fifties found *That Red One* (fig. 44) and so many other great pictures still available. It was nearly the same with Georgia O'Keeffe. Even though she had become better known and more widely collected than Dove, many outstanding works remained

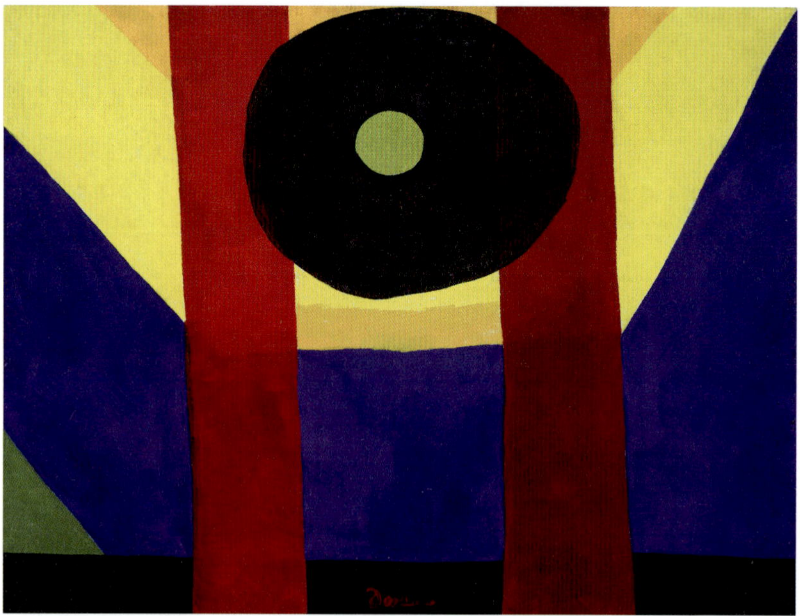

Fig. 44. **ARTHUR G. DOVE,**
That Red One, oil and wax on canvas, 1944. Museum of Fine Arts, Boston.

unsold, including the iconic *Deer's Skull with Pedernal* that Bill bought in 1953. Excellent paintings by Charles Sheeler, Marsden Hartley, and Stuart Davis similarly were similarly available, testimony to the slow acceptance of modernism in the US. These artists were all frequently exhibited members of the modern canon, yet there were few buyers for their work; for years, American collectors remained wedded to the School of Paris. The Armory Show of 1913 is rightly described in every textbook as a key turning point in American art, but it affected very few people at the time. Wider acceptance of Picasso and Matisse began in the US only around 1940, and was largely due to the efforts of Alfred H. Barr and the Museum of Modern Art, as Hugh Eakin explains in his book *Picasso's War.*[3] As Lane's experience demonstrates, wider appreciation of the American moderns lagged behind the European.

From the start, Bill regarded himself as a serious collector and one with a mission. He established his foundation late in 1953, partly for tax purposes and partly as something he could use to insulate himself from inquiries. He was both a public figure with all of his lending, and a very private one. Lane owned about half of the collection personally, with the other half belonging to the foundation, but he always lent in the name of the foundation. He had just bought three terrific industrial pictures by Charles Sheeler from Halpert, and he quickly wrote the dealer, "If you are able to detect goose pimples between the lines, he is to blame for it."[4] He lent his whole collection to the Addison Gallery at Andover, where his friend Bartlett Hayes was the director; the show opened on November 20, 1953, and was called "Paintings from the William H. Lane Foundation." Museums operated a little more quickly in those days, for just a month before, on October 27, he had written Edith Halpert, "Plans for an exhibition at the Addison in November seem to be shaping up."[5] This was the first of an astonishing forty-three exhibitions that Bill sent out to local New England museums over the next twenty-eight years, the last being the show that I viewed at the deCordova in 1981. In most cases, the exhibitions featured a number of painters, but occasionally they would be devoted to just one artist. The shows went to the museums at Fitchburg, Worcester, Amherst, UConn, Bowdoin, Wellesley, Vassar, and elsewhere in New England. Bill was the registrar and packer; he typically drove the thirty or so loosely wrapped paintings to the venue, and he and his secretary did all the paperwork. Though he was running a business, he had enough time to manage an extraordinary second career as an educator and a champion of the American moderns.

Lane took up his educational mission with gusto, in a way carrying on the work of Alfred Stieglitz (1864–1946), whom he never met, but about whom he had learned a great deal from Edith Halpert. Bill didn't want to hear about European parallels or sources, or about Fauvism or Cubism, and at times would utter proclamations that came directly from Stieglitz; he'd say, "No isms, dammit," or "This is an *American* picture!" By the time Lane knew Halpert, she and her gallery were in decline, and according to many sources, she was becoming increasingly irascible. But all I ever heard from Bill Lane were words of admiration and gratitude for her, and when we did our exhibition, he suggested that we dedicate the catalogue to her.[6] Many of Lane's major acquisitions came from Halpert, while he turned to other dealers for Abstract Expressionism, a style Halpert never quite understood, for paintings by Gorky, Hofmann, and Kline. Lane also bought works by the best of the Boston Expressionists, Hyman Bloom and Karl Zerbe. He thus developed his own independent eye. Looking back, it seems almost impossible to comprehend that these pictures were so little valued by collectors and the market during the fifties and early sixties, when Bill was buying. *Life* magazine had already featured Edith Halpert and her artists; their names were known, and the Whitney, Brooklyn, the Columbus (Ohio) Museum of Art, the Phillips Collection, and occasionally MoMA, were showing them. New Yorkers Edith and Milton Lowenthal were active buyers in the same years; but unlike Lane, they aimed for breadth rather than depth, and often bought just one work by each artist.[7] Most of the sophisticated, knowing collectors of the day were not interested; the School of Paris still dominated American taste, and when people did buy contemporary American paintings, they were likely to choose figurative works by Ben Shahn, Raphael Soyer, Milton Avery, Edward Hopper, or Reginald Marsh. Bill Lane, on the other hand, fell in love with abstraction.

A turning point occurred in February 1982 during our planning of the exhibition. We had agreed with Bill on the selection of works and were starting to think about catalogue design and other possible venues. Then James (Jay) Maroney, a brilliant deal maker, called me to say that Stuart Davis's *Hot Still-Scape for Six Colors—7th Avenue Style* of 1940 (fig. 45) was on the market, and would the museum be interested? The price was $1.5 million. I said yes, please hold it for us, though I had absolutely no purchase funds available. I knew the picture well, having admired it at Sotheby Parke-Bernet at the Edith Halpert Estate sale in 1973 (coincidentally, a sale run by the same Jay Maroney). Its color and structure, its vibrant joyfulness, and especially the way its unusual red hues energized every other color, overwhelmed me. I thought it was Davis's greatest painting, and a key work of American modernism. The MFA's acquisition funds were empty, and I couldn't think of a donor who would venture one tenth of the price. I had no chance. So I drove out to see Bill Lane, knowing he loved Davis's work, but aware that he had never paid more than a few thousand dollars for anything. I didn't know him well at that point, and I felt like a fool on a doomed mission.

I knocked on the Lanes' front door; Saundra led me upstairs, where I found Bill sitting in his worn, mustard yellow armchair, surrounded by books and art. Then I noticed, over the chair, a small color reproduction of *Hot Still-Scape*. Wow. I asked him, why do you have that little reproduction hanging there? He said, "That's the great one that got away." I paused, then I said, "I think we can solve this problem." I told him about Maroney's call; we discussed the picture, agreeing that it was one of the best of all American paintings. We talked about the huge price but concluded that we would have to pay it before someone else did, and Bill said, "Well, I'll pay for half if you pay for half. We can own it jointly." I said OK. I drove home, singing and dancing in my head. The future was clear, if only I could get director Jan Fontein's approval. We would have

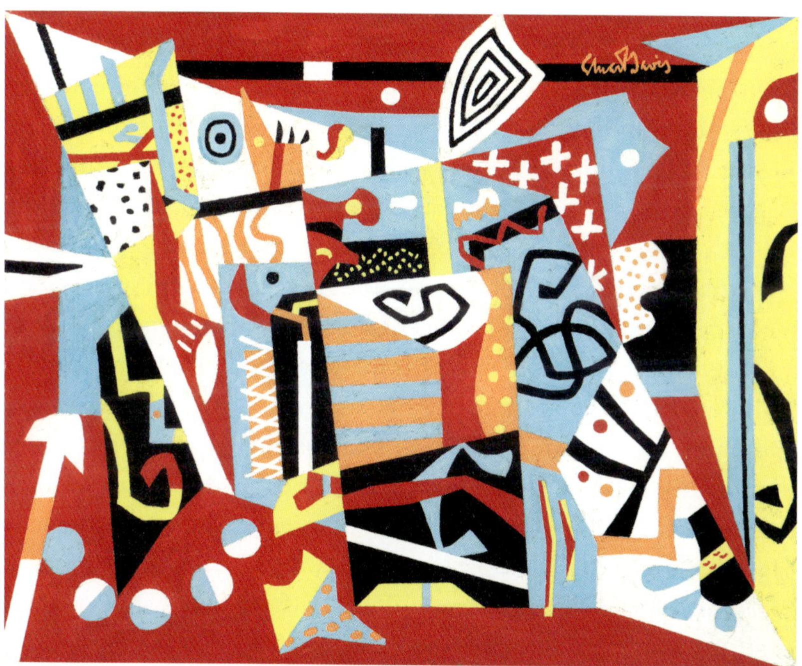

Fig. 45. **STUART DAVIS,**
Hot Still-Scape for Six Colors- 7th Avenue Style,
oil on canvas, 1940. Museum of Fine Arts, Boston.

to deaccession some good paintings to raise our share; and we would need to persuade the Board of Trustees that venturing into such a joint ownership with a collector whom we didn't know well was a reasonable risk. Two weeks later, I ferried Fontein and the museum president, Howard W. Johnson, out to meet Bill. Howard Johnson was a quiet, impressive man; a Chicagoan, former president and by then board chair at MIT, he had a gift for honest communication and he was a keen judge of character. Bill Lane himself had a more Western than Eastern character: He knew his own worth and the importance of his collection, but he had no pretension, and he never said anything he didn't mean. He and Howard and Jan immediately fell into an easy rapport, with me standing back, cheering silently. They agreed that the museum would draw up a joint ownership contract, with Bill being entitled to hang *Hot Still-Scape* at home for half of each year; in fact, to our relief, he never once asked for it. If I could find three quarters of a million dollars for our share, it would be a done deal. I had as usual drained the purchase funds, so our only option was to deaccession a valuable painting or two. I had already sold several Heades and a Lane earlier to pay for the Gilbert Stuarts of George and Martha Washington that the Boston Athenaeum was selling, and I couldn't come up with anything else that could be deaccessioned without a loss to the integrity of the collection until I thought of the George Caleb Bingham *Wood-Boatmen on a River* in the Karolik Collection. The artist's name and subject matter made it valuable, but it had been painted during Bingham's decline and was in such poor condition that we never exhibited it. The trustees authorized me to conduct a private auction among the leading dealers, and Larry Fleischman of Kennedy Galleries bought it for just about what we needed. I thought it was a good trade, as I realized that Lane's becoming the MFA's partner in *Hot Still-Scape* could easily lead to our acquisition of the whole collection. That would be immense, because Bill's collection dovetailed beautifully with the few really fine modern paintings we already owned, including our two Edward Hoppers. I thought it would be a perfect marriage.

I felt enormously pleased by Bill Lane's reaction to the painting and the price, but the more I think about it, the more astonished I am. Most collectors have trouble when prices in their field double or triple; even if they can still afford to collect, they are likely to resent the new price levels. When I worked in Washington in 1968, I got to know Hermann Warner Williams, the director of the Corcoran Gallery. As an assistant curator at the Met, he had worked on the "Life in America" exhibition thirty years earlier. When I met him, he had just been offered a fine Heade marsh scene for $5,000, but had decided against it on the basis of price: "I just don't like the way those boys have been pushing up Heade's prices," he told me.[8] Now here was Lane, not a rich man, hearing that his favorite painting had seen a price increase of about two hundred times since Halpert first sold it in 1941. Ninety-nine collectors out of a hundred would have sent me packing. Bill Lane didn't, because he cared so deeply about art. I once read a foolish book about collecting by Richard H. Rush, where he opined that investment value is a major consideration for every collector.[9] For real collectors, nothing could be further from the truth.

Opening night for the Lane Collection took place on April 12, 1983. Jan and Howard understood what was at stake, and had wisely made Bill a trustee of the museum several months before the opening. No one could have acted less like Karolik: Bill attended the meetings, but mostly listened and learned. At the black-tie opening dinner, I felt nervous. I had never heard Bill speak in public, and I had no idea what he was going to say. But it went perfectly: After Howard Johnson, Jan Fontein, and I spoke, Bill took the floor and in his incredible bass voice thanked the museum, and spoke movingly about the meaning of art and the importance of these painters. No one in Boston knew the Lanes before that; now everyone did. What I had dreamed of was actually happening. Bill and Saundra loved the exhibition and the catalogue, which had been beautifully designed by Carl Zahn. In my essay I discussed the major painters in the collection and their spiritual, stylistic, and historical connection to Alfred Stieglitz, while in her piece our assistant curator Carol Troyen examined the career of Edith Halpert, whose Downtown Gallery had supplied Bill with so many works and who had influenced him so greatly. Bill and Saundra liked people, and in the process of our working on the exhibition they became friends with Registrar Linda Thomas, the exhibition designers Tom Wong and Judith Downes, head of publications Carl Zahn and many others on all levels. After Boston, the exhibition moved to the San Francisco Modern and then the Amon Carter Museum in Fort Worth. The Lanes and I and some other colleagues went along, and we all enjoyed our shared success on the road.

Bill Lane wasn't about to go back to Lunenburg with his clippings and memories to renew his quiet, isolated life. He had grown, and he had tasted what his collection could mean. Bill was now attached to the Museum of Fine Arts; he felt close to the staff and trustees. The curator's life is strange that way. You approach the collector because it's part of your job. You get to know each other. You do the exhibition. Then sometimes in the process a real, deepening friendship develops, as it did with Lane and myself. Now that the big exhibition was over, we had a shared loyalty to the art and the MFA, and to each other. We had our disagreements, but at the conclusion of each project we accomplished together, Bill had only words of praise and gratitude. Throughout the next decade we did one show after another, with Saundra Lane playing a crucial support role as Bill's wife and as my friend. As I pressed him to make the big gift of the paintings collection, Saundra—twenty-five years Bill's junior, and obviously a future widow—was steadfast in her approval of the museum and me, and never once showed the slightest concern about her own future well-being. She was a remarkable, generous person.

Part Two: PHOTOGRAPHY

TALKING WITH Bill as we planned the paintings exhibition, working only from the side of his vault with its racks of paintings, I couldn't help noticing the layers of black solander boxes on the opposite side. It became clear that they were full of photographs. After our exhibition of the paintings, Bill slowly, hesitantly, began to show them to me. He felt even more moved by the photos than by the paintings, and he was deeply torn about their future. Slowly I learned the story of how he came to acquire one of the greatest of all photography collections. It had begun with the death of Charles Sheeler on May 7, 1965. He and Bill had become close friends, and he had shown Bill his photographs. While Sheeler had exhibited his photos in the US and abroad during the time they were being made, roughly the years from 1915 to 1930, after that he kept them largely under wraps. His dealer, Edith Halpert, was concerned that collectors would see his paintings as "only photographic," and she encouraged him to lie low as a photographer so that the paintings would sell.[10] That was still Sheeler's way of thinking in the 1950s, when he began discussing them with Lane, and it became the mindset of his widow Musya as well. They realized that much as Sheeler valued his photographs, there was almost no market for them or for any photography at that time—as incredible as this seems today—and if Musya was to continue to enjoy an income after his death, it would stem from Halpert's ability to keep selling his paintings.

After Bill had discussed the matter with Edith Halpert, he wrote Musya Sheeler on November 1, 1966, offering to buy "the entire collection of photographs," "with the understanding that they will be carefully examined and preserved and then judiciously deposited in the appropriate public collections."[11] Halpert was Bill's ally in this pursuit, and Bill kept her fully informed, though I don't know whether or not he paid her a commission. The discussion continued for over a year, with the lawyers for the estate eventually drawing up a purchase contract. On March 29, 1968, Lane agreed to buy all of Sheeler's photographs, including—according to his own inventory—1,755 prints and 71 color transparencies, for $20,000, just over $100 each for prints that now sell for upwards of $100,000 apiece. Yet the price was fair, for the medium was just beginning to have traction with scholars and the market. The Museum of Modern Art founded its department of photography in 1940, and with the appointment of the legendary John Szarkowski as curator in 1963 began a series of exhibitions devoted to the photography of Eugène Atget, André Kertesz, and Walker Evans. Szarkowski knew Sheeler's work, and he knew where the photographs were; he told me once that he regarded his inability to secure them for the Modern as the greatest disappointment of his career.

A key figure for Lane's intense pursuit of photography was Ansel Adams, who advised him informally from the start. Lane's friendship with Adams dated from 1954, when Lane and Charles Sheeler traveled to San Francisco together after attending the opening of Sheeler's big exhibition at UCLA. A lengthy correspondence resulted, as well as many visits back and forth. Between 1967 and 1973, Lane also formed a large, important collection of Adams' own photographs, including a number of early rarities. Apparently, no one before Lane had studied his work with such care and with such an eye for quality. Adams wrote him, "It was a Great Day for photography when you came this way!!!"[12]

Bill and I quickly agreed that we should do a major exhibition devoted to the work in all mediums of Charles Sheeler, Bill's friend and his favorite artist. It would be a groundbreaking exhibition, the first show ever of Sheeler's greatest paintings and drawings seen together with the outstanding images from his photographic oeuvre. I came to love photography, though I had no idea that I was embarking on a decade of study of Bill's holdings, and would do five photo shows over the years. The MFA in 1987 produced a beautiful two-volume catalogue designed by Carl Zahn, one devoted to Sheeler's photography, the other to his paintings and drawings. Every owner of the paintings and drawings responded favorably to our loan requests, and of course we needed only one photography lender, Bill himself. In my essay, I concentrated on unraveling a number of mysteries regarding chronology and the size and makeup of Sheeler's most important series, making use of the standard tools of connoisseurship while sticking very strictly to the objects. Bill liked it. Carol Troyen ranged more widely in her writing, paying considerable attention to the influence of Cézanne and others, and describing feelings of loneliness and isolation that she observed in Sheeler's work. The show was much admired, though probably only specialists were aware of its uniqueness in exhibiting Sheeler's paintings, drawings, and photographs in the same exhibition. In the catalogue we felt free to make direct visual comparisons, though in the galleries—perhaps erring on the side of caution—we exhibited the photos separately. Bill Lane and I spent untold hours examining the photos, studying them minutely, and I came to believe that Sheeler ranks as one of the preeminent photographers of the century. I found his photos more interesting than all but a handful of his best paintings; I tended to skirt this question in our conversations, as Bill found magic in everything Sheeler had done, but he better than anyone understood the greatness of the photos.

Even before the big Sheeler purchase was final, Bill began to pursue the work of the California photographer Edward Weston. Ansel Adams told him that Weston's four sons all needed money and were thinking of selling their holdings of their father's work. Ansel put Bill in touch with the Weston "boys," who were in their fifties and early sixties. Beginning in the summer of 1967 with Brett Weston, a photographer much influenced by his father and a friend of Ansel's, Lane agreed to buy all of the Edward Weston prints in his possession. The mutually agreed price was $150–$200 for platinum prints, $75 for signed eight-by-ten-inch prints, and $30 for unsigned ones and for four-by-five-inch prints. Over the next two years, he worked out purchase contracts on the same terms with Brett's three brothers, Chan, Neil, and Cole, and with Chan's son, Ted. Cole had the largest number of prints, 973, while grandson Ted had the fewest, 161. In all, Bill Lane purchased 2,217 prints from the Westons, by far the largest such holding anywhere. The Westons were very pleased, and so was Bill.

What were the Westons thinking? One would imagine that one of them might have held back or decided to sell only half of his holding, but no, all four went all in. The sons had ambivalent feelings about their father, whom they viewed as a neglectful, self-involved dad; in some ways, they were probably glad to be rid of their heritage. Moreover, no one could foresee the boom in photography that lay just around the corner; Bill made his purchases just on the cusp of the widespread acceptance of the medium. And what was Bill Lane thinking? Why not just buy a collection of, say, fifty or a hundred works by each photographer he admired? His one attempt to do this ended in failure. In June 1968, he wrote Georgia O'Keeffe inquiring about buying a group of Stieglitz photos, and within a month he had selected twenty works.[13] For reasons that are unclear, this purchase never materialized. With Sheeler, Edward

Weston, and the others, the way was clear, and he bought in huge volume. He had a sense of mission—the mission being to preserve a given corpus in good hands. As he wrote Brett Weston in December 1967, "It is my desire to protect the integrity of my purchase by acquiring a measure of control over the remaining work of Edward Weston . . . "[14] Bill Lane's acquisitions were thus absolutely extraordinary in their ambition and their timeliness.

Bill and I soon began discussing an Edward Weston exhibition, but we quickly discovered that there might be a problem with regard to publishing a catalogue. The University of Arizona in 1981 had bought from the family a separate group of Weston prints they owned that had been in a traveling exhibition at the time of Lane's purchases, along with all of his negatives and copyright to all of his work, for a sum in the neighborhood of $4 million. This was just fourteen years after Lane's acquisitions from the Westons: It demonstrates how quickly photography had gained in recognition and value. The price was good news for the Weston sons, who finally reaped a windfall from their father's work. The people at the Center for Creative Photography at the university were friendly to our inquiries, but made it clear they claimed copyright on all Edward Weston works, and any catalogue of ours would have to acknowledge that. Lane immediately foresaw this as a major potential problem for future publications, and so we decided to challenge Arizona's claim on the basis that all of the Weston photos had been "published" in earlier years, in legal terms, and that their claim was too late.

Two fortunate things happened. First, MFA director Jan Fontein concurred wholeheartedly with Bill's feelings; he agreed that the MFA would be the lead party in terms of dealing with lawyers and with Arizona, and that we could go on the offensive if necessary, so long as Bill paid the legal bills. Months passed before we found the right attorney to take on our case. Fortunately, a brilliant South African lawyer had recently joined the museum's law firm: This was Margaret H. Marshall, who later became chief justice of the Massachusetts Supreme Judicial Court, and happily she agreed to work with us. "Margie," as she is called, possesses the keenest legal mind that I have ever worked with. Once we consulted her and laid out the facts as best we could, she quickly outlined a proactive legal strategy; within months Arizona had conceded the issue, and we were free to exhibit and publish Lane's Westons. Late in 1987, Alan Shestack succeeded Jan Fontein as director, and our projects continued to receive unstinting directorial support, as Alan himself was an early collector of photography and he totally understood the significance of what we were doing.

I immersed myself in the vast trove of Westons and in the literature, and we decided to do a series of exhibitions called "Weston's Westons." I devoted the first show to Weston's figurative work, as I found there was so much to learn from it, from the elegant, misty views of single figures of around 1920 in the then-fashionable Pictorialist mode, followed by his early experiments with Cubism, to the portraits of friends and the classic nudes of the mid-thirties, then finally to the very different wartime photos. In this way I could study the whole of his oeuvre and his life. By this time I was aided by both by the designer Carl Zahn—himself a lover of Weston's work—and by Karen Quinn, an amiable, smart young scholar who got along very well with the Lanes. I found the whole project deeply moving, working with Bill, traveling to California with him and Saundra to meet Weston's sons as well as Edward's wife and model, Charis Wilson. I will never forget seeing Chandler, Brett, Neil, and Cole wrestling playfully on the living room floor, while arguing about their parents. The Weston boys clearly liked Bill and felt totally at home with him, and I was surprised not to pick up any sense of regret on their part for having sold him their prints. On another occasion, we visited Charis—still lovely and fit some fifty years after the iconic images of her were made—and found her swimming on her back in the nude at a friend's pool, exactly as she had in a photo a half-century earlier. I had the sense to invite Charis to come and speak at the MFA during the run of the exhibition; she and her daughter Rachel came east and despite being startled by the cold weather, they loved Boston and were loved in return. The highlight of our joint talk to a sold-out Remis Auditorium came when I asked Charis what the secret of her success as a model was. Without a pause she said, "Well, I always knew when to take my clothes off." It brought the house down.

Part Three: WINDING UP

IN 1989 I decided we should try to nail down the paintings collection for the museum, and Bill and Saundra were in accord. The Lane Collection was now valued in the millions, and as it was by far the couple's major asset, they reasoned that making a partial gift and partial sale to the MFA would be fair. I agreed, and Jan Fontein and Stephen D. Paine, the trustee head of our Collections Committee, went along enthusiastically. For this special occasion, everyone was willing to mortgage our purchase funds—that is, to spend the income a year or two in advance—and so the acquisition did not necessitate any further sales from the collection. And fortunately, many of the best Lane paintings were in the foundation, and thus were necessarily gifts, while the less valuable ones that we purchased came from Bill and Saundra themselves.

Bill and I negotiated the purchase and sale over several months. I wanted to get the great paintings for the museum, while he wanted to keep some of the best privately owned ones for himself to enjoy, and possibly (though he never said this) for a rainy day. I trusted that he would eventually give us the rest, but as I have learned, in the art world, a bird in hand is worth ten or twenty in the bush. Promised gifts and intended gifts can evaporate like a morning mist. So we discussed, and we argued. One picture I very much wanted was the Gorky *Good Hope Road,* as there were no other possible Boston sources for a great Gorky, and I was trying badly to build up our Abstract Expressionist collection. But Bill had the picture propped in front of the fireplace in his music room, where he spent a great deal of time, and did not want to give it up. Finally, he gave in. Curators like collectors always remember their mistakes and long lament the ones that got away, and missing out on Sheeler's great oil, *Newhaven,* of 1932 still bothers me. I didn't quite appreciate its importance at the time, as one of the amazing American domestic interiors that the painter transformed into the cubist idiom. I think I could have had it included if I had argued more forcefully, or given up other things. In any case, Saundra sold it years later, and it is now in the Seattle collection of Bill and Melinda French Gates.[15] We obtained everything else we wanted in the agreement of 1991, all of the other Sheelers, Doves, Hartleys, O'Keeffes, and Davises, as well as excellent examples by Ralston Crawford, Niles Spencer, Patrick Henry Bruce, Jacob Lawrence, the Boston painters Hyman Bloom and Karl Zerbe, and superb holdings of Franz Kline and Hans Hofmann—seventy-five works in all. At my urging the trustees wisely named the large gallery where the collection hung "The William H. and Saundra B. Lane Gallery." The museum's development people demurred, as they prefer receiving cash for this kind of "naming opportunity," but fortunately they were overruled, and the museum has consistently honored the Lanes in this way ever since.

Bill Lane died on July 15, 1995, after more than a year of declining health. The service was held in a big Roman Catholic church in Leominster, and Jan Fontein, the former director, and I gave the eulogies at Saundra's request. Also attending were a number of MFA staff members, though I don't believe any of the Museum of Fine Arts trustees made it. Bill was cut from a different cloth. There was much more to this brilliant man than I can quickly outline. In matters of race, he was progressive. All of his frames were made by Leon Brathwaite, a Black framer in Boston. He and Bill enjoyed each other's company. Bill Lane loved music as much as art, and he was highly knowledgeable about it. During the 1960s he acted as manager for his good friend Roland Hayes, the great African American tenor, and during the seventies and early eighties he was a supporter and board member of Sarah Caldwell's Boston Opera Company. In the years I worked with Bill, he was following the career of the mezzo-soprano Frederica von Stade, whose voice he loved. He also had the latest hi-fi equipment and he frequently listened to Italian opera. His and Saundra's favorite, as they would often recount, was Verdi's *La forza del destino*, for this was the opera at which they had met. Bill, freshly divorced, would always have two tickets for every Boston production, and he would wait to see if a likely-looking woman would come to the box office looking for a last-minute rush seat. None did until one night in 1962, when a pretty young teacher named

Saundra Baker showed up. Bill gave her the ticket, they sat together and talked, and they were married a year later when Saundra was twenty-five and Bill was fifty. In many ways, it was a perfect match. Saundra had been born in Chelsea, Massachusetts, the only child of a difficult mother and a mostly absent father who served in the merchant marine. She had never known a stable household or financial security, but she was bright and motivated and completely without guile or pretense. Saundra earned a master's degree in teaching after college, and she loved music and art. On their first date, Bill and Saundra went to the MFA and admired the Impressionists, especially the subtle, complex *Ravine* by Van Gogh, never dreaming of the role they would later play at the museum. For his part, Bill was looking for a new start at marriage, and finding the innocent, lovely Saundra must have seemed the answer to his prayers.

Bill Lane was a friendly, smart Irishman from central Massachusetts, the kind of man you'd place as the popular owner of the local hardware store, instead of one with a passion for music and art. He liked hard-working people and like Karolik had no interest in the upper crust and its small talk, though he made exceptions for such Boston art lovers as Bill Osgood, Charlie Cunningham, and Steve Paine. Not much of Harvard seems to have stayed with him. Bill had little use for cities or their clubs or fancy restaurants: He was literally a meat and potatoes guy, one who loved mowing the grass in Lunenburg on his little green John Deere tractor. I introduced him once as a "businessman," and he corrected me: "No, I'm a manufacturer." He was tough, but always straightforward; he entirely lacked cynicism or deviousness. Bill connected easily with men over shared interests—the lawn, the art, the music—but he didn't have similar relationships with women, except for the dealer Edith Halpert, and of course Saundra.

Lane's great collecting years were ones of personal unhappiness and loneliness, as with so many collectors. He responded to paintings that were colorful, well organized, and subtly poetic; he loved inventive, abstracted views of nature, and photographs with the same qualities without the color. His long, single-handed flights over the Western landscape were highly important to him, as emotional release, and as teaching him what mountain and desert looked like from the sky. It seems simplistic, but a number of the works he loved look like aerial views. Most importantly, Bill Lane was the purest collector, the most innocent one I ever knew. His financial return could have been astounding if he or his estate had chosen to cash in, but money was irrelevant to him, as it is for real collectors; it was only the art that mattered.

AFTERWARDS

I MOVED TO Harvard in 2002 as curator of American art. Saundra Lane joined my visiting committee and we remained friends, but her heart stayed with the Museum of Fine Arts. Saundra formed a wonderful relationship with another great collector, another Bill: This was William E. Teel, a widower, and a keen collector of African art that was slated to go to the Museum of Fine Arts. Teel was a warm, soft-spoken person who respected Saundra, and the two enjoyed over a decade of travel and enjoyment before Bill's death in 2013. Wanting to form her own photography collection, she sold off a dozen important duplicate prints by Sheeler, including a few of the classic Doylestown images and two major paintings by Stuart Davis and Sheeler, so that she now had considerable wealth at her disposal. Saundra became a well-known figure at the galleries and the photography fairs, and she demonstrated that she had an eye and a passion of her own. In 1996, the year after Bill Lane's death, she purchased an Edward Weston that he had always wanted, the famous classical image of Charis, nude, curled up in sunlight (fig. 46). It was a memorial purchase, and a brilliant one, and we included it in our "Photography and Modernism" exhibition at the MFA three years later. She went on a few years later to buy another extraordinary Weston, *Fish Gourd on Striped Serape*, a modernist work of great rarity, paying some $172,000 for it—far more than Bill Lane had spent for all his photos, and evidence of the amazing rise of the photography market in fewer than forty years. Saundra also branched out much further than Bill had, and she became interested in the whole history of the medium from the experiments of Fox Talbot and

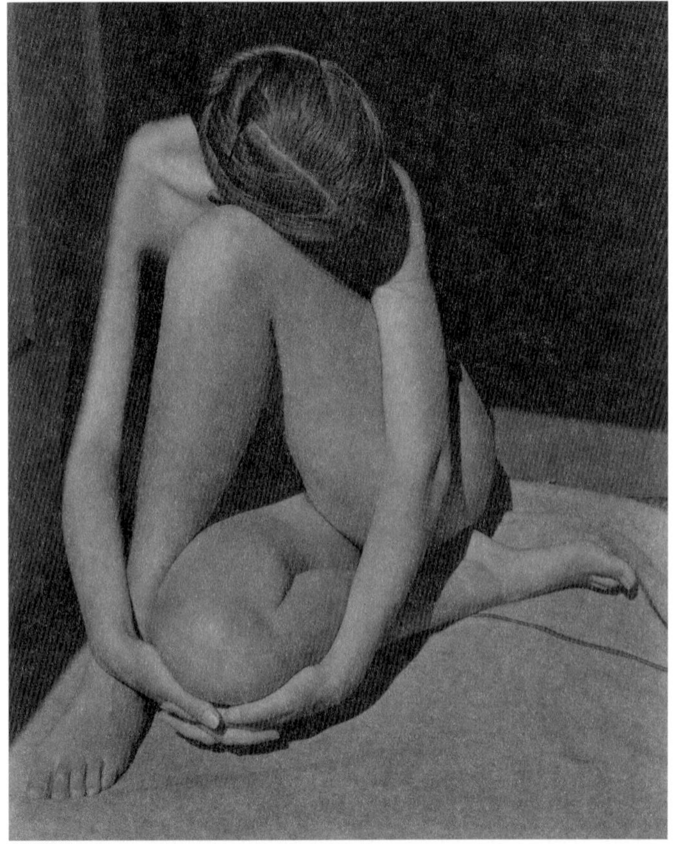

Fig. 46. EDWARD WESTON,
Nude, photograph, gelatin silver print, 1936. Museum of Fine Arts, Boston.

Charles Hippolyte Aubry to such Pictorialists as Heinrich Kühn and Adolf de Meyer, then to the key early modernists in Europe, including Josef Sudek and Eugène Atget, and finally to such varied artists as Diane Arbus, Robert Adams, and Mike Smith. She published her collection, together with some of Bill's things, in an elegant book titled *An Enduring Vision*, in 2011. Then the following year, facing the slow onset of Alzheimer's, the saddest of illnesses, she gave the MFA the entire collection of photographs, including all the Westons, all the Sheelers, everything that Bill had bought and everything she had, along with the American paintings and drawings still in her possession. It must rank as the greatest donation in the museum's history. Given her character, it would have been unthinkable for her to do anything else. Her gift cemented the MFA's holdings of American painting of the twentieth century, and it instantly made the museum an international center for the study of photography.

---

[1] Harvard University, *1935–36 Report Card, Class of 1937* (Harvard University, 1936), William H. Lane Papers, Archives at the Museum of Fine Arts, Boston.

[2] Harvard University, *1935–36 Report Card.*

[3] Hugh Eakin, *Picasso's War: How Modern Art Came to America* (Crown, 2022).

[4] William H. Lane to Edith Halpert, October 27, 1953, William H. Lane Papers.

[5] Lane to Halpert, October 27, 1953.

[6] Theodore E. Stebbins Jr. and Carol Troyen, *The Lane Collection: Twentieth-Century Paintings in the American Tradition* (Museum of Fine Arts, 1983); Lindsay Pollock, *The Girl with the Gallery: Edith Gregor Halpert and the Making of the Modern Art Market* (Public Affairs, 2006).

[7] See Lisa Mintz Messinger, "Edith and Milton Lowenthal Collection," *Metropolitan Museum of Art Bulletin* 54, no. 1 (1996): 8–56, for their eight gifts to the Met and a listing of the entire collection.

[8] Hermann Warner Williams, conversation with the author, 1967.

[9] Richard H. Rush, *Art as an Investment* (Prentice-Hall, 1961).

[10] Lindsay Pollock, *Girl with the Gallery*, 202.

[11] William Lane to Musya Sheeler, November 1, 1966, William H. Lane Papers.

[12] Ansel Adams to William Lane, September 1, 1967, William H. Lane Papers.

[13] William Lane to Georgia O'Keeffe, June 29, 1968, William H. Lane Papers.

[14] William Lane to Brett Weston, December 27, 1967, William H. Lane Papers.

[15] Two other excellent Lane Collection paintings, Dove's *Sunrise I* and Stuart Davis's *Unfinished Business* went into the superb small collection of Deborah and Ed Shein. See *American Modernism: The Shein Collection* (National Gallery, 2012).

13

Alice Kaplan, Only the Best

When I'm in love, and I love it, and it's a beautiful object, I've got to get it.

—ALICE M. KAPLAN, Smithsonian oral history interview, 1978

IN 1974, David Daniels, a collector and head of the Drawing Society, asked me to write a history of American drawings and watercolors, a field I knew practically nothing about, and I agreed. It was one of the best decisions I ever made, as it led me to visit and study every private collection and every museum I could think of, in order to see everything they had, and Harper & Row produced a lovely book. Early in the process, Daniels and Wilder Green, director of the American Federation of Arts (AFA), said, "You should meet Alice Kaplan." They were planning a traveling exhibition based on my still nonexistent volume that would be circulated by the AFA, and Alice Kaplan, they said, was president of its board. She would have to raise funds to pay for the exhibition and the book, so it was important for me to make a good impression on her. I'll never forget meeting her and seeing her collection for the first time.

Alice was special. She was tall, confident, welcoming, and commanding all at once, an Auntie Mame without the singing. We immediately became friends, as she did with nearly everyone she met. Her collection reflected her personal flair, comprising works from the US, Central America, Africa, Europe, India, and China in every medium dating from 2500 BCE to the present. It was beautifully installed; every work seemed to speak to the ones near it, and each seemed the best of its kind. Seeing it was a dazzling experience. Alice remains in many ways my favorite collector. Other collectors' homes seem perfect in my mind's eye—I think of Elizabeth Gosnell Miller, Julian and Jo Ann Ganz, David Daniels and his drawings, and Joe Helman—but I found Alice's collection inspiring for its extraordinary range and its amazingly consistent quality. She bought art for the only reason that ultimately makes any sense: because she hungered for it. The real collector sees an object, is struck by it, and has to have it. This is not a rational process; the collector covets the object the way teenagers dream of their first loves. There is an automatic sensual response. And there is, of course, a second, more rational stage, when desire is brought under some kind of control, research may be done or advice sought from an art historian or restorer, and the bank account is checked. I also admired Alice for her late start. She did not begin collecting seriously until she was nearly sixty. In 1955, she had been married for thirty years to Jacob M. Kaplan, the wealthy philanthropist and owner of the Welch's Grape Juice Co., and had raised four children. As she said, "What am I going to do? Go around and have lunch every day and go to—I mean, what am I going to do?"[1] So instead of taking up lunching and playing bridge, she went back to school and eleven years later received her master's degree in art history from Columbia. There and at the Institute of Fine Arts, she took courses with some of the best art historians of the day, including Julius Held, Meyer Schapiro, Robert Goldwater, Barbara Novak, and Rudolf Wittkower. Mr. Kaplan supported her collecting, but it was very much her creation; as she said, "he wasn't involved."[2] He was never at home when I visited, and I have no idea what their life together was like, but certainly Alice had a lot of time on her hands. She was one of those women who at a later time would have headed a major company. As it was, she got deeply involved in the Adlai Stevenson presidential campaigns of 1952 and 1956, then began serving on one board or visiting committee after another, in each playing a leadership role as she organized benefits and fund raisers with enormous success. Besides serving as president of the American Federation of Arts for a decade, in the period when I came to know her she raised the funds for the fiftieth anniversary of the Armory Show for the Henry Street Settlement, for Columbia University, the Morgan Library, the Committee to Save the Cooper-Union (later the Cooper-Hewitt Museum), and the American Folk Art Museum. Her personality, her organizational skills, and her passionate commitment to her causes made it impossible for her many friends to turn her down.

The odds against a relatively small-time private collector ending up with even one superlative work are significant. Inexplicably, Alice Kaplan owned a number of masterworks in every medium, from five continents and five thousand years of human history. Normally, the first advice I give to collectors is to specialize—not just in painting or sculpture, in Asian or African art, but in a specific school or style. But Alice did exactly the opposite, securing an extraordinary group of American folk paintings, the two best Maurice Prendergast watercolors anywhere, an amazingly wide variety of drawings of the highest quality (including examples by Egon Schiele, Honoré Daumier, Jean-Auguste-Dominique Ingres, William Blake, Giovanni Battista Tiepolo, Rembrandt, and Peter Paul Rubens). She also had a superb Burgundian stone carving of a Virgin and Child, several bronze plaques from the Biniculture (Edo State, Nigeria), a colorful mummy mask from Peru's Chimu culture, several gold pieces from Colombia, a sensitive Aztec pottery head, a richly decorated Ching Dynasty twelve-panel standing screen, two fine Han vessels, a Khmer goddess from Cambodia, a Gandhara standing Buddha whose grace recalls the sculpture of classical Greece, a Ptolemaic torso, and a Cycladic head of the Spedos type. All this sounds messy, as if one had stumbled across a fabulous unknown antique store on a back street, but it wasn't. Somehow, everything worked. Mrs. Kaplan's home was supremely comfortable, sumptuous but livable. When you sat down, you weren't afraid of knocking over something valuable. In the entrance hall one saw all kinds of drawings hung on a dark chocolate-brown wall, an astonishing array. Alice got advice when she needed it, from her former teacher Julius Held, the Rubens expert, among others; but my sense is that she made her own decisions and served as her own decorator as well. All you can say is that Alice had the art collecting equivalent of perfect pitch for musicians.

Mrs. Kaplan acquired three of the greatest of all American folk portraits before folk painting joined the canon. Her Ammi Phillips painting *Mrs. Ostrander and Her Son, Titus,* with its incredible linear qualities, is outstanding, but even better, I believe, is another Phillips, *Boy with Primer, Peach, and Dog,* now owned by the Philadelphia Museum. It has everything: rich local color, a superb gold border outlining the boy's coat and buttons, and a sensitive human likeness, not to mention the red book in the boy's hand and the cheerful dog. Yet my own favorite is the *Portrait of Sarah Prince* (also known as *Girl at the Pianoforte*), by the deaf-mute itinerant artist John Brewster Jr., that she bought in 1966 (fig. 47). It bears all the hallmarks of the untrained artist in the crude hands and figure, and in the laboriously detailed piano keys and the sheet of music, but the striking face of the sixteen-year-old sitter reaches another level. Here one feels the painter's enchantment with his subject, and one can only wonder how he achieved such a likeness years before the invention of photography. This masterpiece had been lent to the Abby Aldrich Rockefeller Folk Art Museum by its owner, the New York dealer Martin Grossman in 1959, and one can only shudder at the notion that that museum ever let it leave its premises. After Alice's death, it remained with her equally talented daughter, the late Joan K. Davidson, until it was brilliantly purchased by my first employer, the Yale University Art Gallery, in 2017, when it was valued in the five-million-dollar range. As part of the same transaction, Yale also acquired Alice's great Blakelock, *Moonlight,* as the gift of Mrs. Davidson. Alice had taken a course at Columbia with the young Barbara Novak who even then was teaching her students about Luminism. Mrs. Kaplan in 1960 went to Hirschl & Adler Galleries looking for a Fitz Henry Lane; they didn't have one, but in the process she spotted the Blakelock *Moonlight* and purchased it. Neither Novak nor anyone else had told her about this artist; she simply saw a work that moved her and bought it. It's one of the painter's two or three outstanding works.

Alice made her first serious purchase in 1955 when she chose a large monochrome painting by Joaquín Torres-García entitled *Construction*

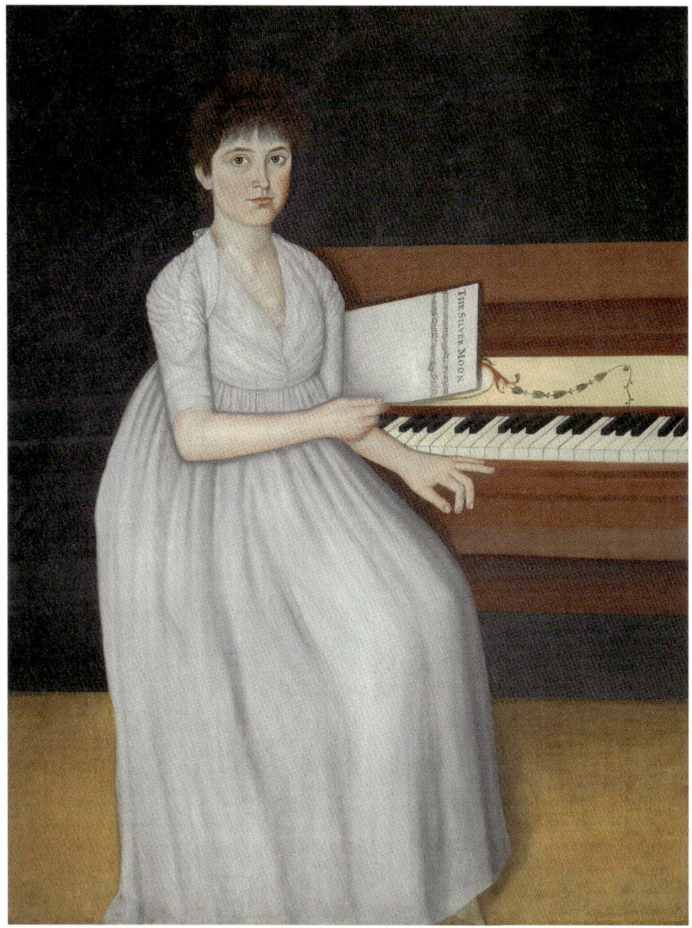

Fig. 47. JOHN BREWSTER, JR.
Portrait of Sarah Prince, oil on canvas, ca. 1801. Yale University Art Gallery.

in White. In its disciplined linearity, it foretold her future interests, while also suggesting how little she would be influenced by current trends. A few years later, in 1959, she began a decade of active collecting when she bought her first two Benin bronzes while also acquiring an extraordinary drawing in black crayon, with touches of red watercolor, by Egon Schiele: Already her focus on the sensuality of line was in evidence. No one was buying such things at the time: The Schiele, the first of several she would acquire, cost her $300 at the Galerie St. Etienne.

Although Alice and I often talked about her collection, I still cannot explain why she was so successful. How did a private collector, not a scholar, a curator, or a specialist, come to own all these wonderful objects? In her first year of serious collecting, Mrs. Kaplan promised a friend to attend a Parke-Bernet auction being held for the benefit of Irvington House, an institute for medical research, and to buy something. At the viewing, she recalls, she saw an "attractive, pleasing" portrait of a woman in a black dress holding a red book.[3] Although it was unsigned and unattributed, she made the winning bid of fifty dollars because she liked the painting. Only in 1961, when one of the first articles on Ammi Phillips appeared, was her purchase attributed to the artist. Mrs. Kaplan purchased a second Phillips in 1964 (the magnificent one of Mrs. Ostrander and her son); in 1966 came the Brewster, in 1974 a third Phillips, and then, in 1977, four more, including two husband-and-wife pairs. Thus, Alice made her initial purchase purely on the basis of eye, an instinctive reaction to quality; at the time, it must have seemed unlikely that there would ever be a firm attribution. There were no experts who could have advised her on these works, and there was very little literature. Yet somehow she obtained better folk portraits than Abby Aldrich Rockefeller had, years earlier.

Alice Kaplan was confident in her eye, she had the time and the money, and she seems to have created her own good luck. Her Prendergast watercolor, *Square of San Marco, Venice,* I believe to be the artist's supreme work on paper. The watercolor appeared out of nowhere at a New York auction in 1973; Mrs. Kaplan liked it but was outbid. When the man who prevailed needed to sell it a year later, he remembered her interest; this time she bought it without quibbling (another rare and useful quality for collectors), paying a premium for her earlier mistake. One wonders, where were the Horowitzes, the Fraads, and all the other collectors of American Impressionism? Similarly, many people—myself among them—would opt for another of her American paintings, the 1888 trompe l'oeil entitled *Mr. Hulings' Rack Picture* by William Harnett, as being the preeminent object in her collection (fig. 48). Harnett is arguably the greatest American still life painter, and his acknowledged genius makes his work expensive. When Parke-Bernet offered it for sale in March 1969, Kennedy Galleries bought it and sold it to a collector. I was astonished to learn that the buyer had returned it a year later. What a mistake! Even as it was being unwrapped, Alice, who was not a regular customer, had happened in, making her own good luck as usual. Fleischman showed it to her, and the rest, as they say, is history. Through her willingness

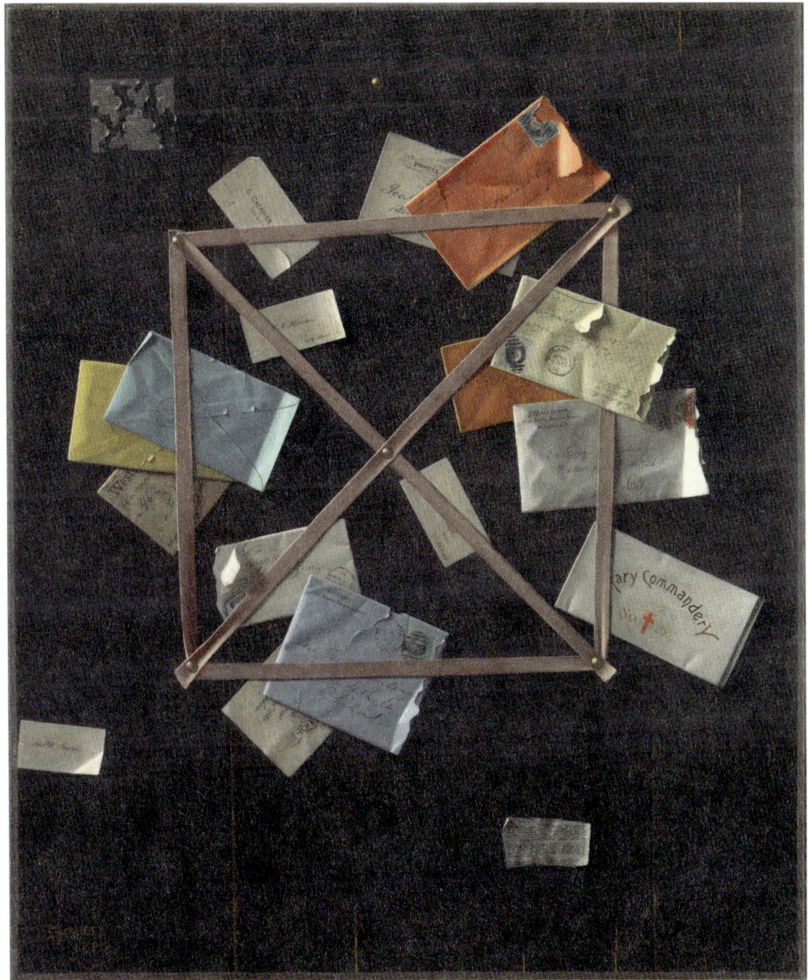

Fig. 48. WILLIAM M. HARNETT,
Mr. Hulings' Rack Picture, oil on canvas, 1888. Private Collection.

to act quickly, her good luck and perspicacity, Mrs. Kaplan was in the right place at the right time and acquired one of the greatest American paintings. I had the pleasure of borrowing it from her for my "New World" exhibition of 1983.

What appealed to Alice Kaplan were works with a limited range of color and great elegance of line. She collected classicism rather than expressionism. This is obvious in the gentle outline of her exquisite Curlew weathervane and in the Harnett, as it is of the folk paintings, and even of the Indian sculpture. She is drawn to the crisp, sensual linearity one sees in her Ammi Phillips and in her drawings by Schiele and Ingres. In Brewster's *Sarah Prince,* lines converge from every direction to meet at the sitter's right hand. Nearly all the drawings suggest the tension of human figures in motion. A superb Spanish still life records a moment in time just after an apple has been peeled and lies teetering on a ledge. And the ancient objects make this tension even clearer: The great Aztec head, with its serene, linear surface and its earth colors, seems about to cry out in pain. The Khmer divinity gestures toward us with her mouth, her body, and her sensuous, pleated skirt.

Alice never bought anything from Leo Castelli; she was a client instead of his rival André Emmerich. She did not, however, buy Emmerich's Color Field artists but rather went for the dealer's other area, that of pre-Columbian art. She surely was aware of Morris Louis, Ken Noland, and the others, but those works were too colorful, too undisciplined, and perhaps too highly promoted for her taste. What she got from Emmerich instead were three superb Columbian gold pieces, including the great male figure pendant in the Popayan style as well as the powerful woven mantle from the Chancay culture in Peru, which features the strong, geometric design that characterizes so much of her collection. In addition, Alice also bought contemporary art from the start, and her choices reflected the same taste that guided her in the ancient fields: her love of line, subtle coloration, and evocative form. Her drawing by Elie Nadelman, her sculptures by Jacques Lipchitz, Saul Baizerman, and Gonzalo Fonseca (who was married to her daughter Elizabeth), and her paintings by Giorgio Morandi all reflected her love of simplicity. Each of these works had the quality she sought, but of these artists, only Nadelman and Morandi have been promoted to the canon, demonstrating once again how difficult it is to separate winners from losers, or perhaps the fortunate versus the unlucky, among living and recent artists. The small, faintly colored still lifes of the Italian Morandi had won attention in 1948 when he was awarded the medal at the Venice Biennale, and the New York audience would have heard about him beginning in 1949 when the Museum of Modern Art acquired its first examples. However, Alice was still in the vanguard when she made her first purchase of his work in 1962; the subtlety of his works and their connection to Minimalism has led to the constant growth of his reputation, so that his paintings now cost in the millions.

Alice's forays into contemporary art demonstrate the difficulty and complexity of that field. She bought art that she responded to, including works by Leonard Baskin and Gregory Gillespie. Baskin was a brilliant artist, a master draftsman, sculptor, watercolorist, printmaker, typographer, book designer, and publisher as founder of the Gehenna Press. He was an avaricious, learned collector of books, European sculpture, Renaissance medals, and American Tonalist paintings. His imagination roved over artists of the past, from Goya to Blake to Eakins. Stylistically and temperamentally, he was a successor to Karl Zerbe, Hyman Bloom, and the Boston Expressionists. Art was no laughing matter for him: The son of a rabbi, he was devoted to the human figure, the world of animals and mythical creatures, and to the expression of humanity's mysteries and its pain. In 1960, as she was starting out, Alice acquired the *Owl* that Baskin had laboriously carved from wood the year before. It's a piece of haunting poetry, with its tiny head, the large, carefully carved feathers on its body and the smaller detail of its textured chest. It's a unique, handmade work, realistic but also abstracted, one that looked cutting-edge in its day. When Alice bought the piece from the dealer Grace Borgenicht, Baskin was a coming figure, a potential great. Yet time passed him by because of the arbitrary way in which changing tastes and the creation of canons happen. An entirely opposite kind of art rose to favor at just this time, the mechanically reproduced art of Andy Warhol with its imagery lifted from newspaper photos. Baskin was all about the hand of the artist, while Warhol totally eschewed the personal touch. Baskin's art spoke to the humanist tradition, Warhol's to popular culture and its cult figures from Marilyn to Elvis, and Western culture opted for the originality and excitement of Pop Art rather than the old-fashioned look of art that stemmed from European sources.

Gregory Gillespie, on the other hand, was less sanguine temperamentally than Baskin; he remained angry and dissatisfied all his life. He poured all his talents and all his emotional fervor into a realist style of painting that, like Baskin's work, became increasingly out of step with the prevailing direction of the field. Like Baskin, he had strong supporters, including the loyal group of realist painters in the Northampton area who regarded him as their leader, the Forum Gallery where he always showed, and some loyal collectors. And also like Baskin, Gillespie was a student of art history, spending eight formative years (1962–70) in Italy studying Masaccio, Crivelli, and the Italian masters. The highly original style he developed relied on his knowledge of Renaissance paintings and Surrealism, combined with an inventive use of photography and collage and his own rich inventory of imaginary creatures and juxtapositions. Alice Kaplan went to the first of Gillespie's seven exhibitions at the Forum Gallery, and the painting she selected, *Roman Interior (Still Life)* (fig. 49) accorded well with her taste, being one of the simplest and most geometric of Greg's pictures; it also included the reds that Alice loved on the rare occasions when she went for color. The painting depicts the corner of a bare room, perhaps a kitchen, with a table in the corner; the room and the table are flattened, while a small, deep window or hole cuts through the thick wall to reveal the Castel Sant'Angelo in the distance. It's the painter at his best, in a period when he was solving painterly problems rather than dealing with the moods that saw him in later years literally painting himself into a blue corner, paintings that evidence his growing depression and eventual suicide.[4]

Alice Kaplan was an outstanding collector who had a brilliant eye, decisiveness, and means, and the good luck of frequently finding herself at the right place at the right time. Each object was purchased

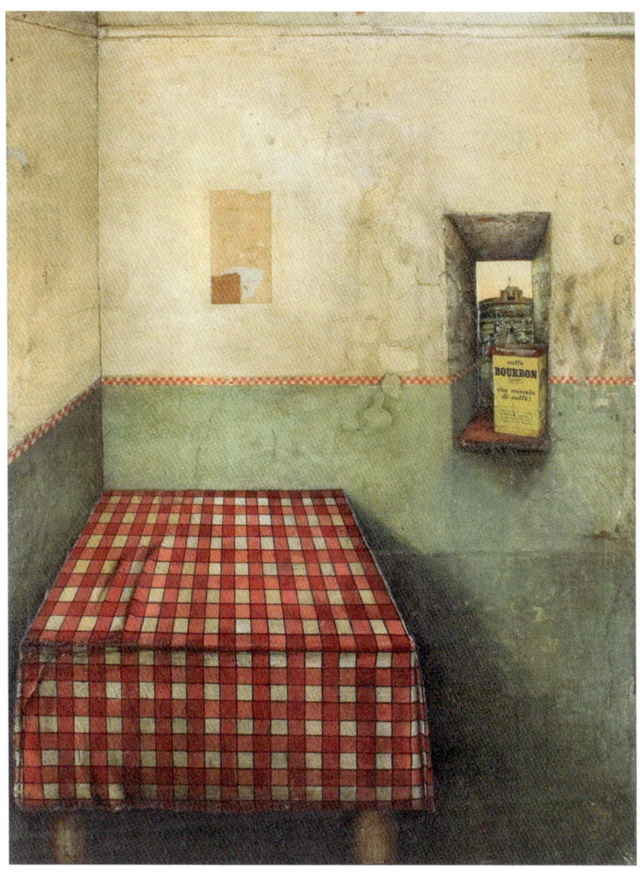

Fig. 49. GREGORY GILLESPIE,
Roman Interior (Still Life), oil and mixed media on wood, 1966–67.
Private Collection.

because she loved it; when she fell out of love, she would give the offending work away to a family member or a museum. Her collection tells us several interesting stories and offers insight into the modern field and how a canon is shaped. I would argue that everything in her collection was well chosen, while conceding that only two of her modern works, the pair of paintings by Morandi, have been the kind of winners that her Harnett, the Prendergasts, the folk paintings, and others proved to be. Market value and critical reputation usually work in tandem: The Baskin, the Gillespie, and most of her modern collection fail on both accounts. For Alice to be considered equally farsighted in the contemporary field, she would have had to buy Warhol, Lichtenstein, or Johns during the 1960s, but their work just didn't appeal to her. Nonetheless, I believe she was the best collector I ever knew.

---

[1] "Oral History Interview with Alice M. Kaplan, 1978 February 21–March 8," interview by Paul Cummings, Smithsonian Archives of American Art, February 21–March 8, 1978.

[2] "Oral History Interview with Alice M. Kaplan."

[3] Theodore E. Stebbins Jr., "Alice Kaplan, Collector," *Portfolio: The Magazine of the Fine Arts,* May/June 1982, 84; see also Linda Bantel, *The Alice M. Kaplan Collection* (E. P. Dutton, 1981).

[4] Donald D. Keyes, *A Unique American Vision: Paintings by Gregory Gillespie* (University of Georgia Museum, 1999); Theodore E. Stebbins Jr. and Susan Ricci Stebbins, *Life as Art: Paintings by Gregory Gillespie and Frances Cohen Gillespie* (Harvard Art Museums, 2003).

14

The Problem of Collecting Contemporary Art: Richard Brown Baker, Joseph Helman, Monroe Price

I now hold that it's a small problem to differentiate between a bad and a good work of art.

—RICHARD BROWN BAKER

You can take a measure of yourself by looking at the art that engages you, that you like, that you collect, that you don't even have to collect. If you think about it, you'll get a take on yourself and on the world and what your place is in it.

—JOSEPH A. HELMAN

COLLECTING THE work of living artists can be both joyful and risky: joyful in terms of living with art and getting to know the artists, dealers, and fellow art lovers, but risky if one counts on seeing the money again. In this chapter, I describe three serious, dedicated, but very different New York collectors. I know or knew each one well, and I think I understand their collections, their strategies, and their feelings about what they accomplished. They represent three very different approaches to the canon, with Joe Helman skillfully managing the late-twentieth-century greats, Richard Brown Baker establishing a personal canon that has never gained traction, and Monroe Price paying no attention to canons or to anyone else's opinions. I'll start with Baker (1912–2002), who was a trustee of the Yale University Art Gallery when I began my career there. His story is a complicated one. After occasionally acquiring a print or watercolor as a young man, Baker turned to contemporary art in 1954 and began buying in earnest the following year. Over the next forty years, he purchased some 1,651 works, an average of forty per year, or a painting, drawing, or sculpture a week when he was in town. He had high ambitions from the start, wanting his collection to be "great," while setting a goal of buying "ahead of the millionaires" as he wrote in his journal.[1] At forty-three, Baker badly needed to find success somewhere; he had retired early from government service and he had failed as a writer and then as a painter. He conceived his collection as a future gift to Yale, where he hoped it would provide a definitive survey of the art of the later twentieth century, building on what the Société Anonyme Collection had done for the earlier years. Unfortunately, the collection would never attain this lofty mark. Following a unique set of self-imposed rules, Baker became an extraordinary conceptual work of art himself, a one-man experiment in looking and buying. For four decades he would write up every day's tour of the galleries in his diary, recording each purchase along with his observations. He never sold a single work, and he also had a strict self-imposed rule against going back to buy an artist whom he hadn't initially responded to. Never was a collection more of an autobiography.

Baker was a self-styled Puritan (he once said "Self-denial is our Puritan goal," but like many things he said, he didn't practice it at all), handsome and debonair, with a gentlemanly, deferential manner.[2] He came from Providence, and it was quietly but wrongly assumed by many that he was a Brown of Rhode Island, a descendant of Nicholas Brown and the founders of Brown University.[3] Yet no one could have had a more promising start than his, as a Phi Beta Kappa in the Yale Class of 1935, where he majored in English literature, then a Rhodes Scholar at Oxford, where for three years he studied politics, economics, and philosophy. He enjoyed a handsome but not lavish income from family trusts. During the war he worked for the Office of Strategic Services, and later in a low-level position at the CIA, though around the Yale University Art Gallery it was whispered incorrectly that he'd been an important operative there. Resigning from that job in 1949, he moved to New York to become a writer, but after several years, he realized that he lacked the necessary skills. He studied art briefly with Hans Hofmann, and as late as his twenty-fifth-reunion report, he described himself as an "abstract painter."[4] He never showed me one of his paintings.

After beginning slowly, Baker blossomed as a collector in 1955 with thirty-four remarkable acquisitions, almost all of them abstractions by European and American painters, including Georges Mathieu, Pierre Soulages, Giuseppe Santomaso, Robert Motherwell, and Hans Hofmann, among others, before closing out the year by buying a great Dubuffet oil and the superb Jackson Pollock *Arabesque* of 1948 from the Janis Gallery (fig. 50). In early March 1956, during his second year as a committed collector, Baker purchased Franz Kline's *Wanamaker Block* for $2,000, also from Janis. Brimming with confidence, he wrote in his journal, "I now hold that it's a small problem to differentiate between a bad and a good work of art."[5] He went on, "If I did acquire a lot of duds, nobody would pay any attention to my collection, and few therefore would know of my errors in judgment."[6] He had no idea how lucky he'd been, and he assumed his luck would continue. Yet he was

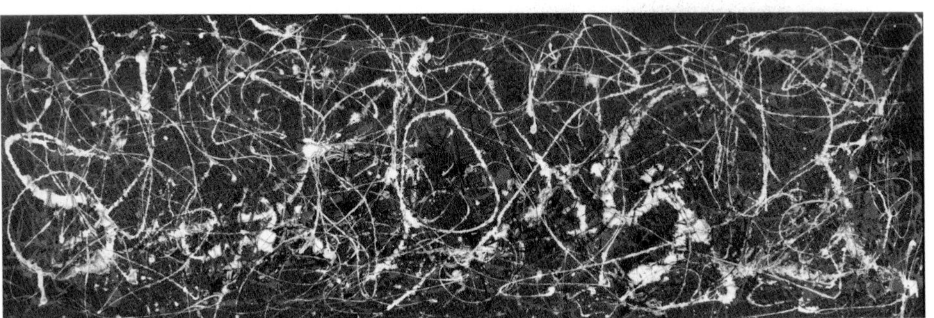

Fig. 50. JACKSON POLLOCK,
Number 13A: Arabesque, oil and enamel on canvas, 1948.
Yale University Art Gallery.

still deeply insecure about his direction in life; in September 1956, he thought about seeking a job in a new field and took a series of Johnson O'Connor aptitude tests. He failed to record the results in his journal and made no changes to his life.[7]

The Pollock and the Kline quickly made Richard's reputation, and his increasing celebrity in the New York art world brought him renewed pleasure. Baker was now mixing at openings with Alfred H. Barr, James Johnson Sweeney, Ben Heller, Nelson Rockefeller, and other leaders of the New York art world.[8] Within weeks of its purchase, the Kline was requested by MoMA for its influential international exhibition, "The New American Painting" that took the best of Abstract Expressionism to eight European countries. The Pollock added even more luster. The picture had first been shown at Betty Parsons's gallery in January 1949, where it went unsold with a price tag of $1,200, and it was still available—now at Janis—in December 1955, when Baker paid $2,500 for it. Despite Pollock's rising reputation—he was well-known by this time in modernist circles—the price had only doubled in seven years. Richard had looked at various Pollocks earlier, but *Arabesque* was the first to strike him hard: As he said, "The moment I saw it I was enchanted."[9] He rarely articulated his likes and dislikes any more deeply than this. Richard was gratified by the ever-greater offers he received for it over the years. In 1962, the dealer André Emmerich offered him $100,000 for it, assuring him that its value was unlikely to increase any further.[10] A quarter century later, Richard recorded a visit from Evan Janis, who proposed that he sell the Pollock for him for $12 million, far more money than he had ever possessed; yet he never deviated from his policy of never selling a work, noting in his diary, "I suspect I get as much of an ego boost out of rejecting that large sum as I would from receiving it."[11] Living off trust funds, Richard, like many of his social class, viewed money-making with disdain.

Baker continued in 1957 and 1958 at a slighter lower pace, purchasing fifty-one works over the two years, including a superb Hofmann. His collection brought him visits from prominent people in the art world, including Andy Warhol, whose work he never fully embraced, and the critic Dore Ashton, among others, and after just three years as a committed collector, he was invited early in 1959 to show his collection at the Rhode Island School of Design in Providence, the first of dozens of such exhibitions in his lifetime and after.[12] Richard proudly pointed out, in the slender eight-page catalogue, that his fifty-six paintings had been executed by artists from twelve nations, mostly within the past three years.[13] He was hungry for the attention and the plaudits these exhibitions brought him, from the courting museums and the lively openings to the interviews, panels, and reviews. Servicing requests for loans became a major part of his life; in addition to his scouting the galleries, he served as curator, registrar, art handler, publicist, and proud owner, all in one.

Baker would often repeat his mantra, "Get there first, with adequate credit, and decide promptly."[14] However, in reality he rarely followed this course. During his great buying run of the mid-fifties, he was actually acquiring painters who were already well known to the leading dealers and collectors, and whose work had been shown at the Museum of Modern Art, the Carnegie International, and elsewhere. The Abstract Expressionists had become a canon by then, supported by a growing number of publications and exhibitions. Richard was actually getting there second, then buying well: At the end of the day, this might actually be the best way to collect contemporary art. These purchases demonstrated both Richard's good eye and his good ear; though he didn't read much art criticism, by this time he had excellent contacts among the curators and dealers, and he followed their lead. However, in November 1961 in the back room at Leo Castelli's gallery on Seventy-Seventh Street, he actually "got there first" when he saw several paintings by Roy Lichtenstein, an unknown artist yet to have an exhibition who had recently given up his abstract style in favor of one based on comic strips. Baker went back for a second look, then purchased *Washing Machine* for $575, describing it in his journal as one that "beautifully, crisply depicts an arm pouring yellow suds into an electric washing machine."[15] Three months later, Castelli opened his first Lichtenstein exhibition, and Richard purchased a second work, the now famous *Blam*, this time paying $1,000. The exhibition sold out, and the painter's prices began a swift ascent, but not before Baker had acquired a third picture, *Thinking of Him*, in December 1963. It is easy to forget how totally foreign Pop Art looked when it first appeared, what an affront it seemed to accepted standards (and Abstract Expressionism), and how long it took for many collectors and critics to accept it. Richard's quick acceptance of Lichtenstein showed him at his very best; it was the way he always hoped to operate but rarely would again.

In 1974, director of the Yale University Art Gallery Alan Shestack agreed that we should mount an exhibition of outstanding works from Baker's collection; Yale lacked Pollock, Kline, and Lichtenstein, and our aim was to secure a future gift of Richard's best works. In the fall term of 1974, I taught a seminar of outstanding graduate students whose mission was to select the exhibition and write the catalogue. It was not an easy show to select, for by that time Richard owned 908 widely varied works, with others constantly arriving. We quickly agreed on the masterworks by Pollock, Kline, Dubuffet, and the three terrific Lichtensteins, and then decided to enrich the showing of Abstract Expressionism with Richard's paintings by Motherwell, Hofmann, and Marca-Relli, an easy call, as was including such Pop artists as Indiana, Dine, Wesselmann, Rauschenberg, and Rosenquist and the fine Color Field pictures by Kenneth Noland and Jules Olitski. Then two alternatives presented themselves: We could either exhibit more of the outstanding works from Richard's first active decade, which would have shown him as a remarkably prescient, highly focused collector whose best years were long past, or we could try to present him as a perceptive buyer of contemporary art over the last twenty years. We diplomatically decided on the latter course, aiming to show the whole range of the collection as it then existed. We decided to include minor works by Agnes Martin, Frank Stella, Richard Diebenkorn, and others, along with a large group of realist and photorealist paintings and some sculptures that indicated the direction in which Richard was heading. Our aim was to flatter him and to represent him as still having a brilliant eye in 1965–75, which in fact he no longer had. At the time, we had no idea how insecure Richard was, as he showed us all of the works in his apartment in the same quiet, dispassionate way. We thought we were leaning over backwards in including some pretty minor recent acquisitions, while Richard felt that we hadn't done enough. When I read his journal years later, I learned of his disappointment with our selection; he wrote, "It should be a lesson in humility to me that they have given their approval to no more than thirteen of the 286 works that I have acquired since the 1970's began."[16] But he was pleased with the exhibition that opened in April 1975, and he had only praise for the catalogue; they accomplished what we had hoped and played a role in Richard's later gifts to Yale.

In 2011, almost a decade after Richard's death, the Yale University Art Gallery produced a useful decade-by-decade history of his collection, putting the best possible face on his forty-year career.[17] From it one sees that his best days as a collector actually ended in 1967 with his purchase of a large Cy Twombly from Castelli. During the decades that followed, he missed the major movements in the US and Europe, including the minimalism of Donald Judd and Richard Serra (one would have thought that Serra would be easy for him, given his predilection for Kline and the others); feminist art (Louise Bourgeois, Barbara Kruger); Arte Povera; Installation Art; Latin American Art; European neo-Expressionism (Kiefer, Baselitz, Chia, Immendorff); photography (Cindy Sherman) or video, or the surrealist assemblages of Joseph Cornell, among others. He bought few works by women, and fewer as time went on. When he did buy Jasper Johns, Frank Stella, Richard Diebenkorn, Ellsworth Kelly, Andy Warhol, Agnes Martin, or Brice Marden, it was hesitantly and after the fact, in the form of a print or a very small painting. Richard in these years plunged instead into photorealism, building a collection of a school that seemed promising to many during those years. Then during the eighties and nineties he lost the scent altogether, as he turned largely to fantastical, garish neo-Expressionist paintings by Peter Saul, Peter Blake, Luis Cruz Azaceta, and a host of others. On a level well below them, he bought thirteen cartoonish pictures on gay themes by Eric Stotik (fig. 51), a group of drawings of men and boys by Bill Vuksanovich, animal pictures by Rick Bartow, and several intense realist paintings of Steven Assael, along with numerous derivative abstractions by other painters. Richard turned to raw portrayals of violence while in his journal frequently bemoaning the violence he was encountering in his life.[18] Few of these painters

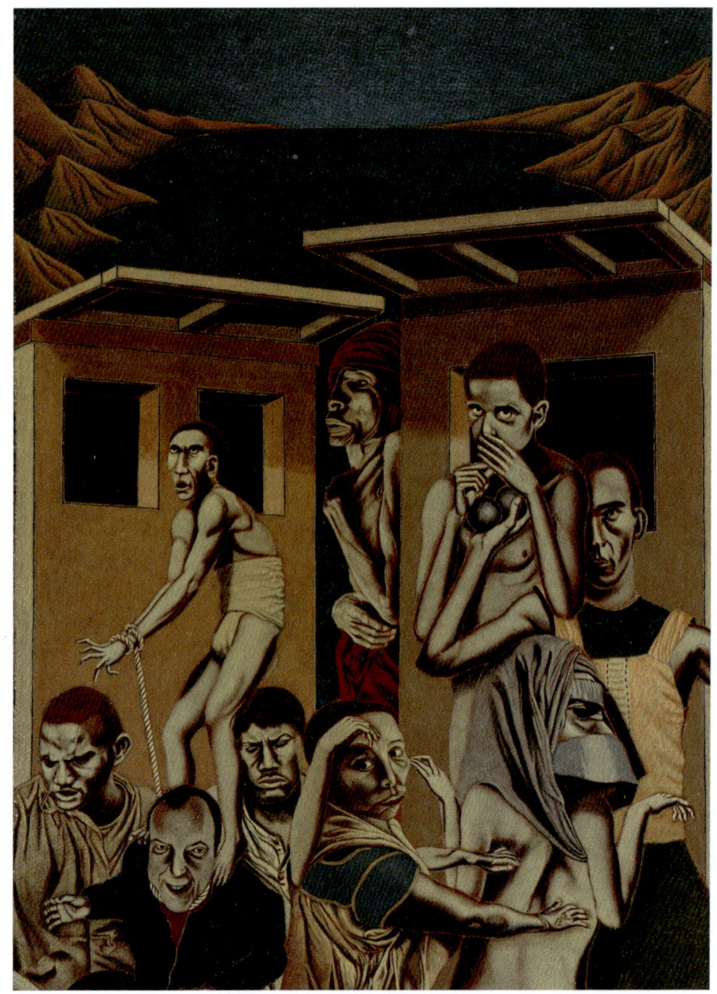

Fig. 51. ERIC STOTIK,
Vol. 148 No. 310, acrylic on linen on wood, 1989–90. Yale University Art Gallery.

are still remembered, Peter Saul being one of the exceptions. As the always-honest critic Robert Storrs put it, "The hard truth is that much of the time Baker operated like a prospector heading into the territories without a map or a compass."[19] He gave up going to Castelli, stopped paying attention to MoMA, and never sought professional advice. He should have given up collecting, but what was he to do instead? So he bravely went on; as with Karolik before him, buying art was all he knew how to do. His diaries of these years are full of laments about his weakening confidence; time and time again, he realized that he had missed the best artists. Thus, when Yale, on Richard's death, found itself owning 1,344 American and European works from his collection (the 336 British works went to the Rhode Island School of Design) it possessed both a remarkable benefaction of some major paintings and a huge future problem in terms of the care, conservation, and curatorship of many minor ones. At most, a fifth of the collection has real merit by today's standards while the rest seems destined for permanent storage. Storrs rightly sums up "the nearly inchoate aggregate of Baker's collection."[20] Today, of the 1,344 works, just five paintings and three works on paper hang at the Yale University Art Gallery, with another dozen or so on view elsewhere around the university.[21] It would be interesting to know how much it costs the university annually to store and care for the collection, but whatever the amount, it can probably be justified as part of the hidden cost of owning the Pollock, the Rauschenberg, and the Twombly.[22]

Baker graduated from Yale in 1935, in the depths of the Depression, when nativism and homophobia were rampant. In 1960, Baker's class produced a twenty-fifth-reunion report, and a classmate wrote of Richard: "He is still a bachelor—and little wonder: What wife could keep up with a man who gets around so much?"[23] Being single made him atypical, but the class reporter found an easy explanation for it in his frequent travel; the idea of having a gay classmate would have seemed unimaginable to his college friends. Richard was with the CIA as a foreign affairs officer until his resignation in March 1949. Washington had become a particularly uncomfortable place for gay men because of the "Sex Perversion Elimination Program" instituted by the Park Police in 1947. As a closeted gay in government service, he was exactly the kind of person that Senators Wherry, Hill, and McCarthy were trying to hunt down, and in fact, in 1950, the State Department ousted ninety-one gay men as security risks. Describing the mid-fifties, Edmond White wrote that "the three most heinous crimes known to man were Communism, heroin addiction, and homosexuality."[24] Thus, it seems likely that Richard's resignation from government and his move to New York reflect the terrible pressure he must have been feeling, though his diary doesn't mention his sexual orientation until the mid-fifties when he records a visit to a "B&G" (blow and go) cafeteria in Chicago.[25] He was always open about his sexuality in his journal, so he effectively came out for posterity. But sadly, the Gay Liberation movement came too late for him; Richard remained locked into his fears and totally closeted until his death, living one life with his gay friends, and another with the prominent, wealthy collectors at his clubs and on the Governing Board at the Yale University Art Gallery. In those years, I never heard the slightest hint that he was gay.

Like many collectors, Richard became addicted to the art world action and to his constant visits to the dealers, but his lack of reading, his failure to consult, and his complete reliance on his own instincts led him astray. He was aware of his weaknesses, writing, "I wonder whether I have been frittering away my money on insignificant items," adding, "Possibly I have lost my daring."[26] He was fearful of posterity's judgment: "Time will have to be my judge, time may prove severe upon me."[27] By the early 1970s, his diary demonstrates a declining interest in art, as it grants more and more attention to gossip, travels, friendships, and personal reflections. He lamented that he had no one to talk to, and it irked him that he spent so much time discussing the past, but he concluded, regarding his journal, "I am obsessed by these writings. I cannot escape thinking of them."[28] Recording his life quietly replaced his earlier aim of making a record of his reactions to art. In mid-1985, he laments that he is seeing only a quarter of New York's one-artist shows, and writes, "I am convinced that I am not in touch with a great deal of artistic creativity."[29] Richard's gargantuan journals, written in longhand and amounting to about 140,000 words per year, or some 5 million words altogether, constitute a quagmire. The critic Thomas Crow gamely speaks of their "literary quality,"[30] and rightly describes them as having no parallel in the art world; indeed they don't, but remind one of the Boston recluse Arthur Crew Inman's (1895–1963) incredible, equally self-involved 17-million-word diary.[31] Richard was aware of his dual obsessions: As he wrote in 1987 in a moment of honesty, "Both diary and collection exist in excess. My mind rejects excess. My behavior succumbs to it."[32] His Puritan standards had been left far behind. Sadly, he didn't write well, and though he says a great deal about himself, he frustratingly reveals very little about his innermost hopes and fears. Yet he bravely bought works of art that moved him and pleased him, and he will be remembered for his triumphs and not his failures.

It would be difficult to find a collector who stands in more contrast to Baker than Joseph A. Helman (b. 1937), though both were full-time members of the art world. Baker was a shy man who had trouble finding his way, while Helman is an immensely able, naturally confident person who connects easily with people. Their backgrounds couldn't be more different, with Baker being highly educated and Helman a gifted dropout from college. Joe's first experience with art happened in 1949 when his grade school class was taken to the St. Louis Art Museum to see the exhibition "Masterpieces from the Berlin Museums" that the US Army circulated to thirteen American museums before returning the works to Germany; it included major paintings by Titian, Rembrandt, Hals, Friedrich, and Picasso. Helman says that at twelve, his eyes were opened, and that he was deeply moved to learn that these great pictures had survived while so many people had not. Thus, the war and the Holocaust were factors for Joe, though not in the immediate way they were for Monroe Price, whom I discuss next.

After leaving college, Joe went to work for a real estate developer in St. Louis and quickly became its leading salesperson; he then went out on his own, developing property, and early on demonstrated impressive entrepreneurial skills. Then, in 1962, he saw an article about Jasper Johns in a magazine. Joe immediately responded to the images and wanted one of the paintings for himself. There is no explaining why Johns's unusual imagery appealed to this aspiring collector. Helman went to a local frame shop, then a nearby dealer, but neither had a Johns. Someone suggested that he call the St. Louis Museum; he did so, and by a lucky stroke reached Emily Rauh, a young curator who a decade later would marry the widower Joseph Pulitzer Jr.; she directed him to several New York dealers, including André Emmerich, Betty Parsons, Sidney Janis, and Leo Castelli.[33] On his next trip to the city, early in 1963, he went to each. At Castelli's he met with Leo's right-hand man Ivan Karp, who showed him the only Johns painting in the gallery, *Painting with Ruler and "Gray"* of 1960. It had just come back from the painter's solo exhibition at Ileana Sonnabend's new gallery in Paris, where it had gone unsold. Johns was hardly unknown at this point, his first exhibition at Castelli having been followed up by a successful second one in February 1960. His work had already been seen across the US and Europe; it had been widely written about and was being actively collected. But Helman bought it for $7,000 and quickly paid; Johns's prices were already soaring. This was Helman's first work of art, and the start of an amazing career as a collector, dealer, theorizer, curator, and sometime philanthropist.

The story of Leo Castelli's discovery of Johns and Rauschenberg in 1958, and his subsequent showing of Warhol, Lichtenstein, and the other Pop masters, is well known. His support for these artists and his exhibitions of their work, starting with Johns in 1958, made him a singular creator of a new canon. There were no middlemen; Leo recognized the special qualities of unfamiliar work by a group of young, unknown artists, and showed it; the rest is history. But one wonders, how did Castelli arrive at the point where he could immediately recognize the quality of Johns's work and that of Jasper's friend Robert Rauschenberg as well? Leo had been a friend of artists and critics in New York for years; he was part of the ongoing conversations about avant-garde painting at The Club, a group made up mostly of Abstract Expressionist painters founded in 1949, and he had organized the now-famous Ninth Street Exhibition in 1951. Discussing his own development, Leo said, "My greatest teacher was the Collection of the Museum of Modern Art," and he added, "Peggy Guggenheim was an important influence. It was in her living room that I saw my first Jackson Pollock.[34] By 1957, he was fully prepared and highly ambitious, but he wasn't yet a tastemaker; he was waiting for an epiphany, which happened at Jasper Johns's studio. There's no question that Leo was a genius, but finding great artists wasn't easy, even for him. In his 1958–59 season, for example, the year after he had given Johns and Rauschenberg their initial exhibitions, he presented one-artist shows of the work of Angelo Savelli, Esteban Vicente, Nassos Daphnis, Salvatore Scarpitta, Gabriel Kohn, and Jon Schueler, all of whom did creditable work, but whose names are known today only to specialists. The skilled dealer can do a lot, but he cannot discover greatness where it doesn't exist.

The mystery of collectors is why certain works strike them so powerfully that they must own them. *Painting with Ruler and "Gray"* was a difficult work by any standard, with its painted sections and its wooden attachments on the surface. It's a work that looks back to Abstract Expressionism as well as to Duchamp and Dada while demonstrating Johns's own breakthrough approach in what critics would later call his "device" pictures. Joe Helman had read some contemporary art history by this point, but he could not have thought his way to this purchase. Too much learning is often more of a handicap than a benefit to collectors, because the decision to buy is essentially an emotional act. For Joe as a new collector to acquire the Johns required extraordinary visual instincts on his part, a purely visceral reaction to the work.

Though Helman doesn't own the work today, Jasper Johns remains at the heart of his thinking. For him the key to Jasper is his *White Flag* (fig. 52) and related pictures of 1955. Their importance is simple but

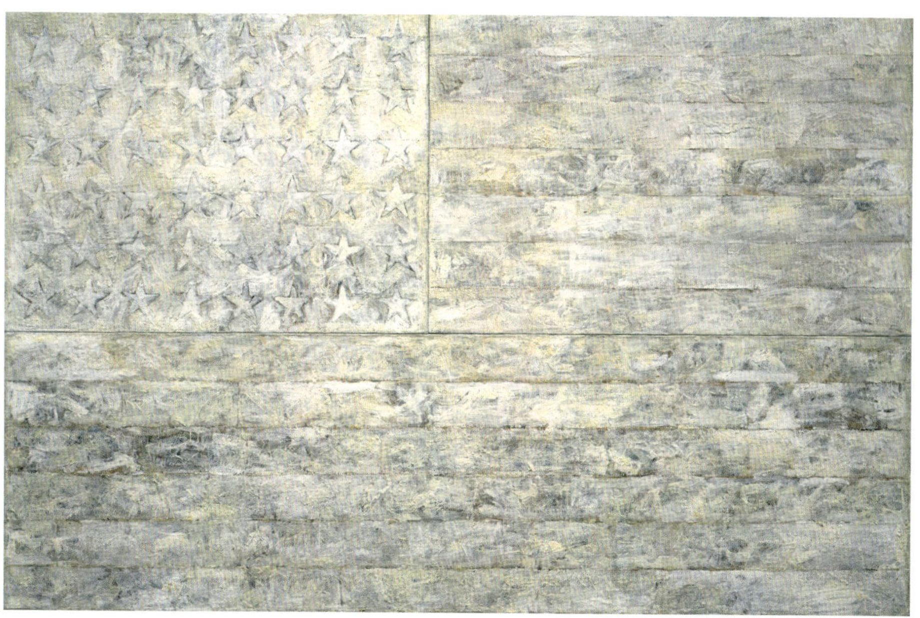

Fig. 52. **JASPER JOHNS**,
White Flag, encaustic, oil, newsprint, and charcoal on canvas, 1955.
Metropolitan Museum of Art.

profound; as Helman puts it, "he's the first guy using iconic American imagery to make iconic American painting." Joe believes that Jasper's breakthrough "changed the world, and led to Roy doing these flat images, to Andy doing photographs, to Judd, Serra, and Kelly."[35] Joe speaks eloquently about how Johns and the others eliminated figure and ground: Flags and targets were used not as images but rather as neutral templates marking out the work. Helman opines that the extraordinary period of American preeminence in art was a short one, running from the end of the Second World War to Vietnam. What he has sought as a collector are the key, transformative works from this brief golden age, barely two decades in length, but one that saw the maturation of two distinct styles, Abstract Expressionism and then early Pop Art. For Joe Helman, these works are not decoration, investment opportunities, or the subject of sales talk, but markers of important moments in the great decade; as he said, "I think the artists who came of age during that period changed America and the world's culture."[36]

Parenthetically, long before knowing Joe Helman, I also came to feel that *White Flag* was one of the central paintings of the era. I will never forget Jasper Johns calling us at Yale in 1972 to ask we would like to borrow the painting. Alan Shestack and I drove to New York to pick it up at Jasper's storage area in a former bank building in the Bowery, and I still remember the experience of seeing so many of his works carefully stored there, with the smallest objects and drawings secured in the bank vault itself. We hoped he might eventually give us the picture, but Jasper had other plans.[37]

After his initial purchase, Helman returned to his profitable work as a real estate developer but spent his evenings reading about contemporary art at the library in Steinberg Hall at Washington University in St. Louis. He became familiar with the writings of Leo Steinberg, Michael Fried, Barbara Rose, Clement Greenberg, and other critical voices in the leading journals, including *Art International, Artforum,* and *Art in America.* He became highly articulate in his theoretical analyses of the advanced art he loved. And he continued to collect. He quickly understood Roy Lichtenstein's importance, and bought *Baseball Player,* 1963, from the painter's second show at Leo's.

In 1968, Helman decided to become a dealer, and opened a gallery in St. Louis. For his first exhibition, he mounted a group show of Roy Lichtenstein, Andy Warhol, Jasper Johns, and Josef Albers, three of Leo's key artists plus Albers as an older master whose abstract paintings would suggest the roots of the younger painters. He followed this with a one-person exhibition of Richard Serra's work. Serra became a favorite; Joe showed him for years and they became close personally. The Helman Gallery became a regional outpost of the Castelli Gallery, one of many in the US and Europe that Annie Cohen-Solal describes in her book on Castelli, though Joe also had good relations with other galleries and their artists.[38] From the start, his champion in St. Louis was Emily Rauh Pulitzer, who gave him, he says, "museum credibility."[39] Joseph Pulitzer Jr. (1913–1993) became his major client. Pulitzer was already a brilliant collector; as a Harvard senior in 1936 he had bought a fine Modigliani and the stunning early Picasso *Woman in Yellow*, before going on to superb works by Cézanne, Monet, Miro, Brancusi, Rothko, and Pollock.[40] Rauh and Helman introduced Pulitzer to a new generation of modernists, in particular to the work of Donald Judd and Richard Serra, resulting in his commissioning Serra's *Topographical Sculpture* (two big steel boxes, one inside the other) for his lawn. Because the lawn wasn't level, Helman brought in his topographical engineer to help ascertain the levels and relationships of the forms. Much the same happened when Pulitzer commissioned Serra to make his *Field Piece*, looking like a half-buried wall, for the property a year later.[41] Helman also sold Pulitzer numerous works by Lichtenstein, Judd, Warhol, and especially Ellsworth Kelly, but he was unable to convince him of Jasper Johns; according to Helman, Pulitzer thought Johns was overpriced, but I wonder also whether Johns's pictures lacked the kind of crispness that he favored.[42] In the process, Helman brought modernism to St. Louis. Being a curator at heart, he organized two superb exhibitions for Washington University, "Color Field: Pollock to the Present," and "Then and Now," which included Serra, Richard Tuttle, Bruce Nauman, and Alan Saret.

Helman took on the canon that Castelli had established, a who's who of Pop Art, and understood its importance and its ramifications. Today

Warhol, Lichtenstein, and the others are seen as central players in the international canon of modern art; this seems inevitable in hindsight, but was far from a given at the time. There were dozens of critics and a hundred rival galleries with ideas of their own. Bettors might well have placed their money on the Color Field painters, whose work was championed by Clement Greenberg, the most admired American critic of the day, and on his young follower Michael Fried. Greenberg had been right on Pollock, why shouldn't he be on the next generation? Boston, for example, had rejected the Castelli artists; curator Ken Moffett and the leading collectors there believed that a different group of young painters were the best of their time. Following Greenberg and Fried, they scorned the "Neo-Dada" of Johns, Rauschenberg, and the others and instead saw Kenneth Noland, Morris Louis, and Jules Olitski, the practitioners of painted "flatness" as defined by Greenberg, as the heirs to Pollock. When I was at graduate school at Harvard, my fellow student Michael Fried in 1965 organized an exhibition of Noland, Olitski, and Frank Stella, and argued brilliantly in his catalogue essay for their preeminence.[43]

After a few successful years in St. Louis, Helman moved his family to Rome for two years, having handed over his gallery to his friend Ronald Greenberg. He came back for the Sotheby's sale of the Robert Scull collection in October 1973, aiming to buy Jasper Johns's *Ale Cans*, but failed due to a mix-up with another bidder. The taxi king Scull had been Castelli's best customer in the early years, particularly for Johns and Rauschenberg, but he also had superb paintings by de Kooning, Kline, and Barnett Newman purchased from other galleries. Looking through the sale catalogue gives one pause for thought. For example, there are two fine works by Lucas Samaras, an artist I have always admired, but who has never quite made it to the top rank. Helman and I discussed this, and Joe said, "Just think of what the situation would be if Leo had taken him on!"[44] The thought startled me, then I realized he was right: It's a two-way street, the artists make the dealer, but the dealer also makes the artists. In Leo's hands, Samaras, with all his ability and originality, would very likely be considered a major figure today.

In 1974 Joe Helman and West coast dealer Irving Blum decided to open a gallery together in New York, and Blum/Helman was born. Blum is an energetic art lover whose taste coincided well with Helman's, both of them being close to Castelli. Blum had been at it longer than Helman, having operated the Ferus Gallery in Los Angeles where he exhibited Ed Kienholz, a creator of gritty assemblages, and Joseph Cornell, the maker of extraordinary, small Surrealist boxes, among others.[45] In 1962 he won a place in history by showing Andy Warhol's thirty-two paintings of Campbell's Soup cans. He and Helman's first exhibition together was devoted to Richard Serra's work. Helman had first seen Serra's pieces at Richard Bellamy's gallery in 1967, and he persuaded Leo to take him on, while bearing half the cost of his stipend himself. One wonders, could Leo have taken on a Black artist like Norman Lewis or Martin Puryear? Might history have been changed? Blum/Helman exhibited Serra frequently, as they did Ellsworth Kelly (Joe says that he showed his work sixteen times over the years, including group shows) and Andy Warhol, along with Claes Oldenburg, Bruce Nauman, Roy Lichtenstein, and occasionally Robert Rauschenberg. These were Leo's artists; some, like Kelly, Helman could exhibit frequently, as Leo didn't pay much attention to them, and by the eighties, Blum/Helman was representing both Kelly and Serra. The gallery also gave exhibitions to a wide variety of others, including Richard Tuttle, Alan Saret, Neil Jenney, Robert Moskowitz, Francesco Clemente, José María Sicilia, Donald Sultan, sculptor Bryan Hunt, ceramist Andrew Lord, and occasionally photographer Peter Beard. The partners agreed on the promise of the younger artists like Lord, Sultan, and Hunt; they promoted them energetically, and the artists sold well at their regular exhibitions even if posterity has been less kind.

Helman understood from early on that if he was right about the art, the market would keep rising and he could get both the greatest pleasure and the greatest financial reward by keeping some of the key works. Over the ensuing years, as a seminal piece would come along, he would add it to his collection. He went after *Four Marilyns* by Warhol (fig. 53) in 1988 and got it at auction for $495,000, a very high price at the time; but he was prescient, as other works in this series of five have sold for nearly $40 million in recent years. In 1984 his regular client Si Newhouse came to the gallery to tell him that he'd bought

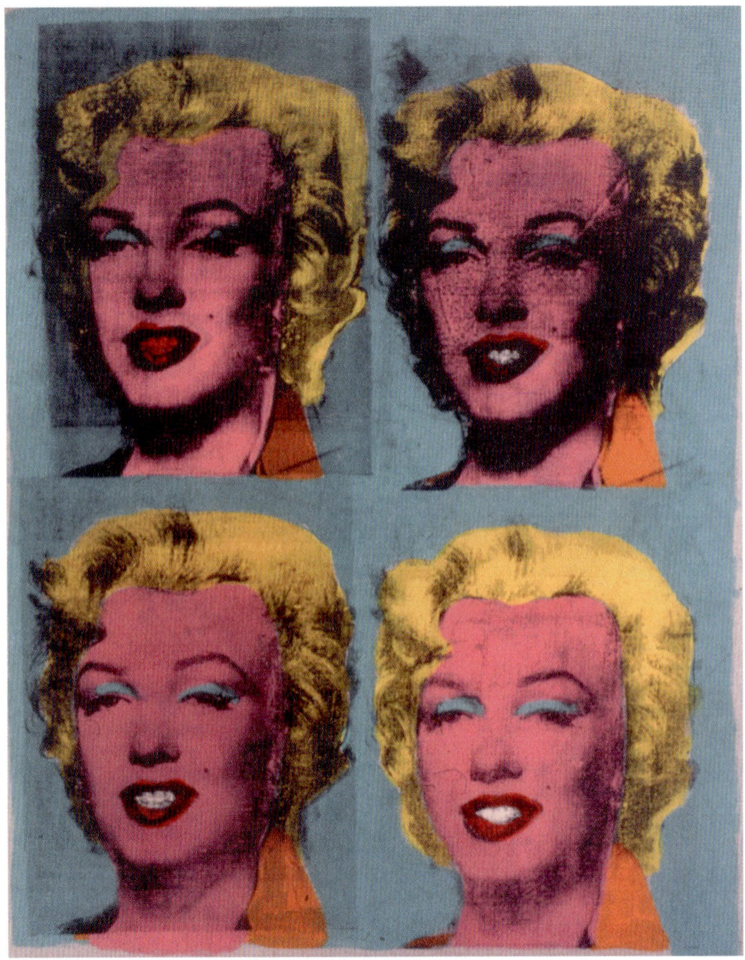

Fig. 53. **ANDY WARHOL,**
Four Marilyns, oil on canvas, 1962. Helman Collection.

Lichtenstein's *Aloha* (fig. 54) for $1 million from Emily (Mrs. Burton) Tremaine, but felt that he had paid too much and regretted it. Joe said he'd take it off his hands at his cost, and he bought it. It remains one of Joe's great favorites, having been a star of Leo's second show of the painter's work; Joe believes it exemplifies the iconic Americanness of the painter's work with its sexy subject painted in red, white, and blue to honor Hawaii's recent admittance to the Union.

It's a pleasure to visit Joe's New York apartment; for me it's a chapel of modernism. I love museums, but nothing equals the joy of seeing great art in someone's home. In the living room, one sits facing the classic Warhol over the mantel, with great Lichtensteins on either side. On the far left, on the floor, is a giant soft canvas Oldenburg of raisin bread that he got years ago from Janis. It's the size of a sofa, and for Joe, it recalls *Portrait of Madame Récamier* by Jacques-Louis David. To the right is a brightly painted plaster ice cream sandwich by Oldenburg, from the exhibition of similar work in 1961 at "The Store," which Helman regards as the founding moment of the new art, and one finds numerous Oldenburg watercolors around the apartment. Facing the

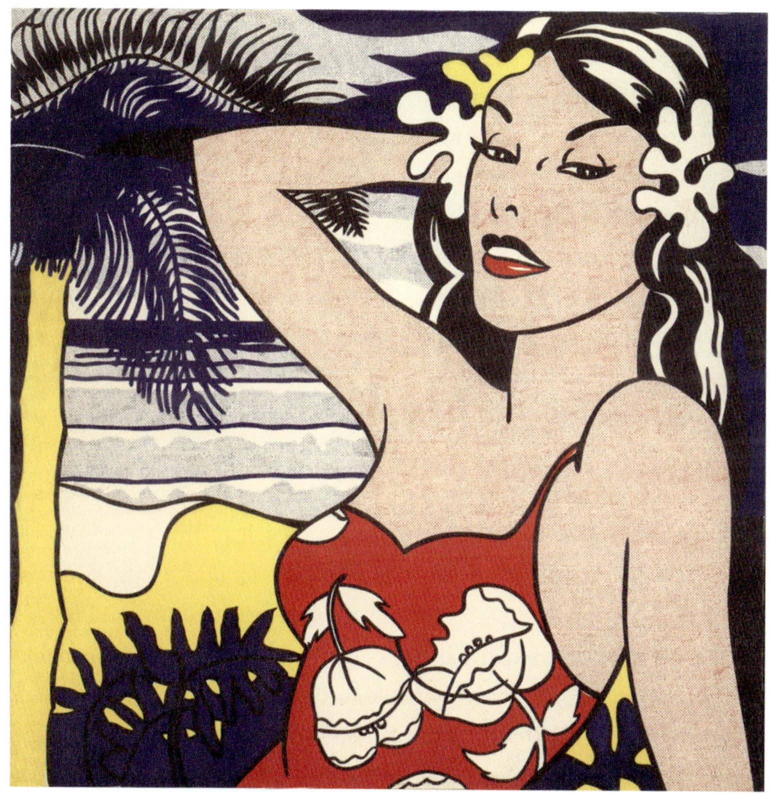

Fig. 54. ROY LICHTENSTEIN,
Aloha, oil on canvas, 1962. Helman Collection.

fireplace is an elegant, simple Ellsworth Kelly of two adjoining rectangles, one in red, the other black, a perfect example of Joe's taste for rigor and simplicity. In the dining room one sees a Rauschenberg of about 1987 from his little-known *Stop Sign Glut* series; it appears to me the best of this group. On the left is another Lichtenstein, *Overturned Wine Glass with Peeled Lemon* of 1972, a deceptively brilliant work. Opposite it is Ellsworth Kelly at his simplest and most profound, painting rectangles of red and white. In the corner stands a tall pipe leaning against a large square piece of lead on the wall; this is Joe's favorite kind of work, as it's a seminal piece by Richard Serra from 1968, and it's one where Joe himself played a key role in its making. Serra was just starting to make "prop" pieces of lead, but because lead disintegrates, they were falling down. Joe found the St. Joseph Lead Co. in Pittsburgh, and they made Serra four flat pieces of lead forty-eight inches square with an antimony alloy to make it firmer. Serra used them to make four works, of which Joe's is the first; others went to Harvard, MoMA, and the Cleveland Museum. After this, he switched to steel. Joe also has two superb works by Donald Judd, who ranks among his favorite artists. One is a breakthrough "specific object" of 1963, a large rectangular plywood box painted green, with a yellow pipe sliced in half running through it lengthwise. It is solid and silent, a mystery to behold, a work that proclaims the artist's departure from expressionism. The other Judd, made a few years later, seems its opposite: a horizontal wall piece made of brass and aluminum painted red, inexplicably elegant in its colorful simplicity.

One wonders, how about Jasper Johns? I kept thinking, he's the key to all of this, there must be one in the collection. But there isn't. Joe retained his first acquisition—*Painting with Ruler and "Gray"*—until he divorced and moved to New York in 1974 to open Blum/Helman. He tells me he needed the funds, but could have found them elsewhere; he sold his treasure in a way to prove to himself that he was now a real dealer. Non-collectors will never understand this, but there's pain in the life of every collector, no matter how gifted. Every collector I know has lasting regrets about the one they didn't reach for, or the one they had and lost. Joe handled a number of great paintings by Johns in later years, including *False Start, Jubilee,* and *Target,* but by then the prices were out of reach. He tried to reacquire *Painting with Ruler and "Gray"* but was unable to. And being highly disciplined, he hasn't compromised on a lesser example.

Joe is a confident entrepreneur who has an expansive vision of his role in the art world; he doesn't hesitate to take on big projects. After the death of the Fascist dictator Franco in 1975, Spain slowly began to open up to democracy and to Western culture. Through his friendship with the architect José Luis Sert, Joe became familiar with Spain and he undertook two important projects aiming to bring modern art to that country. First, in 1983 in collaboration with Carmen Gimenez (who came to the Guggenheim Museum in New York as a curator in the early nineties) Helman organized "Tendencies in New York," a show at the Palacio de Velázquez in Madrid that introduced the Spanish audience to contemporary American art; it included some of the most highly regarded younger painters of the day, including Donald Sultan, Susan Rothenberg, Julian Schnabel, David Salle, Keith Haring, Eric Fischl, and Jean-Michel Basquiat. It was an important event for Spain and led directly to the founding of the Reina Sofía as Madrid's museum of modern art.

In the early nineties came an even bolder project, as Joe Helman worked with the important Spanish sculptor Xavier Corberó (1935–2017) to bring a group of monumental American sculptures to Barcelona. That city, looking to the Olympics it would host in 1992, committed major funding to renewing its urban spaces. Corberó persuaded the city to include a public art program, and acquired monumental pieces by the Spanish sculptors Eduardo Chillida, Antoni Tàpies, and Juan Miró for its parks. Corberó enlisted Helman in the project, and Joe persuaded some of the major American artists to design massive pieces for the city and to make gifts of them. The project was an amazing success, and Barcelona now boasts an unequaled group of monumental American sculptures.[46] Roy Lichtenstein's *The Head of Barcelona,* a colorful, abstracted woman's head looking windblown, stands high above the Port Vell waterfront, and Claes Oldenburg's *Matches,* a giant matchbook cover with yellow matches sticking up, some 68 feet tall, is in Vall d'Hebron. More earthbound are Beverly Pepper's amazing *Fallen Sky* and Richard Serra's *Wall,* two curving white walls 170 feet in length on the Plaça de la Palmera de Sant Martí. Robert Hughes lavished praise on the former, writing: "Beverly Pepper got a whole park adjacent to the long-disused Estació del Nord and turned it into a huge earthwork around which children play; their favorite part of it is *Fallen Sky,* a whaleback hill rising from the green turf, sheathed in slabs of cobalt and turquoise ceramic." Bryan Hunt executed a bronze, *Rites of Spring,* that is sensitively installed among a series of arched columns that survive from an industrial building, while another of Joe's favorites, Ellsworth Kelly, contributed two graceful *Totem* pieces to a small park in Barcelona. Everything was in place in time for the summer Olympics. There are very few curators or collectors anywhere who have made such a telling contribution to the life of a city.[47]

A third, very different, collector of contemporary art is Monroe Price, whom I have known since 1958, when we found ourselves in the same honors seminar at Yale, studying Politics and Economics. Monroe's background is very different than mine: When he was three months old and living with his parents in Vienna, his father was arrested and beaten on Kristallnacht, when the Holocaust began in force. A few months later, the family was able to procure the necessary papers, and emigrated to the United States. Their way of life was destroyed, their home, their savings, and all but a handful of belongings gone; many family members were murdered at Auschwitz. His father, who had managed the family weaving plants, first got a job in Macon, Georgia, in the cotton business, then moved the family to Cincinnati, where Monroe attended the excellent Walnut Hills High School. The principal of that school recognized Monroe's promise; fortunately his brother headed admissions at Yale, and so Monroe was directed there, and was awarded a full scholarship.

After brilliant careers at Yale and the Yale Law School, and following stints clerking for Justice Potter Stewart and working for the Warren Commission, Monroe taught at the UCLA School of Law and began to specialize in American Indian law. He founded California Indian Legal Services and in 1973 published *Law and the American Indian,* a text that served for years as the standard reference in the field. He decided not to collect Native American art, which he was drawn to, because he didn't want to risk having the tribes misunderstand his motives for assisting them. Monroe tells me that in 1964–65, he began collecting art in Paris where his talented art historian wife Aimée Brown Price was on a Fulbright. Here he met a number of future friends, including the painter/musician Art Rosenbaum (1938–2022), whose work he began collecting. He started going to the flea markets and auctions, looking for things that moved him and that he could afford, and then followed the same pattern in every city that he visited or lived in; there were many, due to his being in high demand around the world as a lecturer on human rights and media law. Though his work led him to Asia, Africa, and Mexico, his focus as a collector was always on the art of central Europe, where his roots lay. The collection is his, but Aimée has been his key support, and one finds in their home some fascinating works by her friends and former students.

When I first visited the Prices I encountered a cavernous, dark apartment whose every wall and every surface were cluttered with paintings, drawings, and strange objects. I looked around, seeking something familiar, a place to start the conversation, but there was nothing that I recognized. The images I encountered were powerful ones; they were moving and expressive. Monroe buys works that affect him emotionally, ones that reflect his family's displacement from Vienna. He carries the experience of irredeemable loss along with an instinctive understanding that inanimate objects can embody one's deepest feelings. He says that at each new home his father would hang a picture of "his most respected and honored antecedent," Gabriel Engelsmann, chief rabbi of Rechnitz, as well as portraits of his father and grandmother, while his mother put up photos of her family as well as drawings and paintings of nearby areas that they had known. Monroe's parents also possessed a vitrine that held small silver objects, porcelain figurines, and tiny teacups, with the whole functioning like a sacred memorial to the past.[48]

While the pursuit of art was central to the lives of Richard Baker and Joe Helman, collecting for Monroe is a byproduct of his work. What matters most to him are his activities as a teacher, scholar, and leader in the international effort to measure propaganda, to preserve free speech, and to examine the role of newspapers, television, and the internet in dispensing information and disinformation. Monroe's collection, gathered in cities from Mexico City to Moscow, is the product of his after-hours rummaging through out of the way galleries and flea markets. Seeing Helman's collection, I was awestruck to see so many outstanding works by legendary artists. Seeing Price's, by contrast, I felt humbled by my ignorance, and by the hours it took me to grasp the meaning of the collection. After recovering from the shock of seeing so much unfamiliar

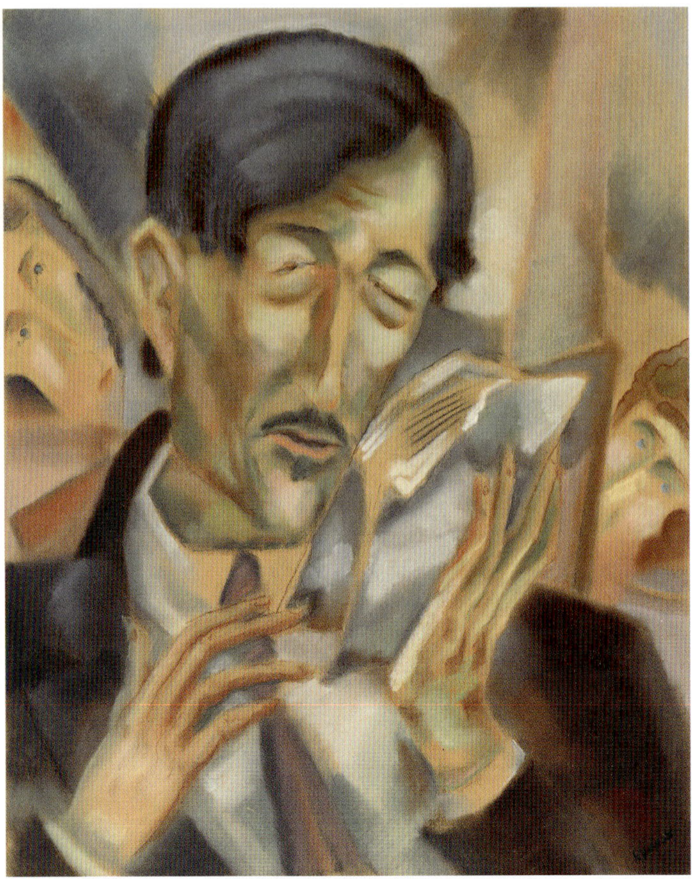

Fig. 55. **PETER KRASNOW,**
Sadakichi Hartmann, pastel on paper, 1929.
Smithsonian, National Portrait Gallery.

art, I began to look, piece by piece. There was a big oil by the Los Angeles painter Peter Krasnow of a colorful reclining figure, as well as a sculpture of a tree and a painted cabinet by him. The Prices recently gave to the National Portrait Gallery their excellent pastel portrait of the critic Sadakichi Hartmann, whose work I discuss in chapter 2 (fig. 55). I also saw a bright cartoonlike collage by Danny Elfman, several fabulous, colorful paintings by the Mexican American artist Carlos Almaraz (fig. 56); a cartoonlike mural by Art Rosenbaum.

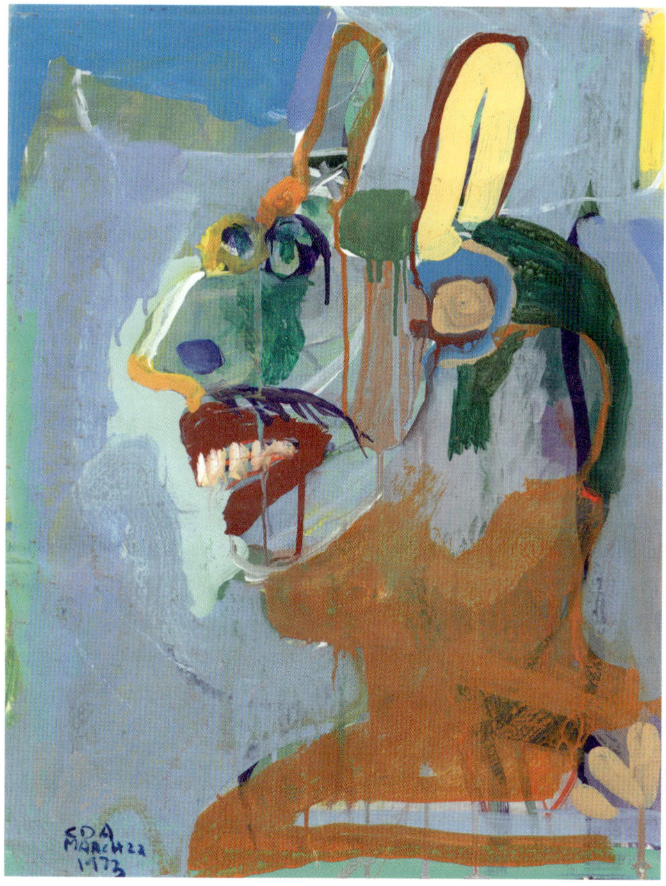

Fig. 56. **CARLOS ALMARAZ,**
Man in a Mask (Rabbit Ears) (Self-Portrait), acrylic on paper, ca. 1974.
Smithsonian, National Portrait Gallery.

Some of the pictures are traditional in style and subject, such as the oil by the German Heinrich Kley of industrial scaffolding, which reminds one of Leger's work, while others are shockingly direct like the Stephen Ettinger painting of amputees or the Boardman Robinson satirical drawing titled *Send Out More of Those $2 a Day N——s*. There are dozens of prints and drawings by the Ukrainian Vasily Kasiyan and by Renata Ginsburg Wichmann, and strongly colored expressionist oils by the Hungarian Lajos Sváby. I was moved by the set of twenty colored woodcuts by the Swiss artist Edmond Bille entitled *Une danse macabre*, each one with its own special take on cruelty and death as administered by the troops. All these artists were known and well regarded in their home countries in their day, though most of their names are unfamiliar today. There are men and women artists, posters (including one devoted to Julius and Ethel Rosenberg on the eve of their executions), there is a big standing hair dryer with many wires that looks like a new form of torture machine or a Tinguely, and one finds various kinds of once-useful industrial objects that have been turned into sculptures. There's a whole collection of antique toasters. Many of the artists are Jewish, and many are not. One of Monroe's favorite artist friends is the English painter Francis Hoyland (b. 1930), whose large book of poster-paint drawings, a little reminiscent of Edward Hopper, illustrate the life of Christ. At the bottom of a drawer, I found a print by George Bellows, and thought, a familiar name at last.

If you look into the drawers in Price's pantry, you find dozens of old photo albums, all with page after page of snapshots of middle-class European families traveling, honeymooning, or sightseeing in capital cities or popular resorts. They are images of ordinary life in the thirties, with people dressed up and trying to smile for the camera, affectionate, self-conscious couples, old folks and young, stolid, good people all. Each album is different, depending on the family's itinerary, pretentiousness, or ability with the camera. Each photo speaks to lives, plans, hopefulness, but each speaks unmistakably about death as well, as Susan Sontag tells us such photos must, even without our knowledge that disaster was just over the horizon for many of these families.[49] These albums are heartbreaking stand-ins for all the lost photos and lost memories of Monroe's own family, for his parents and grandparents, aunts and uncles, and cousins, for the peaceful lives they led in Vienna and for the lives they would have kept on living, had history allowed.

The paintings and drawings, the "sculpture" and the photos, all speak to a lost world in their styles and in their manner of protesting the horror of ongoing events. Stylistically, many are examples of international Depression–era realism, with strong elements of political satire and with occasional bits of Dada thrown in. Monroe has little interest in the avant-garde, nor in abstraction or theory or conceptual art: What concerns him is the story and the strength of the image. His approach is a forerunner of today's art that speaks to morality and justice, and does so through realism. Price buys what he can afford, strictly by instinct, without being influenced by reading about art, or by what others are acquiring, or by the slightest interest in investment. His collection deserves preservation, not for its financial value or the glory of the collector but rather to preserve the memory of a painful era and the ability of numerous little-known painters and printmakers to record it.

---

[1] Serge Guilbaut, "Collecting Bohemia in Post–World War II New York: The Richard Brown Baker Story," in *Get There First, Decide Promptly: The Richard Brown Baker Collection of Postwar Art,* ed. Jennifer Farrell (Yale University Art Gallery, 2011), 71.

[2] Richard Brown Baker, "Richard Brown Baker," in *Two Modern Collectors: Susan Morse Hilles, Richard Brown Baker,* ed. Yale University Art Gallery (Yale University Art Gallery, 1963), 38.

[3] Richard Brown Baker, Journal, Richard Brown Baker Papers, Yale University Archives.

[4] Yale University, *25th Reunion Report, Class of 1935* (Yale University, 1960).

[5] Richard Brown Baker, "Notes on the Formation of My Collection," *Art International,* September 1961, 44.

[6] Baker, Journal, March 1956, box 20, Richard Brown Baker Papers.

[7] Baker, Journal, September 1956, box 23, Richard Brown Baker Papers.

[8] Guilbaut, "Collecting Bohemia," 68.

[9] Farrell, *Get There First,* 184.

[10] Thomas Crow, "The Onset of the 1960s in the Collecting Life of Richard Brown Baker: 'Without the Taking of Risks, a Great Collection is Not Formed,'" in Farrell, *Get There First,* 91.

[11] Baker, Journal, December 3, 1987, box 48, Richard Brown Baker Papers.
[12] Farrell, *Get There First*, 27.
[13] Rhode Island School of Design, *A Collection in the Making, Lent by Richard Brown Baker* (Rhode Island School of Design, 1959).
[14] Farrell, *Get There First*, 34.
[15] Baker, Journal, December 1961, box 23, Richard Brown Baker Papers.
[16] Baker, Journal, December 2, 1974, box 41, Richard Brown Baker Papers.
[17] Farrell, *Get There First*.
[18] See for example his journal entry in January 1955, "I think all gentleness and delicacy to be crushed (though not exterminated) in this Megalopolis of liquor, lust, and rush." Baker, Journal, January 1955, box 23, Richard Brown Baker Papers.
[19] Robert Storrs, "A Man About Town," in Farrell, *Get There First*, 105.
[20] Storrs, 112.
[21] Andrés Garcés, Yale University Art Gallery, email to the author, February 15, 2023.
[22] Baker's agreement with Yale allows for some deaccessioning, but to date nothing has been sold.
[23] Yale University, *25th Reunion Report, Class of 1935*, 14.
[24] Edmund White, *The Beautiful Room Is Empty*, as quoted in Neil Campbell and Alasdair Kean, *American Cultural Studies: An Introduction to American Culture* (Routledge, 2015), 250.
[25] Baker, Journal, January 1955.
[26] Baker, Journal, May 2, 1975, box 41, Richard Brown Baker Papers.
[27] Baker, Journal, May 2, 1975.
[28] Baker, Journal, 1980, box 41, Richard Brown Baker Papers.
[29] Baker, Journal, May 1985, box 41, Richard Brown Baker Papers.
[30] Crow, "The Onset of the 1960s," 88.
[31] Arthur C. Inman, *The Inman Diary: A Public and Private Confession*, ed. Daniel Aaron (Harvard University Press, 1985).
[32] Baker, Journal, December 3, 1987, box 48, Richard Brown Baker Papers.
[33] Joe Helman, conversation with the author, April 24, 2022. Marjorie B. Cohn, in *Classic Modern: The Art Worlds of Joseph Pulitzer Jr.* (Yale University Press, 2012), tells this differently.
[34] Ann Hindry, *Claude Berri Rencontre Meets Leo Castelli* (Renn, 1990), 82.
[35] Helman, conversation with the author , November 2, 2022.
[36] Helman, conversation with the author , November 2, 2022.
[37] Johns sold the painting to the Met in 1998 for an enormous amount.
[38] Annie Cohen-Solal, *Leo & His Circle: The Life of Leo Castelli* (Knopf, 2010).
[39] Helman, conversation with the author, February 16, 2024.
[40] Cohn, *Classic Modern*.
[41] Cohn, 286–95.
[42] Helman, conversation with the author, February 16, 2024.
[43] Michael Fried et al., *Three American Painters* (Harvard University, Fogg Art Museum, 1965).

[44] Helman, conversation with the author.

[45] Laura De Coppet and Alan Jones, "Irving Blum," in *The Art Dealers: The Powers Behind the Scene Tell How the Art World Really Works* (Clarkson N. Potter, 1984), 150–59.

[46] See Kevin Booth, *A Guide to Free Art in Barcelona* (Poble Sec Books, 2016).

[47] See Colman Andrews, "Traveling in Style: The Best Outdoor Show in Europe," *Los Angeles Times*, March 1, 1992; Robert Hughes, *Barcelona* (Vintage Books, 1992), 42.

[48] See Monroe Price, *Objects of Remembrance: A Memoir of American Opportunities and Viennese Dreams* (Central European University Press, 2009).

[49] See Susan Sontag, *On Photography* (Farrar, Straus and Giroux, 1977).

15

Alice Walton, Educator and Museum-Builder

We needed to learn how to unlearn the canon.

—MINDY BESAW, Crystal Bridges curator, 2022

Everybody deserves access to art. Art is hope, it's opportunity, it's education, it's all of the things we all want.

—ALICE WALTON

THE LAST hurrah for the traditional canon of nineteenth- and early-twentieth-century painters began in 2005 when the Walmart heiress Alice Walton (fig. 57) announced her plans to establish a new museum of American art in Bentonville, Arkansas. Walton was following in the footsteps of Isabella Stewart Gardner, Gertrude Vanderbilt Whitney, Abby Aldrich Rockefeller, Lillie Bliss, Mary Quinn Sullivan, Electra Havemeyer Webb, and Peggy Guggenheim, American women who founded important museums before her. She spent over $1 billion building it, then at least the same amount filling it with as much canonical art as could be found. Her aim was to bring important art to Northwest Arkansas and to attract a large free audience, and she succeeded in both. The museum opened

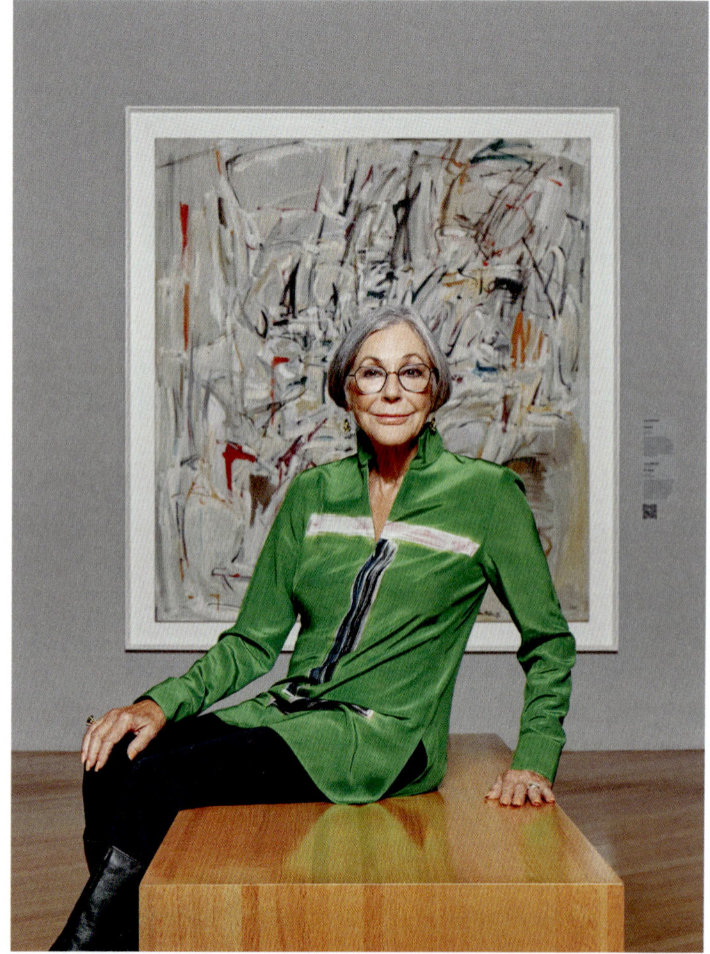

Fig. 57. ADAM AMENGUAL,
Alice Walton at Crystal Bridges, photograph, 2021.

on November 11, 2011, and since then has had over twelve million visitors. Advised by the former National Gallery curator John Wilmerding aided by a rotating cast of other experts, Walton did her best to emulate the great museum collections of the Northeast, with the result that Crystal Bridges now stands in the top fifteen or twenty of all museum holdings of American art. It lacks the masterworks and depth to equal the collections at the National Gallery, the Met, Boston, Philadelphia, and a few others, but its ambitious programs and its deep resources suggest that it will play an important role in the field in years to come.[1] The building designed by Moshe Safdie is superb and in my view ranks among the best museum architecture of the era.

From the moment of entry, the visitor enjoys a different experience than at any other museum. You see the sign "Crystal Bridges," then drive down a picturesque wooded road to reach the museum's unpretentious entrance, a curving one-story concrete structure. Nothing could be more unlike the traditional museum temple that one finds at the Met, the Getty, and Philadelphia. The old museums aimed to awe with their grandeur, while this one exudes friendliness from the start, with staff members directing visitors to the elevators. Surprisingly, these take visitors down, not up to the gallery level. Visitors emerge into a large gathering space that opens to a shop, galleries, and a large, sunlit restaurant with lake views on both sides.

Nature and the outdoors play a greater role here than at any other museum I know. Crystal Bridges, guided by landscape architect Scott Eccleston, has made extraordinary use of the land with its trees and meandering streams: Visitors can walk on the four miles of paths, or they can choose the Art Trail or the "Listening Forest," or seek out the canoe made onsite by the Marshall Islander Wa Kuk Wa Jimor. Or best, they can visit the exquisite Bachman–Wilson House by Frank Lloyd Wright, which was brought piece by piece from New Jersey to the museum grounds, where it was carefully rebuilt in a perfect woodland setting. Wright is all about linearity and right angles, Safdie about materials that seem to bend and flow, but the two architects have in common their elegant use of wood and concrete in contrasting tones, their love of water, and the way their buildings nestle into their natural settings. Bringing the Wright house to the grounds of the museum was a brilliant move.

Walton's initial aim was to acquire the best possible works by the major members of the canon as it was defined in Wilmerding's book of 1976, my "New World" exhibition of 1983, and the like. In some cases she succeeded very well while in others the results were mixed, because in many instances works of great quality were simply not available for love or money. And buying by committee is always an imperfect process;

there were simply too many voices crying for attention, and no one just saying yes, we have to have it. Yet overall, the Crystal Bridges collection of paintings before 1950 or so is distinguished; it provides a worthy destination for lovers of American art of that period, or for scholars, students, or the general public. The colonial and federal periods are well represented by the painters who were celebrated by Dunlap and Tuckerman. Crystal Bridges lacks an important history painting, because the ones by Copley, Trumbull, West, and the others were acquired by museums years ago. However, a good effort was made to fill this gap with historic portraits of Washington by Gilbert Stuart and Charles Willson Peale and with imposing full-lengths by Trumbull and Sully, together with a few works like Samuel F. B. Morse's portrait head of Lafayette. Moreover, the outstanding group of six Franks family portraits by New Yorker Gerardus Duyckinck makes up for the absence of late-seventeenth- and early-eighteenth-century New England portraits while also letting visitors know that there were important Jewish families in the colonies. Walton frequently worked with Dara Mitchell at Sotheby's, purchasing, among others, the Constable-Hamilton Portrait of Washington by Gilbert Stuart, being sold by the New York Public Library, for over $8 million in 2005. The Peale family is represented by Charles Willson Peale's full-length Washington, Rembrandt Peale's a self-portrait, and by a still life of middling quality by his brother Raphaelle; one longs for works by other members of this talented group, especially Sarah Miriam and her sisters and cousins. The collection includes a handful of unusual outliers, such as the unique *Indians of Virginia* from about 1675 by James Wooldridge, a new name for me, as well as Edward Marchant's *Thomas Family* and Francis Guy's *Winter Scene in Brooklyn*.

The museum also did well with the Hudson River School, acquiring three paintings by Thomas Cole, good examples by Bierstadt, Cropsey, and Kensett, and an outstanding picture by Frederic Edwin Church, *Home by the Lake*, 1852, acquired when the collection of Jo Ann and Julian Ganz of Los Angeles was broken up. In 2005 Crystal Bridges acquired one of its key works: Asher B. Durand's *Kindred Spirits* of 1849 (fig. 58), arguably the cornerstone painting of the Hudson River School, and a New York treasure since being commissioned by the important early collector Jonathan Sturges. Like Stuart's Constable-Hamilton portrait of Washington, it was sold by the New York Public Library. The Met failed to rise to the occasion and made an inadequate effort to keep the Durand in the city.

In the early years, up to the recession of 2008, Walton and her competitors were buying into the teeth of a booming market, when American pictures were bringing higher prices than ever before. Walton's activities helped drive the market, but she had competition from other immensely wealthy collectors like Bill Gates and John S. Middleton, who were quietly purchasing many important works themselves as described in Chapter 11.

Luckily for Walton, Richard Manoogian was selling off his great collection in these years, and she got some superb paintings from him,

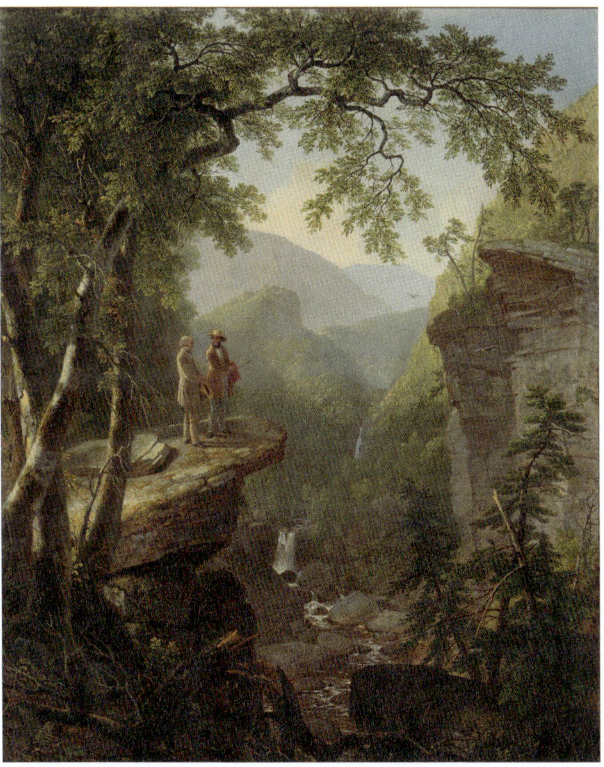

Fig. 58. ASHER B. DURAND,
Kindred Spirits, oil on canvas, 1849. Crystal Bridges.

including Richard Caton Woodville's *War News from Mexico* of 1848 that had long been owned by the National Academy of Design, Arthur F. Tait's masterpiece *A Tight Fix,* and Martin Johnson Heade's sixteen *Gems of Brazil.* She also purchased the twenty-five Heade oil sketches owned by the St. Augustine Historical Society. Walton altogether acquired some forty-four works by Heade, who became her favorite nineteenth-century painter; but strangely, she didn't collect oil sketches by the other masters of the medium, such as Church and Bierstadt.

Outstanding works by some of the most important painters were simply not available. A billion dollars takes you just so far. A raft painting by George Caleb Bingham, a history painting by John Trumbull, a Prout's Neck oil by Winslow Homer, or a rowing scene by Thomas Eakins simply could not be bought as they were already owned by museums or in a few cases by private collectors with great wealth of their own. Crystal Bridges came close to securing what would have been its ultimate masterpiece when it nearly succeeded in buying a half interest (with the National Gallery) in Thomas Eakins's *Gross Clinic* in 2006–7. But Philadelphia rose to the occasion to protect the work, in the way New York failed to do for *Kindred Spirits.* Nonetheless, there are wonderful late-nineteenth-century paintings at Bentonville, along with surprising gaps. Eakins is known in Bentonville only by three fine male portraits, with none of the women that show the painter at his most sensitive. There's a good group of Sargents, led by his *Robert Louis Stevenson,* once owned by John Hay Whitney; Chase, Bunker, and Dewing are also well represented. But surprisingly, women are in short supply, both as artists and sitters. The Cassatt *Reader* is a decent early picture, but there's no Cecelia Beaux and no Lilly Martin Spencer. In addition, the Whistlers and the Homers are weak (though Mrs. Walton has a fine Homer oil from the mid-seventies at home, a promised gift that will someday be at the museum). The Boston School, which can still be purchased, is found here only in Frank Benson's *Summer Day,* one of the less convincing former Horowitz pictures. On the other hand, the still life paintings are good ones. With La Farge, the museum wisely concentrated on his watercolors, including the superb *Peonies in a Breeze,* once in the Middendorf Collection. Three fine mid-century still lifes were bought from William H. Gerdts, and the late-century masters, including Decker, Haberle, and Peto, are well represented. Still, the lack of a Harnett seems surprising. Walton was offered the magnificent *Mr. Hulings' Rack Picture*—perhaps the greatest of all American still lifes, one formerly owned by Alice Kaplan and the Ganzes—but she rejected it. A mistake, in my view, but Walton, like such great museum-builders before her as Isabella Stewart Gardner and Henry Clay Frick, is building her museum with works of art that she responds to personally. She also likes to bargain on price; this has caused her to miss several great works. One of the biggest surprises at Crystal Bridges is the lack of folk paintings and "outsider art." Alice Walton is known for her populist views and her ambition to bring art to the people of the American heartland: Folk painting has an immediate appeal, and outsider art (now called folk art or work of the untrained) was often made by talented Black artists whose forbears were enslaved. This weakness seems strange, especially given the current direction of the museum, where two new wings designed to house two of Walton's great enthusiasms, American craft and the art of Native Americans, were begun in 2021.

With regard to the art of the early twentieth century, Walton responds strongly to the work of George Bellows; she owns four terrific oils and the magnificent big drawing *The Knockout* from the Fraad Collection. For Edward Hopper, there is a fairly good oil and two fine watercolors. Her special favorites, however, appear to be the modernist painters of that era: Georgia O'Keeffe, Arthur Dove, John Marin, and Stuart Davis. Each is represented by nearly a dozen paintings while their contemporary Marsden Hartley is found here in some twenty works spanning the whole of his career, a wonderful, definitive holding. These are painters that Alice feels deeply about. She has described Hartley as "one of my favorite artists," adding, "I love the emotion and the feel and the spirituality of his work."[2] Crystal Bridges in 2007 wisely bought a half interest in the Alfred Stieglitz Collection owned by Fisk University. This brought the new museum about a hundred American and European works on a two-year rotating basis, including several icons of American modernism it could never have found elsewhere, including *Painting No. 1* of 1913 by Hartley, O'Keeffe's *Radiator Building—Night, New York* of 1927, and Charles Demuth's big *Calla Lilies,* also from 1927. This part of the collection is strong, and Crystal Bridges looks especially good if you visit while the Fisk paintings are in residence.

Another of Alice's favorite artists is Andrew Wyeth; her museum lists twelve works on its website, and the two major paintings, *The Intruder,* and *Airborne,* are promised gifts. She purchased *The Intruder* of 1971 at auction in 2007 for $5,753,000, well above its estimate; clearly its desolate mood struck an important chord with her. Another melancholy Wyeth, a depiction of a dead bird lying on a windowsill, is entitled *Chimney Swift.* In an interview, Alice commented, "Andrew Wyeth—the mystery, the loneliness that is expressed . . ."[3] The collection doesn't own an N. C. Wyeth, which one would think would be a natural here, but it does have an appealing Norman Rockwell illustration, *Rosie the Riveter.*

Contemporary art at Crystal Bridges seems something of an afterthought. It would be unfortunate if the audience thought that all her large, colorful paintings really represented anything like a survey of American modernism. The years after 1946, after all, saw American painting throw off its provinciality and become recognized internationally for the first time. The areas of weakness seem not the result of unavailability, but rather of price resistance. Crystal Bridges does own two fine works by Jackson Pollock, an early painting and a classic abstraction on paper, *Number 30 (Birds of Paradise),* from 1949. There is also an excellent de Kooning drawing, but no major paintings by any of the Abstract Expressionists except for Rothko: Great works by these canonical figures are available, but at prices in the hundred-million-dollar range. Mrs. Walton could do that, but chose not to as she developed other priorities. The museum does own representative paintings by Joan Mitchell, Hans Hofmann, Helen Frankenthaler, and Ellsworth Kelly; these are good pictures, though they illustrate only one aspect of modern art. Pop Art is even more modestly represented in Bentonville: One finds a fairly good Rauschenberg, a fine painting on paper by Johns along with a tiny Johns flag, and modest examples by Warhol, Oldenburg, Wesselmann, and Lichtenstein.[4] There is no indication here that art can be challenging or angry, sexual or political; there is little sign of conceptual or installation art, no video work, little minimalism, no earthworks. Their absence makes you realize how rich and varied our recent art has been, and how much of it relates to emotional and societal anger, and to humor as well; such emotions are rarely on view here. One of the most popular works at the museum, judging from the line of visitors waiting for access, is Yayoi Kusama's *Infinity Mirrors Room*. It is an engaging work: One enters the room and is dazzled by the effects of balls of color and light that surround one, but it seems more entertaining than artistic. Some of the best recent art is found on the grounds, where one encounters a colorful Kusama flower strikingly installed by a pond, and a great work by Louise Bourgeois entitled *Maman*, a gigantic forbidding spider. Equally fine is the James Turrell *The Way of Color*, a commissioned construction that allows visitors to experience the light of sunrise or sunset in a special way. Outdoors one also finds several appealing glass pieces by Dale Chihuly, including one called *Turquoise Reeds*, that seem to grow along the banks of a creek.

When I first visited Crystal Bridges in November 2016, the collections were arranged in traditional museum fashion, chronologically, one work at a time, with factual labels, as they had been since the museum opened in 2011. By 2018, just two years later, everything had changed. In a very short time, Alice had quickly recognized the moral imperatives of the new inclusionary, anti-racist canon. Crystal Bridges had the funds and the energy to pivot to a new stance, and it went on another, less costly, buying campaign, hastening to add some of the best Black, Native American, and female artists to the collection so that a different story could be told. An Indigenous Committee was formed to assist in the reinstallation of 2018, and in 2023 a curator of Indigenous art was appointed. Also in 2018, Mindy Besaw at Crystal Bridges was put in charge of the staff committee charged with reinstalling the collection, with the curators aiming to "unlearn the canon."[5] This is the same process that was underway at the Met, the MFA, Philadelphia, and many other museums, though it was rarely expressed so explicitly. If one goes to Crystal Bridges' website today, you learn that the five collection highlights are Francis Guy's *Winter Scene in Brooklyn* of 1820, a big outdoor glass piece by Dale Chihuly, Henry Ossawa Tanner's *Good Shepherd,* 1917, Alma Thomas's *Lunar Rendezvous,* 1969, and *Precious Jewels by the Sea,* painted in 2019 by Amy Sherald. The little-known Guy, never a member of any canon, painted several brilliant pictures of middle-class Brooklyn; Chihuly, the best-known American glassmaker, is a favorite of Walton's. The other three artists are highly regarded African Americans, with Sherald, the newcomer, having quickly become one of the best-known American painters. Earlier, Walton had bought large-scale works by Kerry James Marshall, Félix Gonzáles-Torres, and the Native Americans Fritz Scholder and Jaune Quick-to-See Smith. Well-known abstractionists from the traditional canon like Morris Louis and Agnes Martin are now handsomely installed together with abstract paintings by such Black painters as Sam Gilliam, Alma Thomas, and Julie Mehretu, and with figurative work by Reggie B. Hodges, Mickalene Thomas, and Genesis Tremaine. These works were well chosen; Mehretu's *Retopistics: A Renegade Excavation,* Marshall's *Our Town,* and Mickalene Thomas's *Guernica (Resist #3)* are among the best paintings in the modern collection.

Crystal Bridges' permanent collection was dramatically reinstalled in 2016. Now, in the first gallery, rather than coming on the six Levy-Franks family portraits lined up in a row, one finds only Richa Franks in her red dress hung near seven very different pictures ranging from a colorful portrait by Frank Big Bear and a "portrait" of George Washington by the outsider artist Howard Finster, to Alfred Maurer's provocative full-length rendering of *Jeanne* dating from 1904 and a striking video portrait by Susie J. Lee. This grouping is lively and varied, and lets the visitor know that this isn't going to be another dull museum lineup. In subsequent galleries, one finds noteworthy loans from Tulsa's Gilcrease Museum that temporarily fill some major gaps in Crystal Bridges' collection while inadvertently drawing attention to them: Bierstadt's grand *Sierra Nevada Morning* provides a better place to talk about Manifest Destiny than Crystal Bridge's example by Bierstadt, while the Winslow Homer *Watching the Breakers* and the Whistler *Nocturne* announce other major holes in the Crystal Bridges collection. These loans were available because the Gilcrease was closed for a period; it will be interesting to see whether similar loans from other institutions will be sought in the future. Just as one begins to wonder what happened to many paintings from the permanent collection, one finds them stacked high on two corner walls in the following gallery. One labeled "Notions of Beauty" is devoted to portraits by Eakins, Sargent, Whistler, and Bellows, while the other, labeled "Nostalgia," holds a wide variety of landscapes and still lifes. The effect is like the study storage areas one finds in many museums, and it works well unless you want to examine one of the paintings carefully. I am told that this installation is not a temporary measure, but a permanent one.[6] Overall, the new hang probably proves more inviting than the old one for first-time museum visitors, while being disappointing for experienced art lovers; the seemingly random installation with some important works "skied" has the effect of weakening the apparent quality of the collection, at least to eyes like mine.

Crystal Bridges has much more to offer than the permanent collection. Besides the outdoor attractions mentioned above, one finds in the museum itself a number of ancillary temporary exhibitions, each one thoughtfully conceived and handsomely installed. These will change over time, but will doubtless be replaced by offerings of similar quality. In October 2022, one found a beautifully presented fashion show "Fashioning America: Grit to Glamour," while a different suite of galleries was devoted to another ambitious exhibition, this one entitled "We the People: The Radical Notion of Democracy." A third exhibition, "Entre/Between," was devoted to the history and plight of Latinx people in the Americas; it had two sites, with paintings at Crystal Bridges, and video works and performances at the Momentary, its sister museum a few miles away. What all this means is that Crystal Bridges is now richly programmed with a varied exhibition schedule supported by a large and obviously skilled staff of curators, researchers, registrars, designers, and educators, as one finds at the major museums.

Walton is particularly concerned with children, and an excellent program with free lunches and free transportation has been established for schoolchildren from K–12 from Northwest Arkansas and beyond; about fifty thousand young people benefit yearly from their visits. On my last visit, I saw one class after another heading to a lunchroom or viewing the galleries, all of them looking happy. Alice is pleased that so far, well over three hundred thousand children from twenty states have visited as part of the school field trip program.[7] However, Crystal Bridges lacks one important component of a major art museum, and that is a conservation studio. With all the movement of the collection, all the exhibitions coming and going, and all the works on paper, this is worrisome; damage needs to be prevented by conservators, then repaired if it occurs. Apparently all the conservation is done by the Dallas Museum, a six-hour drive away, though I was pleased to learn that Crystal Bridges does retain several trusted conservators to examine works on the premises when needed.[8]

With all its money, its collection, and its programs, Crystal Bridges is now in a position to organize major loan exhibitions; few institutions would lightly reject its loan requests. In 2021 it organized a groundbreaking exhibition called "American Waters" with the Peabody Essex Museum in Salem, Massachusetts, an ambitious institution with deep roots in maritime history, and one that is finding its modern identity through an inclusionary, anti-racist approach. The idea for the exhibition itself began years earlier in the minds of curators Dan Finamore and Austen Barron Bailly at the Peabody Essex, then gained new life and new funding when Bailly moved from that museum to Crystal Bridges. The exhibition was revolutionary, as it redefined the meaning of marine painting and entirely overturned the traditional canon of marine artists. The earlier studies by John Wilmerding and Roger Stein were ignored.[9] It would have seemed impossible to present American marine painting without Winslow Homer, so long viewed as the giant of the genre, and without Frederic Edwin Church, Martin Johnson Heade, Thomas Birch, and Albert Ryder, and with only minimal representation of Fitz Henry Lane, yet they did it, and did it well. Bailly suggested to me that it would have been a problem to say anything new about the much-studied Winslow Homer, adding, "Homer has had his day."[10] The exhibition provided another example of how the notion of quality has been redefined. Without declaring the old canon null and void, the curators proposed something new, a selection of works where ideas and themes, not individual painters, reign. A vastly wider story was told here than in earlier studies; the sea meant more to more people than we ever dreamed.

Alice Walton's immense wealth is matched by her energy, her imagination, and her ambition to improve access to American art across the nation. In 2017 she developed the Art Bridges Foundation to serve as the primary vehicle for implementing her ideas nationally. It is entirely separate from Crystal Bridges, and has its own budget, collection, headquarters, legal structure, an establishment board including the directors of MoMA and LACMA, and an endowment of $1.5 billion. In 2019, the widely respected Paul Provost, a Princeton PhD and a student of Wilmerding's, became its CEO for a four-year period. The Art Bridges program has three major prongs, each one noteworthy in itself. First, it supports the in-house development and circulation to museums of all sizes of traveling exhibits, a number of which are devoted to works by Black artists; recent ones included "Black Survival Guide, or How to Live Through a Police Riot," "Black Women in Art," "The Radical Art of Nelly Mae Rowe," "William H. Johnson," "The Spelman College Art Collection," and "Photography of Gordon Parks." Art Bridges supports most of the expenses for these exhibits, including installation and educational material. In addition, a fellowship program seeks to identify young people of color interested in museum work, granting selected candidates three-year fellowships to work in registration, conservation, and other departments at leading institutions.

Secondly, through an even more ambitious initiative, Art Bridges aims to encourage and facilitate a program whereby major museums share works from their vaults with smaller neighboring institutions. Ten important museums, including Boston, Philadelphia, and LACMA, became "lead cohorts," and each selected a number of "cohort partners" to work with. The process moves in stages over several years, eventually resulting in a group of loans going to the smaller venues, with Art Bridges paying for staff and other important support at both the lending and borrowing institutions. Still other museums send out groups of pictures to smaller institutions; the Whitney, Cleveland,

and MoMA are all participating, along with such borrowers as the museums at St. Petersburg, Florida; Boise, Montana; and Kalamazoo, Michigan, and the Jordan Schnitzer Museum in Oregon. One of the real accomplishments of the program has been vastly increased communications between large museums and small. Nonetheless, very little of the art being lent by the "lead cohorts" has been of great quality. The major museums have thousands of works in storage, and may eventually lend them, but so far they are understandably keeping the real treasures on their own walls both to serve their own audience and for reasons of conservation.

Art Bridges is also building its own collection, completely separately from Crystal Bridges, with an acquisition budget larger than that of its sister institution, to the point where it has become one of the major buyers of American art. This collection is designed to be lent to other museums, one or more works at a time. Art Bridges was managed at the start by chief curator Margi Conrads, who let the field know of the new entity's ambitions with the acquisition of Childe Hassam's important flag picture *Italian Day, May 1918*. Then, from 2019 to 2023, Paul Provost bought brilliantly. Nearly all his acquisitions were modern and contemporary works, though one exception is the terrific Sanford Gifford *Twilight in the Adirondacks,* one of the paintings sold by Theodore and Barbara Alfond when they moved to the modern field. Here one finds Henry Ossawa Tanner's *Thankful Poor* of 1894 (fig. 59); it's difficult to imagine a more important acquisition. I asked Alice whether it gave her pause to be enriching the discredited collector Bill Cosby to the extent of $8 million; when I asked her about this, she said that she thought the art came first.[11] There are major works purchased at recent auctions, including Joseph Stella's *Tree of Life* from Barney Ebsworth's collection ($6 million) and Lee Krasner's *Re-Echo* ($9 million). Other buys range from important works by Arshile Gorky, Georgia O'Keeffe, and Richard Diebenkorn, to those by Norman Lewis and Archibald Motley. The overall quality level is higher than one finds in the Crystal Bridges modern collection. I understand Alice's good intentions here, but the idea of these superb works always being on the road makes me nervous, as I'm someone

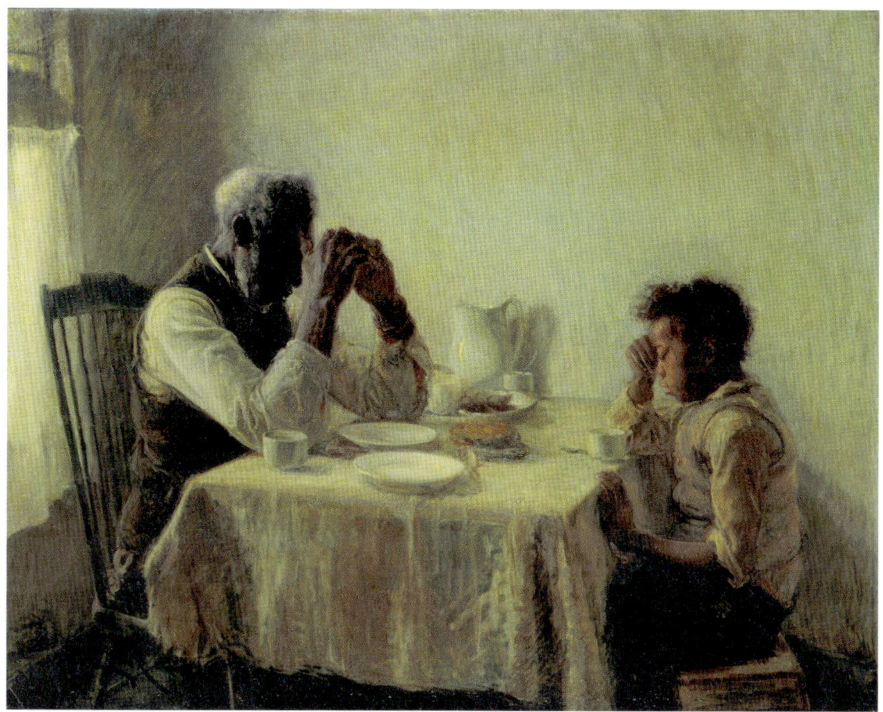

Fig. 59. HENRY OSSAWA TANNER,
The Thankful Poor, oil on canvas, 1894. Art Bridges Foundation.

who has always believed that the first obligation of a museum is the care and preservation of its holdings.

Museums have always struggled with this issue, how to balance the obligation to preserve versus the mission of sharing and educating. The MFA for years had a curator who believed that the precious collection of Japanese prints should never be on view and only could be viewed by qualified experts. Other museums put glass or plexiglass on their paintings, which protects them from careless visitors or vandals but makes it difficult for everyone to see them.

In October 2023, Art Bridges announced a new "Access for All" program, another reflection of Walton's core belief that art benefits people, and that art needs to be brought to larger, more diverse audiences. The new initiative was thoughtfully planned, like everything Alice does. It announced grants totaling $40 million, ranging from $56,000 to

$2 million to sixty-four museums, with institutions like the Taft Museum in Cincinnati, the Springfield (Massachusetts) Museum, and the Columbus (Ohio) Museum of Art receiving an average of $1 million over three years to extend their free hours, institute bilingual programs, and offer virtual tours. Walton stresses that "we support partners and projects rather than grantees and grants." Art Bridges as of 2024 had partnered with a growing network of over 232 museums of every size, while supporting some 886 projects across the country. Thus, Alice's enterprises are now connected financially with a great many American museums, large and small. For me, however, a weakness in her programs lies in their exclusive interest in American art. Contemporary art is global, and many American museums celebrate artists from Asia, Africa, Europe, and South America; nationality becomes a complex and increasingly irrelevant measure. It would be far more cost-effective for Walton to help American museums introduce their audiences to the rich and incredibly varied arts of the world.

Alice's aims for widening the audience and the scope of American art is shared by several other institutions, including the Luce Foundation, the Lunder Institute (discussed above), and notably the Terra Foundation. Daniel Terra's death in 1996 led to a period of confusion for his foundation, but it was reinvented under the leadership of the remarkable Elizabeth Glassman, who served as its president from 2001 to 2019. It now plays an important role both as a grant-making entity and as a lender from its collection. The foundation makes grants of around $12 million annually. Many of its efforts are international; exhibitions have been funded in São Paulo, Lagos, South Korea, and Paris, and many others support exhibitions of Black artists.[12] There is no telling what the politically conservative Terra would have thought of some of the details, but surely he would be pleased at having his name become well known throughout the international art world. In addition, the Terra collection looks better than ever, as many of the weaker works have been sold, and now Motley, Delaney, and other Black painters are being added.

The two entities, Crystal Bridges and Art Bridges, together constitute a new kind of art organization, one bringing art to the people of Northwest Arkansas for the first time, the other one seeking to change the lives of people in small towns and large around the country, teaching regular museum-goers new ways of seeing while recruiting wider swaths of the public to the experience of connecting with art. This aim goes back to Ruskin and the idealistic, educational mission behind many museums in the nineteenth century. What distinguishes Walton's new two-headed enterprise is its huge financial strength and the insistent, out-front social messaging at the core of all its projects; traditional museum considerations of style and aesthetics play a diminished role here, while matters of racial inclusion and good citizenship become highly important.

Finally, what can we say about Alice Walton herself? Born in 1949, she is the youngest of Walmart founder Sam Walton's four children. She was long a dedicated horsewoman, a breeder, rider, and trainer of cutting horses who loves the outdoors, though in recent years she has given up her Texas ranch. Like many collectors, she loved art at an early age; she speaks fondly of painting watercolors on camping trips with her mother. She had two early marriages and two divorces and has no children. Like many other collectors, she knows loneliness and despair; many of her favorite paintings reflect these feelings. You can never leave one's past wholly behind, but Alice appears to have emerged from her troubles as an articulate, highly intelligent, caring person with a driving ambition to benefit her community and the nation. She is knowledgeable and passionate about art and about Arkansas. Like many great collectors and museum builders before her, she will be remembered for her extraordinary impact on the field of American art, not for her personal history. Other collectors will follow, but it's difficult to imagine anyone else coming along with her ambition to reshape art appreciation first locally, then on a national level. On top of building a great art center for her area, Alice now aims to benefit museums and their audiences across the nation. Crystal Bridges' first decade closed with Alice's nominal retirement in November 2021 as board chair and her replacement by her niece Olivia Walton; however Alice remains head of the Art Bridges board, and that's where she is putting her energies. Alice has unprecedented power in the art world, and it's growing. Her decency and good sense are manifest, but I cannot help being nervous about a future when her enterprises are no longer in her hands. There is no way of predicting how Crystal Bridges and Art Bridges will develop without her, once committees take over.

---

[1] Other museums with collections arguably superior to that of Crystal Bridges are Yale, The New York Historical, Brooklyn, Detroit, Cleveland, St. Louis, Art Institute of Chicago, Pennsylvania Academy, Addison Gallery, Fine Arts Museums of San Francisco, and the Virginia Museum. Closely comparable to Crystal Bridges are the holdings of the Worcester Art Museum, the Wadsworth Atheneum, and the Smithsonian American Art Museum, the Amon Carter, and the Carnegie Museum.

[2] Rebecca Mead, "Alice's Wonderland: A Walmart Heiress Builds a Museum in the Ozarks," *New Yorker*, June 27, 2011.

[3] Mead, "Alice's Wonderland."

[4] *ARTnews* reported that Alice Walton was the buyer of *Buffalo II* by Robert Rauschenberg at Christie's in May 2019. Alice denied it to the press and repeated her denial to me when we spoke. If she did buy it, it would be a good addition to the collection. Maximilíano Durón, "Report: Alice Walton Was Buyer of Record-Breaking $88.8 M. Rauschenberg at Christie's," *ARTnews*, June 4, 2019; Alice Walton, conversation with the author, December 13, 2022.

[5] Mindy Besaw, "Re-Envisioning Histories of American Art," lecture, Hood Museum, Dartmouth College, April 7, 2022.

[6] Austen Barron Bailly, conversation with the author, October 7, 2022.

[7] Alice Walton and Diane Carroll, conversation with the author, December 13, 2022.

[8] Alice Walton, conversation with the author, December 13, 2022.

[9] John Wilmerding, *A History of American Marine Painting* (Peabody Museum of Salem, 1968); Roger B. Stein, *Seascape and the American Imagination* (C. N. Potter, 1975).

[10] Bailly, conversation with the author, December 1, 2021.

[11] Alice Walton, conversation with the author, December 13, 2022.

[12] Special thanks to Amy Zinck, the executive vice president of the Terra Foundation.

PART THREE

TODAY

16

The Recognition of Racism and Misogyny

The propriety of the nation must be startled; the hypocrisy of the nation must be exposed.

—FREDERICK DOUGLASS,
What to a Slave Is the Fourth of July?, 1852

The ultimate art coming from black folk is going to be just as beautiful, and beautiful largely in the same ways, as the art that comes from white folk, or yellow, or red; but the point today is that until the art of the black folk compels recognition they will not be rated as human.

—W. E. B. DU BOIS,
"Criteria of Negro Art," 1926

A NEW ERA began during the late sixties and seventies when Black artists, energized by the Civil Rights movement, began to make themselves heard in the white art world. The murder of Martin Luther King Jr. in 1968, the battles over the Civil Rights Acts, and the difficult dismantling of Jim Crow were on everyone's minds. There was no ivory tower for the artists, as they were living in an angry time of riots and high tension in the cities. A significant event in the arts was the Whitney Museum's exhibition of 1968, "The 1930s: Painting and Sculpture in America." It included the work of eighty artists but failed to include a single Black one, not even Jacob Lawrence, whose work was in the museum's collection. Benny Andrews, Faith Ringgold, and others organized a protest that was, as Ringgold writes, "the first black demonstration against a major museum in New York."[1] Andrews and others organized the Black Emergency Cultural Coalition, which picketed the major art museums protesting the exclusion of minority artists. As a result, the Whitney in 1969 mounted its first solo show of a Black painter, Al Loving, followed three years later by an exhibition of the work of Alma Thomas, the first Black woman to be so honored. As part of this effort the Whitney in 1971 presented the exhibition "Contemporary Black Artists in America," organized by Mac Doty. Turmoil followed as each Black artist argued over what to make of a white curator being in charge, especially one who glorified abstraction as the universal artistic language, and debated among themselves whether to participate.[2] The Black Emergency Cultural Coalition (BECC) protested the Whitney exhibition and organized a counter-exhibition at the new Studio Museum in Harlem.[3]

The Met was moving in the same direction, haltingly trying to right old wrongs with regard to Black artists. The story of its infamous "Harlem on My Mind" exhibition of 1969 has been told many times. It was an ambitious presentation of photos, films, television, and photomurals illustrating life in Harlem from 1900 to 1968. The show was conceived by the museum's young director Thomas Hoving as a well-intentioned gesture that he hoped would remedy the lack of communication "between black people and white people," but both his preface to the catalogue and the whole project were deeply flawed. Hoving demonstrated his own racism in describing his Black servants, the "sunny" maid and the "sour" chauffeur, and in commenting that he couldn't conceive of meeting with Black people as equals.[4] The introduction, written by a Black high school student, was demonstrably anti-Semitic; the author wrote that "our contempt for the Jew makes us feel more completely American in sharing a national prejudice."[5] A backlash occurred immediately, and henceforth the catalogue included an inserted, half-hearted apology from the author. Demonstrators, including many Black and white artists, picketed the museum on opening night, and several works in Met galleries were vandalized.[6] The exhibition itself was roundly criticized for its failure to include Harlem residents in its planning and especially for its exclusion of any original works by the Harlem artists. The organizers seem to have been completely unaware of the varied cultural productivity of the Harlem Renaissance and its many distinguished painters and writers, yet it succeeded unintentionally in rousing many angry Black artists to action.

The Met in 1972 responded to the mess caused by "Harlem on My Mind" by establishing a Community Programs Department, a well-meant, useful initiative that had the Met working from on high with three local venues, the Bronx Museum, the Storefront Museum in Queens, and El Museo del Barrio, dedicated to Puerto Rican artists. An early hire was Lowery Stokes Sims, who worked on sending out artworks from the Met to these partners. In 1975, Henry Geldzahler, the Met's curator of twentieth-century art, hired the energetic, productive Sims as his assistant curator, making her, I believe, the first Black curator at one of the major Eastern museums. She worked on a variety of white and Black artists, from Horace Pippin to Stuart Davis on her way to becoming a central figure in the field and a champion of Black artists. In 2000 she became director of the Studio Museum in Harlem, where she put on important shows, stabilized the finances, and hired Thelma Golden as curator.

Progress was slow. Racism and misogyny were embedded in our culture. For every advance in terms of opening the major museums to Black artists, trustees, and senior staff members, there were reversals. A telling example of this is seen in the short career (May 1970–January 1972) of John Hightower as director of the Museum of Modern Art. Hightower proposed electing the museum's first African American trustees and showing artists of color, and he maintained close communications with Faith Ringgold and Benny Andrews. But he had gotten ahead of the trustees, one of whom wrote, "We cannot show or buy any more works of art by Negro or female artists without letting down our standards."[7] This represented the prevailing attitude not only among MoMA trustees but of the whole white establishment, and Hightower was fired shortly afterwards.

Few in the white art world were aware of the Black culture that strongly supported its artists and galleries for years while connecting the artists and their backers from the south to Los Angeles, Chicago, and New York. The most admired Black artists effectively became a separate canon, one that was recognized in the Black community but little known outside it. These important developments were rarely reported in the white textbooks and art magazines, though they were well covered in the Black press, including the *Amsterdam News* (serving Harlem), *The Chicago Defender*, and the *Baltimore Afro-American*, and in *Ebony* (a Black answer to *Life* magazine), as well as in *The Crisis*, the magazine that W. E. B. Du Bois had founded in 1910. In 1936, the painter Aaron Douglas laid out the aims of the Black artist: "Our chief concern has been to establish and maintain recognition of our . . . complete social and political equality." Douglas reported on the constant negative propaganda "from nursery rhymes to false scientific racial theories" that demoralized the artists and hindered wider recognition.[8] Yet the artists' careers were nurtured through the years by private collectors, supportive galleries, and such entities as the Harmon Foundation, with its important grants and exhibitions and most importantly by the historically Black colleges and universities (HBCUs). Richard J. Powell and Jock Reynolds brought these institutions and the artists to wider attention with their farsighted efforts in the 1990s to bring modern conservation methods to some of the outstanding paintings, sculpture, and photographs owned by the HBCUs. The catalogue for the traveling exhibition they organized, "To Conserve a Legacy," described the museums at Clark Atlanta, Fisk, Hampton, Howard, North Carolina Central, and Tuskegee universities and introduced the uninformed to artists that many were not aware of, including painters Samella Sanders Lewis and Frederick C. Flemister and photographer Frances Benjamin Johnston. It also presented important yet unfamiliar works like Charles White's powerful mural at Howard, *Progress of the American Negro* and Hale Woodruff's six-panel mural *Art of the Negro* at Clark Atlanta.

Most of the works included in "To Conserve a Legacy" were figurative, though there were a number of abstract paintings as well. Figurative art was considered unsophisticated by many tastemakers, both white and Black, and the Black arts community long debated the question of abstraction versus realism as it sought a Black aesthetic.[9] The scholar Sarah Lewis discusses this complex question in her eloquent essay, "African American Abstraction," where she posits, "The question was how these artists could 'respond to the Civil Rights Movement through their art, and without having to go the figurative route.'"[10] Lewis makes the case that while the majority of work by Black painters is figurative, abstract works may be equally expressive of racial concerns.

Black artists were largely shut out from mainstream white exhibitions and galleries, though there were a few exceptions. Samuel Kootz showed Romare Bearden until 1948 as Arne Eckstrom did for long afterwards, Marian Willard represented Norman Lewis from 1946 to 1964, and Bertha Shaefer exhibited Hale Woodruff during the fifties. Edith Halpert at the Downtown Gallery presented an exhibition of "American Negro Artists" in 1941 and she showed Horace Pippin; most importantly, she learned of Jacob Lawrence from Alain Locke and represented him for years after showing his Migration of the Negro series. These instances are significant historically, but in the end, the establishment dealers accomplished far less in supporting Black painters than the Black colleges and universities. Woodruff, for example, grew up in Nashville, studied at the Art Institute of Chicago and at Harvard, then with the aid of the Harmon Foundation worked for four years in Paris. In 1931 he began teaching at Atlanta University (later Clark Atlanta), where he founded an annual competition for Negro Artists that ran from 1942 to 1970; it provided a key venue for aspiring artists. According to artist/writer Tina Dunkley, over the life of the competition, some nine hundred Black artists from across the nation sent their works to compete; works that won purchase awards entered the permanent collection. The successful artists included Jacob Lawrence, Elizabeth Catlett, Romare Bearden, John Biggers, Lois Mailou Jones, and John Wilson, all unknowns at the time.[11] Woodruff worked for the Works Progress Administration (WPA) during the thirties, and in 1936 went to Mexico to study with Diego Rivera; he then executed a series of six murals for Talladega College in Central Alabama, three of them depicting the famous slave revolt on the Amistad in 1839. These powerful works were unknown to many until 2012, when they were conserved by the High Museum and sent on a national tour.[12] Like many of his peers, Woodruff collected African art and was keenly interested in the roots of Black culture in the US. In 1946 he quit Atlanta and began teaching in New York, where with Romare Bearden, Charles Alston, and Norman Lewis, he helped found an artists' collective called the Spiral Group (1963–65) and moved to a more abstract style; the group's stated purpose was "discussing the commitment of the Negro artist in the present struggle for civil liberties." One of the members was Merton D. Simpson, a painter who in the sixties and seventies became a leading dealer of African art. Spiral's successor was the Cinque Gallery, also in New York, founded by Bearden, Lewis, and Ernest Crichlow; it showed many of the greats before closing in 2004.[13]

The innovative collage-maker Romare Bearden also gained some prominence at this time. He showed regularly from 1961 on at Cordier-Eckstrom, a highly respected New York gallery that specialized in the avant-garde and had retrospective shows at the Corcoran in 1965 and MoMA in 1971. The exhibition at MoMA introduced his inventive collages to a wider white audience and helped sales at Cordier-Eckstrom. The brilliant young MFA curator Clifford Ackley purchased two collages from that gallery's 1971 show, and a dedicated private collector, Dr. Abram London, bought one titled *Soul History* (fig. 60) at the same time. "Bram," as he was known, was a friend of mine who introduced me to Bearden through this work, one he gave to Harvard in 1997. Yet even then, at the height of his lifetime recognition, Bearden suffered from harsh criticism, as when *New York Times* critic Hilton Kramer found his work "a little too decorative, a little too pat."[14] In retrospect, this feels like racism at work, though given Kramer's flawed eye, one cannot be sure. Kramer demonstrated a similar narrowness when he praised the abstractions of Norman Lewis and Alma Thomas while criticizing the figurative paintings in the exhibition as "political propaganda pure and simple."[15]

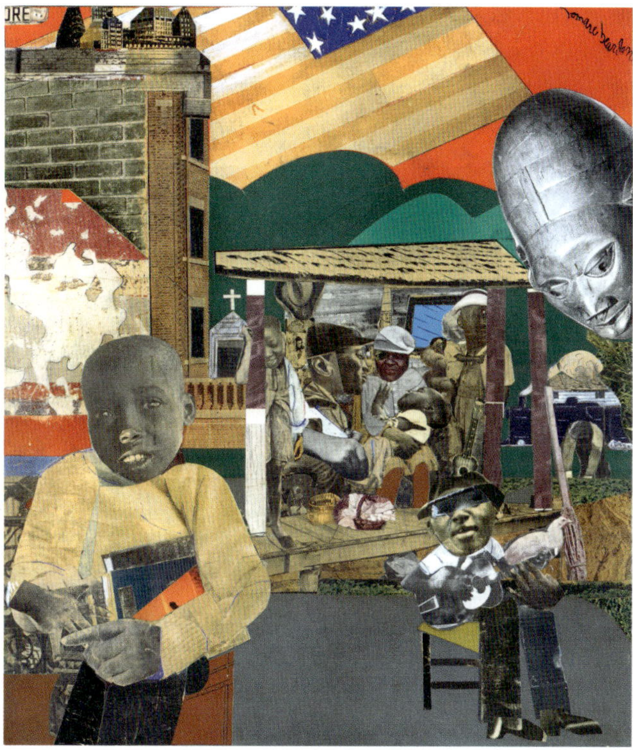

Fig. 60. ROMARE BEARDEN,
Soul History, collage, graphite, colored pencil, and gouache on masonite, 1969.
Harvard Art Museums.

Equally important was the Chicagoan Charles White, the painter of the WPA mural mentioned above, and later an important teacher in Los Angeles whose students included Kerry James Marshall and David Hammons. White inspired the formation of Gallery 32 in L.A. in 1968, a gathering place for art and protest where Betye Saar and others fought the battle for Black women. Saar's *Liberation of Aunt Jemima,* 1972, was both art, satire, and political protest. The late sixties saw Black artists across the country coming together, making art while fighting for their civil rights. Chicago's AfriCOBRA, an artists' collective, was founded in 1968. Its artists held two exhibitions, and many traveled to Africa to reconnect with their roots in African culture and art. Los Angeles was also home to an active Black arts community centered around the Brockman Gallery that lasted until 1990. All of these efforts were focused on fighting racism in a passionate struggle to create a Black art independent of the white art mainstream.

In New York, the Studio Museum in Harlem, also founded in 1968, became an important gathering place and exhibition venue for the Black artists, as did the Artists Space movement (1972), Printed Matter/St. Marks, the Franklin Furnace, and Just Above Midtown, the gallery established by Linda Goode Bryant in 1974 that foregrounded the work of African American artists.[16] Bryant boldly inserted her Black-run gallery into Fifty-Seventh Street, the heart of the white art world, and it somehow survived for over a decade. The white art world generally disregarded these events but the cumulative effect of such exhibitions, together with the work of the ICA Boston, MOCA Chicago, the Perez Museum, and the New Museum, led gradually to the widespread changes of attitude and policy we see today.

In 1970, I was a junior member of the Yale faculty. My own real-world education began that year. Two leading Black Panthers had been arrested in New Haven, and a violent, bloody crisis seemed imminent as the Panthers marched on the university on May Day. I have strong memories of the rampant fear throughout the school and the city as the Panthers and 15,000 protesters came down Chapel Street: Would they ransack the Art Gallery? Would we in suburban Branford be attacked? Suddenly all the Gallery's glass walls seemed highly vulnerable. The Panthers were up in arms over "the jailing and unfair trial" of two Panther leaders accused of conspiring to murder one of their own, as Henry Louis Gates wrote later (he was a Yale sophomore at the time), and many students and faculty quickly took their side. I was too unaware to take any position. Fortunately for Yale, President Kingman Brewster and chaplain William Sloane Coffin possessed the abilities, courage, and flexibility to save the university from violence through skilled communications with student leaders and the Panthers themselves.[17] The very different tragedy at Kent State occurred just two days later. As a member of the establishment, I was only a fearful observer, but my eyes began to open.

Change was happening in these years. The women's movement and the rise of feminism during the sixties, coming as they did in the years of the Civil Rights movement, played important roles in opening doors for women artists and in preparing the ground for the acceptance of Black artists. Linda Nochlin's famous article "Why Have There Been No Great Women Artists?" was published in *ARTnews* in 1971 and led to a growing number of articles, exhibitions, and protests. 1985 saw the founding of the Guerilla Girls, an anonymous group of feminist artist/activists wearing guerrilla masks, formed in response to a major MoMA exhibition, "An International Survey of Recent Painting and Sculpture." The participants observed that of the 165 artists from seventeen nations, just 13 were women. Regarding older art, they found an even worse situation: The Met's catalogues of its early paintings, published between 1980 and 1994, revealed that of the 288 artists whose work it owned, just 6 were women, and exactly 2 were Black painters (Joshua Johnson, Robert S. Duncanson).[18]

The late twentieth century also saw increasing exhibitions and recognition of women artists, though mid-career whites were the major beneficiaries. Only during the last two decades has one observed widespread efforts among the major Eastern museums to recognize the broad spectrum of women creators, including Black and Hispanic practitioners. The makeup of major contemporary surveys began to change, with the Whitney Biennial, for example, reaching sexual parity for the first time in 2010 with twenty-nine women and twenty-six men being shown. Then the Whitney in 2015 took a massive step physically and aesthetically with its move downtown and the opening of the grand new building by Renzo Piano. The opening exhibition "America Is Hard to See" demonstrated far more inclusive views than heretofore, with its foregrounding of political art, the references to Vietnam and the AIDS epidemic, the work of women, and especially the inclusion of numerous Black artists. The Museum of Modern Art's reinstallation of 2007 fell badly short in terms of inclusion of women, but when it reopened in 2019, vastly more were included, and its 2017 exhibition "Making Space: Women and Postwar Abstraction" was serious and successful.[19]

The art world has found it difficult to characterize the work of Jean-Michel Basquiat (1960–1988) (fig. 61), whose dramatic rise in the 1980s occurred before the widespread embrace of diversity and the work of

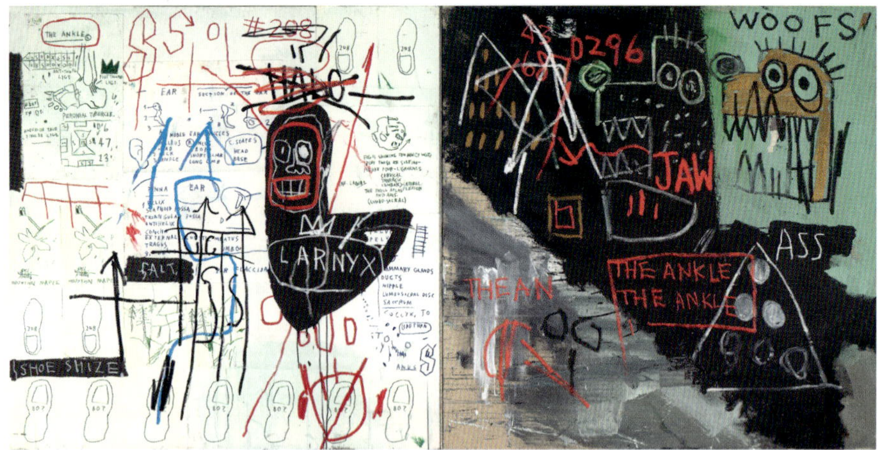

Fig. 61. **JEAN-MICHEL BASQUIAT,**
Diagram of the Ankle, xeroxed paper, oil stick, and acrylic on two hinged canvases, 1982. Yale University Art Gallery.

Black artists. Basquiat was the child of a Haitian father and a Puerto Rican mother, but his sudden fame was seemingly caused more by his art than his story. At eighteen Basquiat was painting graffiti in New York as SAMO, while at twenty-one he was included in an exhibition at P.S. 1, was profiled in Artforum, and had become a friend and collaborator of Andy Warhol; soon afterward he was being courted and exhibited by powerful dealers from Hollywood to Zurich, including Bruno Bischofberger, Mary Boone, and Larry Gagosian, while being included in the Whitney Biennial and Documenta. By 1985, his picture appeared on the cover of The New York Times Magazine, he was making over $1 million a year, and had become a heavy drug user. His tragic death of an overdose at twenty-seven occurred shortly thereafter. Dealers and collectors drove the boom, prices rising quickly after his death until reaching over $1 million in 1999, then continuing upward until one of his paintings sold at Sotheby's in 2017 for $110.5 million. That stood as the all-time record for a modern painting until a Warhol went higher in 2022.

Despite Basquiat's meteoric rise, or perhaps because of the way it happened, the art world has had trouble placing him. Numerous dealers and a few collectors like the Rubells got there early, and the

Whitney built a good holding after receiving the gift of a Basquiat painting in 1984. However, there is no Eastern museum where one can see his work in depth; for that, one must go to the Broad in Los Angeles. Collector Eli Broad understood the painter's significance early on, and acquired thirteen of his works, many of them painted in Los Angeles when Basquiat was living at the home of dealer Larry Gagosian. Due to a combination of curatorial doubt and the fast-moving market, most major museums in this country do not own his work to this day: The National Gallery, the Philadelphia Museum of Art, the Art Institute of Chicago, and the MFA have nothing at all by him, while the Museum of Modern Art has only some drawings. Crystal Bridges owns a fine 1981 oil, while the Met received two major paintings as gifts in 2021. The textbook writers have been equally doubtful: Wayne Craven describes him briefly in his survey of 1995, Frances Pohl allots his work just one sentence, while Jennifer Roberts, the leading Harvard scholar who wrote the modern chapters in American Encounters, does not mention his name. On the other hand, Watson and Navaroli, authors of the most recent survey, deal sensitively with how Basquiat was commodified as an "exotic," rather than a powerful Black artist who used his art to speak to the painfully real issues of a racist society.[20] Similarly, some exhibitions and surveys of Black artists include Basquiat, while others do not; among the best treatments is the one in Sharon F. Patton's *African-American Art* of 1998.

Basquiat was the first Black American artist to gain a national and international reputation. His work is complex and sophisticated: He's a descendant of Picasso and Rauschenberg, his paintings speak clearly of his early years painting graffiti, and they reflect his awareness of the work of African masks and the Abstract Expressionists as well. Long before George Floyd, he had the 1983 killing of graffiti artist Michael Stewart by the New York police on his mind. The faces in his paintings like *The Irony of the Negro Policeman* are nearly always Black, and they look like tormented skulls. Basquiat did not rise up through the Black network of education and patronage that I have described; rather, he was singular in being lionized by the white art world before much of it was aware of Black art. His intelligence and his instincts led him to find an answer to the question of whether Black art should be figurative or abstract: His was both.

Several universities provided key leadership in bringing the issues of racism and slavery to wider attention in the white world. Brown University president Ruth Simmons in 2003 launched the university's report on slavery and justice, a model of unflinching research.[21] It revealed that Rhode Island was the source of 60 percent of all slaving voyages originating in North America, that many of Brown's leading trustees and supporters, including its eminent founding family, were deeply involved, and that much of the economy of the state relied on slavery and the slave trade well into the nineteenth century. One result was the outdoor erection of a subtly buried ball and chain called *The Slavery Memorial* by the well-known African American sculptor Martin Puryear. Around the same time, Harvard Law School took a hard look at its founder. In September 2006, Janet Halley, the incoming Royall Professor of Law, gave a thoroughly researched lecture titled "My Isaac Royall Legacy" in which she concluded that the funding of the Royall chair and the law school about 1816 were "derived, directly and indirectly, from the sale of human beings and the appropriation of their labor."[22] Royall's wealth came from his plantations in Antigua and his slave trading; when he moved to Medford, Massachusetts, he brought with him about 19 enslaved persons. The Law School canceled the Royall Professorship, the oldest of its kind in the US, and redesigned its shield so it would no longer feature the Royall family crest.[23] At Georgetown University, a student paper in 2014 described how its Jesuit leaders in 1838 engineered the sale of 272 enslaved persons it owned in order to pay the school's debts. Further research revealed that Georgetown owned some 1,650 enslaved people, and the university has now identified some 12,500 of their descendants who have been granted preferred admission status in perpetuity.[24] My alma mater, Yale University, was late, finally launching a "Yale and Slavery" research project, which resulted in 2024 in an excellent history of enslaved people at the university from its earliest days, and an outline of related future projects.[25]

These and many other developments were part of a national reconsideration of race and slavery in the twenty-first century, with academics frequently leading the way. The land acknowledgment movement, originating in university faculties in Native Studies, has been taken up by many art museums and universities that now make written reference to the Indigenous people who originally inhabited the land. In just a few years, the argument that the Confederacy had fought nobly for a lost cause and states' rights has been widely rejected as recognition grew that it had battled instead for slavery and a slave-based economy. Monuments to Robert E. Lee and other leaders began to be removed throughout the South, often under violent protests. Thomas Jefferson, long celebrated as one of the greatest presidents, is now also known for the family he fathered with an enslaved woman. A recent book demonstrates that Washington was not so different from the other Virginia planters of his time in that he not only owned hundreds of slaves but authorized severe punishment when one was found lazy or rebellious. The Washingtons energetically pursued a young female slave to New Hampshire after she escaped from their household in Philadelphia.[26] Growing awareness of race on the part of the white community was furthered by the publication in 2016 of Jill Lepore's groundbreaking history of the US, *These Truths,* and was reflected in the growing visibility of the Black Lives Matter movement and the widespread protests following the horrendous videotaped murder of George Floyd on May 25, 2020. Many universities went about renaming buildings, as Yale did with its Calhoun College in 2017, and as Princeton did shortly afterwards in removing Woodrow Wilson's name from its school of public affairs. Both changes caused resentment among the alumni; I have Yale classmates still lamenting the loss of Calhoun College. When I was a student there, the residential Pierson College had some student rooms known as the "slave quarters," and members of its teams were nicknamed "the slaves"; this was only changed in 1980.[27] Many people still argue that you cannot alter history, but scholars point out correctly that history is constantly changing; James M. Banner makes this clear in his recent book, *The Ever-Changing Past: Why All History Is Revisionist History.*[28]

Turning back to older art museums, the Pennsylvania Academy of the Fine Arts, long an anti-modern institution, has forged a new identity in promoting diversity. In 2010 it received from the collector Linda Lee Alter some five hundred works in all mediums by women of every age, race, and sexual orientation. Included are well-known figures like Miriam Shapiro, Nan Goldin, and Betye Saar, along with a number whose names are still unfamiliar. Alter herself is a distinguished artist and a longtime backer of women's causes, and her important collection was published in a fine book entitled *The Female Gaze*.[29] Three years later the Academy went all in when it sold one of its two Edward Hopper oils for $36 million and dedicated half the proceeds to contemporary acquisitions that would broaden the collection, with the other half allocated to modern and historic works. In 2012 the Academy organized a large-scale exhibition of the work of Henry Ossawa Tanner with a catalogue to match, and three years later presented the first major exhibition of the work of Norman Lewis, the long-overlooked Black Abstract Expressionist. Then in 2019 it received a gift of seventy works by African Americans from Constance Clayton. Most recently, in 2022, the Academy presented an exhibition called "Women in Motion," a survey of woman artists who studied or exhibited there; this project received support from the Horowitz and Terra foundations and from Alice Walton.

The MFA Boston has also made significant progress. In 2019 it presented an impressive show of over two hundred works called "Women Take the Floor" that included many recent gifts, purchases, and loans of paintings by Americans Joan Mitchell, Lee Krasner, Helen Torr, Lois Mailou Jones, and many others, along with the portrait of *Linda Nochlin and Daisy* by Alice Neel that I acquired in 1983 for the Museum of Fine Arts (fig. 62). The effort to identify women artists and ones of color has necessarily led to expanding the definition of museum-quality art, as so many women worked in what were long considered lesser mediums. Curator Nonie Gadsden in Boston did this effectively by including photography, pottery by white and Pueblo potters, fabrics and weaving (including Sonya Clark's *Hair Craft Project*, a multipart work that wouldn't have found a museum home just a few years ago), silver, prints, books, and sculpture (including five pieces by Meta Vaux Warrick Fuller). This was a show that marked an important turnaround for the MFA, but sadly, it had no catalogue, and we learned long ago that exhibitions without catalogues tend to be forgotten.

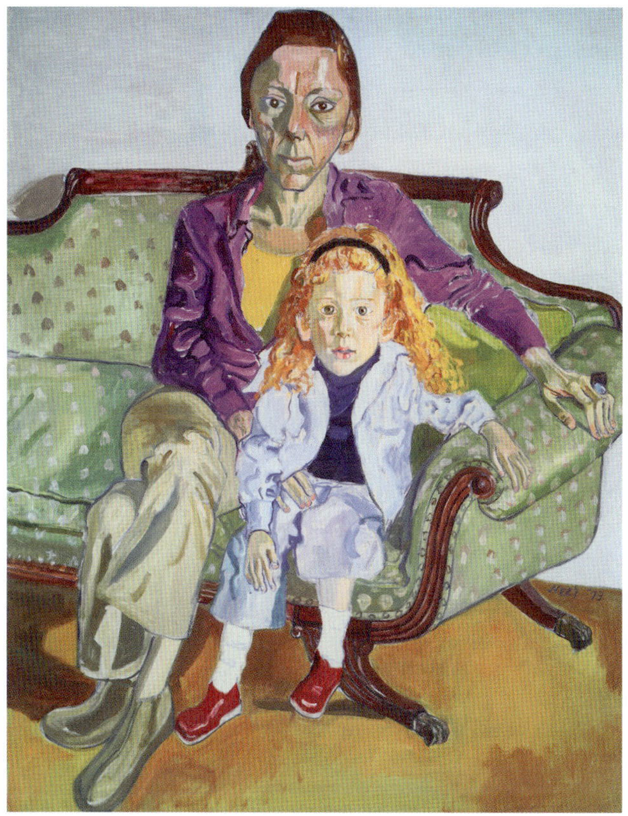

Fig. 62. ALICE NEEL,
Linda Nochlin and Daisy, oil on canvas, 1973. Museum of Fine Arts, Boston.

One finds a good overview of the developing methodology, with all its merits and its confusion, in two hefty textbooks published during the first decade of the century: *Framing America: A Social History of American Art* (2002) by Frances Pohl from Pomona College and *American Encounters: Art, History, and Cultural Identity* (2008), by a team of six well-known university professors with Yale degrees led by Angela Miller. Both books have been described as reactions to Wayne Craven's conservative survey of 1995. The writers of both have the question of the canon very much on their minds: Pohl describes how recent scholars have engaged with feminist, Marxist, psychoanalytic, and poststructuralist methodologies in "rejecting or supplementing the elite canon that privileged white male artists and 'masterpieces,'" while Miller and her colleagues aim to study the art made by "diverse peoples" outside of the mainstream side by side with the works in the traditional canon—"those familiar landmarks," as she calls them—while suggesting new interpretations for them.[30] Both surveys aim to reinterpret, revise, and expand the canon, in effect presenting a new set of aesthetic standards for the twenty-first century. The books agree that American art has been dramatically redefined. For my generation and earlier ones, it consisted of the work of white male artists working mostly in the Northeastern US, who looked to England and Europe for their models. Indigenous and Spanish colonial art were seen as areas of study left to other specialists, but the recent texts accept these arts as equally American, as deserving of equal standing with products of the Anglo/Euro tradition.

Both *Framing America* and *American Encounters* lead off with several chapters devoted to the Indigenous art from across South and North America and the Spanish colonial missions of the southwest. Mediums such as pottery, quilts, needlework, embroidery, printmaking, photography, wood carving, and caricatures are brought to the fore, and one increasingly finds the traditional distinction between the fine arts and material culture erased, as it is in many recent museum installations. Both volumes demonstrate significantly expanded interest in the art of women and African Americans and especially in how Native Americans and Black people are portrayed. Subject matter and its interpretation take on major importance, with Pohl considering many works in their political and historical contexts, while Miller and her colleagues see art through race- and gender-colored glasses. The standbys of the old art history, the consideration of chronology, quality, patronage, and artistic influence, are much weakened.

The writers of both volumes include many members of the traditional canon of painters, but they give diminished space to them as they have so many other artists and mediums to cover. The two surveys lead off with the Freake-Gibbs painter and Captain Thomas Smith, before taking up Dunlap's favorites, West, Copley, and Trumbull. There were no major Black painters at work in this era, but both books attempt to make up for this by emphasizing the occasional images of Black men in the colonial paintings. There is more than a hint in both volumes of the old "what is American in American art" question, and a casual reader would hardly be aware that these Americans ever worked in Europe or painted European subjects.

These books are thoughtful and articulate, but in their enthusiasms, inconsistencies, and occasional omissions, they demonstrate the complexity and occasional chaos of today's fast-moving art world. A student relying on either one would gain a somewhat skewed understanding of the history of American art. Pohl, for example, fails to mention John Smibert or his famous *Bermuda Group* of 1729 at the Yale University Art Gallery, long regarded as one of the founding works of American art; one wonders whether she omitted it because it depicts Bishop George Berkeley, who penned the lines "Westward the course of empire takes its way," a seeming prediction of Manifest Destiny. Pohl has spent her professional life in California, and includes more works from Western collections than do Miller et al. For their part, Miller and her colleagues somehow fail to mention either Edward Bannister or Robert S. Duncanson, two important Black painters of the nineteenth century, and they also leave out the long-admired still lifes of Raphaelle Peale, Martin Johnson Heade, John F. Peto, and William Harnett. Both volumes grant art a more powerful societal role than was traditionally understood. When an earlier scholar suggested that a painting was "important," he or she usually meant that it stood out in terms of quality, price, critical reception, or its influence on other artists; art in general was seen to play a role mainly in the insular world of critics, collectors, and curators. But the recent writers see artists as central players in the society, more powerful and more calculating than the earlier historians had found them. Miller and her colleagues, for example, assert that "the visual arts played an active role in shaping national identity" during the antebellum years.[31] My generation understood artists as painting in order to make a living, advance their careers, and win peer recognition, while taking up subjects they thought would sell; but in one of the new texts we read of George Caleb Bingham "seeing a chance to shape the public's opinion of the West" when he sent his *Fur Traders Descending the Missouri* to the Art-Union to be engraved.[32]

Both Pohl and Angela Miller and her colleagues implicitly regard Winslow Homer as the most important American painter of the nineteenth century, judging from the number of words and illustrations allotted to him, while Thomas Eakins also ranks highly for them. They deal with the painters in ways that earlier writers wouldn't have recognized. Pohl employs Homer's *Morning Bell* in her discussion of American workers, and discourses perceptively on Homer's *Prisoners from the Front* and his *Visit from the Old Mistress* of 1876, but then astonishingly stops, with no mention of the Prout's Neck marines for which he is best known.[33] Miller et al. take a very different approach, considering *Dressing for Carnival* and *The Gulf Stream* and the Black figures central to both, while admiring the painter as "an astute social commentator."[34] Thomas Eakins is also seen in a new light. Pohl writes that his "often heroic images" may have helped the new class of professional men "reassert their masculinity," an interesting echo of the stress on masculinity by the critics of a century before. Miller similarly sees Eakins as "pursuing issues of gender relentlessly" in the medical and sporting pictures and in his portraits.[35]

The two books diverge significantly once they reach the twentieth century. Pohl is particularly effective in dealing with politics and sexuality in the teens and twenties, and she usefully illustrates unfamiliar material, including wartime posters and magazine covers. While Pohl emphasizes the figurative, Miller writes that "abstraction was perhaps the fundamental feature of aesthetic modernism."[36] Writing about the years of Abstract Expressionism and Pop Art, Pohl gives a richly nuanced picture of the scene as she describes the influence of the Cold War and the atomic bomb, while challenging the critic Clement Greenberg's focus on the masculinity of the paintings. Johns and Rauschenberg are described as "a couple" who challenged "the virile and existential assumptions of Abstract Expressionism."[37] Clearly she intends to right old wrongs: Cy Twombly is omitted and Pollock and de Kooning are considered only briefly, while the work of Joan Mitchell, Hedda Sterne, Lee Krasner, Helen Frankenthaler, and several other women is explored. Miller's book was written six years after Pohl's, and explains postmodern theory well, while including more

Black and Indigenous artists. Both books minimize the work of the old guard while proposing a number of heretofore unfamiliar women and Black artists for the new canon. Miller et al. consider Bill Traylor, Lonnie Holley, and others to be "vernacular" artists, rather than "folk" or "outsider," as those terms are now considered demeaning. Thus, there are several parallels between these books and the direction of many museums, where it is increasingly believed that the age of the heroic white male and the masterpiece is over.

---

[1] Faith Ringgold, *We Flew Over the Bridge: The Memoirs of Faith Ringgold* (Duke University Press, 2005), 168.

[2] Susan E. Cahan, *Mounting Frustration: The Art Museum in the Age of Black Power* (Duke University Press, 2016), 114–16.

[3] See Caroline Wallace, "Three Lessons from the Artists' Protests of the Whitney Museum in the 1960s–70s," *Hyperallergic*, April 27, 2017.

[4] Thomas P. F. Hoving, "Preface," in *Harlem on My Mind: Cultural Capital of Black America, 1900–1968*, ed. Allon Schoener (Random House, 1969), 10.

[5] Candice Van Ellison, "Introduction," in Schoener, *Harlem on My Mind*, 14.

[6] Cahan, *Mounting Frustration*, 72–74.

[7] As quoted in Cahan, 219.

[8] Aaron Douglas, "The Negro in American Culture," as quoted in Sharon F. Patton, op. cit., 143.

[9] See Sharon F. Patton, *African-American Art* (Oxford University Press, 1998).

[10] Sarah Lewis, "African American Abstraction," in *The Routledge Companion to African American Art History*, ed. Eddie Chambers (Routledge, 2019). Lewis's recent book, *The Unseen Truth: When Race Changed Sight in America* (Harvard University Press, 2024), is another outstanding contribution; it examines art and racism in the US in broad, original terms.

[11] Tina Dunkley, "Clark Atlanta University Art Galleries," *The New Georgia Encyclopedia*, last edited March 28, 2021, georgiaencyclopedia.org.

[12] [9] Stephanie Mayer Heydt, *Rising Up: Hale Woodruff's Murals at Talladega College* (High Museum of Art, 2012).

[13] Patton, *African-American Art*, 212.

[14] Hilton Kramer, "Black Experience and Modernist Art," *New York Times*, February 14, 1970. In the same article, Kramer reviewed an exhibition of sculpture by Barbara Chase Riboud at Bertha Shaefer and found that "She has not yet found a style equal to her ambition."

[15] As quoted in Lewis, "African American Abstraction," 164.

[16] MoMA in 2022 joined with the Studio Museum in Harlem in presenting the exhibition "Just Above Midtown: Changing Spaces," celebrating the accomplishments

of Linda Cooke Bryant and the rich programming of her gallery. For an excellent survey of the role of the HBCU, see Shawnya Harris, "Historically Black Colleges and Universities, in *Southern/Modern: Rediscovering Southern Art from the First Half of the Twentieth Century,* ed. Jonathan Stuhlman and Maryha R. Severens (Mint Museum, 2023).

[17] Henry Louis Gates, "Introduction," in *May Day at Yale, 1970: Recollections: The Trial of Bobby Seale and the Black Panthers* (Prospecta Press, 2016), n.p.

[18] Doreen Bolger Burke, *American Paintings in the Metropolitan Museum of Art,* vol. 3, *Artists Born Between 1846 and 1864* (Metropolitan Museum of Art, 1980); Natalie Spassky et al., *American Paintings in the Metropolitan Museum of Art,* vol. 2, *Artists Born Between 1816 and 1845* (Metropolitan Museum of Art, 1985); John Caldwell and Oswaldo Rodriguez Roque, *American Paintings in the Metropolitan Museum of Art,* vol. 1, *Artists Born by 1815* (Metropolitan Museum of Art, 1994).

[19] The French were far ahead in recognizing women, as suggested by the important exhibition at the Pompidou Center in 1975: Christine Macel and Karolina Ziębińska-Lewandowska, eds., *Elles font l'abstraction (Women in Abstraction)* (Pompidou Center, 1975).

[20] Keri Watson and Keidra Daniels Navaroli, *This Is America: Re-Viewing the Art of the United States* (Oxford University Press, 2024), 375.

[21] Brenda A. Allen et al., *Slavery and Justice: Report of the Brown University Steering Committee on Slavery and Justice* (Brown University Press, 2006).

[22] Janet Halley, "My Isaac Royall Legacy," *Harvard BlackLetter Law Journal* 24 (2008): 117–31.

[23] See Allen, *Slavery and Justice* and Harvard University Presidential Committee on Harvard and the Legacy of Slavery, *The Legacy of Slavery at Harvard: Report and Recommendations of the Presidential Committee* (Harvard University Press, 2022). Harvard reported making serious progress in early 2023 with the appointment of Ruth Simmons, Brown's former president, as senior advisor to the president of Harvard on engagement with historically Black colleges and universities. See *Harvard Magazine,* May/June 2023, 13–14.

[24] See Rachel L. Swarns, *The 272: The Families Who Were Enslaved and Sold to Build the American Catholic Church* (Random House, 2024). In March 2021, the American Jesuits announced a hundred-million-dollar program, with half the income for race reconciliation projects, one quarter for grants and scholarships, and some for the support of descendants facing health emergencies.

[25] See David W. Blight, *Yale and Slavery: A History* (Yale University Press, 2024).

[26] Jessie MacLeod, "Ona Judge," George Washington's Mount Vernon, mountvernon.org.

[27] See Sarah Maslin, "In Pierson's Lower Court, a Tainted History," *Yale Daily News,* September 2, 2013. This lasted until 1980.

[28] James M. Banner Jr., *The Ever-Changing Past: Why All History Is Revisionist History* (Yale University Press, 2021).

[29] Robert Cozzolino, *The Female Gaze: Women Artists Making Their World* (Pennsylvania Academy of the Fine Arts, 2012).

[30] Frances K. Pohl, *Framing America: A Social History of American Art* (Thames & Hudson, 2002), 10; Angela L. Miller et al., *American Encounters: Art, History, and Cultural Identity* (Pearson, 2007), xiii. Regarding the latter volume, Angela Miller tells me that Janet Catherine Berlo wrote the sections on Indigenous cultures and the self-taught artists; Bryan J. Wolf and Margaretta M. Lovell shared the period before the Civil War, and Wolf wrote on Homer and Eakins; David Lubin wrote on genre painting while Angela herself discussed the post–Civil War years up to about 1960, with Jennifer L. Roberts contributing the last two chapters covering 1960 to the present. Angela Miller, email to the author, November 3, 2022. Both books have much to recommend them. Pohl's textbook has been a great success, being still in print after five editions, while the Miller survey did not sell well, despite its distinguished authors.

[31] Miller, *American Encounters,* 171.

[32] Miller, 226.

[33] Pohl tells me that her book is still in print, having gone through five editions, and that in recent editions she includes both Joseph Blackburn's *Isaac Winslow and His Family* (but no Smibert) and Winslow Homer's *Fox Hunt.* Frances K. Pohl, email to the author, October 13, 2024.

[34] Miller, *American Encounters,* 290.

[35] Pohl, *Framing America,* 253; Miller, *American Encounters,* 371.

[36] Miller, *American Encounters,* 401.

[37] Pohl, *Framing America,* 446.

17

Museums Reset

The truth is that as soon as the reasoning intelligence takes upon itself to judge works of art, nothing is any longer fixed or certain: you can prove anything you wish to prove.

—MARCEL PROUST,
In Search of Lost Time, Volume VI

When you come to the end of one time and the beginning of a new one, it's a period of tremendous pain and turmoil.

—JOSEPH CAMPBELL

BUBBLES BURST. Throughout history, bubbles have typically been caused by speculators, but in the case of traditional American paintings, the big buyers at the height of the market before 2008 were not short-term speculators but rather immensely wealthy people like Bill Gates, John Middleton, Tony and Lulu Wang, and Alice Walton, who got into collecting late and were fixated on American art rather than art in general. These buyers sought the very best and could afford any price. So, Sargent's *Siesta*, the picture Ray Horowitz loved but couldn't afford at $24,000 in 1962, went for $23.5 million to John Middleton in 2004. Bill Gates paid $10 million for Chase's *Fairy Tale* that the Horowitzes stretched for at $30,000. All of this skewed the market, dividing it in two, with a handful of recognized masterpieces still bringing huge prices, while the value of most of the earlier American paintings declined dramatically.[1] Numerous factors contributed to the dramatic change in the market, including the financial crisis of 2008 and a changing sense of America's place in the world.

As the boom in American art faded, questions of racism, long swept under the rug by white Americans, gradually became part of a broader national discussion. At many museums, the only Black staff members were guards and custodians. Increasing numbers of art museums began efforts to improve the racial balance of their professional staffs, along with their boards, exhibitions, and acquisitions. The museums' permanent collections are being rethought and reinstalled with the aim of diversifying the artists and better explaining the art; this typically involves explanatory labels and texts for the galleries, new acquisitions, and occasional interventions of contemporary works. The search was on for paintings by women, Black, Indigenous, and Latinx artists. All this naturally reduced the market, not to mention the wall space in the museums, for traditional "American" (white male) paintings. Many institutions also went about appointing curators of African American, Outsider, Folk, and Latinx art, frequently seeking non-white candidates for these posts.[2]

What follows is a personal review of museum activities; it is necessarily selective, as I haven't been able to visit every museum or talk with every curator that I would have wished. However, it seems clear that a number of Southern and Western museums took the lead in terms of social justice/BIPOC responses, and of anti-racism in particular. The Birmingham Museum of Art, for example, under director Richard Howard courageously hosted the museum's first exhibition of a Black artist (the painter and printmaker Corietta Mitchell) in March 1963, just after the church bombing. Howard acquired a Tanner in 1971; the following year saw the first purchase of a work by a living African American artist (David Driskell), with funds provided by the important civil rights activist and entrepreneur A. G. Gaston. A tradition of collecting and exhibiting significant Black, outsider, and local artists was established early. Thus, Birmingham's recognition of new criteria for judging art was neither sudden nor recent; rather, the city itself turned around quickly during the sixties and seventies, and the museum became part of this development.[3]

Another major institution, the High Museum in Atlanta, began collecting Southern and African American Art in 1975, with an early landmark being the acquisition of thirty of Bill Traylor's amazing drawings in 1982. In 1994, it became the first general interest museum to appoint a dedicated curator of Folk and Self-Taught Art. Since then, it has acquired perhaps the premier collection in this field, building on the gift of the T. Marshall Hahn Collection in 1996 and the numerous donations that followed. The High has continued to champion the work of Black and untrained artists ever since, presenting one important exhibition after another, including ones devoted to Civil Rights photography, the National Gallery's "Outliers and American Vanguard Art," as well as monographic shows of the work of Julie Mehretu, Romare Bearden, and most recently, David Drake the potter.

Similarly, the Museum of Fine Arts in Houston has moved strongly toward inclusion since the appointment of Peter C. Marzio as director in 1982. Recognizing the city's large Hispanic and Black populations, Marzio led the field in his aggressive efforts to diversify the collection with Hispanic/Latinx art and the work of Black and outsider artists, while presenting exhibitions devoted to the Quilters of Gee's Bend, the painter/assemblage maker Thornton Dial Sr., and many others. In 1987 it organized the groundbreaking exhibition "Hispanic Art of the United States" that traveled nationwide. Marzio also cultivated the oil heiress Caroline Wiess Law, resulting in the donation of her modern collection (Picasso, de Kooning, Lichtenstein) and her 2003 bequest of more than $400 million to fund modern acquisitions; Houston has bought brilliantly and diversely since then. The tradition continues under Gary Tinterow, director since 2012. The American galleries have been reinstalled; leading them off is a text titled "The Myth of the West," telling visitors that "Native people and their cultures survived even in the face of persecution and genocide" and going on to ask "What is myth, and what's reality?"[4] The museum's forty-seven paintings by Frederic Remington used to form the core of the Houston collection, but now just three are on view. Remington's handsomely rendered paintings of cowboys riding, shooting, busting broncos, and fighting Indians were long seen as the height of Western American art, but now they are judged as representing harmful, false myths. No painter has been more thoroughly reevaluated: For Jane Tompkins, his works "embody everything that was objectionable about his era in American history."[5] One sees the beginning of this notion in "The West as America" controversy of 1991 that I describe in chapter 18. Remington's person came to be viewed as offensive as his art. In a letter to writer Owen Wister he expressed his loathing of immigrants, writing: "Jews, Injuns, Chinamen, Italians, Huns—the rubbish of the earth I hate."[6]

LACMA has also been far more progressive than the Eastern museums. In 1976 it organized the influential, pioneering exhibition "Two Centuries of Black American Art," curated by the scholar and painter David C. Driskell, that traveled to Atlanta, Dallas, and Brooklyn. Like Houston, Los Angeles has an ethnically diverse population with many Hispanics; LACMA responded by pursuing the gift of the extraordinary Bernard and Edith Lewin Collection of Mexican Art in the mid-nineties. Ninety-seven of the two thousand works were exhibited in an impressive exhibition in 1997–98; they featured strong groups of paintings by Mexican muralists and a number of their contemporaries. Shortly afterwards, LACMA started a Latinx and Latin American initiative, and hired its first Latinx curator.[7]

The Fine Arts Museums of San Francisco have similarly played an active role in promulgating diversity. In 1998 the de Young Museum hosted the traveling exhibition "Rhapsodies in Black: Art of the Harlem Renaissance" organized by the Corcoran and the Hayward Gallery, London. Since then, curator Timothy Burgard has guided the acquisition of dozens of works by many of the best Black and white artists of the last hundred years, from Jacob Lawrence to Nick Cave. In 2017 the museums acquired by gift and purchase sixty-two impressive works from William Arnett's Souls Grown Deep Foundation, including paintings and constructions by Purvis Young, Bessie Harvey, Lonnie Holley, and Thornton Dial, as well as quilts by Willie "Ma Willie" Abrams and Annie Mae Young; only the Met had preceded them in making such an acquisition from Arnett.[8] Finally, I should mention Burgard's amazing triennial exhibition project, "The de Young Open" that he began in 2020. For its 2023 iteration, some 7,766 area artists submitted individual works that were juried blindly by a committee of curators and Bay Area artists, with 883 of them selected and installed in floor-to-ceiling, salon style, at the de Young Museum for the three-month run of the show. In 2020, about one-third of the works were sold, with the museum itself purchasing sixteen. It is impossible to imagine a more democratic project; it tells us how dramatically the art world is changing.

The Brooklyn Museum was an exception to the generally cautious climate in the Northeast. Responding to the large Black population of that city, in 1969 it formed a Community Gallery dedicated to showing the work of Black Artists in New York. Brooklyn was the only institution that hosted the two key exhibitions of that era, David Driskell's "Two Centuries of Black American Art, 1750–1950" mentioned above, and the Corcoran's even more influential show of 1982, "Black Folk Art in America, 1930–1980," that effectively introduced the canon of self-taught artists who have become well known in recent years.

One of the most influential recent exhibitions was organized by the Rubell Family Collection from its own collection in Miami. The philosophy of Mera and Don Rubell is simple: "We only show art we own."[9] The Rubells are ambitious, farsighted, and hardworking. They visit artists all over the nation, and they buy the ones they like in depth. The Rubells were always interested in Black artists, in 1981 purchasing a major Basquiat in the year it was made and then acquiring others in the following two years. Around 2005 they turned major attention to Black art, and built an important collection. In 2008 they opened an exhibition called "30 Americans," devoted to the work of thirty-one Black artists, including many whose work became more widely known in subsequent years, such as Nick Cave, Barkley Hendricks, Kara Walker, Mickalene Thomas, and Kehinde Wiley. Most remarkably, the exhibition up to 2024 has traveled to twenty-two museums around the country, providing an eye-opener for many people. Professor Eddie Chambers points out the importance of the exhibition's title: The artists are not described as Black or African American, but simply as Americans.[10] A major question for years had been whether the aim should be to create a distinctive Black art making use of African precedents, following the views of the key philosopher Alain Locke, or rather James A. Porter's belief that the work of Black artists must be seen within the context of American art; the Rubells came down forcefully on Porter's side.[11]

One thinks of the venerable museums of the Northeast, including the Met, the National Gallery, Philadelphia Museum of Art, and the Museum of Fine Arts as being the field's leaders; they are the institutions I know best, and they were long the ones that established aesthetic standards for the field. Recently, however, they have been racing to catch up. Considering Boston first: Edmund Barry Gaither, director of the National Center of Afro-American Artists in Boston from 1969 to 2020, organized an ambitious show for the MFA in 1970: It was called "Afro-American Artists: New York and Boston," and included 158 works by 70 artists, favoring those whose work made reference to Africa, with an excellent catalogue. But the show was on view for barely a month, and it came and went with little effect on the museum's programs or its audience. Boston for years was one of the whitest American cities, and its loyalty to the city's colonial history remains deeply entrenched. Boston's schools weren't desegregated until a struggle partly resolved by a court ruling of 1974. In 1970, the MFA acquired its first two paintings by Black Americans: Horace Pippin's *Country Doctor*, and Robert S. Duncanson's *Dog's Head of Scotland*, while it purchased two collages by Romare Bearden from Cordier and Ekstrom in 1971. But things began to change substantially only in the 1990s with farsighted purchases of important works by Faith Ringgold, Glenn Ligon, Betye Saar, Robert Colescott, and Lorna Simpson, initiated by curator Trevor Fairbrother. A massive storage jar by David Drake was acquired in 1997. Then under curator Elliot Bostwick Davis's direction, an impressive Henry Ossawa Tanner was bought in 2005. Thanks to the museum's Heritage Fund for a Diverse Collection, established in 2005, and other donors, major works by Norman Lewis, Kara Walker, Mark Bradford, Allan Rohan Crite, Martin Puryear, Mickalene Thomas, and Kehinde Wiley were acquired by the department of contemporary art. Capping this campaign was the landmark acquisition by gift and purchase of 67 works from the Boston collector John Axelrod in 2011, which added strong works by members of an earlier generation of artists, including Romare Bearden, Hughie Lee-Smith, Beauford Delaney, and Archibald Motley (fig. 63), along with an important group of Afro-Brazilian paintings dating from the mid-twentieth century and another jar by David Drake.[12]

In addition, a decade ago the Museum of Fine Arts began to exhibit the baroque art of the Spanish colonies in Central and South America in galleries adjacent to Boston's treasures of eighteenth-century New England furniture, silver, and paintings. The result was highly successful, and owes a great deal to the splendid purchases made by curator Dennis Carr, along with some fortuitous finds in the MFA storerooms. Among Carr's first buys was the astonishingly heavy, graceful baroque Cuban chest of drawers, which makes the equivalent Boston pieces

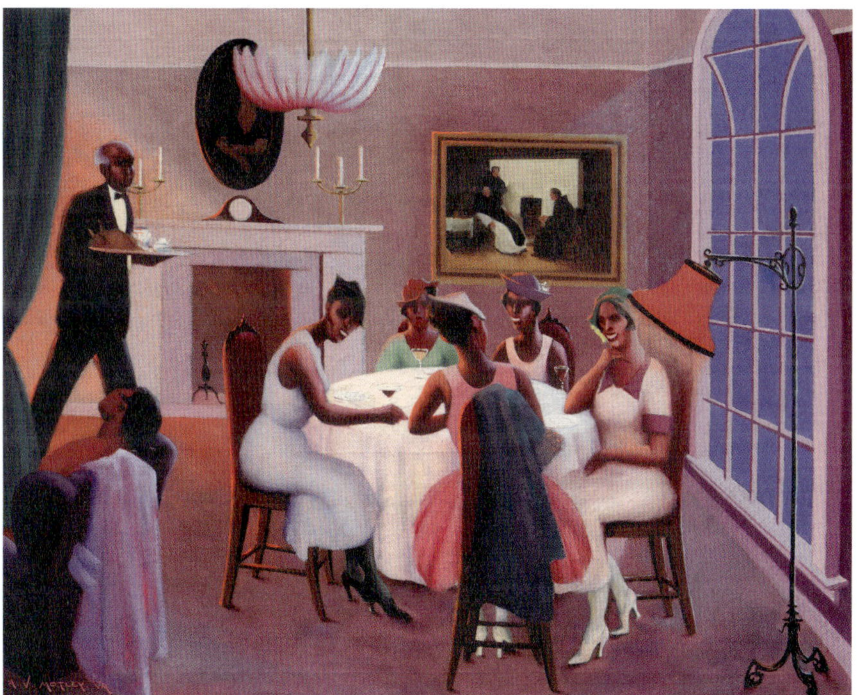

Fig. 63. ARCHIBALD MOTLEY,
Cocktails, oil on canvas, ca. 1926. Museum of Fine Arts, Boston.

look tame indeed. In 2015 came a flurry of purchases, including a striking desk and bookcase from viceregal Mexico, also from the mid-eighteenth century; its energetic geometric wood and bone inlays and its pseudo-chinoiserie decorative painting on the interior are extraordinary. Silver plaques from Bolivia and communion pieces from Guatemala are also revelatory, and make telling contrasts with New England silver of the same period. Illuminating for many visitors are the set of sixteen small paintings of about 1775 by the Mexican artist Ignacio de Castro depicting *The Castes of New Spain*, which codify the exact social ranking of each mixture of the races found in the populace.

After I left the MFA in 1999, I became curator of American art at the Harvard Art Museums. One of my most important contributions there was bringing in the Didi and David Barrett Collection of Self-Taught, Folk, and Outsider Art. The Barretts had been collecting the material for several decades, stemming from Didi's service as a trustee of the Museum of American Folk Art in New York. They introduced me to the work of such Black artists as Bill Traylor, Bessie Harvey, Thornton Dial Sr. (fig. 64), Nellie Mae Rowe and numerous others, and I responded to it. But some people at our supposedly open-minded university, both faculty members and old-time collectors, found the art unworthy of Harvard's venerable traditions, not I believe for racial reasons so much as that the art looked so unfamiliar, so crude and untraditional to them. But today I am pleased to see increasing use of the Barrett Collection at the museum, though I am still waiting for the curators to install one of the Barrett's richly textured Thornton Dials next to the paintings of Pollock, Kline, and Alberto Burri.

The Metropolitan Museum of Art is the nation's greatest museum and has traditionally led the field. It was brilliantly directed by Philippe de Montebello from 1977 to 2008, but with the dawning of a new era, it became clear that the Met had fallen behind in terms of diversity. The museum turned the corner with the appointment of the Austrian-born and trained Max Hollein as director in the late spring of 2018. He came to the Met after a successful nineteen-month tour as director of the Fine Arts Museums of San Francisco. Hollein confirmed to me that he had learned a great deal from the sexually, ethnically, and politically

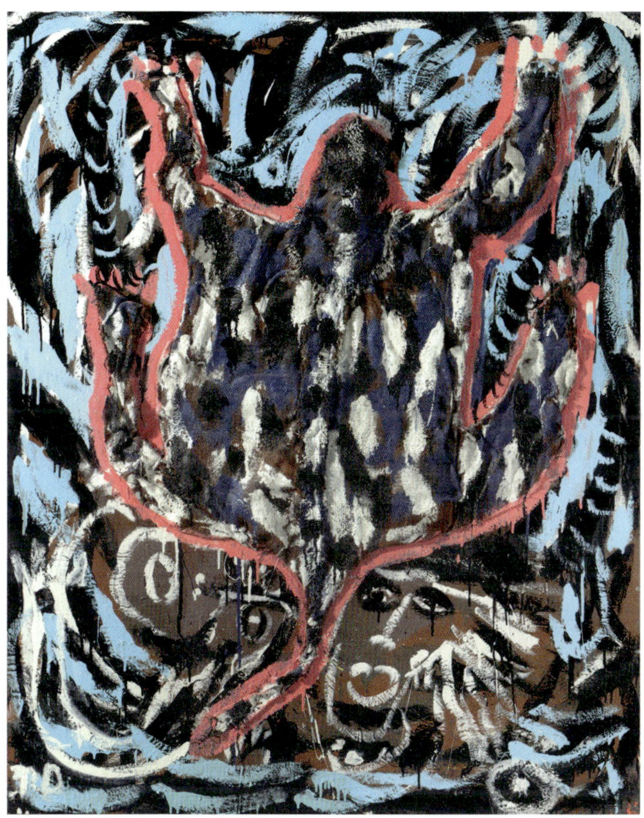

Fig. 64. THORNTON DIAL,
Life Begins with Crawling, enamel, carpet, and burlap on wood, 1992. Harvard Art Museums.

diverse culture of that city and from the projects that he found himself overseeing, including the exhibition "The Summer of Love Experience: Art, Fashion, and Rock & Roll," and the acquisition of sixty-two works from the Arnett Foundation that resulted in an impressive exhibition called "Revelations."[13] In July 2020, just weeks after the killing of George Floyd, Hollein issued a bold, detailed policy statement at the Met proclaiming that "our government, politics, systems, and institutions have all contributed to perpetuating racism and injustice."[14] Hollein mandated anti-racism training for staff and trustees, increased hiring of Black, Indigenous, and people of color, emphasized collecting art by

BIPOC artists, and outlined a series of diverse projects, many of which have already been accomplished. He told me that as an Austrian he was keenly aware of the Holocaust, and that this experience played a role in his quick understanding of American racism and our history of slavery.[15]

In 2019, under Hollein's direction, the Met commissioned two massive paintings by the Canadian First Nations painter of Cree ancestry, Kent Monkman, for the Great Hall, thus signaling the museum's commitment to anti-racism and anti-colonialism. *Welcoming the Newcomers* parodies the traditional white view that Columbus "discovered" the new world. Monkman sets history straight; now the Native Americans residents are in charge, echoing Professor Ned Blackhawk's thesis that Indigenous people are at the center of American history; in this work, they welcome a mixed-race group to safety, while some white men cling to an overturned lifeboat offshore. Monkman's companion picture *Resurgence of the People* echoes Leutze's *Washington Crossing the Delaware,* but here it is an overloaded boatload of Indigenous people making it through choppy seas with Native women paddling. Monkman, like many Black and Indigenous artists, presents a satiric but in his view, a just rewriting of history. Exhibitions all around the Met illustrated its commitment to diversity, including "Fictions of Emancipation: Carpeaux Recast," an inventive "Afro-Futurist Period Room," and in the American Wing, the permanent installation of the outstanding Charles and Valerie Diker Collection of Native American art, a recent gift.

These dramatic developments were capped by a highly ambitious exhibition in 2024, "The Harlem Renaissance and Transatlantic Modernism," organized by curator at large Denise Murrell.[16] It stood in purposeful contrast with the disastrous "Harlem on My Mind" presentation of 1969. The Met's new show was broad-reaching, with numerous loans drawn from the collections at historically Black colleges and universities. For the first time, the Harlem artists were shown together with such European modernists as Picasso, Matisse, Munch, as well as Chaim Soutine, Kees van Dongen, and Germaine Casse. These painters added gravitas to the exhibition, while making it clear that the Americans were not the equal of the European masters in terms of technique. Visitors might have assumed that the use of "Transatlantic Modernism" in the title pointed to stylistic comparisons of the Europeans with the Americans, but no: Questions of style are no longer of great concern to art historians. Instead, paintings by the Europeans were apparently selected for the way they rendered the poses and skin color of Black subjects, as comparisons to the Harlem pictures.

At "The Harlem Renaissance," the opening label told visitors that "Black artists developed radically new modes of self-expression." In fact, their modes of expression were conventional; the artists' impressive accomplishment is that they persevered and did good work in a highly racist society. Their aim was to tell their own stories, to represent their friends and families, rather than emulate MoMA's view of avant-garde art. Aaron Douglas, Romare Bearden, Jacob Lawrence, and William H. Johnson all worked effectively in styles derived from Cubism, though none pushed the boundaries of that style. As the catalogue points out, one finds parallels in the work of Archibald Motley and others to German painters and the Neue Sachlichkeit, but otherwise the major European trends of those years are not in evidence. The best-known Black artists were well represented, but we were also introduced to such talented lesser-known figures as Laura Wheeler Waring, Malvin Gray Johnson, and Samuel Joseph Brown Jr. Winold Reiss's sensitive portraits of Alain Locke, W. E. B. Du Bois and other key figures were scattered throughout: Together with a number of his books, including Alain Locke's important volume *The New Negro,* with illustrations by Reiss, they added significantly to the exhibition. In it, Reiss was never identified as white (the labels saying only that he had been born in Germany); he was a gifted artist with close connections in both the Black and Indigenous communities and was rightly included in the show.[17] Lois Mailou Jones was, strangely, represented only by an atypical still life, one that wasn't listed in the catalogue. Quality as such goes unmentioned in the book, but Murrell's judgments are indicated by the weight given to some artists and the minimal representation of others: Archibald Motley, whose work is increasingly admired, led with fifteen paintings, followed by the great photographer James Van Der Zee and the painters William H. Johnson and Aaron Douglas, the latter being accorded a room of his own. I found some reviews of the show to be inexplicably lukewarm; for me, seeing it proved an uplifting, moving experience. What I came away with was the memory of having met an extraordinary group of people. The portraits of women were especially memorable for the calmness and dignity of the sitters, and for the sadness one sees in their eyes. I found the show beautiful and well installed. It was an important one, though it couldn't make up for the museum's (and the white establishment's) past neglect, but it did point to a more inclusive future.

The Met's longtime rival, the National Gallery of Art, made a delayed entry to the modern art party but has quickly caught up. When I was there as a Fellow in 1967–68, the rule against hanging any work by a living artist was still in place. However, in the early 1970s, this changed dramatically, as the need to display contemporary art in the new East Wing designed by I. M. Pei became clear. E. A. Carmean Jr. was appointed the Gallery's first curator of modern art in 1974; his well-funded exhibitions and acquisitions from the modern canon were impressive. Far more experimental was the exhibition called "Outliers and American Vanguard Art," organized by curator Lynne Cooke in 2018.[18] This was an astonishing venture for the Gallery, as numerous objects were crudely made by its traditional standards, and so many were by women and minority artists, never a strong suit for this institution. The exhibition of 250 works by eighty artists was colorful, inventive, and full of surprises, with artists ranging from Bill Traylor and Henry Darger to the Douanier Rousseau, Edward Hicks, and Marsden Hartley and the Gee's Bend quiltmakers. The results were impressive, even if the aim of outlining a clear theoretical framework for the whole proved difficult for the catalogue authors; the connection between the work of the "outliers" and the modernists never became clear. One wondered exactly how Cindy Sherman came to be included, and I longed for a Picasso sculpture, or for some nod to Duchamp, Dada, Dubuffet, or Arte Informale to suggest the roots and parallels to some of the assemblages.

This important show was followed at the National Gallery in 2022 by another powerful presentation, "Afro-American Histories," a remake of an exhibition from São Paolo, and by the purchase of forty works by Black artists from the Souls Grown Deep Foundation. This acquisition included works by such outstanding figures as Thornton Dial, Bessie Harvey, and Nellie Mae Rowe; in addition, included were a number of quilts by Mary Lee Bendolph and Irene Williams of the Gee's Bend community.[19] The Gallery has also recently built a superb holding of paintings by many of the best Black, Native American, and Hispanic contemporary artists; this impressive effort was led by the gifted curator Harry Cooper, who came to the Gallery in 2008.[20]

The federal art museums in Washington have a special problem: They can never tell when a cranky senator might drop in and object to something. Memories are still fresh of how the Corcoran in 1989 canceled a Mapplethorpe photography exhibition after objections by Senator Jesse Helms, with unfortunate results for the museum director's career, and how the Smithsonian's "The West as Art" in 1991 caused such a furor (as I have described in chapter 18). Curator Eleanor Harvey at the Smithsonian Museum of American Art confirmed that she and her colleagues are aware of past history, and that they tread cautiously.[21] The National Gallery of Art, just a few blocks away, was long a conservative institution often characterized as an old-boys club, but as I have mentioned, the recent exhibitions of Black artists and the adventurous acquisitions helped establish a new direction. This course was confirmed by the appointment of Kaywin Feldman as director in 2019 and of E. Carmen Ramos as chief curator in 2021; together they urged an acknowledgment of the changing times and a new awareness of race. The museum's American galleries have taken on a new look, as the long tradition of labels limited to artist, date, and credit line has been replaced by one that encourages explanatory texts. Now in the American galleries there are not only labels for individual works but also interventions with contemporary paintings mixed with older works. Bierstadt's *Last of the Buffalo* receives special treatment, with a text noting that the seeming message of the painting—that Native Americans were responsible for the slaughter of the buffalo—is historically inaccurate. Copley's *Watson and the Shark* is coupled only moderately effectively with two large, recently acquired paintings by Kerry

James Marshall. But the Gallery's full-scale plaster version of Saint-Gaudens's *Shaw Memorial* is treated sensitively, and is accompanied by Archibald Motley's moving portrait of his mother, who was enslaved at birth.

Most museums are following similar playbooks, the curators all being aware of what their peers are doing. A key question often arises: How much weight to give to the old canon and its "masterpieces." At one end of the spectrum we find The New York Historical, which has buried in storage its extraordinary holdings of Hudson River and genre paintings, including Thomas Cole's *Course of Empire,* in an effort to be topical and to give a number of Black and Indigenous artists their due. Apparently art is no longer considered an important aspect of history. This kind of initiative can succeed only if the great paintings are replaced with stimulating, informative installations; they so far are sadly lacking at the New York Historical.[22] Crystal Bridges, with its large staff and excellent funding, has also reduced the impact of its permanent holdings, but without removing the best works. It has made these changes successfully while making clear the museum's role in teaching civics and history through art. Diversity is more easily accomplished in modern and contemporary art than in the older fields; a curator can buy or borrow desired works by the Black, Hispanic, Indigenous, and women artists, then hang them judiciously with the collection. One sees an outstanding example of this at Yale in the galleries installed by the gifted Keely Orgeman. Dealing with the eighteenth and nineteenth centuries is more difficult because relevant paintings and sculpture—ones illustrating the lives of free or enslaved Black people or key historical events—are few and far between, and often the ideal paintings simply do not exist.

The recently completed installation of American art up to 1860 at the Philadelphia Museum is thoughtful and effective. Curator Kathleen Foster tells me that they began by identifying the major treasures in the collection such as Peale's *Staircase Group,* then placing them on important walls and sightlines, before filling out the galleries with all the varied works needed to flesh out the stories they wanted to tell.[23] Hanging on the entry wall in the first gallery are several loans, including historic portraits of Lenape chiefs Lapowinsa and Tishcohan by Gustavus Hesselius dating from 1735 together with a great treasure, a tribal wampum belt memorializing the peace treaty of 1683 (a text explains how the treaty was later violated). A long label in the next area tells us that "nearly all the works in the American galleries bear connections to slavery," a truth still shocking to some and one that went unrecognized in earlier years.[24] Philadelphia did not need to make many purchases to fill in the gaps; it already owned fine Spanish colonial paintings, but it did buy a superb Peruvian silver monstrance that compares nicely with the museum's fine examples of Philadelphia silver.

The next gallery opens with the extraordinary Copley double portrait of Philadelphians, Mr. and Mrs. Thomas Mifflin, who visited Boston just before the Tea Party. The artist portrayed the loving relationship of a wealthy Quaker couple, with Mrs. Mifflin and her weaving occupying center stage while her husband looks on admiringly. Copley, Stuart, and Sully are shown alongside Pennsylvania German frakturs, pottery, and painted chests, with no apologies for the appropriate emphasis on showing the museum's strong holdings in local artists and artisans. Next, one is met by Charles Willson Peale's landmark painting, *Staircase Group*. To its left is one of the most moving of American portraits, Peale's 1819 rendering of Yarrow Mamout (1736–1823) (fig. 65), a remarkable man of eighty-three who had been kidnapped into slavery in Africa, then brought to Annapolis where he was enslaved until being granted his freedom in 1796.[25] Peale sought him out to paint in his old age, and the result is a likeness of astonishing warmth and humanity, a far more engaging portrait than, say, the painter's rendering of the wealthy Cadwalader family that hangs nearby. Mamout represents another example of curatorship at its best: The Philadelphia Museum purchased the portrait in 2011 for over $2 million when the Historical Society of Pennsylvania sold it, deaccessioning some works to raise the funds. The huge price gives evidence of the new taste: Peale portraits rarely bring in excess of $40,000 unless the subject is George Washington, but the one of Mamout has everything that is most desired now, as a truly superb painting and one of a once-enslaved Black man. An equally good rendering of a white man would be far less valued by curators or the market,

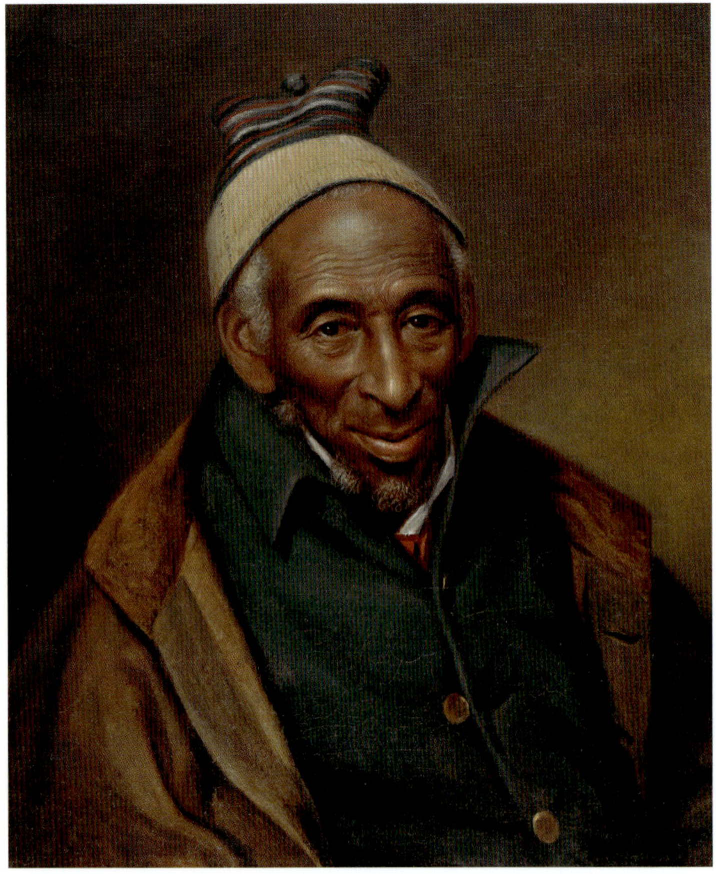

Fig. 65. **CHARLES WILLSON PEALE**, *Yarrow Mamout*, oil on canvas, 1819. Philadelphia Museum of Art.

suggesting again the extent to which social, non-aesthetic factors play a major role today in judging art.

Nearby one finds still lifes by Raphaelle Peale and several family members, along with Charles Willson Peale's unique portrait of his wife in tears lamenting the death of their baby daughter who is pictured, deceased, in her lap. Peale exhibited the painting in his museum under a warning sheet, as some museums do today with potentially troubling works. Close by, we see objects that recount stories of displaced Indian tribes, of the China trade, and of an enslaved Black profile maker named Moses Williams who was owned by Peale himself.

One proceeds to a gallery devoted to vernacular art of Pennsylvania, including paintings by Edward Hicks, a striking salt-glaze stoneware water cooler, and a handsome painted tall clock and chest, while in the final area one finds silver, furniture, and paintings by free Blacks in Philadelphia, a portrait by Joshua Johnson, local glassware, and landscapes by Thomas Cole and Thomas Doughty. This reinstallation of the early American art will be followed by another that will reorganize the museum's great holdings from Thomas Eakins and Winslow Homer to the mid-twentieth century.

The MFA Boston had the same aims but worked with a different methodology, one where ideas could trump the old notions of quality. It began a series of reinstallations with twentieth-century art. Since 2020, a visitor entering its American Wing has been greeted with two colorful, satirical paintings by the important Native American Tommy Wayne Cannon (1946–1978), known as T. C. Cannon. These works replaced the equestrian portrait by Copley of *George IV When Prince of Wales*, a grandiose picture that signaled Boston's long allegiance to English colonial values. Curator Ethan Lasser turned the tables and made clear that the Wing would now be devoted to the art of all the Americas. Standing front and center for a time was a colossal bronze head of a Black figure by the Boston sculptor John Wilson (1922–2015); it told us clearly of the museum's intention to honor citizens—both visitors and artists—rarely recognized in the past by this institution. O'Keeffe's *Deer's Skull with Pedernal* hung nearby, her painting sharing a wall with a striking portrait of a Native American wrapped in an American flag by Fritz Scholder (fig. 72 in chapter 18), a work that powerfully asks what it means to be an American. O'Keeffe has been criticized for her paternalistic relations with her Native neighbors, and for portraying the Pedernal, a sacred Native American site, but her position in the canon seems secure for now.[26] From here, one proceeded to six permanent collection galleries, each devoted to a different story—war, the Southwest, jazz, folk art and modernism, Latin America, and abstraction.

The face of the Boston collection has changed dramatically. The most dramatic addition is the *Women's Tailor* of 1957 by the Spanish-Mexican Surrealist Remedios Varo (1908–1963) (fig. 66) that was paid

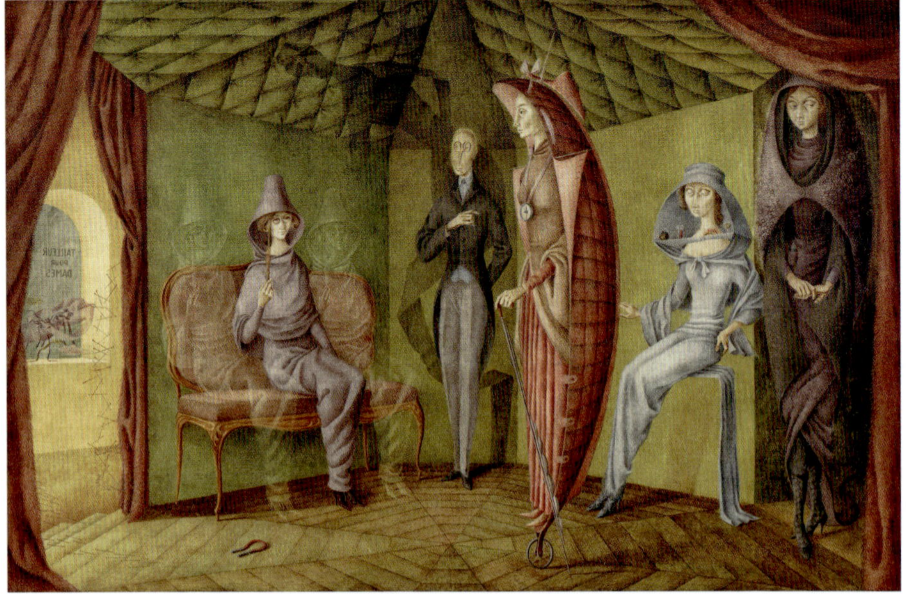

Fig. 66. **REMEDIOS VARO,**
Tailleur pour dames (Ladies Tailor), oil on board, 1957.
Museum of Fine Arts, Boston.

for in 2021 by the sale of two of the museum's weaker O'Keeffe paintings and one by Charles Sheeler. Deaccessioning from a museum collection is tricky, but as this demonstrates, it can be done well. The MFA is badly lacking in Surrealist works and in the work of women; if any acquisition ever filled a gap and opened up a new area of study, this one does. Moreover, it hangs superbly with related paintings the museum bought earlier, including a bold self-portrait by Siqueiros and a moving depiction of two servant women by Frida Kahlo.

In 2023 the MFA mounted a superb exhibition of the pottery of Toshiko Takaezu, who was born in Hawaii of Japanese parents. Despite the long history of American prejudice against Asians, from the Chinese Exclusion Act of 1882 to the wartime internment of many Japanese who were American citizens, not to mention the constant wars the US has fought in Asia since the Philippine War and the continuing evidence of discrimination against Asians in the US, the art world has been generally accepting of artists with Asian roots. One thinks of the long, distinguished tenure of Seiji Ozawa as conductor of the Boston Symphony starting in 1973; Isamu Noguchi, whose work has been admired by the avant-garde since the 1940s; Nam June Paik, the video artist; the sculptor Ruth Asawa; the much-loved cellist Yo-Yo Ma; and of course Maya Lin, the daughter of Chinese immigrants, who designed the Vietnam Memorial in Washington, DC, in 1981. These artists paved the way for younger generations of Asian and Asian Americans whose work has been shown by adventurous museums, including the Guggenheim in New York and the ICA in Boston.[27]

Only fifteen or so of the ninety works from the William H. Lane Collection were on view at the MFA in late 2023, but I was relieved that a number of the classic pictures by O'Keeffe, Dove, Hartley, and Stuart Davis were still hanging. Stuart Davis's *Hot Still-Scape,* which I sweated blood and tears to acquire (as described in chapter 12) was in a gallery devoted to American music rather than one displaying modern masterworks. We celebrated the picture's place at the top of Davis's oeuvre; in its new context, it looks well, though with its stellar quality seemingly downplayed. But where, I wondered, were paintings as Marsden Hartley's *Painting No. 2* of 1914 from the Lane Collection or such other standouts as Charles Sheeler's *View of New York* and Joseph Stella's iconic *Brooklyn Bridge*? For the Boston curators, it was more important to illustrate the breadth of American culture than to include every great example of American modernism. The masterpiece of old is now a work that can be put into storage: My generation of curators aimed to teach art and how to discern quality, while today's practitioners aim to teach visitors about racism, history, and our changing society.

The Baltimore Museum of Art, for a time, adopted more aggressive means to embrace diversity and the role of Black artists, resorting briefly to shortsighted (to my mind) deaccessioning. When Chris Bedford arrived at Baltimore as director in 2016, he quickly instituted a program of selling works from the collection in order to fund purchases of contemporary works by Black and women artists. In 2018 the museum sold seven paintings by Warhol, Rauschenberg, Franz Kline, and others for $16.1 million, then used the funds to buy contemporary works by women and people of color. Bedford had great confidence in his judgment, saying that "the works we bought for very little money will be acknowledged as unquestioned masterpieces."[28] In twenty years, we'll know more about how this turned out, but I would suggest that Bedford should study the history of such predictions before being quite so certain. Then in 2020 he announced a plan to sell three of his museum's most important modern paintings, Warhol's *Last Supper*, an important Clifford Still (the museum's only example), and a Brice Marden given by the painter. A public protest caused the auction to be canceled at the last moment. After Bedford left for San Francisco in 2021, the museum continued to lead the field in its emphasis on a multi-racial staff and board (its current board chair and director are both people of color) and in its exhibitions and acquisitions, but without resorting to such sales. To suggest another example, the Everson Museum in Syracuse, New York, in 2020 sold its small but important Jackson Pollock—one of the outstanding works in its collection, and its only painting by the artist—for $13 million in order to buy works of women and artists of color.[29] I don't believe that the admirable aims in these cases—to diversify the collections—justified the irreversible sales. In my experience, deaccessioning works best when the sales are made from virtual duplicates or from the weakest works of a strong holding, and when the purchases are clearly important additions to the collection. Neither Baltimore nor the Everson came close to meeting this standard.

The same issues are affecting large and small museums across the country. Jeffrey Richmond-Moll, curator at the Georgia Museum of Art, writes that entrenched understandings about American art necessarily are being challenged, "particularly those that reinforce traditional hierarchies, alleviate the complicity of individuals and institutions from systems of oppression and exploitation, and heroize the achievements of white male artists."[30] Similarly, the Portland Museum in Maine has reinstalled its collection, guided by three considerations: "Maine's role in transatlantic slavery, environmental change, and the ongoing presence of Wabanaki and other Indigenous nations."[31] Each museum follows its own course in its installations, but as of late 2024, very few were ignoring the powerful currents of diversity and inclusion.

The Museum of Modern Art provided a model of a successful intervention when it reinstalled the collection in October 2019. Visitors entering the large room of classic Cubist pictures, anchored by Picasso's famous *Demoiselles d'Avignon*, were shocked to find an unfamiliar painting on the long side wall, Faith Ringgold's *American People Series #20: Die*, of 1967 (fig. 67). *Die* depicts a bloody massacre in Cubist terms, with men, women, and children both white and Black being slaughtered by a white man with a gun and a Black one wielding a knife. Ringgold had long been known to Black and Latinx art communities for her roles as a painter, spokesperson, and performance artist, but before this had been largely invisible to the white establishment, and MoMA saw its way to purchasing this painting and a group of her other works only in 2016, when the painter was eighty-six years old. Juxtaposing Ringgold and Picasso made people think and look, as interventions do at their best.

Many Black artists whose work is now being discovered by the major museums have long been known in the Black community. Ringgold's paintings were frequently exhibited at the New Museum, an institution that became a force in the field under founding director Marcia Tucker and her successor since 1999, Lisa Phillips. That museum included Ringgold in two important exhibitions, "Frameworks of Identity in the

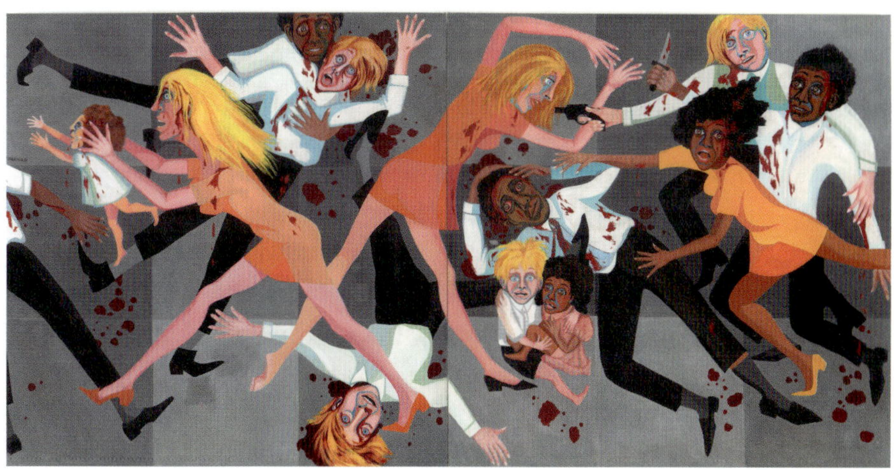

Fig. 67. **FAITH RINGGOLD,**
American People Series #20: Die, oil on canvas, 1967. Museum of Modern Art.

1980s" (1990) and "A Labor of Love" in 1996; it showed a survey of her works in 1998 and then in 2022 the museum presented a definitive retrospective it called "Faith Ringgold: American People." What we learn is that Black artists have long been there, surviving and growing without the patronage or recognition from the white establishment until very recently.

Many of the other senior artists who are members of the newly recognized canon of African American artists have also been significantly supported by exhibitions at the New Museum. Robert Colescott was the first Black artist to have a solo exhibition at the Venice Biennale (1997). However real recognition of his forceful, satirical paintings began only after his death, and came to a climax with the 2021 auction sale of his *George Washington Carver Crossing the Delaware* for $15,315,900 to George Lucas for his new museum of narrative art (it hung briefly and effectively at the Met near Leutze's *Washington Crossing the Delaware* in 2023) and with his splendid retrospective exhibition at the New Museum in 2022.

Kehinde Wiley and Amy Sherald, the painters of the Obama portraits that were unveiled in 2018 before going on a national tour in 2021–22, have become nationally celebrated, with museums and collectors now scrambling for their work. Our first Black president made his interest in Black artists well known and hung their works in the White House. Having a painting by Wiley has become an almost-necessary credential for a museum wishing to prove its bona fides in committing to the new values. Wiley's work was well known before the Obama commission; it is found in many major museums, nowhere in more exciting form than at the Huntington Library in San Marino, California, where the painter's mother took him for art classes as a youth. All of Wiley's work incorporates the depictions of power and wealth that he first observed at the Huntington's sumptuous gallery of full-length British aristocratic portraits. This room holds perhaps the greatest museum collection of grand manner British paintings, works that for a time in the early twentieth century were the most admired and most expensive paintings in the world, as suggested by the world record price of some $778,000 (almost $13 million today) that Henry Huntington paid for

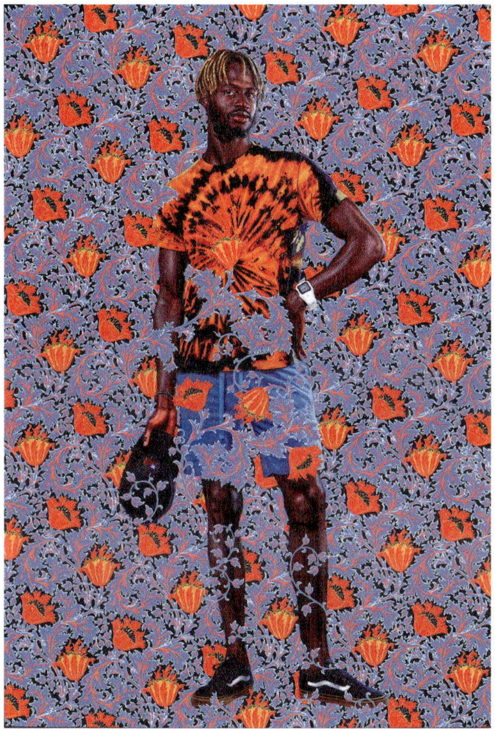

Fig. 68. KEHINDE WILEY,
A Portrait of a Young Gentleman, oil on linen, 2021. Huntington Library.

Thomas Gainsborough's *Blue Boy* in 1922.[32] Opposite the *Blue Boy* today is Wiley's *Young Gentleman* (fig. 68), with its pose directly inspired by the Gainsborough. Neither of the young protagonists, each encased in his own culture, upstages the other; instead, their unspoken dialogue creates a new reality for the visitor.

Eighteenth-century London was a center of the slave trade. In recent years, British art historians have been exploring the legacy of slavery and its effects on the work of both British and American artists. One of the best exhibitions of Black American artists, rivaling anything done by an American museum, was "Soul of a Nation," organized by the Tate Modern in 2017, with the major essays by Tate curators. It traveled to Crystal Bridges, which helped fund it, then to four other American museums. It focused on the art of 1963 to 1983, with useful text and many photographs outlining the key moments of these complex times.[33] Also coming from London, from the publisher Routledge, was the invaluable *Routledge Companion to African American Art History,* with some forty essays on nearly every aspect of the art from the Harlem Renaissance to a consideration of "Post-Blackness" and recent exhibitions.[34] Nearly every article includes an extensive bibliography; in total, they present a picture of the already enormous and still growing literature in this field. Then in 2024 the venerable Royal Academy in London produced a powerful exhibition on the question of colonialism and enslavement entitled "Entangled Pasts, 1768–Now: Art, Colonialism, and Change."[35] Visitors were surprised at the number of British paintings that include Black figures. We are reminded that Copley's *Watson and the Shark* (MFA, Boston) was painted in London for the English audience; it is one of many key loans from American and British museums and private collectors. The exhibition balanced colonial paintings with relevant works by living American and British artists, including a powerful, multifigure sculpture *The First Supper* by Tavares Strachan that stood in the Academy's courtyard, an equally memorable fleet of slave ships by Hew Locke, Sir Isaac Julien's film about Frederick Douglass, and brilliantly selected works by Kara Walker and Mohini Chandra, among many others. The effective installation reinforced the theme of the exhibition, particularly in the Octagon where mirrors reflected a central bust of a muscular Black man up into the area where statues of white luminaries have long been placed.

Finally, one of the most dramatic developments in the American field has been the fast-rising importance of David Drake, an enslaved Black potter in Edgefield, South Carolina; he has become a central figure in the new canon, to the point where ownership of one of his pots has become nearly mandatory for forward-looking museums. To the uninitiated, this seems to have happened overnight, while in fact Drake's rediscovery has been years in the making. In an excellent essay, Adrienne Spinozzi recounts a century's worth of research, publications, and museum acquisitions leading to the feeding frenzy of today.[36] Working mainly in a pottery owned by Lewis Miles, who also owned

Drake himself, Drake made well-crafted alkaline-glazed stoneware vessels from 1829 to 1864. His work is remarkable for the size and grace of his storage jars, for their handsome glazing, and especially for the fact that he often signed and dated his pots; about thirty-five of them also include short poems or aphorisms.[37] Dave tells the story of his life on his pots. We learn that he experienced romance ("what's better than kissing—while we both are at fishing"), he had at least one run-in with a mountain lion ("I saw a leopard & a lions face/then I felt, the need of Grace"); he was practical and proud ("Great and Noble Jar/ hold sheep, goat or bear"); he was sometimes paid for his work ("I made this jar for cash, though it's called lucre trash"); he was religious ("If you don't repent, you will be lost"); he understood his status ("Dave belongs to Mr. Miles"), and indeed he put Miles's name or initials on most of his pots, as was doubtless required; and on two occasions he lamented the loss of family and friends ("I wonder where is all my relation" and "think of me when/ far away").[38] Dave lost a leg, when we do not know, with one report pointing to a railway accident, and he developed great upper body strength, enabling him to handle his eighty-pound pots. He clearly became a well-liked character, with the local paper reporting in 1859 that the kids liked "to watch old Dave as the clay assumed beneath his magic touch the desired shape of jug, or jar, or crock, or pitcher, as the case may be."[39] Drake had become literate—exactly how, no one knows—at a time when teaching the enslaved to read and write was punishable under South Carolina's Negro Act of 1740. Scholars vary on whether his writings placed him in danger or whether, as seems more likely, "Mr. Miles supported Dave in his work."[40] Whatever the case, Dave spent his entire life in bondage, without freedom, as a human being whose every move was dictated by his owners. He was both a survivor and a creator who developed his own voice.

Dave's pottery was sought out by the Charleston Museum as early as the 1920s, and word slowly spread among local collectors. Then, after the High Museum purchased a piece in 1988, some Northern museums picked up the scent, with both the Philadelphia Museum and the MFA buying his pots in 1997. In 2012 one of his pots sold for $130,000, and by 2020 another went for $369,000 to the Fine Arts Museums of San

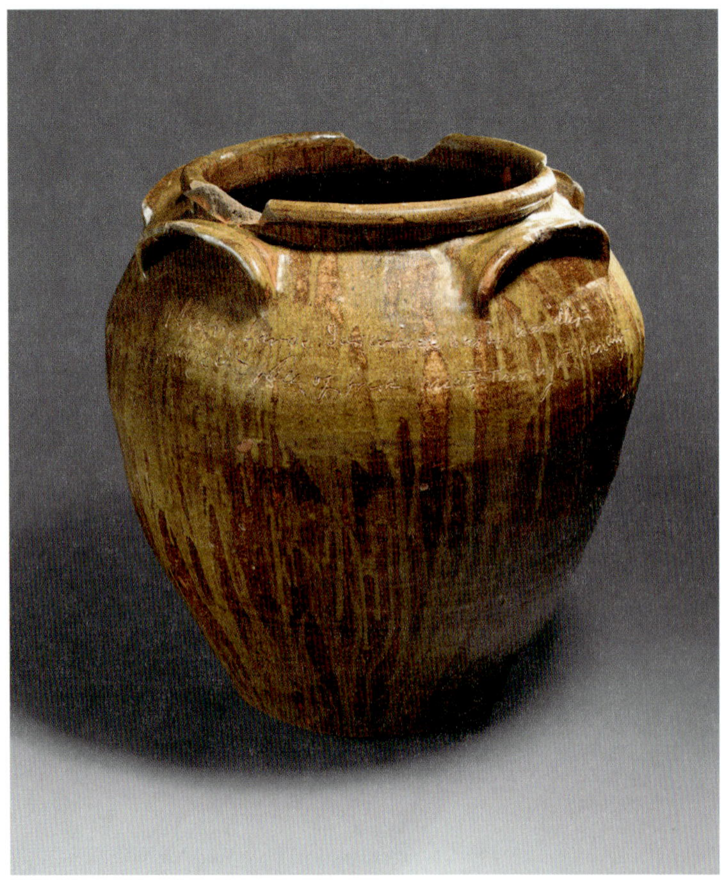

Fig. 69. **DAVID DRAKE,**
Twenty-Five Gallon Four-Handled Stoneware Jug,
stoneware with alkaline glaze, 1858. Crystal Bridges.

Francisco. Then, in August 2021, Dave's largest known vessel, one with four handles and a twenty-five-pound capacity (fig. 69), sold at auction for $1.56 million to Crystal Bridges, an institution willing and able to pay top prices for objects it covets. Drake's work came to wider public attention in the northeast with the exhibition called "Hear Me Now: The Black Potters of Old Edgefield, South Carolina," shown at the Met and the MFA in 2022–23 and supported by the Terra Foundation and the Henry Luce Foundation.[41] Drake's work might seem unremarkable at first glance, but in the new era, for the new canon, he is immensely significant for the unique tale his pots tell, for the part of American history they encapsulate. As we learn from recent studies, he was not the only enslaved craftsperson/artist of the antebellum era, but the drama of his life story, the quiet eloquence of his verses, and the majesty of his pots, make him a special figure.[42]

---

[1] On market bubbles, see Charles Mackay, *Memoirs of Extraordinary Popular Delusions and the Madness of Crowds* (George Routledge & Sons, 1869).

[2] See Robin Pogrebin, "The Whitney Museum Names Its First Latino Senior Curator," *New York Times*, February 18, 2023; "MFA Appoints Michael J. Bramwell as Curator of Folk and Self-Taught Art," *Artforum*, May 25, 2022.

[3] This information courtesy of Graham Boettcher, director of the Birmingham Art Museum, conversation with the author, February 21, 2023.

[4] Alison de Lima Greene, conversation with the author, July 25, 2023.

[5] Jane Tompkins, *West of Everything: The Inner Life of Westerns* (Oxford University Press, 1993), 183.

[6] Letter from Remington to Owen Wister, as quoted in Michael Kimmel, *Manhood in America* (Oxford University Press, 2018), 102. Recent acquisitions at Houston include a landscape by Edward Bannister; an interesting figurative work by the Caribbean painter Agostino Brunias, *Free People of Color with a Servant*; and a large Lakota painting on a buffalo hide depicting a battle between the Lakota and the Pawnee.

[7] See Miguel Angel et al., *Mexican Masterpieces from the Bernard and Edith Lewin Collection* (Los Angeles County Museum of Art, 1997). I also thank Bruce Roberston for this information.

[8] See Timothy A. Burgard, *Revelations: Art from the African American South* (Fine Arts Museums, 2017).

[9] Robert Carleton Hobbs et al., *30 Americans*, 4th ed. (Rubell Museum, 2017), 6.

[10] Eddie Chambers, "Introduction," in *The Routledge Companion to African American Art History*, ed. Eddie Chambers, xxiii.

[11] See Mary Ann Calo, "The Significance of the Interwar Decades to Scholarship on African American Art," in Chambers, *Routledge Companion*, 16.

[12] The MFA published an impressive catalogue of all its African American material with an introduction by Lowery Stokes Sims, *Common Wealth: Art by African Americans in the Museum of Fine Arts, Boston*, ed. Erica Hirshler (Museum of Fine Arts, 2015).

[13] See Timothy Burgard, *Revelations: Art from the African American South* (Fine Arts Museums of San Francisco, 2017).

[14] Daniel H. Weiss and Max Hollein, "Our Commitments to Anti-Racism, Diversity, and a Stronger Community," Metropolitan Museum of Art, July 6, 2020.

[15] Max Hollein, conversation with the author, July 1, 2024.
[16] Denise Murrell, ed., *The Harlem Renaissance and Transatlantic Modernism* (Metropolitan Museum of Art, 2024).
[17] Reiss illustrated Alain Locke's *The New Negro Aesthetic* (1925), with credit on the title page, but later editions omitted his name and the illustrations due to controversies about his inclusion. See George Hutchinson, *In Search of Nella Larson: A Biography of the Color Line* (Harvard University Press, 2001), 282–83.
[18] Lynne Cooke, *Outliers and American Vanguard* (University of Chicago Press for the National Gallery of Art, 2018).
[19] Zachary Small, "National Gallery of Art Acquires 40 Works by Black Southern Artists," *New York Times,* December 30, 2020.
[20] The artists included Carrie Mae Weems, John Wilson, Rosie Lee Tompkins, Winfred Rembert, Rashid Johnson, Hank Willis Thomas, Betye Saar, Njideka Akunyili Crosby, Zanele Muholi, James Luna, and the little-known Abstract Expressionist George Morrison, along with William Kentridge, who is white.
[21] Eleanor Harvey, conversation with the author, March 8, 2024.
[22] In October 2024, the institution changed its name to The New York Historical (dropping the hyphen and "Society").
[23] Kathleen A. Foster, conversation with the author, September 2, 2023.
[24] Philadelphia Museum of Art, Wall Text, American Gallery (2022).
[25] James H. Johnston, *From Slave Ship to Harvard: Yarrow Mamout and the History of an African American Family* (Fordham University Press, 2012). Peale notably wrote Yarrow's obituary four years after painting him and put it in the Philadelphia paper.
[26] Patricia Marroquin Norby, "Visual Violence in the Land of Enchantment" (PhD diss., University of Minnesota, 2013).
[27] See William Rubin, ed., *"Primitivism" in 20th Century Art: Affinity of the Tribal and the Modern* (Museum of Modern Art, 1984).
[28] Mary Carole McCauley, "Baltimore Museum of Art Sold Seven Paintings for $16.1 Million: The Money Paid for These 'Superstars' of Tomorrow," *Baltimore Sun,* May 10, 2021.
[29] See Angelica Villa, "Following $12M. Pollock Sale, Everson Museum Acquires Contemporary Works by Shinique Smith, Ellen Lesperance, More," *ARTnews,* January 17, 2021.
[30] Karl Kusserow, ed., *Object Lessons in American Art* (Princeton University Art Museum, 2023), 180.
[31] See Megan Gray, "Portland Museum of Art Brings Items out of Storage and Up to Date," *Portland Press Herald,* June 4, 2023. See also Murray White, "The Fine Art of Remaking a Collection," *Boston Globe,* October 20, 2023.
[32] By comparison, Sterling Clark paid $170,000 for his magnificent Piero della Francesca eight years earlier, the largest outlay of his career.
[33] Mark Godfrey and Zoe Whitley, *Soul of a Nation: Art in the Age of Black Power* (Tate Modern, 2017).

[34] Chambers, *Routledge Companion to African American Art History.*

[35] Dorothy C. Price, et al., *Entangled Pasts, 1768–Now: Art, Colonialism and Change* (Royal Academy of Arts, 2024).

[36] Adrienne Spinozzi, "Confronting, Collecting, and Celebrating Edgefield Stoneware," in *Hear Me Now: The Black Potters of Old Edgefield, South Carolina,* ed. Adrienne Spinozzi (Metropolitan Museum of Art, 2022). The author describes an important study of the Edgefield potters dating from 1993, a pioneering exhibition of Drake's pottery at the McKissick Museum in Columbia, South Carolina, in 1998, and Leonard Todd's book of 2008, *Carolina Clay: The Life and Legend of the Slave Potter Dave* (W. W. Norton, 2008).

[37] Arthur F. Goldberg and James Witkowski, "Beneath His Magic Touch: The Dated Vessels of the African-American Slave Potter Dave," in *Ceramics in America,* ed. Robert Hunter (Chipstone Foundation, 2006), 58–92. Thanks to Michael Bramwell for bringing this to my attention.

[38] Spinozzi, *Hear Me Now,* 180–81.

[39] "Old Pottersville and Dr. Landrum," *Edgefield Adventurer,* May 11, 1859, as quoted in Goldberg and Witkowski, "Beneath His Magic Touch," 62.

[40] Goldberg and Witkowski, 85.

[41] Spinozzi, *Hear Me Now.*

[42] A *New York Times* review of the Met's exhibition praised the Crystal Bridges pot as "something of as sacred object," before suggesting that "it may qualify as one of 19th century America's great sculptures." Roberta Smith, "The Magnificent Poem Jars of David Drake, Center Stage at the Met," *New York Times,* September 22, 2022.

18

Native Americans Reconsidered

How thoughtful of God to provide such a life-stream such as art.

—T. C. CANNON

The settler and pioneer have had justice on their side: this great continent could not have been kept as nothing but a game preserve for squalid savages.

—THEODORE ROOSEVELT, *The Winning of the West*, 1889

MY FRIENDS and I grew up during and after World War II watching the war films and Westerns of John Ford and Howard Hawks, and after school we played at fighting the Japanese in the Pacific and at what used to be called "cowboys and Indians."[1] Ford's film *The Man Who Shot Liberty Valance* typifies Americans' attitudes toward the Old West, a myth that is still widespread today. As one character in the film reminiscences, "I could see once again the vast herd of buffalo and savage redskin roaming our beautiful territory with no law to trammel them except the law of survival, the law of the tomahawk and the bow and arrow. And then, with the westward march of our nation, came the pioneer and the buffalo hunter, the adventurous and the bold." In concluding, he sums up the West as it was long understood: "It was once a wilderness, now it's a garden." The cowboy was always brave, white, and handy with a gun and his fists; he became an American archetype. Our view of him changed slowly as more truths came out and as violence became less attractive. Today's take on the cowboy is represented by an exhibition of 2023–25 that was presented in two of our great cow towns: Denver and Fort Worth. It demonstrated that the cowboy in reality might be Black, Mexican, or gay,[2] and that he was typically "an overworked, underpaid hireling, almost as homeless and dispossessed as a modern crop worker."[3] Our knowledge of Native Americans was formed by books like James Fenimore Cooper's *Last of the Mohicans* of 1826 (its title alone implying the fate of the tribe) and *The Oregon Trail* published in 1849 by Francis Parkman. The latter book described Natives as "thorough savages" always at war with one another, people whose "religion, superstitions, and prejudices were the same handed down to them from immemorial time . . . who know nothing of the power and real character of the white men."[4] The nation is still struggling to unlearn these values.

The Smithsonian's exhibition of 1991, *The West as America: Reinterpreting Images of the Frontier, 1820–1920*, was an important harbinger of the future. In it, curator William H. Truettner made a determined effort to reconsider the well-known paintings of the American West by Catlin, Bingham, Bierstadt, and Remington, among others, to judge them not for their aesthetic and scenic qualities as had been done for so long but rather for what they said or didn't say about the history and ideology of Manifest Destiny and the effects of racism and institutionalized brutality. Truettner and seven coauthors articulated in the massive catalogue how the paintings represented "contrived versions" and "carefully fabricated time-honored scenes," thus rejecting the traditional views of Western films, textbooks, and of a great many Americans.[5] The writers found that the works of art failed to speak to the barbarous treatment of the Indians, the greed of the fur traders and other pioneers, the environmental ravages caused by mining, railroads, and industry, and they posited that the paintings were mostly made for a powerful class of Eastern investors who stood to gain most from westward expansion. As Alan Wallach has pointed out, by the time of the exhibition, many academic art historians had turned to revisionist art history in which objects are examined in relation to their social, political, or cultural contexts, while their museum colleagues typically remained wedded to the old notion of art as "transcendent, timeless, and universal"; he recognized that Truettner was considerably in advance of his colleagues at other museums.[6]

The exhibition caused an immediate uproar, not because of the paintings themselves or the catalogue essays but due rather to the fifty-five text labels next to the paintings in the galleries that called Daniel Boone and his compatriots "trespassers on foreign territory," spoke about "white deceit," and drew attention to the sexual innuendo

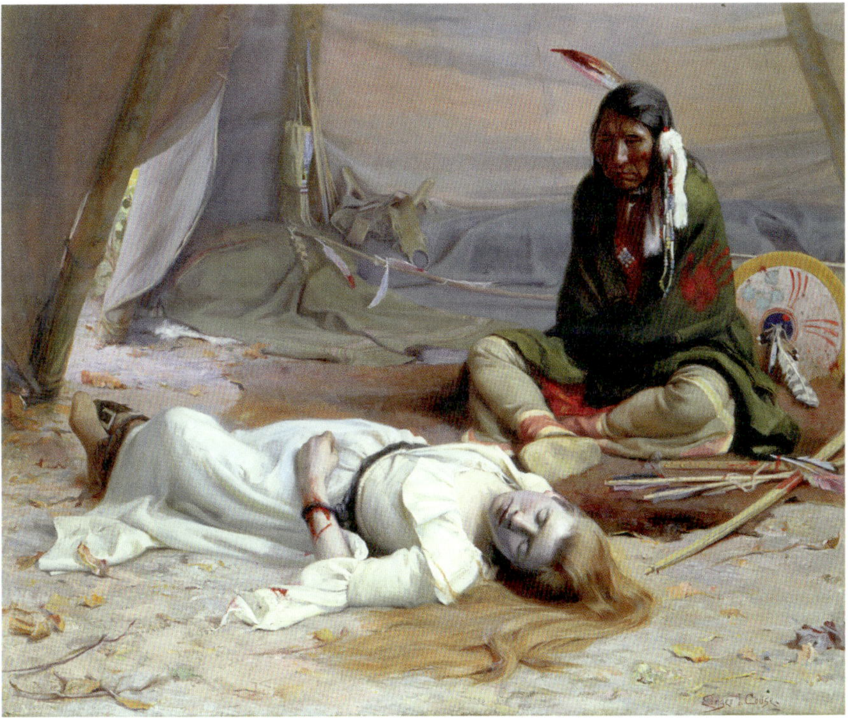

Fig. 70. E. IRVING COUSE,
The Captive (La Cautiva), oil on canvas, 1891. Phoenix Art Museum.

in Eanger Irving Couse's *The Captive* (fig. 70), which pictured a young white woman dressed in white lying at the feet of a seated warrior.[7] One of the first visitors to the show was Daniel J. Boorstin, a prominent historian who had recently retired as librarian of Congress. The conservative Boorstin stood on the opposite end of the ideological scale from Truettner and his colleagues; his books, including *The Americans* and *The Genius of American Politics*, celebrated the courage and ingenuity of the white settlers of the continent, which he described as "a wilderness of dark wood, howling wolves, treacherous swamps, and barbarous savages."[8] Boorstin was an early visitor to the show, and on the first page of the visitors' book he described it as "a perverse, historically inaccurate, destructive exhibit."[9] His remarks quickly caught the attention of press and politicians and led to a continuing uproar over the show. *The Wall Street Journal* chimed in, calling it "an entirely hostile, ideological assault on the nation's founding and history."[10] The exhibition itself was an excellent survey of Western paintings, but the interpretive labels, and the fact that the exhibition occurred in Washington at the taxpayer-supported Smithsonian, provided fuel for the fire.

The curators' interpretation of Frederic Remington's *Fight for the Waterhole* (fig. 71) particularly rankled some visitors; the painting depicts five cowboys defending a water hole in very arid country against distant Indians on horseback. The catalogue reasonably posits that the painting's subject is "the last stand of five outnumbered cowboys."[11] But the left-leaning Alan Wallach defended a text label that explained that "the last stand itself came to symbolize the plight of an embattled capitalist elite.[12] This seemed a bit of a reach for me. He also approvingly cited Bryan Wolf's statement elsewhere that "palette and paintbrush were as much instruments of domination as Colt revolvers or the pony express."[13] Truettner took up this theme, suggesting that the Western paintings had "guided national behavior." He wrote that the murals in the US Capitol "helped launch expansionists' initiatives toward the west," and that the images of fur traders "helped smooth the way for expansion."[14] Nonetheless, "The West as America" was a landmark despite its flaws: It foreshadowed the rejection of the old aesthetic standards and the embrace of new ones that examine the underlying racism, prejudice, and greed lying beneath the surface of westward expansion.

The widespread move toward inclusion at the major Eastern art museums did not include Native American artists until recent years. Until recently, the "winning of the West" was celebrated as one of the key developments in American history. But today the same events, ones that led to the settlement of the West by a wide variety of European immigrants, are read as meaning the destruction of the tribal way of life, the seizure of Indigenous lands and resources, the eradication of the buffalo that were so important for the Native way of life, and the removal of the "murderous savages" (as many called them) to reservations.

Native Americans were long considered to be racially inferior, barbarous, and childlike. They were not granted US citizenship until 1924.[15] Official US policy before the Indian Civil Rights Act of 1968 called for forced assimilation and the eradication of tribal memories, language,

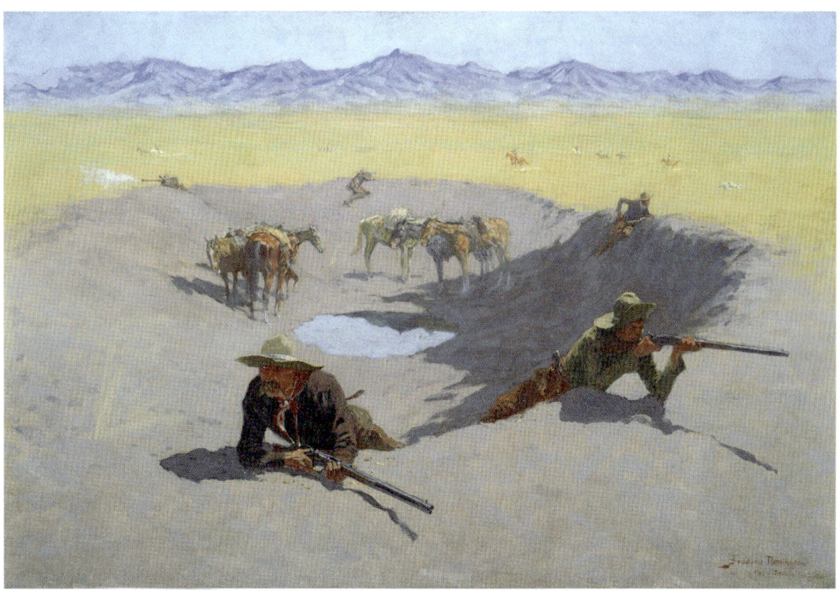

Fig. 71. **FREDERIC REMINGTON,**
Fight for the Waterhole, oil on canvas, 1903. Museum of Fine Arts, Houston.

and traditions. A major component was the sending of thousands of children to distant boarding schools where their Native culture was forcibly drummed out of them.[16] After the passage of the Dawes Act in 1887, which provided for the dissolution of the tribes as legal entities, and the massacre of the Lakota Sioux at Wounded Knee in 1890, physical resistance lessened on the part of Native Americans, and the official view was that "the Indian problem is rapidly disappearing with the approaching extinction of the full-blooded Indian."[17]

White observers long portrayed Indians as members of a "vanishing race," as one sees in Cooper's *Last of the Mohicans* and any number of books, speeches, and paintings ever since. The general theory was that the Indians were doomed, and so they needed to be painted and evidence of their cultures collected before it was too late. Charles Bird King in the 1820s and '30s was commissioned by the government to paint portraits of Indian leaders who came to Washington to negotiate treaties; the aim was to record them before they disappeared. Many mid-century Hudson River School paintings include a single Native figure looking lost and out of place in the wilderness. Hiram Powers sculpted his sad *Last of the Tribes* in 1876, while James Earle Fraser's *End of the Trail* of 1894 presents a tragic image of defeat. Cyrus Dallin's *Appeal to the Great Spirit* of 1908 still stands in front of the Museum of Fine Arts in Boston despite lengthy debates about how it should be read and whether it should be removed or how it should be contextualized.[18] Dallin's own stance as a native rights activist complicates the discussion.[19] A similar debate involves the series of photographs taken by Edward S. Curtis for his huge book project, *The North American Indian*, published over many years up to 1930. No one doubts the importance of the work, but it has been criticized for the extent to which it supports the "vanishing race" theory.

Tribal artifacts were long collected by natural history museums, where they were presented as ethnographic evidence of dead cultures. Just a handful of Western institutions, notably the Denver Art Museum, the Heard Museum in Phoenix, and what is now the Fred Jones Jr. Museum at the University of Oklahoma—all located in areas with significant Native populations—were collecting Native art *as art* by the 1920s. The first modern school of Native painting emerged during the teens in Santa Fe: The "Pueblo paintings" of Tonita Pena (the only woman in the group), Fred Kabotie, and others were guided by white administrators, who controlled the aesthetics, sales to tourists, and modest payments to the artists. The colorful, stylized views of Native figures taking part in the Hopi Snake Dance, the Zia Deer Dance, and other such ceremonies, often derived from Pueblo pottery designs, were "modern" primarily in their dates of execution. Mabel Dodge Luhan was an early patron of this movement, and Marsden Hartley's fulsome articles of 1920 and 1922 helped draw attention to it.[20] The painter John Sloan argued that "the Indian artist deserves to be classed as a Modernist, his art is old, yet alive and dynamic . . ." and campaigned for purchases by the leading Eastern museums.[21] Though his efforts didn't lead to great success, one result was the important Exposition of Indian Tribal Arts that opened in New York in 1931 before traveling to fifteen cities, while another was the inclusion of a selection of Indian arts, including Pueblo watercolors, at the American Pavilion of the Venice Biennale in 1932.[22] Strangely, Grenville Winthrop's advisor, the multitalented Martin Birnbaum, was appointed commissioner of the pavilion; he rejected the premise of Pueblo art as representing a native modernism, and in the catalogue had little to say about the Native works that Sloan had selected (including Pueblo jewelry, pottery, and textiles, besides the paintings), while apologizing for not showing the watercolors of Homer and Sargent.[23]

A truly modern Native art came about with the founding of the Institute of American Indian Arts (IAIA) in Santa Fe in 1962 by the Bureau of Indian Affairs. Its influential early leader, Lloyd Kiva New, rejected the traditional assimilationist policies and the paternalism of white officials and stressed instead that young Native artists should explore mainstream art currents from "a proud and necessary base" of their own cultural roots that he called "Indianism."[24] Painter Fritz Scholder (fig. 72), who had studied with the celebrated California artist Wayne Thibaud, joined the faculty, and he and his student T. C. Cannon (fig. 73) led a breakthrough in the early sixties,

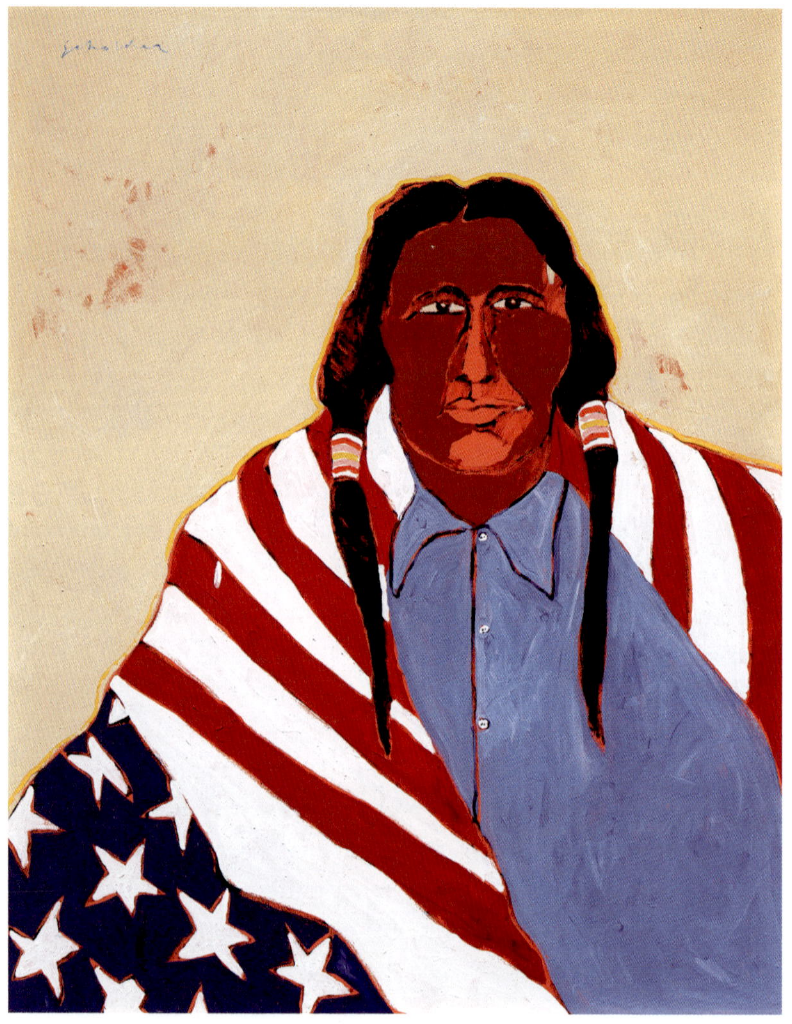

Fig. 72. FRITZ SCHOLDER,
Bicentennial Indian, acrylic on canvas, 1976. Peterson Family Collection.

developing expressive, colorful, often ironic paintings that focused on figures of Native Americans.[25] Their works found an audience in the southwest through exhibitions and sales, and in 1972 the scholar Adelyn Breeskin at the National Collection of Fine Arts (now the Smithsonian Museum of American Art) organized an exhibition of Scholder and Cannon together. Even with that, it was years before the major Eastern art museums or collectors took much notice.

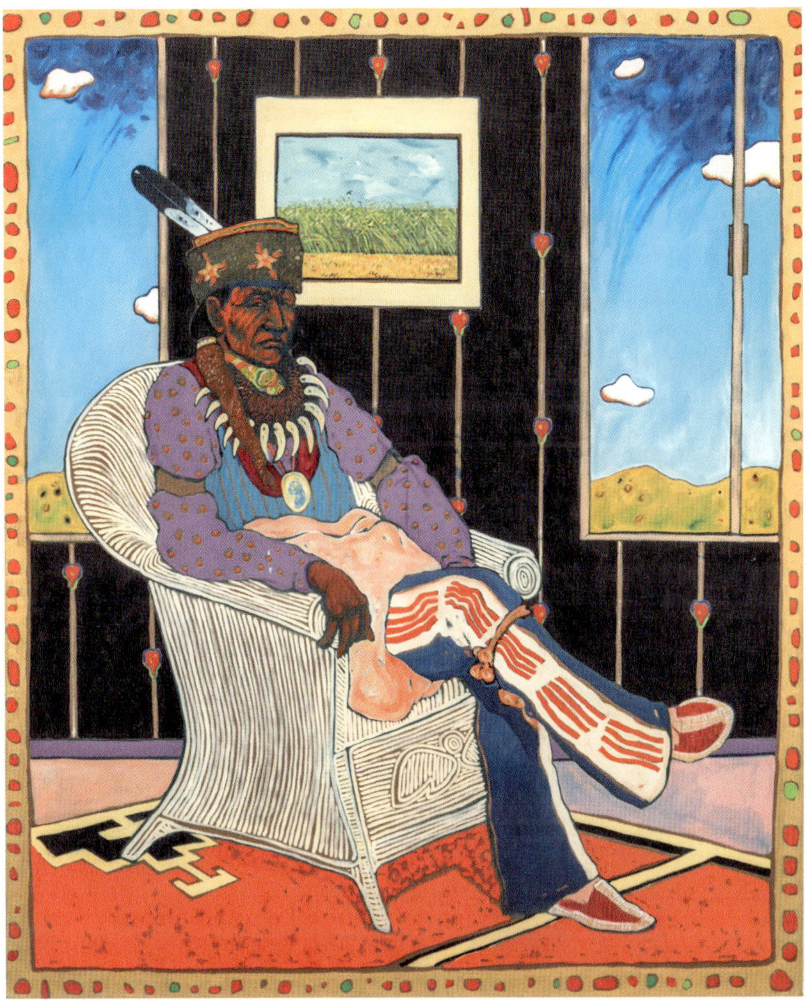

Fig. 73. T. C. CANNON,
Collector #5 (Man in Wicker Chair),
oil and acrylic on canvas, 1975. Peterson Family Collection.

White America became more conscious of Native Americans in these years as anger and activism grew in the Native community. The founding of the American Indian Movement (AIM) in 1968 and the widespread press coverage of the occupation of Alcatraz, the occupation of the Bureau of Indian Affairs offices in Washington, and the violent siege at Wounded Knee in South Dakota over the next few years all raised public awareness of the tribes' harsh living conditions and their continuing efforts to restore their cultural traditions.[26] As with women and Black artists in the same years, anger proved a necessary component of change. Celebrations to mark the five-hundredth anniversary of Columbus's landing in 1492 in the US and Canada also had the unintended effect of stimulating Native artists and scholars, much the way "Harlem on my Mind" had energized Black artists years earlier. "Pre-Columbian" became an ugly term. The curators of a powerful exhibition at the Canadian Museum of Civilization noted, "Perhaps if they'd stolen your land, your culture and your spirit, you'd paint a different picture of history too."[27] Indigenous artists, including James Luna, Kay WalkingStick, Rebecca Belmore, Brian Jungen, and Jaune Quick-to-See Smith, began to be exhibited in group and one-artist shows nationally and internationally, and scholars redoubled their efforts to "upend dominant art history by reversing the paradigm of an Anglo-European master narrative."[28] A handful of scholars, including Ned Blackhawk at Yale, are working to reinterpret American history by centering Native Americans "as a force not just shaped by, but shaping the creation of America."[29] Key for them is correcting the racist stereotypes that portray the Indians as helpless victims rather than members of living cultures by studying their active roles and their important contributions throughout American history.

The Museum of the American Indian, founded in 1916 in New York, moved to an imposing new building on the Mall in Washington under the auspices of the Smithsonian in 2004; it already possessed an outstanding collection of older work and now began acquiring and showing contemporary Native art. The Peabody Essex Museum in Salem, Massachusetts, with its historic holdings of Native American art, led the field in integrating that art into its American galleries. A Peabody Essex exhibition of 2010 featured nine contemporary Native artists, and then in 2018 that museum organized a major show of the work of T. C. Cannon that traveled to the Gilcrease Institute in Tulsa and then to the Smithsonian's National Museum of the American Indian.[30] In the same year, Crystal Bridges organized a superb exhibition, "Art for a New Understanding: Native Voices, 1950s to Now," while continuing to expand its collection and announcing that it would build a new wing for Native art.[31] Crystal Bridges recently purchased a distinguished group of Pueblo paintings from the 1920s and '30s, and late in 2023 the museum announced the hiring of its first curator of Indigenous art.

The Met has made extensive efforts to include Indigenous art in the American Wing. In the summer of 2023, the museum opened an exhibition called "Grounded in Clay: The Spirit of Pueblo Pottery," that was selected not by the museum curators but by living potters from the Pueblo community. The rediscovery of the schematic colored drawings by Mary Sully, a Yankton Dakota artist and the great-granddaughter of the painter Thomas Sully, led to an interesting exhibition the following year. In the American Wing at the Met one also finds several notable acquisitions, including a painting by Jules Tavernier titled *Dance in the Subterranean Roundhouse at Clear Lake, California,* of 1878. It pictures a sacred ceremony by the Elem Pomo tribe, which was forced off its land in northern California; the acquisition was accompanied by an issue of the Met's *Bulletin* written by curator Elizabeth Mankin Kornhauser and her colleague Shannon Vittoria.[32]

The Met, the MFA, the National Gallery, and others began purchasing the new Native art, with prices rising quickly for Cannon, Fritz Scholder, and numerous others; Scholder's paintings now sell for up to $1 million. Late in 2023, the National Gallery invited artist Jaune Quick-to-See Smith, whose own work was the subject of an impressive retrospective at the Whitney earlier in the year, to curate an exhibition of the new generation of Native artists.[33] Included were nearly fifty practitioners working in every media, from painting and photography to beadwork and weaving. In an eloquent essay in the Crystal Bridges catalogue, Paul Chaat Smith suggested that the last few years have been a turning point, and that parity—the treatment of all art as art, no matter who made it, is at hand. Smith boldly suggests that the final test will be when we recognize that "most Indian art isn't very good, just as most Black or Chinese or gay art, most art period, isn't very good either."[34]

Another development was Congress's major revision to the 1990 Native American Graves Protection and Repatriation Act (NAGPRA), which took effect in January 2024. The original law promised "the protection and return of Native American human remains, funerary objects, sacred objects, and objects of cultural patrimony"; the current revisions require all museums holding Native art to inventory their collections and proceed with plans for restitution where appropriate.[35] Museums reacted in various ways, with some scrambling to comply and others dragging their feet.

---

[1] See Philip J. Deloria, *Playing Indian* (Yale University Press, 2022).

[2] "Cowboy," exhibition at the Museum of Contemporary Art, Denver (2023–24), and the Amon Carter Museum, Fort Worth (2024–25), with catalogue by Nora Burnett Abrams and Miranda Lash (Rizzoli, 2023).

[3] Wallace Stegner, *The American West as Living Space* (University of Michigan Press, 1987), as quoted in Carolina A. Miranda, "Mythic Chaps," *New York Review of Books,* October 17, 2024, 33.

[4] Francis Parkman, *The Oregon Trail* (George P. Putnam, 1849), 163. For an articulate analysis of the values promulgated by Western films, with their emphasis on men, suffering, death, and loneliness and their unreality in describing women, Indians, cattle, and horses, see Tompkins, *West of Everything.*

[5] William H. Truettner, *The West as America: Reinterpreting Images of the Frontier, 1820–1920* (Smithsonian Institute Press, 1991), 65, 30. Truettner's thesis relied in part on the important work of Richard Slotkin, author of *Regeneration Through Violence: The Mythology of the American Frontier, 1600–1860* (Wesleyan University Press, 1973). See also Slotkin's most recent work, *A Great Disorder: National Myth and the Battle for America* (Harvard University Press, 2024).

[6] See Alan Wallach, *Exhibiting Contradiction: Essays on the Art Museum in the United States* (University of Massachusetts Press, 1998), 105–27.

[7] Truettner, *The West as America,* 42; Andrew Gulliford, "Review: The West as America: Reinterpreting Images of the Frontier, 1820–1920," *Journal of American History* 79, no. 1 (1992): 203, 200.

[8] Daniel J. Boorstin, *The Genius of American Politics* (University of Chicago Press, 1958), 41.

[9] Gulliford, "Review: The West as America," 201.

[10] "Pilgrims and Other Imperialists," *Wall Street Journal,* May 17, 1991.

[11] Alex Nemerov, "Doing the 'Old America,'" in Truettner, *The West as America,* 329.

[12] Alan Wallach, "The Battle over 'The West as America, 1991,'" in *Art Apart: Art Institutes and Ideologies Across England and North America,* ed. Marcia Pointon (Manchester University Press, 1994), 92.

[13] Wallach, 91.

[14] Truettner, *The West as America,* 50, 41, 43. Truettner was probably referring to *The Landing of Columbus* by John Vanderlyn, *The Discovery of the Mississippi* by William H. Powell, *The Baptism of Pocahontas* by John Gadsby Chapman, and *The Embarkation of the Pilgrims* by Robert W. Weir, all of whose messages are now viewed by some as objectionable.

[15] Ned Blackhawk, *The Rediscovery of America* (Yale University Press, 2023).

[16] See Bill Vaughn, *The Plot Against Native America: The Fateful Story of Native American Boarding Schools and the Theft of Tribal Lands* (Pegasus Books, 2024). President Biden formally apologized for the abusive schools on October 25, 2024 (see *New York Times,* October 26, 2024).

[17] heather ahtone, "Indigenous Art as a Beacon of Survival" in *Art for a New Understanding: Native Voices, 1950s to Now,* ed. Mindy N. Besaw et al. (University of Arkansas Press, 2018).

[18] For the MFA's ongoing effort to contextualize the work, see *Boston Globe,* June 4, 2024.

[19] For a thoughtful view of this issue, see Trevor J. Fairbrother, "Visual Arts Commentary: The Problematics of Multiculturalism at the MFA—on the Dallin Front," *Arts Fuse,* January 30, 2024.

[20] See J. J. Brody, *Pueblo Indian Painting: Tradition and Modernism in New Mexico, 1900–1930* (School of American Research Press, 1997). See also Jessica L. Horton and Janet C. Berlo, "Pueblo Painting in 1932," in *A Companion to American Art,* ed. John Davis (Wiley-Blackwell, 2015). See also Marsden Hartley, "Red Man Ceremonials: An American Plea for American Esthetics," *Art & Archaeology* 9, no. 1 (1920): 7–14.

[21] John Sloan and Oliver La Farge, eds., *Introduction to American Indian Art* (Rio Grande Press, 1931), as quoted in Brody, *Pueblo Indian Painting,* 180.

[22] Brody, 179–80.

[23] Jessica L. Horton, "A Cloudburst in Venice: Fred Kabotie and the U.S. Pavilion of 1932," *American Art* 29, no. 1 (2015): 54–81; Jessica L. Horton, *Art for an Undivided Earth* (Duke University Press, 2017), 227, 232.

[24] Jessica L. Horton, "Inclusivity at Midcentury: George Morrison, Oscar Howe, and Lloyd Kiva New," in Besaw et al., *Art for a New Understanding,* 40.

[25] See Robert A. Ewing, "The New Indian Art," *El Palacio* 76, no. 1 (1969): 33–39.

[26] See Paul Chaat Smith and Robert Allen Warrior, *Like a Hurricane: The Indian Movement from Alcatraz to Wounded Knee* (New Press, 1996).

[27] Gerald McMaster and Lee-Ann Martin, eds., *Indigena: Contemporary Native Perspectives in Canadian Art,* (Douglas and McIntyre, 1992), as quoted in Besaw et al., *Art for a New Understanding,* 12.

[28] Besaw et al., 13.

[29] Dylan Walsh, "Reshaping the Story," *Yale Alumni Magazine,* July/August 2024, 28ff.

[30] Karen Kramer, ed., *T. C. Cannon: At the Edge of America* (Peabody Essex Museum, 2018). See also the brilliant review by Peter Scheldahl, "T. C. Cannon's Blazing Promise," *New Yorker,* April 15, 2019.

[31] See Besaw et al., *Art for a New Understanding.*

[32] Elizabeth Kornhauser and Shannon Vittoria, "Jules Tavernier and the Elem Pomo," Metropolitan *Museum of Art* Bulletin 79, no. 1 (2021): 3–49.

[33] Jaune Quick-to-See Smith et al., *The Land Carries Our Ancestors: Contemporary Art by Native Americans* (Princeton University Press, 2023).

[34] Paul Chaat Smith, "Indian Art for Modern Living," in Besaw et al., *Art for a New Understanding,* 100.

[35] Karen K. Ho, "What the New Federal Regulations for Native American Ancestors and Sacred Objects Mean for Museums," *ARTnews,* February 21, 2024.

19

Changing Taste

What is it about the present that makes it so eager to judge the past? There is always a neuroticism to the present, which believes itself superior to the past but can't quite get over a nagging anxiety that it might not be.

—JULIAN BARNES, *The Man in the Red Coat*, 2019

Any prediction in art is blind guesswork and folly at that.

—HOMER SAINT-GAUDENS

ONCE WE recognize that taste changes and that artists rise and fall, does this imply that every artist's work is doomed to decline in popular appeal and market value? Should we bother to put the art we most admire into museums when it may eventually be disparaged and removed from view? The art world may need a little more humility, but it should not despair. There is no doubt that the canon is constantly being rethought, but at the same time, many painters maintain their reputations over years or even centuries, even as their work is reinterpreted by each generation. The artists most valued by Vasari, for example, including Raphael, Leonardo, and Michelangelo, still hold their rank in the Renaissance canon. And if we look back to the American painters that were most admired by the early-twentieth-century writers and collectors, we find that most of their reputations remain intact: The works of Homer, Sargent, Cassatt, Eakins, La Farge, and Whistler are still highly regarded. Looking further back, Dunlap's canon is still partially intact, with West, Trumbull, and Copley leading, while Tuckerman's favorites, Church and Bierstadt, still hang in places of honor even as the reasons for their appreciation change.

Changing cultural and aesthetic standards have affected the whole art world. The American and contemporary fields are at the center of the storm, but its waves are felt everywhere. One now finds new labels and new approaches that reflect diversity in museum galleries devoted to classical, Egyptian, Asian, and other art. Racism may be a relatively minor factor for most European paintings, but it is still on the curators' minds. In 2024, for example, the Clark Art Institute partnered with the Louvre to present the work of Guillaume Lethière, a French mixed-race teacher and neoclassic painter of distinction who work has been unaccountably overlooked until now. This exhibition did what curators hope for, introducing a significant but little-known artist. But the same urge, to bring overlooked figures to light, can have less sanguine results. The Met in 2023 exhibited the work of Juan de Pareja, whose name and likeness became well known after the museum in 1971 purchased the extraordinary portrait of him by Diego Velázquez. De Pareja was an interesting Afro-Hispanic figure who worked for Velázquez and was enslaved by him until he was nearly fifty, after which he painted a number of modest works on his own. However, his art would never have been shown at the Met or any major museum were it not for his life story, which brings up a key question: How far should the bar be lowered for worthy artists who lacked much talent? Every collector and every curator struggles to balance aesthetic quality with important political and cultural considerations, trying to decide what works to put on the wall and which artists might be better served with a good publication.

The study of art history has come a long way since H. W. Janson could write a textbook of world art in 1962 with no mention of women artists; the scholars of the twenty-first century have taken pains to correct this. There have been hundreds of recent monographic exhibitions and surveys of women's art, with no letting up. An important recent moment came in 2021, when the Wadsworth Atheneum in Hartford and the Detroit Institute of Arts together organized a landmark exhibition entitled "Artemisia Gentileschi and Women Artists in Italy, 1500–1800." The two institutions' curators gathered excellent paintings, pastels, drawings, and prints in exploring the role of talented women in a male-dominated world. As Frederick Ilchman of the MFA told me, "There's a mania now for unearthing women artists."[1]

Excellent, old-fashioned scholarship that makes use of archival digging, connoisseurship, and stylistic analysis is still going on in the European field, and if anything, exhibitions of the best-known artists have become more ambitious than ever. There are few signs in them of the nervousness one finds in projects devoted to American art. The impossible is being accomplished regularly, as one saw in the Gardner Museum's exhibition of 2021, "Titian: Women, Myth & Power," which miraculously brought together the painter's six extraordinary Ovidian subjects commissioned by Philip II of Spain that are now widely scattered. The show featured the Gardner's own *Rape of Europa*, which thanks to a skilled cleaning could finally be seen; this is the work my mentor Jakob Rosenberg most admired in the world. The Gardner is not the only small museum undertaking excellent projects: All an institution needs is institutional credibility, money, curatorial talent, and commitment. Thus, the much-admired Kimbell Art Museum in Fort Worth regularly brings us brilliant exhibitions. In 2022 we in Boston enjoyed the magnificent "Turner's Modern World," a project executed by Frederick Ilchman of the MFA with the Kimbell and Tate Britain, while two years later the Kimbell's George Shackleford organized the superb "Bonnard's Worlds" with the Phillips Collection in Washington. The major urban museums, with their outstanding collections and great borrowing power, continue to play important roles, with the Met and the Art Institute of Chicago leading the way. The Met's legendary curator Keith Christiansen's last hurrah was the unforgettable "Medici" exhibition in 2021; the miraculous "Siena:

The Rise of Painting, 1300–1350" maintained the same high standards three years later. "Siena" was shared with London's National Gallery, while the Met's partner in the very different but equally extraordinary "Manet/Degas" exhibition was the Musée d'Orsay in Paris: In both cases the loans could not have been achieved without these strong international colleagues. Chicago, for its part, gave its audience a great survey of Cézanne's work in 2022 (working with the Tate), while in 2023 its exhibitions featured Van Gogh, Caravaggio, and Camille Claudel, the little-known model, student, and lover of Rodin.

The leading university museums, less stressed about attendance as they are, continue to do important but more rarified projects. At the Harvard Art Museums, Horace Ballard in 2023 organized an impressive showing of twenty-six viceregal paintings from the Carl and Marilynn Thoma Foundation: With a beautiful installation and informative text labels, the exhibition had a great deal to teach the uninformed (that included most of us) about a newly recognized area of American art (fig. 74). The Thomas deserve a chapter of their own, as builders of a superb collection of viceregal paintings that they lend generously. They have literally created a new canon of American art, as every museum is now seeking such material. Sadly, there were no other venues and no catalogue for the Harvard show. Yale, on the other hand, produced a sumptuous book to accompany its ambitious exhibition called "The Dance of Life: Figure and Imagination in American Art, 1876–1917" that traveled to London. The roots of the project lay in Yale's having accepted Edwin Austin Abbey's estate from his widow on her death in 1937. It included some three thousand works, including large finished oils and watercolors; numerous oil, watercolor, and pastel studies on paper; and dozens of Abbey's skilled pen and ink Shakespearean and other illustrations. Yale did its duty by the artist with a fine survey exhibition of Abbey's work in 1939 and another very similar one in 1973.[2] Fifty years later, the new exhibition at Yale omitted the finished paintings and the illustrations to focus on his least-known work, the fine preparatory studies in oil, pastel, and watercolor for his mural projects at the Pennsylvania State Capitol and the Boston Public Library. These were shown in comparison with mural studies by Sargent, Kenyon Cox, John La Farge, and William

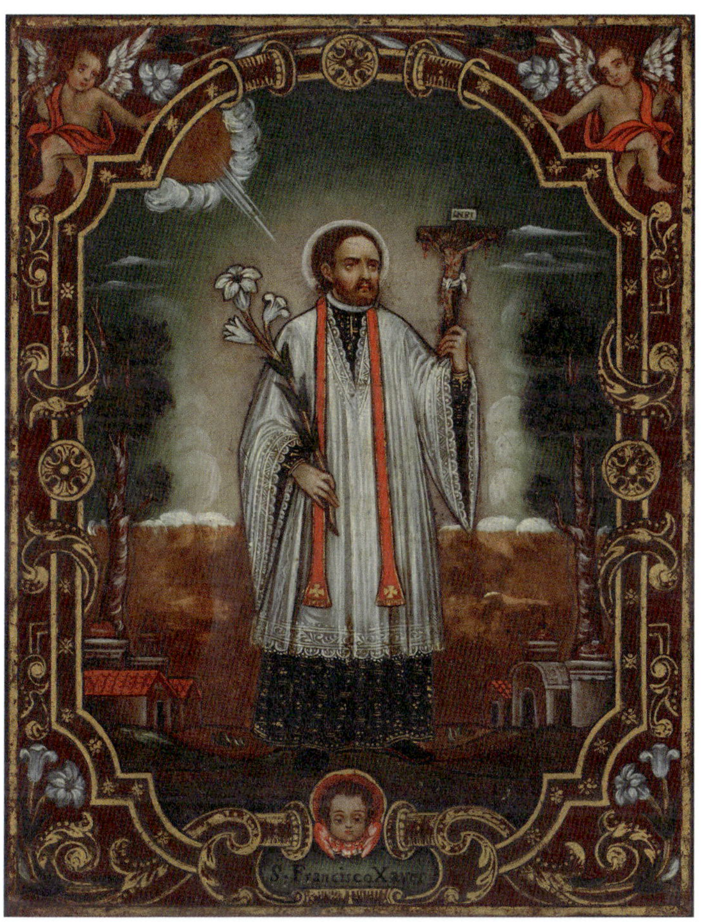

Fig. 74. UNIDENTIFIED ARTIST,
Saint Francis Xavier, oil and gold on copper, 18th century. Thoma Foundation.

Morris Hunt, with works of varying relevance by more than a dozen others added in. A welcome surprise was the inclusion of Sargent's famous painting, *Cashmere,* with its procession of draped figures; the thoughtful, idiosyncratic catalogue makes the case that he and Abbey were neighbors in London and would have known each other's works in progress. Yale undertook a praiseworthy campaign to conserve many of Abbey's hitherto unexhibitable studies on paper and canvas, many of them of large size and technical complexity, including his extraordinary oil sketch for *The Hours* (12.5 feet in diameter, fig. 75). Like the Harvard showing of the viceregal artists, it was an exhibition for specialists and others with considerable interest in American art; both were exactly the kind of projects—ones that opened our eyes to the unfamiliar—that university museums should be undertaking. Abbey was immensely popular in his lifetime and beyond, but the conservatism of his work and the anti-modernism of the American Renaissance in general led to its current neglect. Survey writers through Edgar Richardson (1956) and Wayne Craven (1994) treated Abbey and his fellow muralists with some respect, but Abbey goes completely unmentioned in the textbooks of the twenty-first century, and it seems unlikely that this exhibition will restore his reputation.

Edwin Austin Abbey represents a prime example of a once-admired artist of exceptional abilities who is largely unknown now because his specialties of mural-painting and literary illustration have gone out of fashion, and because his works have been in storage at Yale rather than having life in the market and in widespread museum collections. His case should be proof positive that taste changes. This notion has gradually gained acceptance in the art world, though some holdouts still maintain that aesthetic judgments are permanent. The now-outdated view that quality is fixed and should not be tampered with is represented by the British museum official Charles Saumarez Smith who wrote that the traditional belief in a cultural and artistic master narrative has been fatally undermined by "an assault on the canon: the

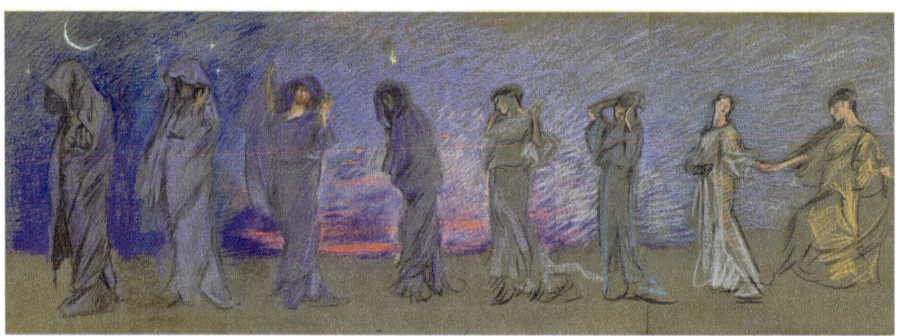

Fig. 75. EDWIN AUSTIN ABBEY,
The Hours, pastel on gray paper and cardboard, n.d. Yale University Art Gallery.

acceptance that all forms of selection and hierarchy are temporary and ephemeral, the product of cultural choice rather than universal values."[3] Smith describes the move toward diversity as part of a multifaceted "attack" on art museums, contrary to the opinion of many today.

One of the noticeable changes of our time involves the monographic exhibition. Such shows formerly featured white painters, but many are now being devoted to Black, Native American, and other unsung artists. Large-scale exhibitions of the work of canonical white painters have not disappeared, but they have become rarer while also becoming narrower and more specialized; earlier shows aimed to introduce the artists to the public, but now the painters are well known and the curators feel obliged to present either new research or a revised way of seeing the work. Museums do them because their collections are rich in their work, because scholars like working on the best artists, and because the popularity of the painters is likely to bring good attendance. In the last few years we have seen three such exhibitions, the Met's "Winslow Homer: Crosscurrents," the MFA's show of John Singer Sargent's portraits called "Fashioned by Sargent," and "Mary Cassatt at Work" at the Philadelphia Museum of Art. Exhibitions of this kind can occur only once every twenty years or so, due to the difficulty of getting the loans. Each of these recent shows was rewarding for both the museums themselves and their visitors, but all were limited in size and scope; the time of great retrospectives such as we saw in the 1990s seems to be over. The Met's presentation of Homer seemed uncertain whether to be a focus exhibition centered on a single Homer in the Met's collection, *The Gulf Stream*, or a broad survey of the artist's career. It was still a wonderful opportunity to see many of his iconic paintings in one place, beginning with *Sharpshooter* of 1863, all his important renderings of Black subjects, and virtually every one of his late Prout's Neck pictures. Yet the exhibition lacked the breadth of the National Gallery show of nearly thirty years before and was flawed also by an uneven selection of watercolors: Anything related to *The Gulf Stream* or the tropics was on view, including several weak examples, while the great Adirondack hunting and fishing scenes were missing. When I see a weak work on a museum wall, I always wonder whether it is owned by an important donor to the institution. The MFA's "Fashioned by Sargent" showed only two aspects of the painter's oeuvre: his portraits and his late outdoor scenes. But it provided the memorable opportunity of seeing a great many of the painter's strongest portraits hung together, just as the Met's Homer show did with his marines. History has come full circle: Sargent first came to attention as a portrait painter, then for years his portraits were regarded as lesser pictures, but now they again look like his most interesting work. The exhibition included some of the dresses and other costumes worn by his sitters; it was the next best thing to having the sitters themselves there. The exhibition and its catalogue missed the opportunity to examine the issues of inequality and gender roles of such great concern today. Philadelphia's "Mary Cassatt at Work," on the other hand, employed current methodology and focused on the theme of Cassatt as a modern woman, doing so not in terms of style and influence so much as "her serious engagement with the realities of gender and labor" in her own life and in her subject matter. There was an admirable, useful catalogue, though the exhibition, with the overload of prints and the paucity of excellent paintings and pastels, failed to present the whole of Cassatt's accomplishments. It is not clear what has caused even the best exhibitions to be limited in scope and ambition, but something surely has.

Exhibitions are best when the curators have something new to say, either through groundbreaking research or by presenting original views. One of the best revisionist exhibitions, one that caused us to rethink the notion that interest in landscape painting is dead, was "Thomas Cole's Journey: Atlantic Crossings" of 2018 at the Met, with its well-researched catalogue by Elizabeth Mankin Kornhauser and Tim Barringer.[4] The authors presented a new perspective on the artist: After years of writers aiming to minimize Cole's Englishness, these curators instead stressed it, and examined Cole in relationship to Constable, Turner, Claude Lorrain, and English and European artists. This project was one of several that has led to a critical reconsideration of Cole's art and of his importance.

The monograph, the in-depth book devoted to a single artist, is also becoming a rarity. Publishers have become wary of such books, and it is often easier and more economical to put the information into an exhibition catalogue. However, Carol Clark's exceptional monograph/

exhibition catalogue/catalogue raisonné devoted to the little-known Western painter Charles Deas is a rarity in bringing together everything one might want to know about the painter. Clark outlines the artist's life and career, brings to light all the known criticism and exhibition records and includes a complete illustrated list of his work.[5] At the same time, exemplary pure monographs unconnected to exhibitions continue to be published. One is Jane Kamensky's impressive study of John Singleton Copley, whose work has been thoroughly—and one might have thought, definitively—examined by Jules Prown, Carrie Rebora, and others in recent years. But Kamensky dug deeper into the archives and the culture of Boston and London, and produced a superb study of the painter and his sitters, patrons, and rivals as people, revealing among other things that Copley owned several slaves.[6] Similarly, in Margaretta Lovell's noteworthy recent book on Fitz Henry Lane, the author investigated Lane's patrons, the life, geology, and economy of his town of Gloucester, the varying rigging and cargoes of the brigs, barks, ships, and schooners he painted and their far-flung ports of call.[7] Both Kamensky and Lovell make use of the earlier literature on their painters, but neither one takes the time to debate methodological questions with their predecessors. Rather, they find important, unstudied questions to examine, in both cases minimizing connoisseurship and the study of style while replacing those matters with a search for meaning in the paintings.

Today's scholars eschew the term "masterpiece" because the concept doesn't fit easily with the new democratic methodology, while the art market, on the other hand, is focused on what it describes as masterpieces. Yet there are no real disagreements between them as the scholars merely substitute other terms for the unspoken one. On the market, what constitutes a masterpiece (the works bringing the biggest prices) has been dramatically rethought: The category now includes portraits of George Washington and other historical figures, works representing Black Americans or Native Americans or by them, and certain works by members of the old canon that are regarded as rare and outstanding.[8] (I cannot explain why images of Washington remain in such demand. They were the subject of major monographs a century ago when admiration for the Founders and for colonial and federal

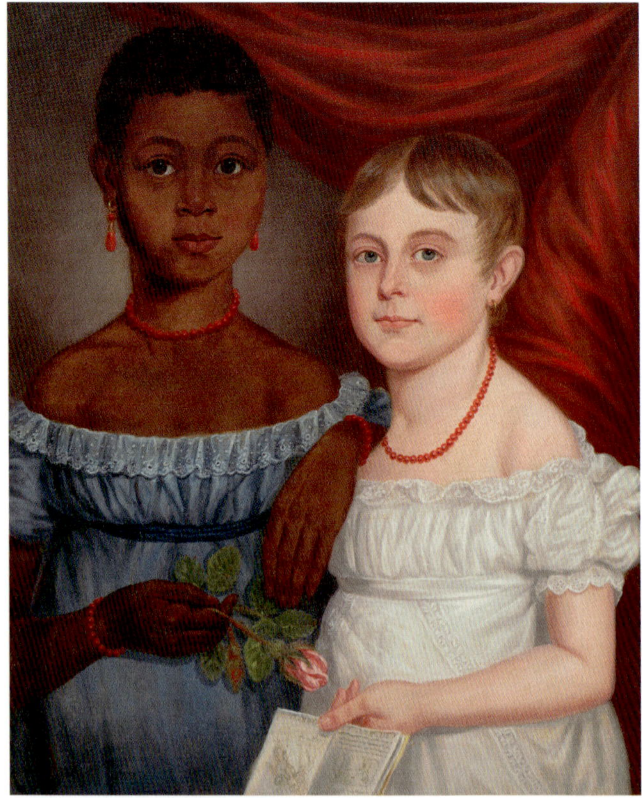

Fig. 76. AMERICAN SCHOOL (?),
Portrait of Two Girls, oil on canvas, ca. 1820–40. Private Collection.

America was at its highest. Those attitudes have been mostly discarded, but Washington sails on, unperturbed.) Auction results in 2023–24 give evidence of this dramatically changed market. At Christie's in January 2023, an *Athenaeum* portrait of George Washington by Gilbert Stuart, one of about a hundred replicas made by the painter, fetched $630,000, while Stuart's lovely portrait of Sarah Wetmore of Boston brought just $25,000. At the same sale, a charming double portrait by an unknown hand of two girls, one white, one Black, was knocked down for $945,000 to a London art dealer (fig. 76).[9] This was a picture that sold at auction in 1995 for $31,000, when it was seen only as a handsome folk painting, perhaps painted in the US, perhaps not. The girls are portrayed as equals: They wear similar Empire gowns and the same coral jewelry, while the taller Black girl rests her left arm affectionately on the other's shoulder. Are they sisters or friends, or had one shared her apparel with the other? Who would have commissioned this picture? Over a dozen museums felt that they had to have it, and bid the price up.

Suggesting that the price paid for the *Two Girls* was not a singular event but instead illustrates the current hunger for Black and mixed race compositions on the part of museums, is the purchase of a family painting attributed to the French neoclassic artist Jacques Amans (1801–1888) by the Metropolitan Museum in July 2023 (fig. 77).[10] Amans

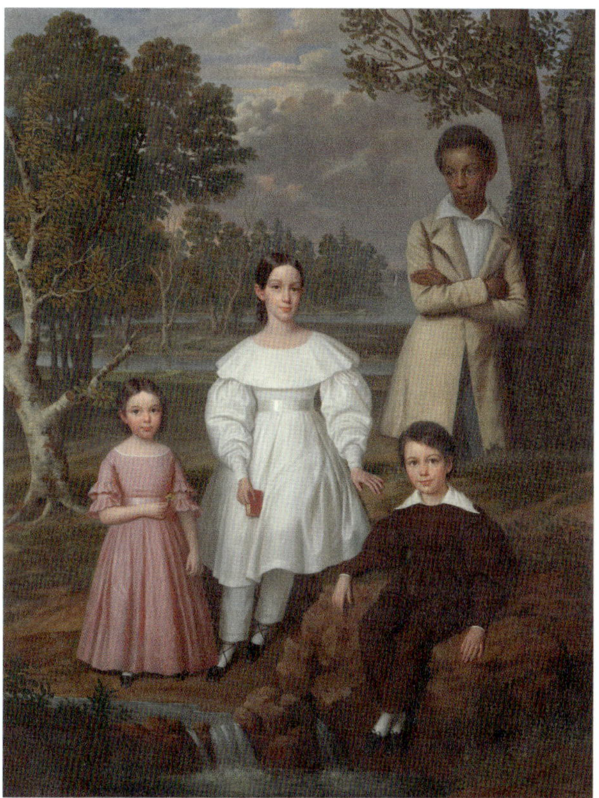

Fig. 77. JACQUES GUILLAUME LUCIEN AMANS, *Bélizaire and the Frey Children*, oil on canvas, ca. 1837. Metropolitan Museum of Art.

worked in New Orleans from 1837 to 1856 and early in his career there was commissioned to paint the three children of a prominent local merchant, Frederick Frey. The picture depicts the youngsters seated in a Louisiana landscape; a daughter of perhaps thirteen is at the center with a younger brother and sister on either side. A darker-skinned fourth figure, a handsome enslaved teenager named Bélizaire who would have been about fifteen, stands at the right, leaning against a tree with his arms crossed. The young man's awkward placement and the fact that his legs disappear into the earth confirm that he was a later addition, one likely made by Amans himself, judging from the paint handling. The intimacy of the figures and the fine clothing worn by all four suggest that Bélizaire was close to the family, or perhaps even part of it. His portrait was subsequently painted out before being recovered by recent restoration. It is a good painting but not one that the Met, or any museum, would have bought for over $1 million until very recently; in fact, it had been deaccessioned by the New Orleans Museum in 2005, when it sold at auction for $7,200. The Met was clearly proud of having acquired this image of a rare biracial group in the South, and publicized it extensively.

The Met's recent purchase brings to mind a related situation at Yale, which owns two full-length portraits of the university's benefactor Elihu Yale pictured with an enslaved youth. One was the first acquisition of the new Yale Center for British Art in 1970, a gift from the 11th Duke of Devonshire. It is a group portrait from about 1719 depicting Elihu Yale seated with three men (two of them his sons-in-law), with a young Black boy at right serving wine while wearing around his neck a silver collar with a padlock; a happy group of white children is seen in the background (fig. 78).[11] The gift of this work seemed a cause for celebration to director Jules Prown, who represented an entire generation seeing what it wanted to see—the historical importance of a portrait of a key figure in the university's history—while not noticing the racism that seems so blatantly obvious today.[12] Recently the Center went to great lengths to label the painting appropriately, while keeping it on view. The university also owns a second large portrait of Yale, who made his wealth as a merchant and slave trader in Madras, *Elihu Yale and his Servant* by James

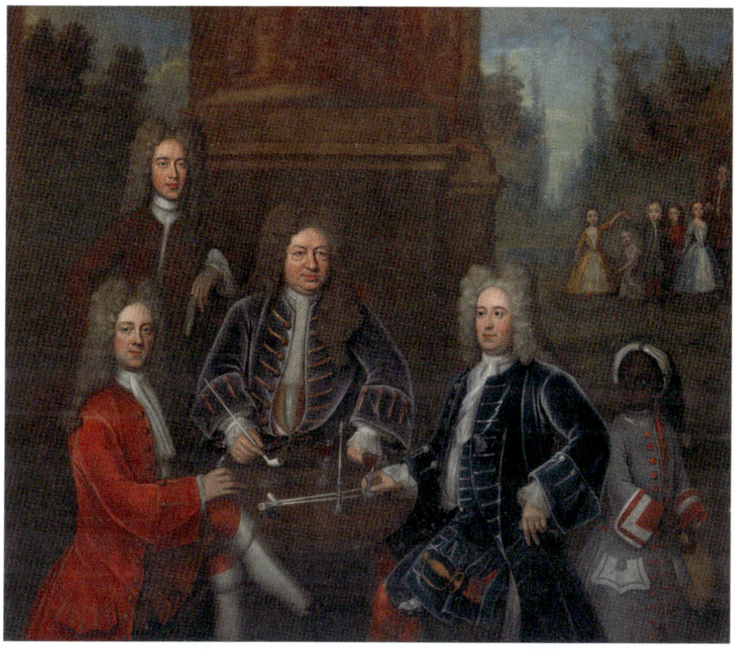

Fig. 78. JOHN VERELST, ATTRIB. TO,
Elihu Yale with Members of his Family and an Enslaved Child,
oil on canvas, ca. 1719. Yale Center for British Art.

Worsdale. In that work, beside the ponderous, seated figure of Yale stands a young, enslaved Black boy wearing a similar metal collar with a padlock. What is truly astonishing is that this picture hung in pride of place in the university's Corporation Room, the seat of the university's power and decision-making, from 1910 to 2007, when a faculty member pointed out its horrifying content and the picture was moved to storage.[13] From these works, it is clear that Elihu Yale took pleasure in being portrayed with a prize possession, the young slave. Both paintings are understood today as deeply racist. Future historians will have to puzzle out the distinction between these portraits and the Met's proud acquisition of a painting that similarly depicts an enslaved young man with members of the family that owned him.

The Christie's sale in January 2024 confirmed the changed market. Once again, there was keen interest in likenesses of Washington combined with a widespread disregard for portraits in general. A fine

Gilbert Stuart likeness of Washington of the Vaughan type sold by the Metropolitan Museum brought $2,833,000. At the same sale, an elegant Stuart oil of Mrs. Jonathan Mason of Boston went for just $23,000. The same pattern applies to the Peale family: Charles Willson Peale's portrait of Washington sold at Sotheby's a day later for $1,633,000, and a Rembrandt Peale of the first president brought $529,000 at Christie's, while likenesses of ordinary sitters by both Peales continue to sell for under $50,000.

The highest priced lot at Sotheby's in January 2024 was a small neoclassic sculpture by Edmonia Lewis called *Hiawatha's Marriage*. It fetched $1,633,000, five times the estimate, due both to the artist's mixed African American and Native American heritage and to her subject. Using Henry Wadsworth Longfellow's famous poem as her source, Lewis pictured the brave Ojibwe leader and his bride Minnehaha standing hand in hand before her tragic death from cold and famine. Few scholars have ever described this sculpture as a great work of art, but the combination of the artist's background and the tale told by the work made it irresistible for the dozen museums from around the country who went after it, including the Amon Carter, the Toledo Museum, the Peabody Essex, and the Columbus (Georgia) Museum of Art, with the Virginia Museum of Fine Arts prevailing. Thus, we learn again that the importance of race in valuing art today can hardly be overestimated. All of the Hudson River School pictures in the sale together brought less than this one work.

From the results at both Christie's and Sotheby's, it is clear that the areas of nineteenth-century painting that held greatest interest to my generation have been significantly downgraded: Hudson River School landscapes; Luminism; the American Pre-Raphaelites; still lifes, including even those of Harnett; most figurative and genre painting; and American Impressionism all now hold far less interest than before for scholars or the market. But an active undermarket exists, with a handful of dealers like Lou Salerno at Questroyal Fine Arts offering Hudson River School and related landscapes, and apparently doing well; there are still some collectors buying the old canon, even if most museums and scholars are ignoring it. And some of the old favorites still bring handsome prices.

Maxim Karolik's favorites, Martin Johnson Heade and Fitz Henry Lane, are still alive in the market but are now viewed highly selectively. Heade's tropical views of orchids and hummingbirds and the best of his marsh scenes still fetch high prices equivalent to those of a quarter century earlier, with a fine orchid composition bringing over $3.4 million at Christie's in January 2024, while most other Heades can be bought for $200,000 or less. With Lane, the premium on perceived masterworks is even more dramatic. The handsome Somes Sound view from the Wolf Collection fetched just over $6 million in 2023, its provenance from a distinguished collection apparently contributing significantly to the price, while more ordinary examples rarely reach $100,000. Not coincidentally, the work of Heade and Lane is still of concern to scholars and curators. Our understanding of Heade's universe has been greatly expanded by Christopher Benfey's research on his life and personal relationships and by recent exhibitions demonstrating how today's artists have connected to his imagery, and interestingly the MFA is planning a future exhibition of Heade's Brazilian work to be shared with São Paolo.[14]

The art market has been turned on its head. The typical eighteenth- or nineteenth-century American painting has lost 50 to 75 percent of its value over the last quarter century. At Christie's, handsome Hudson River School landscapes by Jasper Cropsey and Alfred Bricher sold for around $20,000, as did a rare early Asher B. Durand, the latter an important work by the old standards. Dismayed collectors naturally ask, "But won't they come back?" Based on history, I would guess that some probably will, but most won't. In their books, lectures, and sales pitches, art dealers and advisors tout art as a surefire investment, but in my experience it is far from that. The failure of Bernie Madoff, Lehman Brothers, and Polaroid offer parallel examples in the financial field. One is also aware of the sudden demise of outstanding art galleries like Knoedler or Salander-O'Reilly; the latter was cited by the Robb Report in 2003 as the best gallery in the world, before shutting down four years later with the proprietor going to prison for fraud.[15] For the current art market, the traditional factors that contributed to the notion of quality (and in turn informed price and value) have been significantly modified as considerations of history and race play increasingly important roles.

The painters of the early twentieth century, including George Bellows and the Eight, along with Edward Hopper and such formerly maligned illustrators as Norman Rockwell, dominate today's auction market and the museum field. Among the modernists, women lead the way. Georgia O'Keeffe and Arthur G. Dove were long considered peers, but O'Keeffe has now far outstripped him in the marketplace and in critical interest. Alice Neel was revived by the Met's exhibition after years of being considered a marginal figure. The Abstract Expressionists have been reshuffled, with women including Joan Mitchell and Lee Krasner and the Black painter Norman Lewis joining the canon, while such talented white men as Adolph Gottlieb and Bradley Walker Tomlin are rarely mentioned. Few portraitists of the past, other than Sargent and Frida Kahlo, engender much interest today, but this may be due for revision as we recognize how many of the recently recognized Black painters are known for their portraits; one thinks of Kehinde Wiley, Barkley L. Hendricks, and Henry Taylor, among many others.

Market prices for eighteenth- and nineteenth-century paintings and those for contemporary art were closely comparable before the financial crisis of 2008–9. Prices for Johns, Rauschenberg, and their peers at the auction of the outstanding modern collection of Victor and Sally Ganz in 1997 fell in the same range as the amounts realized for the top nineteenth-century paintings at the Fraad and Horowitz sales of 2004–5. However, the two fields diverged dramatically after 2008–9. The major financial downturn totally derailed the older American art but had only a temporary effect on the modern and contemporary market. Between 2007 and 2013, years of dramatic decline for nineteenth-century paintings, prices for Basquiat, Johns, and Pollock more than doubled. The battle between the Met and MoMA for Rauschenberg's celebrated and very valuable *Canyon* in 2012 caught everyone's attention. Then in 2015 the much-publicized purchase by Ken Griffin of two paintings by Pollock and de Kooning for $500 million established the new runaway market for the top moderns. We know from the prices brought by Ernest Meissonier and Rosa Bonheur in the late nineteenth century (see page 22) that record sales are no guarantee of future value, but today's collectors seem blissfully unaware of the history of changing taste.

In the contemporary field, the boom continues while hundreds of artists and dealers jockey for positions in a crowded field. There are now nearly a hundred living artists whose work sells for over $1 million, a list led by Jeff Koons, Peter Doig, and Christopher Wool, but remarkably one that now includes over twenty Black painters, half of them women. In addition, dozens of deceased modern masters from Picasso to Warhol and Basquiat sell in the many millions: Warhol's Marilyn sold to Larry Gagosian in 2022 for $195 million, and thus holds the current record. Artprice tells us that the market for modern and contemporary art amounted to $90 million in 2000, and now accounts for some $2.7 billion, or half of the total worldwide art market in all nationalities and mediums.[16] Modern generally refers to art of the twentieth century, while contemporary art is by living artists.

For today's collectors and museums, contemporary art is brighter, more attention-grabbing, and far more available than the older, darker, seemingly more difficult to understand productions of earlier American and European painters. Aiding the collectors is a vast network of smooth-talking advisors, scholars, curators, critics, and auctioneers stirring the mix, while hundreds of buyers with huge fortunes made on Wall Street and elsewhere around the world play a highly speculative game that happens to involve art. They are egged on by numerous reports that blue chip art outperforms the S&P 500. Yet they seem blissfully unaware that choosing lasting winners among living artists has always been incredibly difficult, and there is no reason to think the situation is any different now. The last thing on earth that the dealers tell their clients or curators their trustees is that taste is always changing, and will very likely keep doing so.

No one speaks today of an avant-garde, a concept long at the root of modern art. During the heyday of modernism, style meant everything. What Peter Schjeldahl wrote about Mondrian was true for many of the canonical artists and architects of the early twentieth century: "Style for him, from first to last, served a quest to manifest soul-deep spirituality as a demonstrable fact of life."[17] By contrast, today's most celebrated artists are the ones with the hottest markets; they pick and choose their styles and their nations of residence pragmatically according to their usefulness. Many popular painters from all over the world practice various forms of realism, abstraction, photography, and neo-Pop at will. These artists dominate the auction market: "three-quarters of auction turnover in contemporary art is generated by just a hundred artists, out of the 30,000 whose works make it to auction," according to Artprice.[18] The major galleries today are worldwide enterprises like Gagosian, David Zwirner, and Hauser & Wirth, with Gagosian alone racking up about $1 billion a year in gross revenues.

Greed, ambition, and showmanship are widespread in the world of modern and contemporary art. Collectors who study the art and are genuinely moved by it seem a diminishing species. However, there are some idealists among the collectors, one being Agnes Gund, a member of the prominent Gund family of Cleveland. Her aim is to help the artists and the museums she cares most about, including MoMA, the Cleveland Museum, and the Studio Museum in Harlem. Aggie, as she is known, is gifted with a superb eye. She began buying art after coming into wealth on her father's death in 1966; early on she was gathering classic works by Jasper Johns, Robert Rauschenberg, and Cy Twombly, but then turned increasingly to works by women and Black artists like Martin Puryear and Kara Walker. The prices being paid for art have gotten so high that any sane person would wonder what other, better purposes the funds might serve. Gund boldly answered this question when in 2017 she sold one of her most valuable pictures, *Masterpiece* of 1962 by Roy Lichtenstein, for $165 million and put the proceeds into an Art for Justice Fund that works for criminal justice reform. Aggie has become aware of the injustices experienced by Black Americans, including the disproportionately large Black population in American prisons. She is not alone in her idealism, but she stands out for the way she puts her art and her money to good use.

The new mindset in art history is articulated in a recent book from the Princeton University Art Museum called *Object Lessons in American Art*. As Karl Kusserow writes there, "Perhaps the most profound shift is how objects are approached and understood, according to paradigms in which social policy, ethics, and justice factor alongside aesthetic, historical, and cultural concerns."[19] He and his coauthors cover the developing field widely, examining questions of race, gender, and the environment. They write of many issues, including the slaughter and displacement of the Native Americans, and the widespread, continuing impact of enslavement and the effects of the slave economy, from the landing of the English privateer the *White Lion* with its human cargo of "20 and odd Negroes" at Jamestown, Virginia, in 1619 to the present day.

A traveling exhibition "Afro-Atlantic Histories," with its powerful introduction by Adriano Pedrosa (cited in my Introduction), played an important teaching role for me as it may have for others. People who viewed the show in Washington, Houston, or Los Angeles learned that slavery was not simply an issue for the US, but was a worldwide phenomenon. Americans learned again of the extraordinary imperfection of our Constitution: Established "to secure the Blessings of Liberty to ourselves and our Posterity," it simultaneously institutionalized slavery through the Fugitive Slave Clause and the Three-Fifths Clause.[20] Charts and maps in the exhibition informed visitors that twelve million enslaved Africans had been brought to the New World, nearly half of them to Brazil. The nature of slavery was made manifest: Certain human beings, based on the color of their skin, were declared nonhuman, property that could be bought and sold, manhandled, whipped, or raped with impunity.

The exhibition also provided some useful lessons about quality. One thought-provoking wall at the L.A. venue featured five portraits. In the center was the well-known picture by Frederic Bazille called *Young Woman with Peonies,* a profound work by a short-lived French Impressionist, a gift of Paul Mellon to the National Gallery. Brilliant peonies and other flowers dominate the foreground, but the flower seller's look of fatigued resignation is what one remembers. To the left of the Bazille were two pictures of seated figures: In one, a Black woman in a yellow dress leans back with her arms raised as if she were yawning, while in the other, a man sits at a table, his head bent and resting on his hand. What one remembers is the figures' body language; what stands out is the confidence of the woman and the resignation of the man.

These paintings by American artists Dindga McCannon and Hayward Oubre are works that used to be called "primitive" because of their flat, unmodeled forms, but no longer: Now we are able to see them as being about people and their feelings, like the Bazille. On the other side of the Bazille hung two other portraits, both of Black boys. *Johnny Cool* by the Jamaican Osmond Watson (fig. 79) is expressive: The young man seems dangerously thin, and his intense gaze is riveting. The paint handling is unsophisticated; it may not be a great painting according to academic standards, but it is powerful and memorable enough to cause one to rethink how we judge art. Next to it is a portrait of a younger

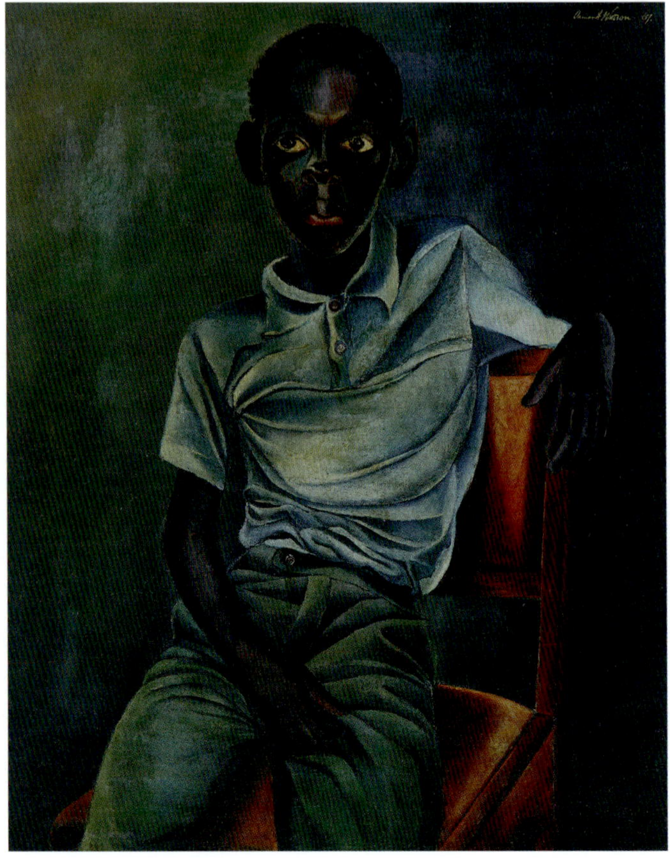

Fig. 79. **OSMOND WATSON,**
Johnny Cool, oil canvas, 1967. National Gallery of Jamaica.

boy by the renowned Brazilian painter Arthur Timótheo da Costa; he had studied in Paris and he modeled his figures well. His young boy's expression is downcast; he could be the son of Bazille's flower-seller.[21] After looking at these five related paintings and many others like them, the question of quality as it has been traditionally posed began to lose meaning for me. I realized that a refined technique and traditional modeling and color do not necessarily result in strong or moving works of art. The paintings by Watson and da Costa have an immediacy that recalls street photography. Such figurative works are meant to touch and inform the viewer, and to my eye, each of the five paintings on this wall did those things very well.

Highly important for the new recognition of Black artists has been the energetic collecting and patronage by private collectors. Black art lovers have supported artists for years; they and the historically Black colleges and universities enabled many painters and sculptors to survive over the last century. The difference is that in recent decades, significant wealth has flowed to Blacks in the sports world, the entertainment industry, and other businesses. This group of new buyers has the means to compete on the highest levels, and has the ambition, the connections, and the philanthropic drive to see Black art fully recognized by the market, the museums, and the press. These collectors, together with numerous museums, have driven values for the best-known Black artists ever higher.

The Brooklyn Museum in 2024 mounted a huge exhibition called "Giants: Art from the Dean Collection of Swizz Beatz and Alicia Keys." Record producer Kasseem Dean, known as Swizz Beatz, and his wife, singer Alicia Keys, have amassed superlative holdings over the years, going back in time to the photography of Gordon Parks and the paintings of Jean-Michel Basquiat and including Kehinde Wiley, Lorna Simpson, Ebony G. Patterson, and Meleko Mokgosi. Entrepreneur and philanthropist Tina Knowles, retired NBA star Carmelo Anthony, model Racquel Chevremont, and developer and curator Jessica Gaynelle Moss are among several dozen other important Black collectors across the country. Another is Pamela Joyner: She and her husband have 425 works in their New York and Lake Tahoe homes, and she reports buying a new one every ten days.[22] These collectors are energized. They know their artists, the dealers, and the museum world well, and they energetically promote the art they believe in. They are following in the footsteps of such pioneering Black collectors as Warren and Charlynn Goins, who began doing this work forty years ago on behalf of Robert S. Duncanson, Edward Bannister, and other earlier Black painters, and who have been generously giving their collection to museums ever since.

A book produced by the Princeton University Art Museum in 2018 makes an effort to expand today's critical methodology; it is titled *Nature's Nation: American Art and Environment*.[23] The title is an ironic echo of Perry Miller's volume of 1967 that was simply called *Nature's Nation*; its essays make an impassioned retort to Miller's exceptionalism.[24] Miller conceived the settlement of the continent as a heroic march of civilization and the expanding country as everything a nation could be, while Karl Kusserow and Alan Braddock, authors of the new book, rethink our art in light of ecology and environmental history, and come to very different conclusions. The richly carved, long-admired eighteenth-century mahogany chests are seen now as part of "an international ecosystem of aesthetics, slavery, and deforestation." Harvard scholar Robin Kelsey tells us that innocent-seeming photographs were typically made with products from the Kodak Company, a leader in "emissions of cancer-causing chemicals," and he goes on to attack the very core of the photographic enterprise, the framing out of undesirable details (cooling towers, housing developments).[25] The eco-criticism they propose may become an important part of the new methodology, though it is difficult to know where it leads. Once we have learned that many of the most treasured pieces of early American furniture, the great high chests from Newport, Philadelphia, and Boston, for example, employed Cuban, enslaved-harvested mahogany as their primary wood, what are we to do? If we label them appropriately, does that discovery still mean those works are less important or less beautiful than we thought? Once we realize that photographs are made from harmful materials, what does that imply for their study or their display? If curators find that venerated objects in their collections were made from Mexican silver mined by enslaved workers, should they take them off view, or merely draw attention to these facts?

Not everyone accepts the new methodology. The lives of stressed-out museum directors have gotten even more fraught as they navigate between determined curators on one hand and nervous supporters on the other. Museums have never been good places for internal discussion, debate, and disagreement. They remain highly class-conscious institutions, where trustees and staff rarely interact and in my experience, seldom talk about the important political, practical, and aesthetic questions they face together. The Met lost the important collection of Erving and Joy Wolf, major donors of funds and objects for more than forty years who had been advised by the museum's curators, when it went to auction in 2023 after her death. I know from our conversations that Mrs. Wolf was not a fan of the new direction of the museum toward diversity, but I don't know whether that affected her decision.[26]

"Wokeness" is a favorite subject of the conservative press. An article by Eric Gibson in *The Wall Street Journal* presents an articulate argument that represents many others in its longing for the old days when "aesthetic values alone" guided the operations of our art museums.[27] Sadly, Gibson hasn't studied enough history to know that this was never the case, both because aesthetic values, typically dictated by small groups of white men, were regularly changing, and because political ideology has always stood behind the perception of quality. Gibson came down hard on Max Hollein, director of the Met, who acknowledged his museum's history of racism. Several museum officials have told me that their trustees and donors read the Gibson article and responded favorably to it. One much-admired director told me, "It has already gotten messy. It's hard making people understand that these changes are not a threat to them or the art they love."[28] Museum donors are still likely to be older, wealthy, white, and entitled, they are confident they know exactly how museums should function, and many of them seem to look for reasons to walk away from their favorite institutions. Now that directors have every reason to fear being considered too "woke," the ground becomes even shakier.

At the MFA, the gifted curator Layla Bermeo is wondering what to do with the galleries of colonial painting that have long been dominated by the paintings of John Singleton Copley. Thirty years ago, as curator, I thought my installation was perfect. We were able to show this premier colonial painter in every aspect, with one great work after another. In the galleries, we could speak to Copley's amazing abilities to capture the materials and the personalities of Sam Adams, Paul Revere, Mercy Otis Warren, Mrs. Ezekial Goldthwaite, all the people who built Boston and created the Revolution, or opposed it. Well, not all. As Bermeo points out, the laborers, sailors, shopkeepers, the middle class, the poor, the children and elderly, and the enslaved people of Boston, all went unpainted.[29] As we had always known, Copley depicted the rich and powerful, the ones who could afford his rates. A new generation of curators finds the lineup of powerful white citizens to be unacceptable because Black or Hispanic visitors to the museum see no one who looks like them, no one they can identify with. What the curators wish for are portraits of the most important Black figures of the Revolutionary period, of Crispus Attucks, who was killed just before Boston's Tea Party, of the poet Phyllis Wheatley, or of Peter Salem, who fought with the Continental Army at Bunker Hill in 1775, but these works simply do not exist. The curators believe passionately that those images, or viable substitutes or interventions, are what the audience needs, and they are searching for creative ways to bring this about.

We don't know nearly enough about why people visit museums and what they hope to gain. There are surely a wide variety of motivations, but my guess is that things have changed little since 1963 when crowds lined up to see the *Mona Lisa* seeking to experience greatness. Greatness can mean beauty, value, rarity, inspiration, craftsmanship, solace, or any number of things, depending on the individual. I learned more about the museum audience (and museum guards) from Patrick Bringley's lovely memoir, *All the Beauty in the World: A Museum Guard's Adventures in Life, Loss, and Art*, than from any number of academic studies and surveys.[30] It's a book that every museum trustee and every curator should read.

The most recent textbook in the field, *This Is America: Reviewing the Art of the United States* by Keri Watson and Keidra Daniels Navaroli published in 2023, offers insight into the views of younger scholars.[31] The authors present an articulate social history of art aimed at students, without footnotes or a bibliography, while aiming "to decenter and decolonialize the art historical canon."[32] Unlike the earlier books by Pohl and Miller, they concentrate on paintings made in the US, interpreting many pictures from the traditional canon and contrasting them with relevant contemporary works. They seek to overturn the historical narrative that generations of Americans grew up with, replacing the glory of the westward movement by defining "settler colonialism" as "the occupation, acquisition, and exploitation of another's land and culture by means of force, displacement, and genocide."[33]

Finally, I'd like to consider the recent (late 2024) reinstallations of American art at New York's two largest museums, the Metropolitan Museum of Art and the Brooklyn Museum. At the Met's American Wing, it is clear that diversity was very much on the curators' minds, and in the galleries one found far more works by Black and women artists than after the rearrangement of 2012. The earlier installation emphasized chronology, typology, and style; the aim was to exhibit the best paintings and sculpture in the collection—its masterpieces, in other words. The new one takes a different tack, one dictated by the times: Now the curators present a richer and more varied picture and include many little-known practitioners. They did so to make the museum collection and its audience more democratic, and there's considerable evidence that people respond to such efforts, that increasing the diversity of the art improves the diversity of the visitors. The Met's great American paintings—the Homers, Sargents, Eakinses, the Coles and the other great landscapes—are still on view, but now, installed next to paintings of varied quality by lesser contemporaries, their impact seems diluted. One came away from the earlier installation with an appreciation of Homer's preeminence, having seen his works hung together in two galleries; with his paintings scattered as they are at present, the importance of the artist seems diminished. Much the same is true of Sargent and Eakins.

The outstanding Black painter of the later nineteenth century was Henry Osawa Tanner, who has now become a canonical figure. In 2023, the Met bought a small, uninteresting painting, *The Flight into Egypt*; which is not on view but a nearly identical larger composition the museum purchased in 2001, is. Installed at the Met is also one of the painter's great works, *The Thankful Poor*, on loan from Art Bridges. That picture was on the market in 2020, as the American Wing was being planned. Why didn't the museum drop everything and go after it? One expects the great museums to act boldly and to lead, as the Met has done on numerous occasions in the past in other instances.

One of the most surprising parts of this reinstallation comes as one enters the American Wing and comes on several galleries devoted to high-style eighteenth-century furniture and labeled "The Calculated Curve." The excellent Queen Anne and Chippendale chairs and tables stand in state on aggressively contemporary round steel bases that look a bit like miniature works by Richard Serra. The walls, painted in a pale purple, are empty, reinforcing the incongruity of these galleries with the rest of the Wing; it is clear that different designers took over here. The laudable intent must have been to isolate the furniture as individual works of art. Similarly, the inclusion of a final gallery devoted to early-twentieth-century modern artists, though handsomely installed, is puzzling. It displays a sampling of outstanding paintings by Georgia O'Keeffe, Charles Sheeler, Edward Hopper, and some others, with no indication that they represent the succeeding generation of leading American painters, and no indication of where more works by these artists might be found in the museum. I am told that these borrowed paintings are scheduled to return to the Modern and Contemporary Art Department in two years' time.[34] A final quibble: Nowhere to be seen is John Trumbull's *Sortie Made by the Garrison of Gibraltar*, one of the masterpieces of the collection and the cover image of the collection catalogue. It was perhaps Jock Howat's finest acquisition when he had the museum purchase it from the Boston Athenaeum in 1976, after the MFA foolishly turned it down. This painting still hangs at the Met, but now inexplicably in the new installation of European paintings. Trumbull would be outraged, for he was arrested and jailed in

London in 1780 as a suspected American spy, and he was nothing if not American.

All this said, the Met's installation has many high points, and the collection is still one of the best. Nothing can take away the brilliance of Sargent's *Madame X*, Eakins's *Max Schmidt in a Single Scull*, or Frederic Edwin Church's *Heart of the Andes*. The Homers are still great, once you find them, and the trompe l'oeil still lifes are outstanding. The landscapes by Kensett, Inness, and the others hang very much as before, and ones by Edward Bannister, Mary Morgan, and William Harper look well hanging together. The three Lilly Martin Spencers are fine additions. Two loans from the Thoma Collection add fresh notes, though nowhere can one find the viceregal (Spanish colonial) paintings that many museums have begun to feature as part of their collections of American art. If one looks, one can find an impressive group of these works in the Met's European galleries. Mary Cassatt and the American Impressionists look well, and the gallery devoted to the Paris Exposition of 1900 (see page 26) is one of several impressive ones. The big Leutze holds down the center of the Wing, surrounded by Bierstadt, Church, and others. The landscape galleries are pleasing, though I object to hanging an unfinished Kensett without describing it as such. And I particularly liked the new grouping of Copley, West, and Matthew Pratt with American furniture and the adjacent gallery devoted to George Washington, both on the mezzanine level.

The Brooklyn Museum also has an outstanding collection of American art, one of the ten best in the nation. For years it seemingly tried to be the Met, but couldn't; now it has apparently decided to be Brooklyn and to serve its own audience. Curator Stephanie Sparling Williams has reinstalled the American collection under the title "Toward Joy: New Frameworks for American Art," and apparently she was given free rein. Williams writes, "Black feminist and BIPOC perspectives act as through lines in this vast presentation," and in an introductory panel she speaks of "settler colonialism, global imperialism, genocide, enslavement, and environmental degradation." The galleries reflect the revisionist thinking of many younger scholars; the text that most closely describes their methodology is the recent textbook by

Watson and Navaroli that I have described above. Yet the installation is not heavy-handed; there are none of the lectures one might expect on Manifest Destiny, enslavement, and the like, but rather a sense of uplift, of teaching visitors about unfamiliar African, Indigenous, and Black American ways of seeing.

The four hundred works on view at Brooklyn include many of the notable works by white men in the collection, the great Bierstadt *Mt. Rosalie* for example, and others by Thomas Cole, Eastman Johnson, Thomas Moran, and Martin Johnson Heade, as well as John Singleton Copley and Gilbert Stuart. But democracy rules, and there are few concessions to traditional notions of quality and importance. Each gallery has a theme. The one called "Several Seats" (from a Black and Latinx phrase of reproach, "Take several seats") features a long row of historic portraits hung at nearly floor level, with labels written by New York drag and ballroom performers, and behind them a row of old park benches where visitors may sit. The gallery "To Give Flowers" (another Black adage) has a striking wallpaper taken from a design by Lois Mailou Jones on which visitors see Laura Wheeler Waring's portrait of a woman holding flowers, as well as paintings by Georgia O'Keeffe and Childe Hassam, a maize god from Mexico, and Hisako Hibi's *Topaz Sunflowers*, painted in a Japanese relocation camp during the war and purchased by the museum in 2023. The "Surface Tension" gallery examines the human body from a two-thousand-year-old ceramic piece from Mexico to Gaston Lachaise, while "Counterparts" pays homage to the Spiral Group in New York as well as to Lorraine O'Grady's historic "Black and White Show" of 1983.

Brooklyn's colorful galleries are densely installed, with works three or four deep on a wall; photography, painting, ancient and modern sculpture, and occasional furniture are mixed together, a little like an art school exhibition. There is no chronology here, and no canon; instead, one enjoys an installation that is bold and consistent. One can disagree with its premises, one can mourn the old days, but one cannot help admiring the curator's commitment and confidence. Democracy rules and the viewer is provided with a lively, engaging experience. Whether this installation represents the future or not,

I have no idea. But it does tell us that the many years when every museum hung their works in the same way are, at least temporarily, over. Today we find a broad spectrum of possibilities, a range from Brooklyn at the most diverse, multicultural end along with Houston and Baltimore, to the Frick, Chicago, and Cleveland with their carefully installed masterpieces at the other. At the end of the day, installations like these are only temporary and will inevitably be redone by succeeding generations of curators.

---

[1] Frederick Ilchman, conversation with the author, October 19, 2024.

[2] *Paintings, Drawings and Pastels by Edwin Austin Abbey* (Gallery of Fine Arts, Yale University, 1939), with contributions by Royal Cortissoz and George Heard Hamilton; *Edwin Austin Abbey (1852–1911: An Exhibition Organized by the Yale University Art Gallery* (Yale University Art Gallery, 1973), with essays by Kathleen A. Foster and Michael Quick.

[3] Charles Saumarez Smith, *The Art Museum in Modern Times* (London: Thames and Hudson, 2021).

[4] Elizabeth Mankin Kornhauser and Tim Barringer, *Thomas Cole's Journey: Atlantic Crossings* (Metropolitan Museum of Art, 2018).

[5] Carol Clark, ed., *Charles Deas and 1840s America* (University of Oklahoma Press, 2009).

[6] Jane Kamensky, *A Revolution in Color: The World of John Singleton Copley* (W. W. Norton, 2016).

[7] Margaretta Lovell, *Painting the Inhabited Landscape: Fitz H. Lane and the Global Reach of Antebellum America* (Pennsylvania State University Press, 2023).

[8] Stuart's portrait of the Mohawk chief, Joseph Brant, sold at auction in 2014 for $7 million.

[9] The buyer was Philip Mould, an able London dealer and publicity hound.

[10] The lead curator on this purchase at the Met was Elizabeth Mankin Kornhauser. See Alexandra Eaton, "'His Name was Bélizaire': Rare Portrait of Enslaved Child Arrives at the Met," *New York Times*, August 14, 2023.

[11] Attributed to John Verelst, *Elihu Yale with Men of His Family and an Enslaved Child*, ca. 1719, Gift of the 11th Duke of Devonshire, accession number B1970.1. In October 2020, this portrait was replaced by a work by the New Haven artist Titus Kaphar entitled *Enough About You*, a wall sculpture that includes a replica of the original painting in crumpled, barely visible, form, along with a new portrait of the enslaved youth freed of the collar, and now housed in a fine gold frame. This solved the problem for six months' time, after which the Kaphar was returned to its owners and the

original portrait was back in the gallery bearing its new title, *Elihu Yale with Members of His Family and an Enslaved Child.* On Yale's wealth and his collection, see Romita Ray, "Going Global, Staying Local: Elihu Yale the Art Collector," *Yale University Art Gallery Bulletin* (2012): 34–51. On Yale's coming to terms with its enslaving past, see "A Reckoning with Our Past: Yale Examines Its Historical Ties with Slavery," *Yale Alumni Magazine,* January/February 2022. According to the Yale Center for British Art website, similar locked metal collars appear on enslaved figures in some fifty other British portraits dating from 1660 to 1760.

[12] Prown is described as an "Anglo-Americanist" scholar by Kirsten Pai Buick. Chambers, *Routledge Companion to African American Art History,* 86.

[13] Noah Remnick, "Yale Grapples with Ties to Slavery in Debate over a College's Name," *New York Times,* September 11, 2015.

[14] *Cross Pollination: Heade, Cole, Church, and Our Contemporary Moment,* an exhibition of 2021 shown at Crystal Bridges and Thomas Cole Historic Site/Olana State Historic Site.

[15] See Philip Boroff, "Will Larry Salander's Fraud Victims Get Their Money Back?" *Artnet News,* April 18, 2014. For a recent case of a fraudulent art agent, see Sarah Maslin Nir and Zachary Small, "Art Advisor. Friend, Thief," *The New York Times,* Feb. 18, 2025.

[16] See Artprice.com, "Artprice Report: 20 Years of Contemporary Art Auction History, 2000–2020." Artsy, for its part, reckons that modern and contemporary account for 46 percent, or nearly half, of the whole market. Artsy Editors, "The 100 Most Expensive Artists at Auction," Artsy, August 8, 2016.

[17] Peter Schjeldahl, "Dutch Magus: Excavating the Mysteries of Mondrian's Greatness," *New Yorker,* October 3, 2022.

[18] Artprice.com, "Artprice Report," 14.

[19] Karl Kusserow, ed., *Object Lessons in American Art* (Princeton University Art Museum, 2023), 23.

[20] Article 1, Section 2, Clause 3 in the US Constitution provides that slaves would count as three-fifths of a person for the allocation of representatives in Congress.

[21] Special thanks to Ilene Fort for reminding me about the installation of these works in L.A.

[22] Charlotte Collins, "How 9 Black Collectors Are Changing the Art World, Starting at Home," *Architectural Digest,* February 15, 2024.

[23] Karl Kusserow and Alan C. Braddock, *Nature's Nation: American Art and Environment* (Yale University Press, 2018).

[24] Perry Miller, *Nature's Nation* (Harvard University Press, 1967).

[25] Robin Kelsey, "Photography and the Ecological Imagination," in Kusserow and Braddock, *Nature's Nation,* 395.

[26] Erving Wolf died in 2018, Mrs. Wolf in August 2022; Sotheby's sold the entire collection, some 1,364 lots, in April 2023, for about $68 million.

[27] Eric Gibson, "Woke Ideologies Are Taking over American Art Museums," *Wall Street Journal,* September 2, 2022.

[28] Confidential discussion, October 22, 2022.

[29] Layla Bermeo, conversation with the author, January 25, 2023.

[30] Patrick Bringley, *All the Beauty in the World: A Museum Guard's Adventures in Life, Loss, and Art* (Simon and Schuster, 2022).

[31] Keri Watson and Keidra Daniels Navaroli, *This Is America: Re-Viewing the Art of the United States* (Oxford University Press, 2024).

[32] Watson and Navaroli, x.

[33] Watson and Navaroli, 4.

[34] Sylvia Yount, conversation with the author, November 15, 2024.

Postscript

> *In bad periods the most appalling buildings and poems are constructed on principles just as fine as in the good periods; all the people involved in destroying the achievements of the preceding good epoch feel they are improving on them; the bloodless youth of such inferior periods take just as much pride in their young blood as do the new generations of all other eras.*
>
> —ROBERT MUSIL, *The Man Without Qualities*, 1930

> *I don't dare bring up the question of quality in staff meetings these days.*
>
> —A curator of American art at a major museum, 2021

THE AMERICAN art world is no longer a quiet, private place. Since the groundbreaking sales and exhibitions of the 1970s, art and art museums have become highly visible parts of our national life. Museum exhibitions attract press attention and large audiences, along with frequent debates and reviews. Directors no longer make leisurely trips seeking out donors and masterworks, nor do their curators live the sequestered scholarly lives of yore. What has happened is that along with art becoming more and more popular, the art world has gone about leveling its playing field more effectively than many other areas of our society;

the disadvantages faced by women artists and those of color have been significantly reduced. Today there are many more artists and more kinds of art in the mix, all of them competing for limited wall space in homes and museums and for the attention of the market. The new direction was well underway by 2015. As Randy Kennedy points out in an excellent article from that year, momentum was building, but the advances seemed fragile, or perhaps only "a fad" as Thelma Golden speculated at the time.[1] But within a decade, things had changed. Scholar Gwendolyn DuBois Shaw in 2024 could speak of a "new Black Renaissance" marked by an "extraordinary level of visibility for Black artists within the museum and gallery world."[2] The painter Norman Lewis, in 1979 as he was dying, said to his family, "I think it's going to take about 30 years, maybe 40, before people stop caring whether I'm black and just pay attention to the work."[3] His prediction seems to be coming true today, over forty years later. Still, people wonder whether we have experienced a sea change in American attitudes. At the moment, the emphasis on diversity, equity, accessibility, and inclusion seems to be spreading—in the arts, at least—with few publicly expressed negative reactions. Yet my private conversations with museum trustees and donors reveal a good deal of quiet doubt about the current movement. Powerful white men and women will continue to play important roles in deciding the museums' future direction. People forget that our great art museums are not government-funded as in Europe, but depend heavily on the generosity of private donors; a key job of the American museum director is listening to them and keeping them in a giving frame of mind.

Though curators these days are loath to speak of quality, a consideration of it underlies almost everything they do. When the Museum of Fine Arts pursued a painting by Remedios Varo, it had to decide whether the quality and importance of the work justified its price, and whether selling two Georgia O'Keeffes and a Charles Sheeler in order to pay for it was warranted. The curators needed to be expert in Varo and her work, and in O'Keeffe and Sheeler and the other artists whose work might be deaccessioned. I learned long ago from my mentor Jakob Rosenberg that quality decisions are far easier when you are comparing likes, for example, two Rembrandt school drawings, or at least two works of a single period and style. However, life is often not that easy, and in many cases, you need to judge between apples and oranges. Over forty years ago, as curator at the MFA, I sold a mediocre Renoir oil from the collection, one of fourteen we had, to pay for the Jackson Pollock *Troubled Queen*, a powerful, transitional work of 1946 that I thought would bolster the one Pollock we owned, a fine, small drip painting. A few people objected strenuously, but the Pollock has proven its importance over the years while the little Renoir would never have made it out of storage.

I remember my excitement in 1980 when I found a donor who enabled the MFA to buy Joseph Stella's *Brooklyn Bridge*, a rarity, long admired as a masterpiece.[4] It's a painting that speaks to the American city, to engineering prowess, and to the developing modernist aesthetic. But my successors no longer hang the painting. Taste has changed, new criteria are in place. If the curators called me and asked whether I would approve the trade of Stella's *Brooklyn Bridge* for, say, Robert Colescott's *George Washington Carver Crossing the Delaware* (fig. 80), I think I might agree to the trade. I have grown to appreciate the new criteria. The Colescott is a masterpiece too, and one with more meaning for today, with its wit and its ambition to rewrite American history, than the Stella. The Stella is as good as it ever was, but its relevance has been lessened, and I understand the need to hang works that seem relevant in today's climate.

I am a curator and a historian, not a soothsayer. I cannot predict whether the art world will continue on its present path toward diversity, equity, and inclusion, or whether it will turn away from those goals, because we know that art has always been intertwined with economics and politics, and never more than at present.[5] We simply do not know whether the developing commitment to aesthetic standards based on justice and diversity has a limited life span like all the earlier generational changes of taste, or whether it represents a lasting development. Nor do I know which of today's painters will maintain his or her high reputation, as Winslow Homer, Edward Hopper, and Jackson Pollock have to date, or which ones are today's Washington Allstons or George Fullers. For me, art can be satirical or profound. It can speak of tragedy or joy. It can be made by someone with a gifted hand, or it can be sloppy and poorly executed. Its technique matters less than the artist's idea and motive. I

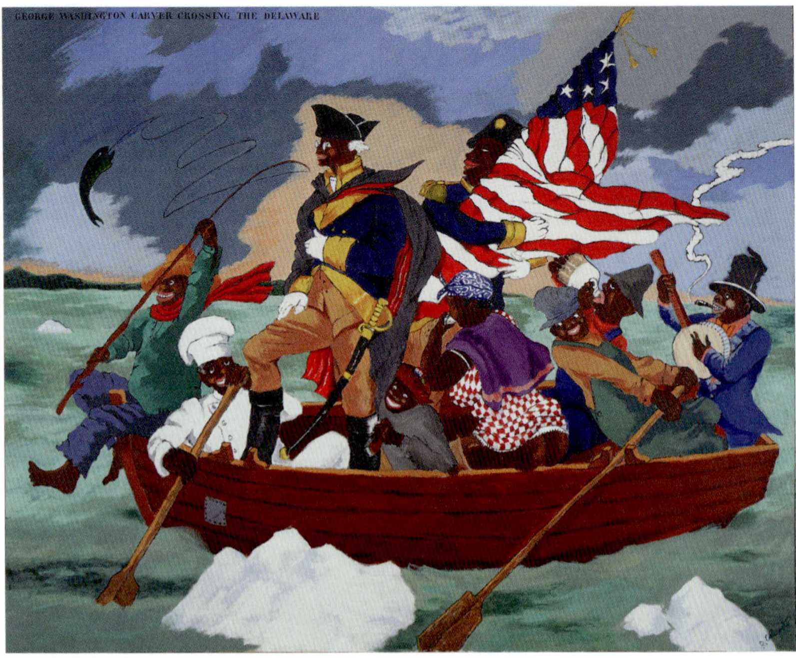

Fig. 80. **ROBERT COLESCOTT,**
George Washington Carver Crossing the Delaware,
acrylic on canvas, 1975. Lucas Museum of Narrative Art.

find many paintings to be beautiful and moving, though I know those terms are no longer in fashion. At the end of the day, art has nothing to do with money; only our response to it matters. Whatever happens, art will continue to represent the highest achievements of each civilization, and to reflect our shared myths and aspirations, our hopes, and our fears.

---

[1] Randy Kennedy, "Black Artists and the March into the Museums," *New York Times,* November 28, 2015.

[2] Gwendolyn DuBois Shaw, *The Art of Remembering: Essays on African American Art and History* (Duke University Press, 2024), 1, 2.

[3] Kennedy, "Black Artists."

[4] For an excellent survey of the time-honored concept of the masterpiece, see Walter Cahn, *Masterpieces: Chapters on the History of an Idea* (Princeton University Press, 1979).

[5] Things have changed quickly in the first three months of 2025, as indicated, for example, by President Trump's executive order of March 27, 2025, "Restoring Truth and Sanity to American History."

Permissions

Introduction

Fig. 1. Thomas Cole, *A View of the Mountain Pass Called the Notch of the White Mountains (Crawford Notch),* oil on canvas, 1839. Courtesy National Gallery of Art.

Chapter One: The Changing Canon of the 19th Century

Fig. 2. Washington Allston, *The Dead Man Restored to Life by Touching the Bones of the Prophet Elisha,* 1811–1813. Oil on canvas, 156 × 122 in. Courtesy of the Pennsylvania Academy of the Fine Arts, Philadelphia. Pennsylvania Academy Purchase, by subscription, 1816.1.

Fig. 3. Daniel Ridgway Knight, *Hailing the Ferry,* 1888. Oil on canvas, 64½ × 83⅛ in. Courtesy of the Pennsylvania Academy of the Fine Arts, Philadelphia. Gift of John H. Converse, 1891.7.

Fig. 4. Edwin Lord Weeks, *The Rajah Starting on a Hunt,* ca. 1885. Oil on canvas. 39⁹⁄₁₆ × 32 in. (100.5 × 81.3 cm). The Metropolitan Museum of Art. Bequest of Maria DeWitt Jesup, from the collection of her husband, Morris K. Jesup, 1924 (15.30.68).

Fig. 5. Frederick Stuart Church, *The Witch's Daughter,* detail, watercolor, 1881. Smithsonian American Art Museum, Gift of John Gellatly, 1929.6.18.

Fig. 6. Rosa Bonheur, *The Horse Fair.* 1852-55. Oil on canvas, 96¼ × 199½ in. (244.5 × 506.7 cm). The Metropolitan Museum of Art. Gift of Cornelius Vanderbilt, 1887 (87.25). Image copyright © The Metropolitan Museum of Art. Image source: Art Resource, NY.

Chapter Two: The Rise of Museums and Professional Critics

Fig. 7. Mary Cassatt, *Mother and Child (Baby Getting Up from His Nap),* ca. 1899. Oil on canvas. 36½ × 29 in. (92.7 × 73.7 cm). The Metropolitan Museum of Art. George A. Hearn Fund, 1909 (09.27). Image copyright © The Metropolitan Museum of Art. Image source: Art Resource, NY.

Fig. 8. Winslow Homer, *Maine Coast.* 1896. Oil on canvas, 30 × 40 in. (76.2 × 101.6 cm). The Metropolitan Museum of Art. Gift of George A. Hearn, in memory of Arthur Hoppock Hearn, 1911 (11.116.1). Image copyright © The Metropolitan Museum of Art. Image Source: Art Resource, NY.

Fig. 9. Alexander Helwig Wyant (American, 1836–1892). *Keene Valley,* ca. 1884–1886. Oil on canvas, 18¹⁄₁₆ × 29¹⁵⁄₁₆ in. (45.8 × 76.1 cm). Brooklyn Museum, Gift of Mrs. Carll H. de Silver in memory of her husband, 13.43.

Fig. 10. George Fuller, *The Quadroon,* 1880. Oil on canvas, 50½ × 40½ in. (128.3 × 102.9 cm). The Metropolitan Museum of Art. Gift of George A. Hearn, 1910 (10.64.3). Image copyright © The Metropolitan Museum of Art. Image Source: Art Resource, NY.

Fig. 11. John Singer Sargent (American, 1856-1925), *El Jaleo,* 1882. Oil on canvas, 232 × 348 cm (91⁵⁄₁₆ × 137 in.) Isabella Stewart Gardner Museum, Boston.

Chapter Three: Important Mid-Century Writers: Goodrich, Sweet, Richardson

Fig. 12. John La Farge, *Portrait of the Painter.* 1859. Oil on wood panel, 16¹⁄₁₆ × 11½ in. (40.8 × 29.2 cm). The Metropolitan Museum of Art. Samuel D. Lee Fund, 1934 (34.134). Image copyright © The Metropolitan Museum of Art. Image Source: Art Resource, NY.

Fig. 13. Thomas Eakins, *Maud Cook,* oil on canvas, 1895. Yale University Art Gallery. Bequest of Stephen Carlton Clark, B.A. 1903.

Fig. 14. Albert Pinkham Ryder, American, 1847–1917. *Constance,* 1896. Oil on canvas, 70.8 × 90.49 cm (27⅞ × 35⅝ in.). Museum of Fine Arts, Boston. A. Shuman Collection —Abraham Shuman Fund, 45.770. Photograph © 2025 Museum of Fine Arts, Boston.

Chapter Four: Americans Discover American Art

Fig. 15. Thomas Anshutz, *The Ironworkers' Noontime,* 1880, oil on canvas, 17 × 23⅞ in. (43.2 × 60.6 cm). Fine Arts Museums of San Francisco, Gift of Mr. and Mrs. John D. Rockefeller 3rd, 1979.7.4. Photograph by Randy Dodson, courtesy of the Fine Arts Museums of San Francisco.

Fig. 16. Eastman Johnson, *The Cranberry Harvest, Island of Nantucket,* oil on canvas, 1880. Putnam Foundation, Timken Museum of Art, San Diego.

Fig. 17. Albert Bierstadt (American, born Germany, 1830–1902). *A Storm in the Rocky Mountains, Mt. Rosalie,* 1866. Oil on canvas, frame: 98⅝ × 158⅛ × 7¼ in., 335 lb. (250.5 × 401.6 × 18.4 cm, 151.96 kg). Brooklyn Museum, Dick S. Ramsay Fund, Healy Purchase Fund B, Frank L. Babbott Fund, A. Augustus Healy Fund, Ella C. Woodward Memorial Fund, Carll H. de Silver Fund, Charles Stewart Smith Memorial Fund, Caroline A.L. Pratt Fund, Frederick Loeser Fund, Augustus Graham School of Design Fund, Museum Collection Fund, Special Subscription, and John B. Woodward Memorial Fund; Purchased with funds given by Daniel M. Kelly and Charles Simon; Bequest of Mrs. William T. Brewster, Gift of Mrs. W. Woodward Phelps in memory of her mother and father, Ella M. and John C. Southwick, Gift of Seymour

Barnard, Bequest of Laura L. Barnes, Gift of J.A.H. Bell, and Bequest of Mark Finley, by exchange, 76.79.

Fig. 18. Frederic Edwin Church, *Home by the Lake*, 1852, oil on canvas, 31⅞ × 48¼ in. Crystal Bridges Museum of American Art, Bentonville, Arkansas, 2008.16. Photography by Dwight Primiano.

Chapter Five: Celebratory Exhibitions and Publications

Fig. 19. John James Audubon, *Gyrfalcon (Falco rusticolus)*, Havell plate no. 366, ca. 1835–1836. Watercolor, gouache and graphite on paper, with mat 52 × 38 in. Purchased for the Society by public subscription from Mrs. John J. Audubon. The New York Historical Society, 1863.7.366. Digital image created by Oppenheimer Editions.

Chapter Six: The Wounded Collector: Grenville Winthrop

Fig. 20. Thomas Couture, *Romans of the Decadence*, detail, 1847. Oil on canvas, 59.37 × 91.12 cm (23⅜ × 35⅞ in.). Harvard Art Museums/Fogg Museum, Bequest of Grenville L. Winthrop, Photo © President and Fellows of Harvard College, 1943.224.

Fig. 21. John Singer Sargent, *The Breakfast Table*, 1883–1884. Oil on canvas, 54 × 45 cm (21¼ × 17¹¹⁄₁₆ in.). Harvard Art Museums/Fogg Museum, Bequest of Grenville L. Winthrop, Photo © President and Fellows of Harvard College, 1943.150.

Fig. 22. Charles Willson Peale, *George Washington (1732-1799)*, 1784. Oil on canvas, 241.3 × 145.7 cm (95 × 57⅜ in.). Harvard Art Museums/Fogg Museum, Bequest of Grenville L. Winthrop, Photo © President and Fellows of Harvard College, 1943.144.

Chapter Seven: The Ambitions of Francis P. Garvan

Fig. 23. George Caleb Bingham (American, 1811–1879). *Shooting for the Beef*, 1850. Oil on canvas, 33⅜ × 49 in. (84.8 × 124.5 cm). Brooklyn Museum, Dick S. Ramsay Fund, 40.342.

Fig. 24. George Benjamin Luks (American, 1867–1933). *Street Scene (Hester Street)*, 1905. Oil on canvas, 25¹³⁄₁₆ × 35⅞ in. (65.5 × 91.1 cm). Brooklyn Museum, Dick S. Ramsay Fund, 40.339.

Fig. 25. Augustus Vincent Tack, *Portrait of Francis P. Garvan (1875-1937)*, oil on canvas, ca. 1930. Yale University Art Gallery. Bequest of Mabel Brady Garvan.

Fig. 26. Thomas Eakins, *John Biglin in a Single Scull*, oil on canvas, 1874. Yale University Art Gallery. Whitney Collections of Sporting Art, given in memory of Harry Payne Whitney, B.A. 1894, and Payne Whitney B.A. 1898, by Francis P. Garvan, B.A. 1897, M.A. (Hon.) 1922.

Chapter Eight: The Troubled Clark Brothers

Fig. 27. Winslow Homer, *Two Guides*, oil on canvas, 1877. Clark Art Institute. Image courtesy Clark Art Institute. clarkart.edu

Fig. 28. George Inness, *Home at Montclair*, oil on canvas, 1892. Clark Art Institute. Image courtesy Clark Art Institute. clarkart.edu

Fig. 29. Edward Hopper, *Sunlight in a Cafeteria,* oil on canvas, 1958. Yale University Art Gallery. Bequest of Stephen Carlton Clark, B.A. 1903. © 2025 Heirs of Josephine N. Hopper / Licensed by Artists Rights Society (ARS), NY.

Fig. 30. William Sidney Mount (1807–1868), *Eel Spearing at Setauket,* 1845, oil on canvas, H: 28.5 × W: 36 in. Fenimore Art Museum, Cooperstown, New York. Gift of Stephen C. Clark. N0395.1955. Photograph by Richard Walker.

Chapter Nine: Maxim Karolik, Discovering a New Canon

Fig. 31. Unknown photographer, *Maxim Karolik,* ca. 1927. Collection of the Massachusetts Historical Society.

Fig. 32. Fitz Henry Lane, American, 1804–1865. *Owl's Head, Penobscot Bay, Maine,* 1862. Oil on canvas, 40 × 66.36 cm (15¾ × 26⅛ in.). Museum of Fine Arts, Boston. Bequest of Martha C. Karolik for the M. and M. Karolik Collection of American Paintings, 1815–1865, 48.448. Photograph © 2025 Museum of Fine Arts, Boston.

Fig. 33. Martin Johnson Heade, *Thunder Storm on Narragansett Bay,* 1868. Oil on canvas. Amon Carter Museum of American Art, Fort Worth, Texas. 1977.17.

Fig. 34. Erastus Salisbury Field, American, 1805–1900. *Joseph Moore and His Family,* about 1839. Oil on canvas, 209.23 × 237.17 cm (82⅜ × 93⅜ in.). Museum of Fine Arts, Boston. Gift of Maxim Karolik for the M. and M. Karolik Collection of American Paintings, 1815–1865, 58.25. Photograph © 2025 Museum of Fine Arts, Boston.

Chapter Ten: Ray & Margaret Horowitz and the Invention of American Impressionism

Fig. 35. John Singer Sargent, *Group with Parasols (Siesta),* oil on canvas, 1904–1905. Private Collection.

Fig. 36. William Merritt Chase, *The Fairy Tale,* oil on canvas, 1892. Private Collection.

Fig. 37. Annie T. Lang, *William Merritt Chase.* ca. 1910. Oil on canvas, 30 × 25 in. (76.2 × 63.5 cm). The Metropolitan Museum of Art. Gift of Mr. and Mrs. Raymond J. Horowitz, 1977 (1977.183.1). Image copyright © The Metropolitan Museum of Art. Image source: Art Resource, NY.

Fig. 38. Theodore Robinson, *The Wedding March,* 1892, oil on canvas, 22⁵⁄₁₆ × 26½ in. (56.7 × 67.3 cm). Terra Foundation for American Art, Daniel J. Terra Collection, 1999.127.

Chapter Eleven: Collecting the Canon During the Boom Years

Fig. 39. Mary Cassatt, *Reading "Le Figaro,"* 1878. Private Collection, Washington, D.C.

Fig. 40. James McNeill Whistler, *Chelsea in Ice,* 1864. Oil on canvas, 17 ¾ in. × 24 in. (45.09 cm × 60.96 cm). Colby College Museum of Art, The Lunder Collection. 2013.293.

Fig. 41. George Bellows, *Kids,* oil on canvas, 1906. Virginia Museum of Fine Arts, Richmond. James W. and Frances Gibson McGlothlin Collection, 2017.153, Photo: Katherine Wetzel, © Virginia Museum of Fine Arts.

Chapter Twelve: William H. Lane, Champion of Modern American Art

Fig. 42. Unknown photographer, Bill and Saundra Lane with Ted Stebbins, 1990. Courtesy of the Museum of Fine Arts, Boston.

Fig. 43. Georgia O'Keeffe, American, 1887–1986. *Deer's Skull with Pedernal,* 1936. Oil on canvas, 91.44 × 76.52 cm (36 × 30⅛ in.). Museum of Fine Arts, Boston. Gift of the William H. Lane Foundation, 1990.432. Photograph © 2025 Museum of Fine Arts, Boston.

Fig. 44. Arthur Garfield Dove, American, 1880–1946. *That Red One,* 1944. Oil and wax on canvas, 68.58 × 91.44 cm (27 × 36 in.). Museum of Fine Arts, Boston. Gift of the William H. Lane Foundation, 1990.408. Photograph © 2025 Museum of Fine Arts, Boston.

Fig. 45. Stuart Davis, American, 1892–1964. *Hot Still-Scape for Six Colors- 7th Avenue Style,* 1940. Oil on canvas, 91.44 × 113.98 cm (36 × 44⅞ in.). Museum of Fine Arts, Boston. Gift of the William H. Lane Foundation and Museum purchase with funds by exchange from the M. and M. Karolik Collection, 1983.120. Photograph © 2025 Museum of Fine Arts, Boston. © 2025 Estate of Stuart Davis / Licensed by VAGA at Artists Rights Society (ARS), NY.

Fig. 46. Edward Weston, American, 1886–1958. *Nude,* 1936. Photograph, gelatin silver print, Sheet: 24.1 × 19.2 cm (9½ × 7⁹⁄₁₆ in.). Museum of Fine Arts, Boston. © The Lane Collection, 2017.2286. Photograph © 2025 Museum of Fine Arts, Boston. © 2025 Center for Creative Photography, Arizona Board of Regents / Artists Rights Society (ARS), New York.

Chapter Thirteen: Alice Kaplan, Only the Best

Fig. 47. John Brewster, Jr., *Portrait of Sarah Prince (1785-1867),* oil on canvas, ca. 1801. Yale University Art Gallery. From the Collection of Alice M. Kaplan; acquired through her daughter Joan K. Davidson with support from the Iola S. Haverstick Fund for American Art; John Hill Morgan, B.A. 1893, LL.B. 1896, M.A. (Hon.) 1929, Fund; Friends of American Arts Acquisition Fund; Leonard C. Hanna, Jr., Class of 1913, Fund; and by a bequest of John M. Schiff, B.A. 1925, by exchange.

Fig. 48. William M. Harnett, *Mr. Huling's Rack Picture,* oil on canvas, 1888. Private Collection.

Fig. 49. Gregory Gillespie, *Roman Interior (Still Life),* 1966–67, oil & mixed media on wood, 43¾ × 32¾ in. Courtesy of Forum Gallery, New York.

Chapter Fourteen: The Problem of Collecting Contemporary Art: Richard B. Baker, Joseph Helman, Monroe Price

Fig. 50. Jackson Pollock, *Number 13A: Arabesque,* oil and enamel on canvas, 1948. Yale University Art Gallery. Gift of Richard Brown Baker, B.A. 1935. © 2025 The Pollock-Krasner Foundation / Artists Rights Society (ARS), New York.

Fig. 51. Eric Stotik, *Vol. 148 No. 310,* acrylic on linen on wood, 1989–90. Yale University Art Gallery. Richard Brown Baker, B.A. 1935, Collection.

Fig. 52. Jasper Johns, *White Flag,* 1955. Encaustic, oil, newsprint, and charcoal on canvas, 78$\frac{5}{16}$ × 120¾in. (198.9 × 306.7cm). The Metropolitan Museum of Art. Purchase, Lila Acheson Wallace, Reba and Dave Williams, Stephen and Nan Swid, Roy R. and Marie S. Neuberger, Louis and Bessie Adler Foundation Inc., Paula Cussi, Maria-Gaetana Matisse, The Barnett Newman Foundation, Jane and Robert Carroll, Eliot and Wilson Nolen, Mr. and Mrs. Derald H. Ruttenberg, Ruth and Seymour Klein Foundation Inc., Andrew N. Schiff, The Cowles Charitable Trust, The Merrill G. and Emita E. Hastings Foundation, John J. Roche, Molly and Walter Bareiss, Linda and Morton Janklow, Aaron I. Fleischman, and Linford L. Lougheed Gifts, and gifts from friends of the Museum; Kathryn E. Hurd, Denise and Andrew Saul, George A. Hearn, Arthur Hoppock Hearn, Joseph H. Hazen Foundation Purchase, and Cynthia Hazen Polsky and Leon B. Polsky Funds; Mayer Fund; Florene M. Schoenborn Bequest; Gifts of Professor and Mrs. Zevi Scharfstein and Himan Brown, and other gifts, bequests, and funds from various donors, by exchange, 1998 (1998.329). Image copyright © The Metropolitan Museum of Art. Image Source: Art Resource, NY. © 2025 Jasper Johns / Licensed by VAGA at Artists Rights Society (ARS), NY.

Fig. 53. Andy Warhol, *Four Marilyns,* oil on canvas, 1962. Helman Collection. © 2025 The Andy Warhol Foundation for the Visual Arts, Inc. / Licensed by Artists Rights Society (ARS), New York. © Estate of Marilyn Monroe.

Fig. 54. Roy Lichtenstein, *Aloha,* oil on canvas, 1962. Helman Collection. © Estate of Roy Lichtenstein.

Fig. 55. Peter Krasnow, *Sadakichi Hartmann,* 1929, pastel on paper. National Portrait Gallery, Smithsonian Institution; gift of Monroe Price and Aimée Brown Price. © Estate of Peter Krasnow.

Fig. 56. Carlos Almaraz, *Man in a Mask (Rabbit Ears) (Self-Portrait),* c. 1974, acrylic paint on paper. National Portrait Gallery, Smithsonian Institution; gift of Monroe Price and Aimée Brown Price in memory of their dear friend Carlos Almaraz, © Estate of Carlos Almaraz.

Chapter Fifteen: Alice Walton: Educator and Museum-Builder

Fig. 57. Adam Amengual, *Alice Walton at Crystal Bridges,* photograph, 2021. Painting in image: Joan Mitchell, *Untitled,* oil on canvas, 1952–1953. Crystal Bridges Museum of American Art.

Fig. 58. Asher B. Durand, *Kindred Spirits,* 1849, oil on canvas, 44 × 36 in. Crystal Bridges Museum of American Art, Bentonville, Arkansas, 2010.106. Photography by Edward C. Robison III.

Fig. 59. Henry Ossawa Tanner, *The Thankful Poor,* 1894. Oil on canvas, 90.17 × 112.4 cm (35.5 × 44.25 in.). Art Bridges Foundation, AB2020.16.

Chapter Sixteen: The Recognition of Racism and Misogyny

Fig. 60. Romare Bearden, *Soul History,* 1969. Collage, graphite, colored pencil, and gouache on Masonite, 50.8 × 43.2 cm (20 × 17 in.). Harvard Art Museums/Fogg

Museum, Gift of Abram M. London, M.D., Class of 1957, © 2025 Romare Bearden Foundation / Licensed by VAGA at Artists Rights Society (ARS), NY.

Fig. 61. Jean-Michel Basquiat, *Diagram of the Ankle,* xeroxed paper, oil stick, and acrylic on two hinged canvases, 1982. Yale University Art Gallery, Charles B. Benenson, B.A. 1933, Collection. © Estate of Jean-Michel Basquiat. Licensed by Artestar, New York.

Fig. 62. Alice Neel, American, 1900–1984. *Linda Nochlin and Daisy,* 1973. Oil on canvas, 55⅞ × 44 in. (141.9 × 111.8 cm). Museum of Fine Arts, Boston. Seth K. Sweetser Fund, 1983.496. Photograph © 2025 Museum of Fine Arts, Boston. © The Estate of Alice Neel.

Chapter Seventeen: Museums Reset

Fig. 63. Archibald Motley, American, 1891–1981. *Cocktails,* ca. 1926. Oil on canvas, 81.3 × 101.6 cm (32 × 40 in.). Museum of Fine Arts, Boston. The John Axelrod Collection—Frank B. Bemis Fund, Charles H. Bayley Fund, and The Heritage Fund for a Diverse Collection, 2011.1859. Photograph © 2025 Museum of Fine Arts, Boston. © Chicago History Museum / © Estate of Archibald John Motley Jr. All reserved rights 2025 / Bridgeman Images.

Fig. 64. Thornton Dial, Sr., *Life Begins with Crawling,* 1992. Enamel, carpet and burlap on wood, 152.4 × 121.9 cm (60 × 48 in.). Harvard Art Museums/Fogg Museum, Collection of Didi & David Barrett '71, Photo © President and Fellows of Harvard College, 2011.41. © 2025 Estate of Thornton Dial / Artists Rights Society (ARS), New York.

Fig. 65. Charles Willson Peale, *Yarrow Mamout,* oil on canvas, 1819. Philadelphia Museum of Art: Purchased with the gifts (by exchange) of R. Wistar Harvey, Mrs. T. Charlton Henry, Mr. and Mrs. J. Stogdell Stokes, Elise Robinson Paumgarten from the Sallie Crozer Hilprecht Collection, Lucie Washington Mitcheson in memory of Robert Stockton Johnson Mitcheson for the Robert Stockton Johnson Mitcheson Collection, R. Nelson Buckley, the estate of Rictavia Schiff, and the McNeil Acquisition Fund for American Art and Material Culture, 2011-87-1.

Fig. 66. Remedios Varo, Spanish, active in Mexico, 1908–1963. *Tailleur pour dames,* 1957. Oil on board, Length × width: 68 ×106 cm (26¾ × 41¾ in.). Museum of Fine Arts, Boston. Museum purchase with funds by exchange from the Alfred Stieglitz Collection—Bequest of Georgia O'Keeffe, and a Gift of the Stephen and Sybil Stone Foundation, 2021.1077. Photograph © 2025 Museum of Fine Arts, Boston. © 2025 Remedios Varo, Artists Rights Society (ARS), New York / VEGAP, Madrid.

Fig. 67. Faith Ringgold, *American People Series #20: Die.* 1967. Oil on canvas, two panels; 72 × 144 in. (182.9 × 365.8 cm). Purchase; and gift of The Modern Women's Fund. Digital Image © The Museum of Modern Art/Licensed by SCALA / Art Resource, NY. © 2025 Anyone Can Fly Foundation / Artists Rights Society (ARS), New York.

Fig. 68. Kehinde Wiley, *A Portrait of a Young Gentleman,* 2021. © Kehinde Wiley. Collection of The Huntington Library, Art Museum, and Botanical Gardens; Commissioned through Roberts Projects, Los Angeles; Gift of Anne F. Rothenberg, Terry

Perucca and Annette Serrurier, and the Philip and Muriel Berman Foundation. Additional support was provided by Laura and Carlton Seaver, Kent Belden and Dr. Louis Re, and Faye and Robert Davidson.

Fig. 69. Dave (later recorded as David Drake), *Twenty-Five Gallon Four-Handled Stoneware Jar,* 1858, stoneware with alkaline glaze, 24½ × 24¼ × 24¼ in. Crystal Bridges Museum of American Art, Bentonville, Arkansas, 2021.29. Photography by Edward C. Robison III.

Chapter Eighteen: Native Americans Reconsidered

Fig. 70. Eanger Irving Couse, *The Captive (La Cautiva),* 1891. Oil on canvas. Collection of Phoenix Art Museum, Gift of Mr. and Mrs. Read Mullan and others, by exchange (1994.7). Photo: Craig Smith.

Fig. 71. Frederic Remington, *Fight for the Waterhole,* 1903. Oil on canvas, 27¼ × 40⅛ in. (69.2 × 102 cm). The Museum of Fine Arts, Houston, The Hogg Brothers Collection, gift of Miss Ima Hogg, 43.25. Photograph © The Museum of Fine Arts, Houston: Thomas R. DuBrock.

Fig. 72. Fritz Scholder, La Jolla Band of Luiseño Indians and American, 1937–2005. *Bicentennial Indian,* 1976. Acrylic on canvas. Height × width: 175.3 × 139.7 cm (69 × 55 in.). Museum of Fine Arts, Boston. The Peterson Family Collection, L-R 30.2022. Photograph © 2025 Museum of Fine Arts, Boston. © Estate of Fritz Scholder.

Fig. 73. T.C. Cannon, American (Caddo/Kiowa), 1946–1978. *Collector #5 (Man in Wicker Chair),* 1975. Oil on canvas, Framed: 182.9 × 152.4 cm (72 × 60 in.). Museum of Fine Arts, Boston. Peterson Family Collection, L-R 91.2020. Photograph © 2025 Museum of Fine Arts, Boston. © Estate of T.C. Cannon.

Chapter Nineteen: Changing Taste

Fig. 74. Unidentified artist, *Saint Francis Xavier,* 17th–18th century, Oil and gold on embossed, chased & engraved copper, © Public domain, courtesy of the Carl & Marilynn Thoma Foundation, photo by Jamie Stukenberg.

Fig. 75. Edwin Austin Abbey, *The Hours,* pastel on gray paper and cardboard, n.d. Yale University Art Gallery. Edwin Austin Abbey Memorial Collection.

Fig. 76. American School (?), *Portrait of Two Girls,* oil on canvas, ca. 1820–40. Private Collection. Image courtesy of Philip Mould & CompanyPhoto © Philip Mould Ltd, London/Bridgeman Images.

Fig. 77. Jacques Guillaume Lucien Amans, attributed to. *Bélizaire and the Frey Children,* ca. 1837. Oil on canvas. 47¼ × 36¼ in. (120 × 92.1 cm). The Metropolitan Museum of Art. Purchase, Acquisitions Fund, Brooke Russell Astor Bequest, Friends of the American Wing Fund, Muriel J. Kogan Bequest, and funds from various donors, 2023 (2023.317). Image copyright © The Metropolitan Museum of Art. Image Source: Art Resource, NY.

Fig. 78. Attributed to John Verelst, ca. 1675–1734, Dutch, active in Britain (by 1697), *Elihu Yale with Members of his Family and an Enslaved Child,* ca. 1719, oil on canvas. Yale Center for British Art, Gift of Andrew Cavendish, eleventh Duke of Devonshire, B1970.1.

Fig. 79. Osmond Watson, *Johnny Cool*, 1967, oil on Canvas, 85.1 × 71.1 cm. Collection: National Gallery of Jamaica.

Postscript

Fig. 80. Robert Colescott, *George Washington Carver Crossing the Delaware: Page from an American History Textbook*, 1975, Acrylic on canvas, 78½ × 98¼ in. (199.4 × 249.6 cm). Lucas Museum of Narrative Art, Los Angeles © 2021 The Robert H. Colescott Separate Property Trust/Artists Rights Society (ARS), New York. Image courtesy of Sotheby's, Inc. © 2025.

Index

A NOTE ABOUT THE TYPE

Rethinking Art in America has been set in Arno Pro. It is the creation of Robert Slimbach—one of our most prolific and influential designers of digital typefaces. The family was created in the tradition of early Venetian and Aldine book types. Arno is also named for the river that flows through Florence, Italy.

Book Design by Brooke Koven
Book Composition by Vicki Rowland